America Imagined

America Imagined

Explaining the United States in Nineteenth-Century Europe and Latin America

Edited by
Axel Körner, Nicola Miller, and
Adam I. P. Smith

AMERICA IMAGINED
Copyright © Axel Körner, Nicola Miller, and Adam I. P. Smith 2012

All rights reserved. No reproduction, copy or transmission of this publication may be made without written permission. No portion of this publication may be reproduced, copied or transmitted save with written permission. In accordance with the provisions of the Copyright, Designs and Patents Act 1988, or under the terms of any licence permitting limited copying issued by the Copyright Licensing Agency, Saffron House, 6-10 Kirby Street, London EC1N 8TS.

Any person who does any unauthorized act in relation to this publication may be liable to criminal prosecution and civil claims for damages.

First published 2012 by
PALGRAVE MACMILLAN

The authors have asserted their rights to be identified as the authors of this work in accordance with the Copyright, Designs and Patents Act 1988.

Palgrave Macmillan in the UK is an imprint of Macmillan Publishers Limited, registered in England, company number 785998, of Houndmills, Basingstoke, Hampshire, RG21 6XS.

Palgrave Macmillan in the US is a division of Nature America, Inc., One New York Plaza, Suite 4500, New York, NY 10004-1562.

Palgrave Macmillan is the global academic imprint of the above companies and has companies and representatives throughout the world.

Hardback ISBN: 978–1–137–01897–7
Paperback ISBN: 978–1–137–53688–4
E-PUB ISBN: 978–1–137–01899–1
E-PDF ISBN: 978–1–137–01898–4
DOI: 10.1057/9781137018984

Distribution in the UK, Europe and the rest of the world is by Palgrave Macmillan®, a division of Macmillan Publishers Limited, registered in England, company number 785998, of Houndmills, Basingstoke, Hampshire RG21 6XS.

Library of Congress Cataloging-in-Publication Data
America imagined : explaining the United States in nineteenth-century
   Europe and Latin America / edited by Axel Körner, Nicola Miller, and
   Adam I. P. Smith.
       p. cm.
   Includes bibliographical references.
   ISBN 978–1–137–01897–7 (alk. paper)
   1. United States—Civilization—Public opinion—History—19th century.
   2. United States—Civilization—19th century.   3. United States—
   Foreign public opinion, European.   4. United States—Foreign public
   opinion, Latin American.   5. Public opinion—Europe—History—
   19th century.   6. Public opinion—Latin America—History—
   19th century.   I. Körner, Axel, 1967–   II. Miller, Nicola.
   III. Smith, Adam I. P.
   E169.1.A445 2012
   973.5—dc23   2012005775

A catalogue record for the book is available from the British Library.

Contents

List of Illustrations   vii

Preface   ix

Introduction   1
Axel Körner

1 Land of Opportunity?   19
   Adam I. P. Smith

2 A Model Republic   51
   Kate Ferris

3 Liberty, Lipstick, and Lobsters   81
   Nicola Miller

4 Barbarous America   125
   Axel Körner

5 A World Apart, a Race Apart?   161
   Maike Thier

6 Slavery and Abolition   191
   Natalia Bas, Kate Ferris, and Nicola Miller

Conclusion   225
Nicola Miller

Select Bibliography   241

Index   259

List of Illustrations

Cover Image: Title: Edward Moran, Unveiling the Statue of Liberty (1886). Edward Moran (1829-1901) was an English artist living in Paris and New York. Therefore, Unveiling the Statue of Liberty is an *English* painting representing a *French* image of the *United States*. Museum of the City of New York.

Young Benjamin [Franklin] in his father's factory	118
Machine to make Yankees	119
Harriet Beecher Stowe, ca. 1870s–1880s	120
Karl May's *Winnetou*, first edition in book format (Freiburg im Breisgau: Verlag Friedrich Ernst Fehsenfeld, 1893)	121
Uncle Tom at the whipping post. Scene from a stage production, ca.1901	122
Brazil and the United States	123

Preface

The origins of this book go back to a comparative research project hosted by the Centre for Transnational History at University College London, entitled "The American Way of Life: Images of the United States in Nineteenth-Century Europe and Latin America." The project was generously funded for four years by the United Kingdom's Arts and Humanities Research Council (AHRC).

The scope of the research for this book was such that it could only be done collaboratively, and one of the book's distinctive features is that it has been devised and written collectively, including the drafting of its individual chapters. Each chapter adopts a thematic approach, focusing on specific national contexts as appropriate to the theme, but then integrates these examples into a wider comparative and transnational framework. Although each contributor took responsibility for a specific theme, hence the individual attributions, the chapters are the outcome of a comparative discussion between all of the authors of this book. As a result of this approach, our book aims to be more than an edited collection of individually composed chapters.

A number of research assistants associated with the project helped to locate and collect primary sources: Esme Cleall, Federico Mazzini, Nico Pizzolato, Katharina Rietzler, Paul Shirley, and Stephen Wilkinson. We would also like to thank UCL's Department of History for its institutional support. We valued the opportunity to present and discuss our project at a number of workshops and seminars, including events organized by the Institute for the Study of the Americas, the Institute of Historical Research, the Central European University, the University of Jena, Brown University, the University of Warwick, and the University of St. Andrews. On all of these occasions we received valuable comments and criticisms. In particular, we would like to acknowledge Kathleen Burk, Stephen Conway, James Dunkerley, Maurizio Isabella, Donald Sassoon, and Guy Thomson, as well as the anonymous reviewers of our project application and the book proposal. We are also grateful to Karl-May-Verlag for granting permission to use an image free of charge. Some aspects of this book have been discussed previously in articles for which references are given in individual chapters as well as in the bibliography at the end of this book.

Introduction

Axel Körner

une page blanche (sauvage) où écrire le vouloir occidental
          Michel de Certeau, in his commentary on
          Jan van der Straet's painting of Amerigo Vespucci[1]

America! America?

Whether as a geographical expression, a political experiment, the realization of Enlightenment ideals, or just an abstract notion of prosperity and progress, during the nineteenth century no word conjured up the idea of the future more powerfully than "America." The metaphor has a long history, famously dating back to Thomas More's "ideal commonwealth," described in his *Utopia* of 1516, which was located in the South Atlantic, but read as a reflection on life in the recently discovered New World.[2] Explorers of the sixteenth and seventeenth centuries saw the New World as an endlessly renewable source of wealth and prosperity for the Old World. For other observers America became a screen onto which to project their political concerns; for example, the Baron Lahontan used his *Voyages dans l'Amérique Septentrionale* (1705) to articulate his criticism of France's *Ancien Régime*. By the time Turgot called for the independence of the colonies in 1750, many Enlightenment thinkers were projecting their visions of a new humanity onto the lands across the Atlantic. The US Declaration of Independence (1776)—followed by the independence of Haiti (1804), most of the Spanish colonies (1808–26), and Brazil (1822)—seemed to confirm the idea that the New World was an arena for political freedom and modern government. By the mid-nineteenth century, however, the utopian promise hitherto associated with the whole of the Americas had come to be represented, at least in European discourses, primarily by the United States of America.[3] In the former Iberian colonies, resistance to this appropriation of "America" by the United States persisted well into the twentieth century.[4] Even so, the successful invention in Spanish-speaking America during the early twentieth century of a tradition based on the idea of *Latin* America indicated a prevalent acceptance there, as in Europe, that it was the United States (rather than any of the former Iberian colonies) that symbolized the utopian potential of modernity.

Thus Alexis de Tocqueville was far from the only person who, in looking at America, "saw more than America."[5] Even for its critics—and there were many—the United States was a great talking point, not only among educated observers but across all strata of society in many parts of both Europe and Latin America. It was continually adduced in elite debates about social change, constitutional reform, the meaning of democracy, industrialization, and even the future world order, but it was also discussed in popular newspapers, illustrated magazines, workingmen's clubs, labor organizations, women's movements, and even in Cuban cane fields. Lincoln's assassination brought crowds onto the streets to mourn not only in Britain, but also in Havana and Buenos Aires. US characters and themes were embedded in popular consciousness by best-selling literary works such as James Fenimore Cooper's novels, which were more popular in Europe than in his native country; Charles Dickens's *American Notes* (1842), written when he was already an internationally celebrated author; or—the most successful of them all—Harriet Beecher Stowe's *Uncle Tom's Cabin* (1852).

A less well-known but equally powerful example of the hold that America had on many people's imagination concerns something that was not even visible to the naked eye. In the 1870s, a generation after the publication of Marx's *Communist Manifesto* (1848), a new specter was haunting Europe in the form of a parasite originating from across the Atlantic, which destroyed an ingredient seen as quintessential to European culture since the era of the Greeks and the Romans—wine. All over Europe local and national governments, chambers of commerce and agriculture, botanists, parasitologists, and agronomists debated the effects of Phylloxera, the parasite that, according to the International Botanical Congress in Florence and the French Ministry of Agriculture, had arrived in Europe from America, through vines specifically imported from the New World in order to cure Europe's vineyards of another disease, mildew.[6] Europeans looked on helplessly as substantial portions of their vineyards were destroyed, which was a catastrophe in particular for the French Third Republic, where wine had become central to the definition of the nation's tormented identity.[7] Meanwhile, from early on the only salvation on offer appeared to be the importation—again from America—of new vines that were claimed to be resistant to the parasite. The experience of Phylloxera highlighted the widespread obsession with America as both the source of all contamination and the only hope of a miraculous cure.

Whether castigated as a threat to civilized order or held up as a promise of earthly paradise, America was ritually invoked as a compass for future developments. Yet, what was meant by "America"? From today's perspective, over a decade after the end of "the American century,"[8] during which certain images of the United States were powerfully promoted by US governments and corporations, it is easy to assume that there is a set of constant and fixed associations (conquest of nature, liberal democracy, industrial capitalism, mass entertainment, and so forth), whether they are celebrated or criticized. The assumption that there is such a universally understood model lies behind much of the literature on Americanization or anti-Americanism. A preliminary survey of nineteenth-century sources suggested, however, that the meaning of "America" differed, sometimes quite sharply, according to the nationality, social status, political conviction, religion, gender, or race of the person invoking the word. During the second half of the nineteenth century most of the countries that observed and discussed the transformation of the United States themselves went through a period of dramatic social, political, and cultural change, a process of modernization and of inventing and reshaping national identities. Ultimately, thinking about the United States meant to follow or to reject specific models of modernization and democracy that were at the core of debates for most of the nineteenth century and still dominated much of the twentieth century. Analyzing images of the United States in comparative perspective provides a key to the ways in which societies reflected upon their own past and future, how they experienced change, interpreted history, and fashioned ideas about selfhood and otherness. Hence, the focus of this book is not the United States itself, but Europe and Latin America and their respective experiences of becoming modern as refracted through images of the United States.

From the Mexican-American War to the Spanish-Cuban-American War

Our book's chronological scope is the second half of the nineteenth century. The analysis starts at midcentury, when the Age of Revolution in Europe and Latin America reached its premature end. In Europe, before 1848, America was one among many points of reference for the revolutionaries and liberal reformers who were united in the aim of creating a new society, but their thinking about what was to come after the end of the *Ancien Régime* drew mainly upon European political thought. However, the end of the Age of Revolution also meant the end of this shared liberal dream. Worries about popular democracy drove the middle classes back into the embrace of the state, with the result that liberal ideals were defeated in France, Germany, Italy, Spain, and the Habsburg monarchy. As a consequence, the US experiment came to occupy a more prominent place in European thinking about the modern age and its liberal promise. It was no coincidence that in 1848–49 the French liberal politician and Americophile Edouard Laboulaye delivered his internationally influential lectures on the history of the United States at the Collège de France. At around the same time, James Knox Polk's ruthless policy of expansionism led to the Mexican-American War (1846–48) and the subsequent cession of Upper California and New Mexico to the United States. This moment was not only significant in the territorial consolidation of the United States but also in what it seemed to signify about the United States' lack of commitment to its own founding ideals. In Latin America, particularly, the Mexican-American War heightened already existing anxieties about the price that the other states of the Americas might have to pay for the successful consolidation of the Anglo-American republic. Moreover, it was during this period that major technological change opened up new opportunities, especially from the 1860s onward, for communication, exchange, and movement between Europe, the United States, and Latin America, notably the transatlantic cable, the increased volume of mail crossing the Atlantic, long distance travel for both business and leisure, and a wider circulation of periodicals, newspapers, and literature.

By the late nineteenth century the United States of America was increasingly perceived as a major economic power with corresponding aspirations to international influence. After the Spanish-American War of 1898, which resulted in informal American control over a nominally independent Cuba and the colonization of Puerto Rico and the Philippines, the United States became widely associated with a new form of imperialism that seemed to contradict earlier images of a republic founded on the ideas of the Enlightenment.[9] US projection overseas became a sustained, concerted, and more deliberate process, during an era when the circulation of people, goods, and ideas was expanding rapidly. Around the turn of the century US direct investment abroad started to increase rapidly, from an estimated $634 million in 1897 to $2.6 billion in 1914.[10] Our book examines what happened before the United States became a world power, when it was ideas and images, traveling in less willed and organized ways, that created impressions of America, rather than its foreign policy. In trying to understand the historical significance of "the American way of life," the second half of the nineteenth century—between the end of the Age of Revolution and the Spanish-American War, when rapid change was experienced throughout both Europe and the Americas—represents a period in itself, which deserves the focused study that has hitherto been lacking.

Investigating these changes in perception and in particular the negative images of the United States that emerged during the second half of the nineteenth century is not the same as tracing the emergence of anti-Americanism, as Dan Diner and Philippe Roger have done for the cases of Germany and France.[11] Anti-Americanism is an ideology that constitutes a particular current of thought in itself. This ideology has contributed to the emergence of negative images, which this book also investigates. However, what is important for our particular approach, and where our book differs from research into the phenomenon of anti-Americanism, is an emphasis on the dichotomy of positive and negative perceptions of the United States. Concentrating on anti-Americanism would be to underestimate the field of ideas from which negative images emerge and to ignore the multiplicity of images that characterize perceptions of the United States. Our focus on images enables us to capture a range of impressions that are less structured, fixed, and also less coherent than would be implied by the ordering principle of an ideology, but which nevertheless may have been significant in shaping attitudes.

Lives of Images

By "images" we do not just mean visual representations, but also textual metaphors and concepts. Like other sources used by historians to explain the social and cultural realities of the past, images are objectifications of subjectively constructed abstractions. They are not necessarily based on any direct experience of what they represent. Some of the most powerful images of the United States were created by people who had never crossed the Atlantic, for example, William Gladstone's famous article in the *North American Review*, "Kin beyond the Sea" (1878), or Laboulaye's entirely imagined *Paris en Amérique* of 1863. But the fact that images are subjective constructions, rather than making them "wrong," actually increases their value for the historian. To adopt Reinhart Koselleck's terminology, images coalesce in certain "spaces of experience" and within certain "horizons of expectation," thus providing a key to mentalities, perceptions, and human behavior in specific historical situations.[12] Social and political realities are always determined by individual or social perceptions, which motivate agency, which in turn confirms, reproduces, questions, or modifies social and political realities. As cultural artifacts images are no longer just objects, but can in themselves become producers of social agency.[13] Reconstructing the particular context from which images emerged allows historians to examine the intersection between structure and event, between individual interpretation and collective perceptions.[14]

Images have often been deliberately deployed to achieve a specific aim through a speech act. Antonio Gramsci argues in his *Quaderni del carcere* that certain clichés of *Americanismo* are so strongly rooted in popular mentalities that they can be used as a means of propaganda and as an ideological pretext to influence political processes.[15] More recently, Ian Buruma and Avishai Margalit inverted Edward Said's *Orientalism* to coin the concept of *Occidentalism* to describe a discourse that consciously distorts images of the West in general and of America in particular, in order to advance certain political or cultural aims.[16] Therefore, referring to America—whether as a positive or negative example—has often been a strategy by which the speaker sought to convince an audience of specific values. However, the meaning of such images was not necessarily determined by the producer or, wholly, by the receiver. Instead, they have lives of their own.

It is this complex relationship between the production and the reception of images, and the cognitive process in which images become meaningful in a specific social context, that makes them such a valuable source of historical investigation. In *The Uses of Literacy* Richard Hoggart challenged the simple concept of a passive adaptation of cultural codes, ideas, and values, emphasizing instead the socially specific "reading" of cultural products based on different life-worlds.[17] Michel de Certeau developed a theory of reception that emphasizes "the creativity of the reader," breaking with the artificial contrast between the production and the consumption of culture.[18] The process of reception is an independent creative process of cultural production, in which "the reader is the producer."[19] Received images take on their own dynamic, being continuously processed and elaborated over time. In Walter Benjamin's words, images appear where "thinking comes to a standstill in a constellation saturated with tensions"; in short, they are bearers of history.[20]

Images of the United States were deployed and produced in the home and at school, by political parties and learned societies, in municipal councils and national parliaments, in advertising companies and at the stock exchange, in trade union meetings and at the chamber of commerce, in universities and on stage. We have surveyed as wide a range of sources as possible: political speeches and diplomatic papers; newspapers, learned journals, and popular magazines; novels, memoirs, and recollections of various sorts; theatre, music, exhibition catalogues, and so on. We are mainly analyzing national debates, in most cases articulated through capital cities, although we noticed differences between the ideas circulating in metropolitan centers and those in second cities or provincial peripheries.

It would be impossible to produce a full record of images of the United States circulating in Europe and Latin America during the second half of the nineteenth century, but our book attempts to present its findings over as wide a range as possible, without duplicating research that has been done, for instance, on travel writing or on images in literature.[21] Those images are not excluded from our analysis, but looked at within a wider framework of sources. Our emphasis is not specifically on the image of America among immigrant communities, because extensive work has already been done on that topic, although the issue of emigration was often at the center of the debates we analyze.[22]

Geographical Scope

This book deals with a truly transnational phenomenon: the construction and circulation of images across nations and continents, across natural, political, and mental boundaries. Discourse about America has always been transnational, preceding the foundation of the United States and extending back to the "naturalist assessment" of the New Continent during the Enlightenment. Although there certainly were images of America that were highly specific to certain nations, it is important to take account of this fluidity of images across borders and of the cosmopolitanism of many of their creators. Whereas most of the existing work on images of America is centered on particular countries, this book studies perceptions of the United States in a transnational as well as a comparative perspective. We aim to explain the semantic content of images through the structural comparison of their similarities and differences, in order to shed light on the contexts in which they emerged. This comparison is two-dimensional, comparing Europe with Latin America, but also individual countries within Europe and Latin America.

One of the reasons for the strong interest in the United States among Europeans and Latin Americans was their understanding of the United States as a descendant from the same European civilization—seen as distant but at the same time related.[23] As Tocqueville confessed, "in spite of the ocean that intervenes, I cannot consent to separate America from Europe."[24] Consequently, observers tended to measure the United States against European realities rather than evaluating the United States in their own right. In this respect the United States had much in common with Latin America, which unlike Africa or Asia was viewed as in many ways related to Europe. Moreover, Europeans often looked at North and South America comparatively as two experiments in forming new civilizations based on European origins.[25] This gives a specific significance to research on images of the United States in Europe and Latin America rather than, for instance, Asia or Africa, or indeed in regions on the periphery of Europe, such as Russia or the Balkans, where kinship with the United States was felt to a lesser degree.[26] While Europeans and Latin Americans understood the United States as a younger descendant of the same culture, for Russians or the populations of the Ottoman Empire it was at best a rather distant relative.

The degree to which the United States mattered to national debates also varied within both Europe and Latin America. Spain, France, and Britain were all directly involved in the US War of Independence, had colonial possessions in the Americas, and remained in a position to influence developments in the United States, which was not the case for the German states, Italy, or the Scandinavian nations. Individual Norwegians and Swedes played a pivotal role in expanding the American frontier, but their collective influence on American politics remained marginal. In nineteenth-century debates on the relationship between church and state, Belgium was often cited alongside the United States, but its young history as a nation-state was so closely bound up with the Netherlands and other European countries that the United States played on the whole a rather limited role in Belgium's own political and cultural debates. Likewise, despite Huizinga's acute descriptions of American society in the early twentieth century, during the nineteenth century the Netherlands showed scant interest in the United States, even during the Civil War. The case of Switzerland is somewhat different, because it sometimes appeared as a fellow federal republic, but Swiss sources on the United States are relatively limited. This is not to say that a study of images of America among smaller national communities and emerging states, or those on the periphery of Europe, would be of no interest, but it would constitute an altogether different piece of research. The promise of a new golden land among European Jews constitutes a truly transnational subject, but it is only indirectly relevant to this book and there are already numerous specific studies of the topic.

The beginning of modern France coincides with the history of the United States, and the American Revolution preceded the French Revolution by just a few years. This made discussion of the American experiment in France almost inescapable. Both countries shared republican experiences and in particular Tocqueville and, later, Laboulaye discussed their own ideas about France's political development through continual reference to the United States. Meanwhile, the making of French national identity, especially after the defeat of 1870, always needed a counterpart, which the French often found in the Anglo-Saxon race, in which they included the United States.

Britain and Spain both had colonies across the Atlantic, which means that their respective histories were closely intertwined. Moreover, Spanish images of the United States influenced debates in Latin America, making Spain a key link between both Americas. While Britain had to come to terms with its early experience of decolonization before accepting the United States as its closest ally, Spain had a more antagonistic relationship with the United States, remaining wary of US expansionism throughout the century, not least because of the question of Cuba. However, Democrats, Liberals, and Republicans in both countries looked to the United States as a constitutional, political, and social model. In Britain these feelings toward the United States were strengthened by a sense of ethnic and political kinship, while Spaniards, like their neighbors to the north, more often turned to notions of Latin and Anglo-Saxon difference to explain their present place in the world.

Italy had no tradition on which to build a modern nation-state, but its political unification coincided with the election of Abraham Lincoln as sixteenth president of the United States. The country's revolutionary tradition since the Napoleonic period resulted in several generations of Italian exiles negotiating concepts of a nation-state from abroad. European and American experiences helped Italians to shape their own concepts of republicanism, federalism, and liberalism. Becoming Italians meant becoming modern, a process in which the United States became a constant point of reference. However, unification did not result in the political and economic prosperity the patriots had hoped for, leading to a constant flow of Italians leaving the country. Although until the early twentieth century other countries in Europe or Latin America constituted the preferred destinations of Italian emigrants, ideas about life in the United States influenced them in their decision to leave.

There were multiple connections between Germany and the United States. While German movements for social reform frequently influenced ideas in the United States, after 1890 the process was reversed when German women's movements found inspiration in the United States.[27] The American university system first took the Scottish system as a model, later the German.[28] A number of recent studies examine specific German debates about the United States, relating, for instance, to the revolutions of 1848 or the early years of Germany's Americanization.[29] While the book refers to some of these debates, Germany's late unification makes it problematic to speak about a national discourse on America, with Prussia, Saxony, or Bavaria presenting very different circumstances from the smaller political units in the southwest or in the merchant city-states of Lübeck, Bremen, or Hamburg. Likewise, the relatively late awakening of national sentiment in Central Europe makes it difficult to include the Habsburg Empire in this book. While Kossuth's popularity in the United States has generated historical interest in Hungarian images of America, it would be challenging to undertake research beyond the Magyar-speaking elites. Regarding the Slavonic languages the source material is scattered and often difficult to separate from the existing German or Hungarian accounts of America in the region.[30]

In colonial Cuba, patriots felt compelled to look to the United States, not only for inspiration but also for practical support in promoting their own various projects for Cuba's political future. This Cuban tendency was reinforced by reciprocal interest from the United States: Thomas Jefferson famously stated in 1820 that Cuba would be a valuable addition to the Union, and four years later John Quincy Adams used the notorious "ripe fruit" analogy to suggest that such an outcome was inevitable. US goods and people were present in Cuba far earlier and more extensively than anywhere else in Latin America, including Mexico. Moreover, many Cubans, not only from the elites, had firsthand experience of living and working in the United States, there, especially, in the tobacco factories of Tampa and New Orleans, but also in New York and Philadelphia. To a greater extent than anywhere else in Latin America, including Mexico, the policies of the United States were a central factor in Cuban politics and the two countries shared a sense that they were part of each other's history. Cuban imaginings about the United States have to be understood in this context. Yet, it will be argued, Cuba was only an enhanced example of what was happening across Latin America, which was that politicians, activists, and intellectuals were all comparing their own experience of modernity with that of the United States.

For Argentina the United States symbolized what was meant by its own *Revolución de mayo* of 1810, namely, the Enlightenment of the masses. Argentina is often thought to be the Latin American country most closely comparable to the United States, and there are indeed valid points of comparison: similarly structured economies based on temperate agriculture, initiatives to attract immigrant workers from Europe, and racist policies, including war, to exclude the native peoples from the national community. It is widely held that the Argentine Constitution of 1853 drew in important respects on the US Constitution and that the US model of primary education had particular resonance in Argentina, but that beyond those two factors Britain and France were far more important reference points throughout the nineteenth century. This view persists mainly because of the attention given to the leading liberal intellectual Domingo F. Sarmiento, who was president of Argentina from 1868 to 1874. Sarmiento is still widely characterized as an imitator of the United States, but he was actually highly selective about the aspects of US life that he introduced into Argentina; moreover, he was unusual—if not unique— among the Argentine ruling class in his enthusiasm for *norteamérica*. The role of images of the United States in nineteenth-century Argentina was both more extensive and less positive than an exclusive focus on Sarmiento has suggested.

Brazil shared with Cuba, Spain, and the United States the problem of the abolition of slavery as a central challenge to its political life. The late foundation of the republic in 1889 gave Brazil a wide range of US experiences to draw upon in building a counterweight to Spanish America. Like Argentina, Brazil saw itself as a rival embodiment of modernity in the Americas, as a South American version of the US experience of modernity. This aspiration was fed in part by historic similarities: continental size, colonial experience, and displacement of native peoples linked to European immigration. The image of the United States encapsulated what Brazil itself wished to become—an industrialized civilization—but Brazilians also saw themselves as more civilized, more humane, and more authentic than the United States.

As this discussion has shown, this is mainly a book about Europe and about Latin America. However, its subject is also relevant for our understanding of US history. Situating the American experience within a transnational framework of responses to its own development, the book also contributes to the growing body of literature that tries to globalize US history, moving beyond the limiting concept of American Exceptionalism.[31] Part of that story is a reexamination of the direction of intellectual and cultural transfers, which was never just a one-way street. Therefore, the book's thematic focus also generates questions about the United States' own sense of self, which was throughout its history affected and even constituted by nationally and culturally diverse influences and understandings of its own character. As is now increasingly being argued, transnational images of the United States were at the core of its own history.[32]

Themes: Prosperity, Domesticity, and Barbarity

The chapters of this book are organized thematically, grouping together a range of images and discourses across countries and decades as is most appropriate to each of our themes, which are prosperity and progress; constitutionalism and civic culture; barbarity and the absence of civilization; kinship and foreignness; race and slavery; domesticity and gender.

The opening chapter—"Land of Opportunity?"— discusses the extraordinarily powerful and durable idea that America was a place where ordinary men and women could make a new and better life. The popular faith that America offered social mobility (or the "right to rise") was based upon both an economic conception of natural abundance, especially of land, in the United States and a political analysis of the open society created by American democracy. Thus these images had important spatial connotations. In the final three decades of the nineteenth century, however, these ideas were challenged in a more profound way than ever before. In its "Gilded Age," the United States became increasingly associated with a vision of modernity that was still technically advanced and large in scale, but that seemed far less appealing to workers and radicals than the democratic modernity of the artisans' and small-holders' republic of the antebellum era.

The second chapter explores the image of the United States as a model—or anti-model—republic, analyzing differing perceptions of the relationship between US founding documents and institutions and its civil society. Debates among the political and intellectual leaders of Europe and Latin America about the United States' particular brand of republicanism and democracy were both shaped by and in turn helped to reshape national political discussions about the form and future of their own systems of government. While some observers, particularly in Spain and Cuba, focused on the American Constitution as the model *par excellence* of self-government and a potential panacea for their own democratic deficit, others followed the lead of Laboulaye, declaring that what was significant about American style democracy was not its constitution but rather its civil society—the myriad alliances, networks, and associations that agitated for political, social, and economic change at the local, as well as state and federal, level.

The third chapter analyzes perceptions of gender and domesticity associated with life in the United States. Europeans and Latin Americans alike were fascinated by stories about these intimate aspects of American life. The chapter explores themes such as education and work; social and sexual freedom; beauty and sexuality; confidence and respect; comfort and convenience. It illustrates both the international competition of images (US women were often compared and contrasted with French and English women) and the importance of disaggregating areas of the United States (gracious and seductive Southern women contrasted with bold, tomboyish Northern women). The chapter also sets the reception of images of US womanhood in the context of the broader question of the gendering of modernity, arguing that by the end of the nineteenth century US idealism had widely come to be seen as confined to the domestic sphere.

The fourth chapter explores images of the United States as a "barbarous" and ultimately "uncivilized" country. For Europeans the self-identification as *Kulturnation* was often viewed in dramatic contrast to the absence of similar markers of civilization in the United States. Widespread embrace of idealism in Europe and Latin America contrasts with the perceived crude materialism of the United States and the supposed grossness and vulgarity of its citizens. One of the turning points in the evaluation of the American model were European debates on the issue of slavery, reaching from learned journals to popular literature, and including stage adaptations of Beecher Stowe's best seller, *Uncle Tom's Cabin*. They set the scene for the subsequent coverage of the excesses of the Civil War, which seemed to confirm both the impracticality of federalism, as well as the uncivilized nature of American society. Throughout the late nineteenth century news about corruption, lynching, and mediocrity supported the idea of America as a profoundly barbarous nation.

The fifth chapter analyzes the widespread use of the concepts "Latinity" and "Anglo-Saxonism" in images of the United States, providing a terminology to describe oneself and the "other," while shaping perceptions of the different countries of the Americas. Exactly because of their vague and malleable nature, Latinity and Anglo-Saxonism became handy catch-all designations in the quest to make sense of the modern world. Both were almost equally shorthand for "progress" and "decadence," "civilization" and "barbarism," or to put it crudely, "good" and "bad"—always dependent on author and context.

The last chapter compares the impact of US models of abolition in Brazil, Cuba, and Spain, the three countries within our remit that still operated slavery. The experiences of the United States were the most significant ones deployed both by defenders of slavery and by abolitionists in these three contexts, although British and French models were also discussed. In ways that stood out even more clearly than in many of our other themes, images of US abolition were refracted through domestic political concerns. Even among supporters of abolition, there was very little consensus about the conclusions to be drawn from the US experience, with very different examples being employed to advocate, at different times and in different places, gradual or immediate abolition. Those who resisted it pointed to the inextricability of abolition and civil war in the United States as evidence that this was precisely how not to go about ending the practice of slavery.

Historiographies

Most historians interested in perceptions of the United States abroad have concentrated their research on individual countries.[33] These works form an important basis for our transnational and comparative approach, but they also differ from our own objectives.[34] Likewise, we draw upon, but have different aims from, the large body of scholarly work analyzing images of America in nineteenth-century European literature.[35] The works of Mrs Frances Trollope, her son Anthony Trollope, Charles Dickens, and Karl May (whose adventure novels of the American West found 300 million readers worldwide) all transmitted images of America well beyond their countries of origin and represent a truly transnational phenomenon.[36] Furthermore, American authors such as James Fenimore Cooper, Mark Twain, Jack London, the Irish-American Thomas Mayne Reid, and—the most popular of all, in Latin America as well as Europe—Edgar Allan Poe were translated into all the major European languages and widely influenced debates about the United States. Some of these images nurtured the dream of American freedom, but in many instances their attraction seemed to lie in their apparent confirmation of many of their readers' doubts about the American way of life. As with all our other images, we try to map the full social context in which literary images were created, looking beyond text, genre, and author.

The other main focus of the existing literature on international perceptions of the United States is popular culture, technological innovation, and the appeal of the United States as a consumer paradise, often looking specifically at the first half of the twentieth century.[37] Within this perspective the United States appears solely as the unchallenged epitome of modernity, without much reference to the wider context of political and social debates that our approach emphasizes. This is largely a consequence of the historians' chosen periodization: for example, Victoria De Grazia's *Irresistible Empire* makes it explicit that "America's advance through Europe" was a process characterizing the twentieth century.[38] There is also a widespread assumption that Americanization can be explained mainly in terms of what the United States chose to project into the outside world. Even when presenting an extensive panorama of Americanization, from politics to economic development and popular culture, most historians pay relatively little attention to what other nations actually made of this particular culture they encountered as a consequence of economic globalization. Diplomatic, economic, and political histories of the United States often include an interesting cultural dimension, but again the focus here is usually on economic, intellectual, and cultural developments during the twentieth century.[39]

A pioneering exception is Robert W. Rydell's and Rob Kroes's *Buffalo Bill in Bologna* (2005), which deals specifically with the workings of transatlantic American mass culture, adopting a perspective inspired largely by critical theory and the theoretical assumptions of the cultural studies approach. Although the book deals more with the export of culture than with the responses to it, the authors show the ways in which mass culture served to construct cultural hegemonies, thereby blunting the edge of class conflict.[40] Some of these ideas can be applied to the reception of American culture elsewhere. Related to this field of research are works on the representation of the United States in World Fairs and on the Chicago exhibition of 1893.[41] Most of these works concentrate on a particular form of representation: the images with which the United States wished to represent itself, celebrating the religion of progress during the industrial age. While we use some of the same sources, we aim to interpret them in the context of wider debates on the United States, incorporating responses to the images America sought to project of itself and thereby historicizing them more effectively. As Paola Gemme has argued in relation to Italy, the idea of America as a model for the Italian Risorgimento was at least partly an American projection.[42]

Our project takes up some of these arguments and places them within a comparative perspective. An agenda closely linked to some of the objectives of our enterprise was outlined in the collection edited by Thomas Bender, *Rethinking American History in a Global Age* (2002). While Bender's book deals with the United States itself (rather than its images abroad), it sets out to challenge the boundaries of any national histories and tries to reconfigure the United States by framing its history through the "plenitude of its narratives."[43] Our book wishes to contribute to the agenda of those historians who take an increasingly global approach to US history in order to break the mold of American Exceptionalism. This is a very contemporary debate, which also reflects how the relationship of the United States to other countries has changed over the centuries and even in our own time.

Notes

1. Michel de Certeau, *L'écriture de l'histoire* (Paris: Gallimard, 1975), 9–10.
2. The main works in a large literature are (ordered by date of publication) Gerbi, *The Dispute of the New World*; O'Gorman, *The Invention of America*; Chiapelli, ed., *First Images of America*; Bitterli, *Die "Wilden" und die "Zivilisierten"*; Pagden, *The Fall of Natural Man*; Todorov, *La Conquête de l'Amérique*; Greenblatt, *Marvelous Possessions*; Brading, *The First America*; Rabasa, *Inventing America*; Madsen, ed., *Visions of America since 1492*; Turgeon, Delâge, Ouellet, ed., *Transferts culturels et métissages Amérique/Europe*; Caesar, *Reconstructing America*; Canizares-Esguerra, *How to Write the History of the New World*; Fernández Armesto, *The Americas*. Craiutu and Isaacs, eds., *America Through European Eyes*.
3. On the history of the incremental identification of the United States as "America," see Murphy, *Hemispheric Imaginings*.

4. See Belnap and Fernández, eds., *José Martí's "Our America"*; Mignolo, *The Idea of Latin America*.
5. Tocqueville, "Introduction," *De la démocratie en Amérique*.
6. A. Zannetti, "Notizia Scientifica. La Phylloxera Vastatrix," in *Nuova Antologia*, January 1875, 212–215.
7. Almost 2.5 million hectares in France alone were destroyed: Richard Smart, "Phylloxera," in *The Oxford Companion to Wine*, ed. Jancis Robinson (Oxford: Oxford University Press, 2006), 525. See also George Ordish, *The Great Wine Blight* (London: J. M. Dent and Sons, 1972), 294ff. The authors are grateful to Kathleen Burk for her help with this part of their research. See also Maike Thier, "*Paris en Amérique*". *French Images of the United States, c.1848–1886*. PhD thesis, University of London, 2009, ch. 5.
8. Alan Brinkley, "The Concept of an American Century," in *The American Century in Europe*, ed. Moore and Vaudagna, 7–21.
9. Wehler, *Der Aufstieg des amerikanischen Imperialismus*.
10. Rydell and Kroes, *Buffalo Bill in Bologna*, 15.
11. Diner, *Verkehrte Welten* and *Feindbild Amerika*; Roger, *The American Enemy*. See also, on European examples, Henningsen, *Der Fall Amerika*; Strauss, *Menace in the West*; Lacorne, Rupnik, Toinet, eds., *The Rise and Fall of Anti-Americanism*; Sebastian Balfour, "'The Lion and the Pig': Nationalism and National Identity in Fin-de-Siècle Spain," in Mar-Molinero and Smith, *Nationalism and the Nation in the Iberian Peninsula*; Schwaabe, *Antiamerikanismus*; Markovits, *Amerika dich hasst sich's besser*; Stephan, ed., *The Americanization of Europe*; On Latin America McPherson, *Yankee No* and his *Anti-Americanism in Latin America*; for an overview: Grandin, "Your Americanism and Mine."
12. Koselleck, *Vergangene Zukunft*, 351.
13. Archer, *Culture and Agency*.
14. Certeau, *L'écriture de l'histoire*, 57.
15. Antonio Gramsci, *Quaderni del Carcere* (Turin: Einaudi, 1975), vol. 1, 347.
16. Buruma and Margalit, *Occidentalism*.
17. Hoggart, *The Uses of Literacy*, 238.
18. Certeau, *L'invention du quotidien*, vol. 1, 249.
19. Ibid., 250.
20. Benjamin, *The Arcades Project*, 475.
21. The representation of American life in European literature is a large and rapidly expanding field of research. For a general introduction, see Evans, *America*.
22. It would go beyond the scope of this introduction to give even a brief survey of the field of immigration studies, but there are a few works that focus in particular on images of America among migrants. For an overview, see Friedman, "Beyond 'voting with the feet.'" Billington, *Land of Savagery, Land of Promise* brings together materials from immigration agencies with travel literature. On Italy: Franzina, *Dall'Arcadia in America* and his *L'immaginario degli emigranti*. On Germany: Helbich, Kamphoefner, Sommer, eds., *Briefe aus Amerika*.

23. See, for instance, Kroes, "America and the European Sense of History."
24. Tocqueville, *De la démocratie en Amerique*, vol. 2, 48–49.
25. The most famous example is Hegel, *Vorlesungen über die Philosophie der Geschichte*, 107ff. See also, on the Italian veteran of 1848 Quirico Filopanti, Fiorenza Tarozzi, "Filopanti Professore Universitario e Insegnante Popolare," in *Un democratico del Risorgimento: Quirico Filopanti*, ed. Alberto Preti (Bologna: Il Mulino, 1997), 93–119, 112.
26. The historical idea of the United States among Afro-Americans constitutes an even more complicated issue for historical investigation. See, for instance, Robin D. G. Kelly, "How the West Was One. The African Diaspora and the Re-Mapping of U.S. History," in *Rethinking American History in a Global Age*, ed. Bender, 123–147.
27. Schüler, *Frauenbewegung und soziale Reform*.
28. Löser and Strupp, eds., *Universität der Gelehrten—Universität der Experten*. Between 1812 and 1914 about 10,000 US Americans studied in Germany.
29. Lerg, *Amerika als Argument;* Klautke, *Unbegrenzte Möglichkeiten;* and Czaja, *Die USA und ihr Aufstieg zur Weltmacht*.
30. Bracewell and Drace-Francis, eds., *Under Eastern Eyes*, esp. 61–120 and 195–222. For a European perspective also see *Amerika und Europa—Mars und Venus?*, eds. von Thadden and Escudier.
31. For a review of the scholarship, see Sexton, "The Global View of the United States."
32. Tyrrell, *Transnational Nation;* idem, "Reflections on the transnational turn in United States history: theory and practice." Bender, ed., *Rethinking American History;* Thelen, "The Nation and Beyond."
33. Exceptions are Vann Woodward, *The Old World's New World;* Thaller, *Studien zum europäischen Amerikabild*.
34. Along with the works cited above see, for Italy, Spini, *Risorgimento e Protestanti;* and Comitato italiano per la storia americana, *Italia e America dall settecento all'età dell'imperialismo*. For French views of the United States: Rémond, *Les États-Unis devant l'opinion française;* Portes, *Fascination and Misgivings;* Villerbu, *La conquête de l'Ouest;* Gavronsky, *The French Liberal Opposition and the American Civil War*. On French liberalism see Gray, *Interpreting American Democracy in France;* Jaume, *Tocqueville;* Brogan, *Alexis de Tocqueville;* Mélonio, *Tocqueville and the French*. The most recent survey for Britain is Burk, *Old World, New World*. For Spain and Latin America: Englekirk, *Bibliografía de obras norteamericanas en traducción española;* Lanero and Villoria, *Literatura en traducción;* Oltra, *La influencia norteamericana en la Constitución Española de 1869;* Garcia Monton, *Viaje a la modernidad*. Reid, *Spanish American Images of the United States*.
35. Similar images in literature have also been discussed by historians of emigration. For Germany: Berger, *Amerika im XIX. Jahrhundert*. For Italy: Franzina, *Dall'Arcadia in America*. The scholarship on English literature about America is vast.
36. Billington, *Land of Savagery, Land of Promise*, xii, 39.

37. See (ordered by date of publication) Christopher W. E. Bigsby, ed., *Superculture: American Popular Culture and Europe* (London: Elek, 1975); Ralph Willett, *The Americanization of Germany, 1945–1949* (London: Routledge, 1992); Reinhold Wagnleitner, *Coca-Colanization and the Cold War. The Cultural Mission of the United States in Austria after the Second World War* (Chapel Hill: University of North Carolina Press, 1994). Alf Lüdtke, Inge Marßolek, Adelheid von Saldern, eds., *Amerikanisierung. Traum und Alptraum im Deutschland des 20. Jahrhunderts* (Stuttgart: Steiner, 1996). Axel Schildt, "From Reconstruction to Leisure Society," *Contemporary European History* 5, no. 2 (1996), 191–222; Reinhold Wagnleitner and Elaine Tyler May, eds., "*Here, There and Everywhere." The Foreign Politics of American Popular Culture*; Moore and Vaudagna, eds., *The American Century in Europe*; Dall'Osso, *Voglia d'America*.
38. de Grazia, *Irresistible Empire*.
39. Volker Berghahn, *The Americanisation of West German Industry, 1945–1973* (Leamington Spa: Berg, 1986); J. Leo Wollemborg, *Stars, Stripes and Italian Tricolor: The United States and Italy 1946–1989* (New York: Praeger, 1990); Thomas Alan Schwartz, *America's Germany: John J. McCloy and the Federal Republic of Germany* (Cambridge, MA: Harvard University Press, 1991); Peter Duignan and Lewis H. Gann, *The Rebirth of the West: The Americanization of the Democratic World 1945–1958* (Cambridge, MA: Harvard University Press, 1992); Reiner Pommerin, ed., *The American Impact on Postwar Germany* (Oxford: Berghahn, 1994); Volker Berghahn, *America and the Intellectual Cold Wars in Europe: Shephard Stone between Philantropy, Academy, and Diplomacy* (Princeton: Princeton University Press, 2001).
40. See the bibliographical essay in Rydell and Kroes, *Buffalo Bill in Bologna*, 47, 175–188.
41. Rydell, *All the World's a Fair*; Gilbert, *Perfect Cities*; Harris et al., *Grand Illusions*; Rydell and Gwinn, eds., *Fair Representations*; Kretschmer, *Geschichte der Weltausstellungen*.
42. Gemme, *Domesticating Foreign Struggles*. Dall'Osso, *Voglia d'America*, 13, notes that Europe's *americanismo* of the late nineteenth and early twentieth centuries was often "prefabricated" by the American elites.
43. Bender, ed., *Rethinking American History*.

I

Land of Opportunity?

Adam I. P. Smith

America, with all its difficulties and defects, is the most prosperous and highly favoured country... on the habitable globe. There can be no place where the poor working man can so easily obtain subsistence for himself and his family, and where the intellect of all classes is, or may be, highly cultivated, or where man is more highly appreciated according to his real value. Success is certain to the man of energy and good repute.

Sheffield and Rotherham, Independent, *March 22, 1869.*

The idea of America as a place where men and women might find not only freedom but also the opportunity for a prosperous life is as old as the European discovery of the New World. It transposed secular aspirations for material success onto a millennialist template that conceived of America as a providentially blessed place. Images of material abundance, freely available land, and an absence of artificial restraints on human endeavor fused to generate an idea of the United States as a new order in which the poor could actually inherit the earth. Yet counterimages of exploitation and hierarchy were present throughout, inflecting the positive vision of American opportunity with notes of ambiguity. Any reckoning with the image of the United States in Latin America and Europe during the late nineteenth century must account for the powerful appeal of the "land of opportunity" motif, and explain its limits.

In European and Latin American visions of a more economically just society, or discussion of the social problems wrought by industrialization and new technology, the United States was often at stake. Stories of poor workingmen making their fortune in the new world, of abundant land and high wages crop up frequently in our sources. At the same time, advocates of a more democratic and politically equal social order invariably invoked the United States as the paradigmatic democratic polity. The core question was the relationship between these two ideas, of economic opportunity on the one hand and political equality on the other. Did one lead to the other? Was "democracy" the mechanism for bringing about a more equal society in which ordinary workingmen could prosper free from the artificial constraints of Old World hierarchy? "Look what the Anglo-Saxon race can do without State-Church, king, or aristocracy!" exclaimed one English newspaper in a discussion of American economic growth. "That is what the ballot, household suffrage, short parliaments, and payment of the members, bring a people to!"[1] Others, however, questioned the proposition that political equality and economic opportunity were fundamentally and axiomatically connected. As early as the 1830s and 40s, some Chartists and land reformers in Britain, for example, were well aware of the difficulties faced by industrial workers in America and some drew the natural conclusion that manhood suffrage was not necessarily the panacea that the People's Charter implied.[2]

In raising the issue of the United States as a land of opportunity, Chartists' principal objective was to alter the social and political framework of Britain, and something similar was true of virtually every invocation of the land of opportunity image. Those who raised it, whether to laud or dismiss it, were invariably offering commentaries on the shortcomings, prospects, or superiority of their own society in relation to the United States, sometimes overtly, sometimes not. Europeans tapped into centuries of thinking about the New World as a land of emancipation and plenty, in which the contrast between the circumstances in America and in their home countries was taken for granted. For Latin Americans, who also generated images of the United States as a land of opportunity, it was less easy to imagine the great republic of the North as a place apart since their countries too were imagined, not least by themselves, as places of abundance freed from the constrictions of the Old Word. After all, Latin American leaders had embarked on nation building in the 1820s, framing Constitutions in the image of that drawn up at Philadelphia in 1787, in the firm conviction that their countries, too, would realize the utopian promise associated with the idea of America, and that their lands would also become lands of opportunity. Despite all the political and economic difficulties of the first stages of their development, Latin American liberals, especially but not exclusively in the more successful economies of Argentina and Brazil, tended to hold firm to the belief that ultimately their nations would overtake the United States and become more gloriously, humanely modern. Consequently, a distinctive theme of Latin American commentary on the United States as a land of opportunity was the sense that the political and environmental factors that led to the distinctive prosperity and economic opportunity north of Rio Grande surely applied south of it as well. If Latin America appeared to lag behind, there must therefore be cultural explanations for the difference. Chilean liberal intellectual Francisco Bilbao was far from alone in arguing that the "world of Columbus" had divided into two parts, the north controlled by "the Saxon religion," which "produced the United States" and the south controlled by "the Latin religion," which "produced the dis-united States [of Latin America]."[3] Thus, images of the United States as a bountiful land of providence in comparison with the Spanish American countries as impoverished, accursed lands fed into the cultural constructs of Anglo-Saxonism and Latinity discussed in Chapter 5.

In broad terms, disillusionment with America as a land of opportunity probably increased in most places during the last half of the nineteenth century. But this is no simple story of declension. Positive and negative images of American society coexisted, waxed and waned. Negative images of low wages, high unemployment, and lack of social mobility were often deliberate inversions of more positive images. Meanwhile, the outcome of the US Civil War offered disenchanted antislavery radicals new reasons to be optimistic about the American experiment, and the figure of Abraham Lincoln, revered in many parts of the world in the late nineteenth century, became the embodiment of the man of the people who rose to the highest office in the land. This chapter will explore the ways in which these persistent images of hope coexisted with bleaker perspectives. Even in the face of much evidence that the industrializing United States was emulating the hierarchies and inequalities of Europe, a vision of America as a place of emancipation remained. For many, despair at the "reality" of inequality and exploitation was counterbalanced by a faith in the capacity of America to "right" itself. For others, the economic prosperity offered by the United States came at too high a cost to its culture and civilization. As early as 1856, Bilbao was making an argument that was to become the refrain of a discourse of Latin American identity in the 1900s, namely, that it would fall to Latin America "to stem the tide of Yankee individualism" and realize the moral promise of the American continent.[4] The United States may have been a land of opportunity in economic and political terms, but in the eyes of many observers it was not seen to be one either culturally or morally.

Enchantment

Before the Civil War, many European radicals and liberals saw the United States as a site of emancipation in which the workingman could thrive free from religious, social, and economic controls and as a republican idyll that ensured rough social and political equality.[5] For many Germans, for example, America was a land of opportunity in all senses of the word. Letters from those who had left were the most significant source of information about the United States for most Germans: as a contemporary put it in the first half of the century, "there exists virtually no German family without its own American correspondent, who incites them to start a revolution."[6] As Chapter 4 will explain, emigration was often a source of negative images of the United States in nineteenth-century Europe, but there was also a burgeoning literature that reiterated romantic images of the rich uncle from America and from rags to riches tales. Advice manuals on emigration developed as a new genre during the first half of the century. In Germany, for example, the most influential work of this kind was Gottfried Duden's *Bericht über eine Reise nach den westlichen Staaten Nordamerikas* (1829), in which the United States was depicted as a "paradise on earth," a lush "land of plenty."

In Britain, the Owenite socialist John Finch reflected the view of many other radicals of his age when he wrote in 1844 of the United States as an "untaxed land, flowing with milk and honey."[7] Working-class emigration societies in Britain promoted America as a place where men could become their own masters. Even industrialization in America, it was claimed, had somehow not brought with it the smoke and soot that blackened, literally and figuratively, the "dark, Satanic mills" of Lancashire and Yorkshire. A middle-class British visitor to the textile manufacturing centre of Lowell, Massachusetts, in the 1840s reported that "there, nothing is discoloured, neither houses, nor mills nor trees."[8] Always underpinning the image of higher wages and better living conditions in American industry was the notion that fortunes were to be made in the vast expanse and abundance of its land. Nothing in the first half of the nineteenth century captured this idea as perfectly as the discovery of gold in California in 1849, which prompted breathless coverage in the European press even in those countries, such as France, with relatively low levels of emigration to the United States.[9]

Natural abundance was usually linked to other, essentially political, factors. In addition to the importance of republican institutions, it was public education and religious freedom that most often appeared in European and Latin American accounts as the key to US prosperity. The "amazing material prosperity" of the "Great Republic of the West," argued one radical English newspaper, was not only due to the "enormous tracts of wilderness which are every year reclaimed" but also to the "immense multitudes of schools, colleges, places of worship, and educational institutions, which spring up every year in all parts of the Union" and the consequent "spread of intelligence and comfort among all classes of the community."[10] In this, as in so many other respects, the United States offered the counterfoil to

English failures: "In this country education is doled out like an alms—bestowed as a boon, and not acknowledged as a right... But in the United States, where the theory of the government is equality of political power in respect to the entire nation, it is considered that to withhold knowledge is to withhold that political power which is every citizen's indefeasible right and unconditional inheritance."[11] The Argentine liberal Sarmiento famously characterized the United States as "the only nation in the world where everybody reads."[12] The capacity to educate all of the different peoples that landed on its shores, from wherever they came, was hailed by many Latin American intellectuals as the secret of US success.

Images of US opportunity were frequently refracted through the lens of religion. Cavour's formula of "a free Church in a free State" was at least partly inspired by the example of the United States, and Italians often encountered America through anticlerical propaganda, which was disseminated by missionary organizations such as the American and Foreign Bible Society and the American Philo-Italian Society.[13] British radicals saw the lack of an established church in the United States as evidence that the "Anglo-Saxon" race in the New World had thrown off the stifling hierarchies of the Old World. And for the Brazilian liberal Aureliano Tavares Bastos, who was highly critical of the centralization of monarchical power buttressed by the Catholic Church in his own country, the key to the "mystery" of the "dynamism" of US society was that, rather than being oppressed by "the dull fanaticism" of Catholic priests, it had been settled by "Quakers and other free sects." Consequently, the "liberal spirit of Protestant reform" with its "morality, love of work... and zeal for individual independence" were transplanted in Anglo-America as they had not been further south.[14] "It is to this absolute freedom of creeds," wrote Tavares Bastos, "and not least to its independent spirit, that the Americans from the North owe their great and rapid prosperity."[15] The Chilean Bilbao, less enthralled by the United States than Tavares Bastos, shared the view that US success lay mainly in its luck in having been colonized by the Protestant, freedom-loving English, rather than the Catholic, hierarchical Iberians. In contrast to the Latin American countries, hampered by all the "black legend" attributes of theocracy, superstition, and authoritarianism ("our cradle was a cradle of iron, the blood of nations our baptism, a hymn to terror the song that greeted our first steps"), the people of the United States were uniquely blessed as "the sons of the first men of modern Europe, of those heroes of the Reformation who bearing the old testament crossed great waters in order to raise an altar to the God of conscience."[16]

There were reasons for midcentury radicals to be skeptical about the promise of American democracy, the foremost of which was the presence of slavery—one traveling English Chartist complained that "he had enjoyed more real and personal liberty in a village in England than he had met with in all the towns he had visited in Texas."[17] Consequently, emancipation and Union victory in the Civil War was a major boost to the idea of America as a land of opportunity. In Britain, ex-Chartists George Julian Harney and Joseph Cowen were among those who organized mass meetings on behalf of the Union during the Civil War, arguing that the workingmen of England should stand up for the cause of freedom in America.[18] For John Bright, the struggle for reform in Britain was as much at stake in the American Civil War as was the emancipation of the slaves. If the Confederacy triumphed, Bright warned, "then European democracy would be silenced and dumbfounded forever."[19] The Civil War seemed to dramatize the enduring conflict between a government of the people and an aristocracy, and the outcome of the war—what Gladstone called in retrospect "one of the most wonderful struggles known to man"—was portrayed, therefore, as the ultimate vindication of popular government.[20] In 1865, Professor E. S. Beesly, a historian at University College London and a regular contributor to the labor newspaper *The Bee-Hive*, argued that with the defeat of the Confederacy, a "vast impetus has been given to Republican sentiments in England." America, he concluded, was a "standing rebuke to England. Her free institutions, her prosperity, the education of her people, the absence of a privileged class, are in too glaring a contrast with our own position to be forgiven."[21] America in 1865 was truly, for many foreigners, as it was for most Americans, the "great nation of futurity."[22] The enfranchisement of the former slaves during Reconstruction was a dramatic vindication of universal male suffrage that revealed a stark contrast with Britain even after the Second Reform Act. "Will the British working men occupy as proud a political position as that now held by the negroes of the States, within six years to come?," asked George Julian Harney in a speech in Newcastle in 1867. "There is stinging humiliation for us as Englishmen in the very question."[23]

Disenchantment

For some, however, the Civil War pointed to a very different conclusion: that the United States was no longer a beacon of either political democracy or economic opportunity. This was an especially common viewpoint among those who had long harbored a deep mistrust of what America represented. An example is the English historian Lord Acton. In an 1865 lecture, he argued that, before the Civil War, America had been a "distant magnet" that exercised a "power of attraction over Europe of which the great migration is only a subordinate sign," but that the war showed that those hopes had been proved false. It had now been revealed, he claimed, that democratic government could survive only by a resort to force more tyrannical than anything exercised in Europe.[24] On similar lines, the English legal scholar Sir Henry Maine argued that American liberty had produced a society of staggering inequality. Only a "superficial thinker," Maine suggested, would equate democracy with liberty, but whereas Tocqueville had warned that American democracy might destroy liberty, Maine believed that the opposite was true: American liberty had been achieved at the expense of democracy. Social Darwinism was the nemesis of the land of opportunity. "There has hardly ever before been a community in which the weak have been pushed so pitilessly to the wall," wrote Maine, "in which those who have succeeded have so uniformly been the strong, and in which in so short a time there has arisen so great an inequality of private fortune and domestic luxury."[25]

Once seen as a society adrift without the anchor of established institutions, the United States, having survived the bloodiest war the world had seen since 1815, now appeared to European and Latin American observers to be astonishingly resilient. Out of the weak antebellum republic had emerged, it seemed, a nation that had shown respect for authority, had found fortitude in adversity, and was prepared to use force to defend power. In the 1870s and 80s, conservatives who earlier in the century damned the American example for its cultural debasement and social anarchy increasingly came to see the American political system with new eyes, not as a threatening, anarchic democracy but as a model of how to contain democratic impulses within a fundamentally conservative structure.[26] For them, increasing inequality in the paradigmatic democratic nation merely served to make democracy seem far less threatening. "The march of democracy in England," mused James Bryce in *The American Commonwealth* (1889), "has disposed English writers and politicians of the very school which thirty or twenty years ago pointed to America as a terrible example, now to discover that her Republic possesses elements of stability wanting in the monarchy of the mother country."[27]

Similarly, in France, the conservative features of the US polity attracted renewed attention. In the debates on the Constitution of the Second Republic in 1848, and again in the making of the Constitution of the Third Republic in 1875, liberals and conservatives alike argued for American-style bicameralism and a strong executive, thereby distancing themselves from the more radical legacy of the French Revolution.[28] In Spain, there were similar analyses of the resilience of American republican institutions (as discussed further in Chapter 2). And, even in Italy, where, as will be illustrated in Chapter 4, the predominant reaction to the American Civil War was horror at futile bloodshed, the liberal periodical *Nuova Antologia* argued that the outcome of the war had established firmer foundations for

American institutions.²⁹ "A good cause has triumphed," wrote the editor, "and now the bases on which the United States were built are much more solid."³⁰

It is natural to assume that this post – Civil War reorientation of conservative perspectives on America must have been mirrored by an opposite transformation on the Left. While conservatives learned to, if not love, then at least come to a newfound respect for American institutions and society, radicals, it is sometimes suggested, transformed their admiration into loathing. For example, in his classic study of the British Left's attitude to America, Henry Pelling argued that, as socialist ideas became more influential in Britain, the British working class became more aware of the contrast between the egalitarian promise and the unjust reality of life for American workers.³¹ Similar views were regularly echoed in Italy, where workers returning from the United States pointed to the exploitation of cheap labor by the US capitalist system. In this reading, the emergence of large-scale industrial capitalism and the rise of wage labor in the "Gilded Age" United States represented a direct challenge to the republican notion that there was an indissoluble connection between political liberty and economic independence as well as to the vision of America as a "workingmen's democracy."

This disenchantment was not without precedents. Even in Germany and Britain, where the impulse to hold up the American model was probably felt most keenly, there had always been notes of ambivalence. Overly positive images were, from early in the nineteenth century, criticized, corrected, and complemented by more skeptical tales, notably those from returning emigrants: Ferdinand Kürnberg's novel from 1855, *Der Amerika-Müde (The One Who Is Tired of America)*, is just one example of a more general weariness with the notion of America as a utopia that was symptomatic of the second half of the nineteenth century. Long before the Civil War, there were occasional worries among British radicals that the Americans were succumbing to the "too ardent pursuit of riches."³² News of periodic economic downturns, of labor agitation and the struggle against land monopoly had, since the 1830s and 40s, been well reported in the British radical press, while French socialists had always been somewhat skeptical of claims about social equality in the United States.³³ Nonetheless, negative images of America as the apogee of capitalist excess became much more common in the 1880s and 90s than they had been before. European radicals in the last two or three decades of the nineteenth century expressed increasing concern about corruption and the role of money in American politics. In turn, under the influence of socialist ideas, they questioned the axiomatic assumption of earlier generations of radicals and reformers that American-style political democracy was the pathway to economic equality. One of the prime consequences of the Civil War for the imagined America, then, was the erosion of the perception that American democracy was necessarily more radically egalitarian than other forms of political organization.

As Pelling has shown, in the decades after the Civil War, there was increasing concern in the English press about the state of the labor market in America. In one 1877 issue of the *Industrial Review*, readers were told an inspiring story of "John and James Dobson, workmen, who left Yorkshire some 20 years ago with very slender means." The Dobsons, apparently, were "now the owners of four large mills near the falls of Schuylkill, where they manufacture carpets and cloth. They employ a capital of 3,000,000 dollars, and 1,500 hands; 10,000 yards of carpet are produced every week." Yet, on the same page, readers were warned that in some parts of the United States "there are twice as many miners as the trade requires."[34]

Above all, the episode that catalyzed the emerging image of America as the epitome not of opportunity for the ordinary person but of capitalist exploitation was the Haymarket Affair. This was an infamous episode in Chicago in 1886 in which a demonstration in support of striking workers led to a bomb being detonated, causing the deaths of eight policemen and an unknown number of civilians. It led to a celebrated trial of eight "anarchists," four of whom were executed and one committed suicide. For socialists, the episode was evidence of "class war" in the United States. H. M. Hyndman of the British Social-Democratic Federation concluded that "corruption" of the legislatures and the power of the "great monopolies" were driving "intelligent workers" to the conviction that "an appeal to downright force is the only solution to the question."[35] Across the English Channel, one writer, a disenchanted former Americanophile, offered a wry riposte to Tocqueville by writing *L'Aristocratie en Amérique*.[36] In the Argentine anarchist press, the Haymarket Affair was interpreted as evidence that the much-vaunted US institutions of democracy had done little to save the workers from the repression of a capitalist state. Their emphasis was on the ferocity of the law as applied by "the capitalist vultures of North America." The convicted anarchists were widely portrayed as innocent men, "apostles and martyrs to an ideal of justice and love."[37] The United States could hardly be a model of a free country given such appalling repression. It was routinely represented in these publications as "the so-called Model Republic."[38] Memories of the hanged workers—depicted as advocates of "full social emancipation"—were invoked in support of virtually all labor campaigns in Argentina during the 1890s.[39]

An anarcho-socialist discourse that condemned the United States as the antithesis of a land of opportunity was in full voice by the 1890s. Juan B. Justo, founder of the Argentine Socialist Party (PSA) and translator into Spanish of Marx's *Das Kapital,* went to the United States because he deemed it the best place to study the current state of industrial capitalism, just as Engels had done in England.[40] Justo adopted a low-key, "factual" tone in his critical evaluation of the failure of the US model of capitalism and "democracy" to deliver the equality he wanted to see in Argentina. In a deliberate and devastating assault on existing images of the United States as a workers' paradise, Justo represented the United States as the "country of the millionaires" in which classes were "as clearly demarcated as in the old European societies." Drawing upon US sources wherever possible, he deployed them to denounce the distribution of wealth, which, according to the US 1890 census, gave 71 percent to the top 8 percent and 4.5 percent to the bottom 52%.[41] In the United States, Justo claimed, the word "society" had come to mean "not the whole nation" but "only the privileged few who pass their time in dissipation and pleasure-seeking." Like many contemporary British and French socialists, Justo was shocked by the high levels of periodic unemployment that seemed hardwired into the American economic order, and also by the degrading nature of much of the work that was available. Whereas English reformers earlier in the century had sometimes seen American techniques for mass production as rather more dignified for workers than the horrific conditions in British factories, Justo at the very end of the century drew attention to what he referred to, in English, as the "sweating system," noting that it relied on women and children.

One key aspect of Argentine comparisons of their country with the United States was immigration, the images of which reveal the volatile mixture of self-confidence and self-doubt that characterized the late-nineteenth-century Argentine elite's sense of their nation's future place in modern civilization. It was often claimed that Argentina was particularly welcoming to its immigrants, thus reinforcing its self-image as the ultimate "cosmopolitan nation." "We call someone who comes from abroad a foreigner [*extranjero*]," announced the liberal former president Nicolás Avellaneda at the opening of a continent-wide exhibition held in Buenos Aires in 1882, "because we have no other word in our language, but it has lost its meaning among us, because a foreigner stops being a stranger virtually as soon as he arrives."[42] By implication, and often by explicit comparison, the United States was less good at integrating its immigrants. There were recurrent images conveying the idea that whatever riches the United States had to offer, it was not likely to be the immigrants who would be the main beneficiaries. Anyone could go there, for sure, but, as imagined in one popular fictional version of the Californian Gold Rush, it was the all-conquering "Yankee element" that would dominate everything, fighting migrants for the spoils if need be.[43]

In Europe as well as in Latin America, it was liberals who were most likely to believe that the US model offered the path to a better society, but by the very end of the century, even they were beginning to share elements of the socialist critique of the United States. In particular, increasing attention was given to problems of urban overcrowding, of unemployment and industrial unrest, with much of the information circulating about these problems produced by US Progressives in support of various reform campaigns. The hypocrisy of millionaire philanthropists who denied their own workers a living wage while being feted for their generosity began to feature in liberal commentary. Argentina's leading liberal newspaper, *La Nación*, published such a piece in 1897, a notable departure, since, as the socialist paper *La Protesta* dryly commented, *La Nación* was usually known for "educating us about the excellent qualities of the republic par excellence."[44]

Persistence of the Idea of America as a Land of Opportunity

Yet the image of "the mightiest republic the world has ever known" as a site of personal transformation and an inspiring example of the beneficent effects of universal male suffrage proved resilient.[45] One of the founders of the German SPD, Wilhelm Liebknecht, maintained his faith in American republicanism until the end of his life in 1900. Liebknecht toured the United States in the company of Karl Marx's daughter Eleanor Marx-Aveling in 1886 and on his return to Germany wrote an enthusiastic travel account in which he lauded the Civil War as a democratic triumph: "where," he asked, "is the heroic European people that could offer something similar?"[46] Also reporting on an 1886 visit to America, the Irish writer Bram Stoker (who was later to find fame as the author of *Dracula*) told a working-class audience in London that their fellow laborers in America were much better dressed, that "everyone of modest means had a holiday home," that domestic service was much rarer because wages were so much higher, and that education was the engine of social mobility.[47] That such images were far from uncommon as late as the 1880s, and not just from professional writers of fiction, revealed the durability of the American Utopia.

This was true above all in Cuba where the image of the United States as "the great refuge for all the oppressed" proved more durable than anywhere else. For many Cuban workers, it was literally a land of opportunity for the significant numbers who went to work in Florida's cigar factories. Images of the good life in the United States persisted in Cuba well into the 1890s: "in this vast country nothing is lacking, or rather, everything is plentiful," so that "the only people who do not live contently here are the bad people."[48] José Martí, who was notoriously critical of many aspects of

US society in his chronicles of the 1880s, emphasizing the divide between "high society" and the masses, presenting in sharp relief the figures of the boss and the robber baron, laying bare the corruption of the wealthy, nevertheless repeatedly evoked "the marvellous prosperity of the United States, [...] never equalled in the annals of human history." Never before "in any people on earth" had there been "such a happy crowd," he wrote, "pursuing such useful labour [...] and enjoying such good fortune."[49] His very first accounts of US society testified to the ambivalence that continued to characterize the images he disseminated. He opened with an idealized vision of the land of opportunity: "I am, at last, in a country where everyone looks like his own master. One can breathe freely, freedom being here the foundation, the shield, the essence of life. One can be proud of his species here. Every one works; every one reads." A few months later, he created equally romanticized images of desperate poverty on the streets of New York: an old man whose "eyes, fixed upon the passers by, were full of tears"; "a poor woman [who] knelt on the sidewalk, as if looking for her grave"; "a hundred robust men, [...] all lying down on the grass or seated on the benches, shoeless, foodless, concealing their anguish under their dilapidated hats."[50] On the labor movement, Martí presented a similarly mixed picture. Commenting on a wave of strikes in 1886, he noted that they were all likely to be defeated (i.e., capitalist power would prevail, as elsewhere), but comparing the United States with Germany, he argued that labor relations were far worse in Germany because there workers lacked the "safety valve" of "the free vote, a free press, [... the chance to] elect a deputy, a senator, a judge, a President." In Germany, he concluded, "violence is just, because justice is not permitted."[51]

Even in Italy republicans argued that it was in America where "the problems on which our future depends articulate themselves and where they will be resolved," conceding that "the explanation for the United States' prosperity lies in the quality of its institutions and the virtue of its citizens."[52] And in Britain and France, even as radical disenchantment gathered pace, mass circulation newspapers devoted more and more space to coverage of the United States, often taking the form of a detailed recitation of statistics, which, in contrast to the Argentine socialist Justo's use of an empirical approach to discredit images of American opportunity, were reported in tones of wonder. An example from England is the *Newcastle Chronicle*, which, beginning in 1865, ran a regular weekly column headed "American items" that mixed amazement at the pace of American economic growth with occasional musings on the possible cultural and material benefits of American institutions. A typical column in 1865, which listed the number of books on the shelves of the public libraries of the United States (some 12 million apparently), concluded that there was a "spirit of self-confidence" in America that "seems to be fostered by the political as well as the physical atmosphere in which the people live."[53]

While intellectuals and socialist leaders became increasingly disenchanted with the promise of the United States, the popular press in Europe often carried more favorable images. A good example is *Reynolds's Newspaper*, which, from 1885 onward (at about the date when many socialists were despairing of America), carried the motto "government of the people, by the people, for the people"—a quote from Lincoln's Gettysburg Address—on its masthead.[54] Until the end of the century, the paper constantly advocated Canada's annexation by the United States on the grounds that "anything that adds to the power and authority of the United States among the nations of the earth is to the advantage of all mankind."[55] For the contributors to *Reynolds's*, the American republic exemplified the liberal maxim that a democratic Constitution and a wider diffusion of political power through democratic processes were the only means of bringing about greater economic equality. Within *Reynolds's* framework of popular liberalism, America appeared in the familiar role of counterfoil to the corruptions of aristocratic England, a guise in which it had first appeared in the writings of English radicals in the 1790s. "The course of Democracy is onward, steadily forward," argued one editorial, because "it is guided by the wisdom and good sense of the people, not by a Saul who towers above the people."[56] In 1887, when William F. Cody's Wild West show was the sensation of the season, "Demos," a regular contributor to *Reynolds's*, wrote a witty piece urging Buffalo Bill to take back to America some of the "relics of an ignorant and barbarous age"—such as a throne, a crown, a House of Lords, the "landocracy," and the "Tory working man."[57] And when Grover Cleveland was forming his second administration, *Reynolds's* could not refrain from pointing out that "fortunately, he has not, like Mr. Gladstone, to consult the whims and caprices of an old lady. There are no ridiculous Court appointments to be made, no sticks in waiting, or mistresses of robes; no buckhounds to be maintained out of the public funds. The United States have happily rid themselves of all that inane tomfoolery."[58] America was the perennial counterpoint to aristocracy and corruption. Furthermore, *Reynolds's* not only eulogized the United States, it also argued—in the melodramatic style that was one of its defining characteristics—that there was an aristocratic conspiracy to keep the English middle classes in ignorance about America. If the truth were known about the operation of republican institutions in the United States, the middle classes in Britain "would not for another year tolerate the rule of an arrogant and overbearing aristocracy."[59]

The continuing appeal of the United States exemplified by a mass circulation newspaper like *Reynolds's* was predicated on the continuing appeal of republican, antistatist, and antimonopolist politics in many countries, despite the rise of Marxist-influenced socialism.[60] Yet, if continued faith in republican institutions partly accounts for the persistence of positive images of America as a land of opportunity, then the perception of political corruption in America posed a profound challenge. In Italy, the impeachment of President Johnson prompted speculation that America "prepared itself again for more bloodshed," while, 13 years later, the assassination of President Garfield was interpreted as yet more evidence of America's moral and material decline since the Civil War.[61] The various scandals of the second Grant administration and the contested presidential election of 1876, together with widespread coverage of corruption in municipal government in the 1870s and 80s, challenged the core idea of America as a site of emancipation and opportunity. By the 1880s, the image of the American politician as a shady rascal out to line his own pockets had become a familiar stock character, lampooned in newspapers.[62] In Britain, the radical-leaning *Weekly Times* lamented that in the wake of the Hayes-Tilden disputed election of 1876 "those who take the most friendly interest in the great transatlantic experiment, and who most firmly believe in its ultimate success, must still be anxious to see how it can be made to work through its difficulties."[63] Yet even the corruption issue could be turned into a narrative of the triumph of the democracy over vested interests. *Reynolds's* praised the breaking of the Tweed Ring in New York and hoped that "when it is seen how the Americans have struggled with and got rid of their municipal tyrants, it is possible Londoners will take heart of grace, and have the metropolis governed as a great city should be governed, and not on the petty parochial principle that at the present time obtains."[64]

It was not that radicals in Britain or elsewhere were unaware of the shortcomings of American society. It was that many believed that whatever flaws were visible in America were the product of wider forces and that the best remedies were contained within America itself. As *Reynolds's* insisted in 1892, "it is absurd for any sane person to pretend that the American system is not better, whatever may be the social and economic flaws in the American structure."[65] The perception that the American labor movement was strong and growing was, for example, a powerful antidote to the contrary perception of rapacious bosses. If American capitalists used physical force more readily than their British counterparts, the American labor movement was seen as being equally, and admirably, vigorous. The sooner the timid British trade unionists "take a leaf out of the book of their American brethren the better" were typical sentiments.[66]

In Spain, too, radicals reading about the conflict between workers and their employers in the United States did not necessarily conclude that

America was no longer a land of opportunity; instead they drew inspiration from the size, organization, and ceaseless activity of America's organized working class. In its first issue in March 1886, the newspaper *El Socialista* lauded the Knights of Labor as a "powerful resistance organisation, perhaps the most important in the world" and admired its ability to mobilize large numbers of men, women, and even children from carpenters and railway workers to telephonists.[67] Above all, *El Socialista* praised the "triumphant" campaign for the eight-hour working day, keeping a running tally over the course of the spring and summer of 1886 of the number of US workers who, it said, had successfully agitated for a reduction in working hours (2,000,000 by August 6, 1886).[68] This editorializing culminated in the assertion in September that the "glorious North American republic" was on the cusp of revolution:

> Modern capitalism [in the United States] has already invaded the last bastion of the reactionaries: the peasants have been expropriated by capital and vomited into the ranks of the Proletariat. This is the beginning of the end of capitalism. The peasants, dispossessed and proletarianised, uniting with the industrial proletariat, will produce the ultimate and most terrible crisis which will destroy the worst of all worlds: the capitalist world.[69]

That there were some who looked to the United States for the Marxist road to revolution is testimony to the infinitely fertile capacity of America to appeal to people's hopes. We see a similar impulse among labor activists in Cuba. The contrast between the coverage of the Haymarket Affair in labor newspapers there and in Argentina is striking. In both countries there was extensive coverage of the riot as well as the subsequent trial and executions, with illustrations and special issues. In both Cuba and Argentina the convicted men were portrayed as innocent martyrs but the emphasis was different. Whereas in Argentina it was very much the oppressive forces of the United States—capitalists and state working together—that conspired against them, in Cuba the incident provoked instead a generalized indictment of all capitalist regimes rather than the US one in particular: "the assassins of the Chicago anarchists [were] all the kings, all the governments, all the bourgeoisie."[70] Rather than using the Haymarket Affair to highlight the deficiencies of the US model, as happened in Argentina, Cuban anarchist leaders preferred to emphasize the class aspects of the incident, representing it as an attack on the anarchist ideal and citing denunciations of it by those whom they saw as their fellow workers in the United States. The events are specifically located in Chicago in Cuban accounts, whereas in Argentina the city tended to be unspecified, implying that they could have potentially taken place anywhere in the United States.

Even if the United States exhibited some of the most frightening aspects of modernity, and even if there were isolated images suggesting that access to opportunity was increasingly race bound, it also remained, stubbornly, a place of potential liberation. By the end of the century, most Latin American images of the United States identified its idealism and commitment to equality and opportunity firmly in the past. Latin American sights were increasingly set on containing the negative impact of an expansionist, materialist power upon its neighbors. Cuban independence leaders were under no illusions about what US intervention in their struggle would bring ("once the United States gets into Cuba, how will it be got out again?," demanded Martí),[71] and the presence of wealthy US tourists on the island generated a range of images—especially cartoons—marked by ridicule, sometimes apparently affectionate, sometimes less so. Even so, to a notable extent, Cuban images from the 1890s convey the persistence of a quite widely shared sense that the American people, if not US governments, were the bearers of the founding ideals.

Abraham Lincoln: Man of the People

The enduring faith in the American republic as a land of opportunity for workingmen was expressed by a widespread veneration of Abraham Lincoln as the epitome of the democratic hero. The tone had been struck by none other than Karl Marx, who, in 1864, drafted a letter on behalf of the International Workingmen's Association congratulating "the single-minded son of the working class" on his reelection. Marx's endorsement of Lincoln, whose "prosaic" style he praised, reflected a strain of radical thought that still hoped that American influence in Europe would further the cause of democratization and emancipation of the working classes. In 1868, Giuseppe Mazzini credited Lincoln with "the real moral, intellectual, economic emancipation of the Whites" in Europe as well as of black people in America.[72] The Durham Miners' leader, John Wilson, was among those whose own experience of a brief stay in the United States had inured him from any sentimental view of America as a democratic paradise, yet in his memoirs no man was as highly praised as "stern, Indomitable 'Old Abe,'" for whom, Wilson wrote, "freedom was an eternal principle; to live in the White House was a temporary fleeting."[73] Lincoln's speeches were tirelessly quoted in the radical press to encapsulate the dignity of labor, the control of government by the people, and the ideal of democracy under the rule of law.

In Europe, the veneration of Abraham Lincoln as the epitome of the democratic hero was one factor that sustained faith in the American republic even as images of American opportunity began to be tarnished, from the 1880s onward, by the anxiety that high wages and social freedom in America were accompanied by long hours of work and a lack of union protection. Lincoln's rise from log cabin to White House was presented as tangible proof of the unique opportunities for social mobility afforded in the United States, opportunities that had been reaffirmed by the result of the war.[74] When Mazzini died in 1872, Italian Republicans modeled the staging of Mazzini's funeral on Lincoln's, including the railway journey through the country, with weeping workers and their wives presenting the Republican leader with a last salute.[75] And in the agitation that preceded the British 1867 Reform Act, "old honest Abraham Lincoln" was repeatedly invoked as an example of a leader who came from the people as a result of "universal suffrage" and who could "stand comparison with hereditary nobility of any country or age."[76] "Honest Abe, the rail-splitter, who piloted [the United States] through the hours of their greatest trial" was invoked frequently enough in the popular press to suggest that his image had substantial popular resonance.[77] Cheap portraits were advertised after his assassination and to hang a print of Lincoln on the wall of one's front parlor was to publicize a radical political allegiance. The widely circulating temperance weekly *The British Workman* published a striking allegorical print of the martyred president with Columbia and Britannia clasping hands and weeping surrounded by the British and American flags and mourning drapes.[78]

Lincoln also played an important role in the imaginative construction of the United States in Argentina, but in a rather different way. At least among the intellectuals who created most of the images of the United States circulating in Argentina in this period, there was less emphasis on the man-of-the-people aspect of Lincoln. Sarmiento's influential biography, rapidly compiled and published soon after Lincoln's assassination, highlighted his role as the nation builder that Sarmiento himself hoped to become, a stern subduer of military power who effectively deployed war as a strategy for national unity.[79] Such a focus is readily understandable given that the main cause of civil war and political discord in Argentina from the 1830s through to 1880 was the distribution of power between Buenos Aires and the provinces. Yet Sarmiento also admired the level of education among the US people and in that context he saw the autodidact Lincoln as the ultimate example of how a society in which learning was valued by all could enable someone as great as Lincoln to come to power "through the influence of his word, his conviction alone, and carrying with him to the Presidency the working people whose hands were roughened if honourable, but whose minds were cultivated."[80]

Writing in explicit challenge to Sarmiento's championing of (some) US practices as applicable to Argentina, the writer Eduarda Mansilla, who was generally skeptical about US claims to have eliminated social hierarchy, implied that Lincoln's bond with his people was perhaps not in practice all that it might be. In a subversive scene, she described the president's annual public audience, when anyone might go to the White House and shake his hand:

> The people are here, silent, reserved, respectful but implacable. Rustic workers, women, children, poor people in shirt-sleeves, dirty, dishevelled immigrants, entered the luxuriously carpeted salon; they all shook that symbolic hand, which directs the destiny of the United States.
>
> "They say," she added mockingly, "that Lincoln had the idea, and carried it out, of having a false arm made, as can be done only in the United States, to use at the evening reception." Overall Lincoln's encounter with the American people was a joyless occasion, to her mind, carried out in complete silence, with no music or conversation: "the celebration of Saxon democracy, with no warmth, no enthusiasm, no happiness."[81]

The image of Lincoln as a man of the people was far more resonant in Cuba, where the US Civil War, which had immediate implications for that island, was followed closely. Individual Cubans fought on both sides of the US conflict, and many people on the island identified themselves as "Lincolnites" or "Confederalists." The official ten-volume *Historia de Cuba* (1952) described how, as the cause of emancipation became bound up with the cause of Cuban independence, "the image of Lincoln, both in modest dwellings and in mansions that housed progressive young altruists, came to be an expression of the deepest Cuban aspirations."[82] The strong Cuban sense that Lincoln was a part of their own history is illustrated by Santovenia's rather speculative claim that "the roots of the Gettysburg address grew in Cuba" (through a connection between Cuban intellectual José de la Luz y Caballero and US Unitarian minister and scholar Theodore Parker).[83] What is certain is that the adventures of two Cubans who fought for the Union and were present at Gettysburg were followed avidly in Cuba through the pro-Lincoln newspaper, *El Siglo*,[84] and that a refrain often heard in the Cuban fields during the 1860s was "Avanza, Lincoln, avanza/Tu eres nuestra esperanza" (Advance, Lincoln, advance/You are our deliverance [lit. "hope"]).[85]

After the final abolition of Cuban slavery in the 1880s, Lincoln's image as the expression of the best qualities of the common man continued to circulate. Martí sharply reoriented the image of Lincoln away from Sarmiento's stern statesman toward Lincoln as natural man. He referred repeatedly to Lincoln's unaffected closeness to the humble people, his capacity to express their sorrows, and his compassion for them, to the extent that he claimed: "the spirit of Christ" was in him.[86] "Lincoln, that sublime son of those 'from below',"[87] as president, wept, Martí noted approvingly, "because his generals were going to shoot, as deserters, a few poor peasant lads who had not learnt to love war."[88] In Martí's eyes, Lincoln's poor, rural upbringing lent him an unrivalled legitimacy as a leader of his people who fulfilled the ideals of US independence: "out of the truth of poverty, with the innocence of the forest and the sagacity and power of the creatures that inhabited it, emerged, in the hour of the national readjustment, the good, sad guide, the woodcutter Lincoln."[89] Lincoln's background enabled him to do what Martí, in his famous manifesto for the cultural independence of Latin America, "Nuestra América" ("Our America," 1891), urged governments in Latin America to do, namely, to govern not according to precepts borrowed from places with a wholly different history, but rather, with knowledge and understanding of "the elements that constitute [their] country."[90]

Martí, who denounced the European-oriented universities in Latin America for blinding young Latin Americans to the beauty of their own history and culture, found it especially important that Lincoln was an autodidact whose wisdom derived from lived experience rather than formal education. Interest in Lincoln's autodidacticism continued to be widespread in Latin America well into the twentieth century.[91] For example, the Argentine Cupertino del Campo's one-page summary of Lincoln's life featured the fact that he had only three months schooling, but "he taught himself by himself, reading and re-reading the Bible and the few books that with difficulty he could get hold of."

The Land Question and American Exceptionalism

The rapid expansion of the United States never failed to amaze foreign observers. The United States' geographical and population growth, the extraordinary advances made in its industrial output after the Civil War, as well as what visitors often perceived to be the dynamism and fast pace of life in American cities, all reinforced the sense that America signified the future. America had always represented modernity because, to friends and foes alike, it meant boundlessness and freedom from the past. And, at least since the days when Benjamin Franklin wowed the salons of Paris, and fired imaginations as far away as San Juan in Argentina, where Sarmiento first read his autobiography, both Europeans and Latin Americans were used to imagining Americans as ingenious and practical. By the late nineteenth century, American modernity and inventiveness had become associated with its vaunted scientific superiority. One of the futures that America represented was the transformation of mankind through technological progress. American engineering was widely seen in Italy and elsewhere as synonymous with ingenuity. An important new bridge over the river Po in the North of Italy was simply called Ponte Americano; and Luigi Manzotti's hugely successful ballet *Excelsior* of 1881 celebrated humanity's progress with images of American inventions and technological advances.[92] Latin Americans had direct experience of the phenomenon, as US engineers went south to pit their wits against the challenges of the Andes, the pampas, and the Amazon. Remarkably similar images of US capacity to conquer nature circulated in both Europe and Latin America. One Cuban drew an extravagant comparison in 1862 between

> yesterday [when] no sound was heard in those wastes save the warhoop [sic] of savages; nothing was seen along the rivers, save some lazy aborigine smoking his leaf papúa, but today how surprising the change [...] all is invaded by man. The air is cleft and woven with the metallic threads of the telegraph, the waters burdened with ships, the soil is covered with railroad lines [...] cities have sprung up, palaces have been erected, roads, bridges, canals and aqueducts have been constructed, and [...] a multitude of 33 millions have appeared which have consummated all that comprehends the fortune of a remarkable nation.[93]

Or, as the English labor newspaper the *Bee-Hive* put it, in an editorial lauding the achievements of the United States in its centennial year, back in 1776, "three million wild Indians then roamed where now busy industries and a prosperous civilisation have replaced the thriftless savage."[94]

In theory, there was a tension between the images of America as a complex modern space generated by rapid industrialization and the persistent image of America as "natural space" defined by its simplicity and authenticity.[95] But, in practice, these contrasting representations often coexisted. The persistent theme of authenticity in popular images of America may even have helped to inoculate America from any possibility of losing its sense of difference. It was also a reminder of the myth of natural abundance—America as a land of plenty—which was the oldest American myth of all and which underlay, sometimes overtly, sometimes only implicitly, the idea of America as a land of opportunity.

Those radicals who, much as they may have wished to do so, doubted the possibility of transplanting American democracy to their home country invariably emphasized the impact of environmental factors, foremost of which was the availability of land, on the character of a people and the political possibilities open to them. As the Liberal British statesman William E. Gladstone put it:

> Passing from a narrow island to a continent almost without bounds, the colonists at once and vitally altered their conditions of thought, as well as of

existence, in relation to the most important and most operative of all social facts, the possession of the soil. In England, inequality lies imbedded in the very base of the social structure; in America, it is a late, incidental, unrecognised product, not of tradition, but of industry and wealth, as they advance with various, and, of necessity, unequal steps.[96]

The abundance of land, according to this argument, was the central fact of America, a point that Frederick Jackson Turner was to make in his celebrated lecture on the significance of the frontier in 1893.

The perception that social mobility was maintained in the United States by the abundance of "free land" goes a long way toward explaining the resilience of the image of America as the "El Dorado of high wages."[97] Among Italian intellectuals, the idea of America as a land of promise received an important boost from Achille Loria's *Annalisi della proprietà capitalistica* (1889), which argued that "free," or unoccupied, land "was the key to a nation's economic growth."[98] In Britain, liberal and radical newspapers argued, well into the 1890s, that the primary cause of inequality was not the structural exploitation of industrial capitalism but the "class interest" of the aristocracy, the basis of whose power was monopoly ownership of land. As Eugenio Biagini and others have argued, popular radicalism in Victorian Britain remained preoccupied with the struggle between the "people" and the landed aristocracy, who radicals saw as the "section of society most hopelessly corrupted by unchecked power, excessive authority and influence and the lack of exertion and daily labour."[99] Writing in the *Newcastle Weekly Chronicle* at the time of the centenary of the Declaration of Independence, the old Chartist W. E. Adams declared that the United States had a "government, not of a class, but of the people—a government of the people, for the people and by the people."[100] Therefore, even in the midst of rapid industrialization in both Britain and the United States, the land question and the struggle with traditional aristocracy remained the central issue for working-class radicals since they saw the evils of monopoly in landed property as the basis of the illegitimate, unequal distribution of social and political power.[101]

In this respect, as in so many others, the United States provided the alternative model. As the *Liverpool Mercury* put it in 1880, "while in England public policy has unremittingly [sic] favoured the accumulation of estates in land by the Few, that of the Republic has as steadily been directed towards their dispersion among the many. This divergence of aim marks with the strongest emphasis the ascendancy of aristocracy in the one country and of democracy in the other."[102] In *Reynolds's*, a regular contributor under the pen name "Northumbrian," who appeared to be an English emigrant to the United States, assured readers in 1887 that "beneath the star-spangled banner, with its glorious memories of noble effort and personal freedom, every man, to generalize, owns either his own house or a plot of land. In England, however, by the caprice of landlords, the whole of the inhabitants of a county might be turned out like sheep upon the road-side tomorrow."[103]

For late Victorian British land reformers who were galvanized by contests in Ireland and to a lesser extent in Scotland and Wales, the United States presented a cornucopia of inspiring images. Landlordism was, in the words of one advocate, no less than "the twin brother of slavery."[104] Great hopes were placed in the Homestead Act of 1862, which, British radicals hoped, would bestow "the "magic of property" on every new immigrant. When Congress passed an act attempting to prohibit the purchase of land in United States Territories or the District of Columbia by noncitizens, *Reynolds's* hailed it, with no discernable irony, as "probably the most tremendous piece of legislative work which any nation has seen."[105] As the author of this piece in *Reynolds's* saw it, the act was evidence that America was attempting to destroy land speculators and the evil of absentee landlordism. It was an example that the newspaper wanted Britain to follow.

There were, argued British observers, two principal consequences of the availability of land in America. Both were points that had been made by the Chartist Land Company and other land reformers before the Civil War. The first was that the abundance of fertile land meant that, as the *Glasgow Herald* put it, "the wages in America can never fall so low as England" because the "safety valve" of the West reduced the oversupply of wage workers.[106] The second point was that the realistic prospect as well as the reality of small proprietorship provided sufficient incentive that workers' productivity increased markedly. For one British observer in 1870, this even applied to the "often thriftless Celt" who,

> when he is told on arrival among his kinsfolk in America that if he will only work up to it and at it, he may in a short time become a landed proprietor, have a house of his own, and laugh on for the rest of his days at the fear of eviction wherein he was bred, rubs his eyes, asks himself if he is awake, and sober, or if the fairies have anything to do with it. He has always been told that to get to be heaven one must die first; but here is something like his notion of the real thing, upon the sole condition of being more alive than he has ever been before. He goes to work, and seldom is his labour in vain.[107]

The idealism of such images was challenged by a counternarrative in the British press of the practical failure of the various Homestead Acts to distribute land to the most deserving. Yet if the reality fell short of the ideal, then European radicals had only to turn to the ideas of one of the best known Americans in the world in the late nineteenth century, Henry George. George's program to restore economic equality in America by abolishing land speculation and imposing a 100 percent tax on rental income provided a powerful image of America as a place where the social and political battle of the people against privilege was being waged and in time would be won.[108] "There was St George; there was George Washington; there is Henry George," trumpeted *Reynolds's*. "The first slew, or did not slay, a frightful dragon; the second founded the greatest commonwealth the world has ever seen; the third has written a book ('Progress and Poverty') which is destined to revolutionise human society, not only in one country but in all from top to bottom." If "the greed of gorged and rapacious capitalists" was threatening to undermine American commitment to the equality of man then the "much favoured Republic of the West" could be redeemed by the Knights of Labor, which was "shaking its fist defiantly in the face of landlords and millionaires."[109]

As the radical press saw it, George's crusade sought to reestablish the republican idea that wealth and political power should be based only on the fruits of one's own labor. His analysis touched a nerve in Britain because of a predisposition to trust the capacity of a vigorously democratic and truly republican government to sustain the common man in a way that the hierarchical British political system never could. The persistence of the image of America as a place where the "right to rise" was protected in spite of the large trusts and the violent strikes was demonstrated by the enthusiasm with which Andrew Carnegie's book, *Triumphant Democracy*, was received by the radical press on its publication in 1886. *Reynolds's* thought that Carnegie—the son of a Chartist who had made his millions in the American steel industry—had demonstrated the contrast between a monarchical state in which "the dignity of labour is looked down upon" and America in which it is valued. Carnegie, whose companies fought violent campaigns against labor rights in the United States, bought 18 British newspapers in the 1880s and ran them in the radical interest. To some in the British radical press, Carnegie, for all his enormous wealth, offered living proof that there was nothing inherently oppressive about capitalism, so long as it was harnessed by a republican and democratic political system. The opening line of Carnegie's book—"The old nations of the earth creep on at a snail's pace; the Republic thunders past with the rush of the express"—could almost have been an unconscious echo of *Reynolds's* observation 30 years earlier that "whereas the work of Reform progresses at a snail's pace in monarchical England, it advances with railroad speed in the kingless climes of the United States."[110] Certainly, *Reynolds's* interpreted *Triumphant Democracy* as a resounding endorsement of its own long-standing view of America.

Conclusion

By the very end of the century even *Reynolds's Newspaper* was struggling to maintain its optimistic vision of the United States. The defeat of the Democratic-People's Party candidate William Jennings Bryan in the 1896 presidential election marked a repudiation of, among other things, Henry George's vision for reinvigorating economic democracy. Bryan, *Reynolds's* told its readers, represented the "opposition to the rings of millionaires who are the real rulers of the United States. What this election has shown is that America, like Europe, is absolutely in the grasp of rich men, and that, for the present, the majority of the people wish to have it so." From Jefferson to McKinley was "a very steep descent suggesting serious political retrogression." To the horror of *Reynolds's* a new aristocracy had emerged in America hostile to republican institutions.[111] This fateful development was then compounded by the "sinister" intermarriage of the "impoverished peers of England" with the daughters of American multimillionaires. "American plutocracy," concluded *Reynolds's*, had, in a dark irony, saved English aristocracy.[112]

The promise of American democracy to offer real opportunities for ordinary men and women, to create a more equal society shorn of the entrenched hierarchies and privileges of the Old World, had, for the time being, dimmed. But even at this bleak moment, the faith in the original American democratic promise and its capacity for reinvention and renewal did not die. The "discontented and disinherited" on both sides of the Atlantic, argued *Reynolds's*, needed now to begin a new struggle to overcome the "great capitalist conspiracy against Republican institutions."[113] They may have been obscured by a "sinister" conspiracy between English aristocrats and American wealth, but it was still American ideals and American voices that offered a template for a more just, democratic society. In 1900, *Reynolds's* fantasized about "what a change would come over the people of this country" if they stopped reading the "lying claptrap and dull platitudes" of the *Daily Mail* and other "Jingo newspapers" and read instead Paine's *Rights of Man* and Henry George's *Progress and Poverty*.[114]

The persistent ambivalence about America's emancipatory potential reflected the larger sense in which images of America were so often caught between two foundational, and theoretically opposing, ideas—that of America as a "natural," even innocent, space and that of America as the epitome of modernity and therefore of complexity and technological advance. The vision of America as a land of opportunity drew on the fertile soil of the first of these two ideas: it was the availability of land above all else that guaranteed opportunity. How the image of opportunity could be integrated into the image of America as a glimpse of a technologically complex and increasingly urban future was less obvious.

Turner's frontier thesis had hypothesized that US exceptionalism—his nation's apparently unique ability to maintain social mobility amid industrialization and gathering technological complexity—was dependent on a finite resource that, according to the 1890 census, had now run out: "unsettled" land. His was a fundamentally bleak prognosis for the American future with little scope for a new life for the tired and huddled masses of the Old World that the United States had formerly offered. But of course the image of opportunity was not extinguished with the census of 1890. Partly this was because land remained cheaper in America than in Europe, but mostly because it was not just the physical availability of land that had underpinned foreign hopes for a better life in America, but the ideologies and political structures that seemed to accompany it. After all, Henry George had already, in effect, offered a riposte to Turner: if there was no more land to be freely settled, then the promise of American democracy required that the land be more equally shared. Moreover, until the First World War, the enormous industrial output of the United States still offered better wages and the promise of a higher standard of living than could be obtained in most other parts of the world, for all the labor conflict, poor housing, and disillusionment that it also brought.

Large-scale emigration to the United States from Italy only began in the twentieth century (in the 1860s five times as many Italians emigrated within Europe as traveled across the Atlantic and as late as the 1880s, Italians were twice as likely to go to Argentina as the United States).[115] But by the 1930s, waves of emigration from the poorer parts of Italy had begun to erode earlier skepticism and even in that country there had developed a fantastical image of the prosperity that might be won in America. The peasants of Lucania conjured up the most powerful of all myths about America when, according to the recollections of Carlo Levi, they pinned dollar bills to their walls, alongside pictures of the local Madonna. "Like the Holy Ghost or an ambassador from heaven to the world of the dead," the greenback, "the last of those brought back from across the sea, or one that had come in the letter of a husband or relative," was a shining promise of an "other world." It was not that America represented an easy life. On the contrary, the Italian peasants understood full well that it was a land, in Levi's words, where a man "goes to work and sweats for his daily bread, where he lays aside a little money only at the cost of endless hardship and privation." Yet, in their eyes it was also, and with no sense of contradiction, an "earthly paradise, Jerusalem the Golden ... so sacred as to be untouchable."[116] It is the intangible, spiritual quality to this faith, impermeable as it was to contradictory evidence, that comes through again and again in our sources.

After all, the image of America as a land of opportunity was always as much a matter of faith in the future as it was a reflection of present reality.

Notes

1. *Morning Advertiser*, undated, quoted in *Reynolds's Newspaper*, February 1, 1857.
2. Bronstein, *Land Reform and Working Class Experience in Britain and the United States*.
3. Francisco Bilbao, *Obras completas* (Buenos Aires: Imprenta de Buenos Aires, 1866, 2 vols.), vol. I, 294–295.
4. Ibid., 286.
5. On the radical image of America in Britain before the Civil War, see Crook, *American Democracy in English Politics*. For a discussion of negative views of America among British radicals in the first half of the century, see Bronstein, "From the Land of Liberty to Land Monopoly"; Claeys, "The Example of America a Warning to England?."
6. Lerg, *Amerika als Argument*, 38.
7. Quoted in Bronstein, "From the Land of Liberty to Land Monopoly," 155.
8. Henry Scoresby, *American Factories and their Female Operatives* (London: Longman, 1845), 11. Cited in Bronstein, "From a Land of Liberty to Land Monopoly," 155.
9. Foucrier, *Le rêve californien*.
10. *Reynolds's Newspaper*, September 28, 1856.
11. Ibid., June 12, 1853.
12. Domingo F. Sarmiento, *Viajes en Europa, Africa y América* (Buenos Aires: Imprenta de Mayo, 1854), 99.
13. Giles Pécout, "Cavour vista dagli Stati Uniti," in *Gli Stati Uniti e l"Unità d"Italia*, ed. Fiorentino and Sanfilippo, 125–132, 126. See also the relevant debate in the Italian parliament on December 6, 1861: *La Politica Estera dell"Italia negli atti, documenti e discussioni parlamentari dal 1861 al 1914*, ed. Segretario Generale della Camera dei Deputati (Roma: GER, 1971), vol. I (1861–1876), 98. Like Mazzini, people in the United States often described Garibaldi as a man of Protestant virtue. Riall, *Garibaldi*, 146–147, 299. The liberal Nuova Antologia looked at the United States as a model in matters regarding the separation of church and state: Francesco Ferrara, "La chiesa e lo stato agli Stati-Uniti di America," in *Nuova Antologia*, March 1867, 562–582.
14. Tavares Bastos, *Cartas do Solitário*, Carta XXVIII, 324.
15. Ibid., 63.
16. Bilbao, *Obras completas*, vol. I, 294–295.
17. *Reynolds's Newspaper*, May 26, 1850. For more skeptical views of America among Chartists who actually went there, see Boston, *British Chartists in America*, 36–46.
18. Todd, *The Militant Democracy*, 70–71.

19. John Bright, *Speeches on Questions of Public Policy*, ed. James E. Thorold Rogers (London: Macmillan, 1868, 2 vols.), vol. 1, 225.
20. *The Times*, April 27, 1887. On British attitudes to America during the Civil War see Campbell, *English Public Opinion and the American Civil War*; Crawford, *The Anglo-American Crisis of the Mid-Nineteenth Century*; Ellison, *Support for Secession*; Blackett, *Divided Hearts*; Adams, *Great Britain and the American Civil War*; Jordan and Pratt, *Europe and the American Civil War*; and H. C. Allen, "The Civil War, Reconstruction and Great Britain," in *Heard Around the World*, ed. Hyman, 3–69. For Italian images of the Civil War see Chapter 4 in this book.
21. *Bee-Hive*, April 29, 1865.
22. This phrase, often used in nineteenth century publications on both sides of the Atlantic, seems to have been coined by John O'Sullivan, editor of the *Democratic Review*, in 1839. "The Great Nation of Futurity", *The United States Democratic Review*, vol. 6, no. 23, 426–430.
23. *Newcastle Weekly Chronicle*, April 13, 1867, cited in Biagini, *Liberty, Retrenchment and Reform*, 81.
24. Lord Acton, "The Civil War in America: Its Place in History," in *Historical Essays & Studies* (London: Macmillan & Co., 1907), 125. (A lecture delivered at the Literary and Scientific Institution, Bridgnorth, on January 18, 1866).
25. Sir Henry Maine, *Popular Government: Four Essays* (London: John Murray, 1885), 50–52.
26. Tulloch, "Changing British Attitudes towards the United States in the 1880s."
27. Lord Bryce, *The American Commonwealth* (London: Palgrave Macmillan, 1888, 3 vols.), vol. I, 339–340.
28. On 1848, see Eugene Newton Curtis, *The French Assembly of 1848 and the American Constitutional Doctrines*. PhD diss, Columbia University, 1917; Portes, *Fascination and Misgivings*, 174.
29. Giovanni Boglietti, "'Repubblicani e Democratici negli Stati-Uniti d' America," in *Nuova Antologia*, August 1868, 766–788.
30. "Rassegna Politica," in *Nuova Antologia*, January 1866, 200–201. Giovanni Boglietti, "Repubblicani e Democratici negli Stati-Uniti d"America," in *Nuova Antologia*, August 1868, 766–788.
31. Pelling, *America and the British Left*. For a similar view, see Boston, *British Chartists in America*.
32. *Reynolds's Newspaper*, May 26, 1850, September 14, 1856.
33. Rémond, *Les Etats-Unis devant l'opinion française*, 774–777.
34. *Industrial Review*, January 13, 1877.
35. H. L. Hyndman, *The Chicago Riots and the Class War in the United States* (London: Swann, Sonnenschein, Lowery & Co., 1886).
36. Frédéric Gaillardet, *L'Aristocratie en Amérique* (Paris: E. Dentu, 1883). On Gaillardet and the French disenchantment with the United States in this period, more generally, see: Roger, *L'ennemi américain*, 139–177.
37. *El Perseguido* V, no. 71, November 11, 1894, 2; *L'Avvenire*, Anno I, no. 1, November 10, 1895, "I mártiri di Chicago," November 11, 1887," front page.

38. For example, "1887–11 Noviembre – 1896," *La Anarquía*, Año II, no. 17, November 1, 1896, front page; *L'Avvenire*, Anno II, no. 15, November 22, 1896, "Dal Nord America," 4; *La Revolución Social* I, no. 14, November 12, 1896, front page.
39. *El Obrero Panadero* (Buenos Aires), I:5, November 22, 1894, 1.
40. Juan B. Justo, *En los Estados Unidos. Apuntes escritos en 1895 para un periódico obrero* (Buenos Aires: Imprenta Jacobo Peuser, 1898).
41. Justo, *En los Estados Unidos*, 27–30.
42. Nicolás Avellaneda, "En la exposición continental de Buenos Aires," March 15, 1882, in his *Discursos. Oraciones cívicas* (Buenos Aires: Librería La Facultad de Juan Roldan, 1928), 216–225, 225.
43. Juana Manuela Gorriti, "Un viaje al pais del oro," in her *Panoramas de la vida*, Imprenta y Librería de Mayo, 1876, vol. II, esp. 174 and 196. It was first published as *Un año en California* in the newspaper *El Nacional* (Buenos Aires) in 1864, reprinted in *La Revista de Buenos Aires* in 1869.
44. Amalia Solano, "Estados Unidos," *La Protesta humana. Periódico anarquista* (Buenos Aires), I:12, October 31, 1897, 4.
45. *Carlisle Examiner*, May 16, 1865.
46. Wilhelm Liebknecht, quoted in Jörg Nagler, "National Unity and Liberty: Lincoln's Image and Reception in Germany, 1871–1989," in *The Global Lincoln*, ed. Carwardine and Sexton, 244.
47. *Reynolds's*, January 3, 1886.
48. Aurelia Castillo de González, *Un paseo por América* (Havana: Imprenta "La Constancia," 1895), 79, 67.
49. José Martí, "Coney Island," in *Obras completas*, December 3, 1881 (Havana: Editorial de Ciencias Sociales, 1975), vol. 9, 123–128, 123. His chronicles of the United States are collected together in vols. 9–13.
50. José Martí, "Impressions of America (by a Very Fresh Spaniard)," *The Hour* (New York), 1880, in *Obras completas*, vol. 19, 103–126, 103 and 123.
51. José Martí, *Obras completas*, vol. 11, 158 and vol. 10, 451.
52. *Almanacco Repubblicano, 1871*, ed. Enrico Bignami (Lodi: Società Cooperativo-Tipografica, 1870), 65–66.
53. *Newcastle Weekly Chronicle*, March 3, 1865.
54. The quotation from the Gettysburg Address was incorporated into the masthead of *Reynolds's Newspaper* from April 5, 1885.
55. *Reynolds's Newspaper*, January 20, 1889.
56. Ibid., August 9, 1885.
57. Ibid., May 15, 1887.
58. Ibid., March 5, 1893.
59. Ibid., August 17, 1851.
60. On this theme, see, for example, *Weekly Times*, May 26, 1872.
61. Leonida Carpi, "Rivista Politica," in *Rivista Bolognese di scienze, lettere, arti e scuole*, January 15, 1867, 109–120; G. Boglietti, "Il Presidente Garfield," in *Nuova Antologia*, October 1881, 181–207.

LAND OF OPPORTUNITY? 47

62. *Reynolds's Newspaper*, January 3, 1886.
63. *Weekly Times*, December 3, 1876.
64. *Reynolds's Newspaper*, April 18, 1886.
65. Ibid., November 13, 1892.
66. Ibid., September 11, 1887.
67. *El Socialista*, March 19, 1886.
68. See, for example, Ibid., May 28, 1886, June 19, 1886, August 6, 1886.
69. Ibid., September 10, 1886.
70. *El Productor* (Havana), November 11, 1891, front page.
71. José Martí, letter to Gonzálo Quesada, October 19, 1889, in *Obras completas*, vol. 6.
72. Quoted in Eugenio F. Biagini, "'The Principle of Humanity': Lincoln in Germany and Italy, 1859–1865," in *Global Lincoln*, ed. Carwardine and Sexton, 88.
73. John Wilson, *Memories of a Labour Leader: The Autobiography of John Wilson, J. P, M.P.* (London: T. F. Unwin, 1910), 173–174. For similar sentiments, see Tom Mann, *Tom Mann's Memoirs* (London: Labour Publishing, 1923); George Ratcliffe, *Sixty Years of It: Being the Story of My Life and Public Career* (London: A. Brown and Sons, 1935); George Barnes, *From Workshop to the War Cabinet* (London: Herbert Jenkins, 1924).
74. See, for example, *Alfonso Jouault Abraham Lincoln, su juventud y su vida política. Historia de la abolicion de la esclavitud en los Estados-Unidos* (Barcelona: Imprenta de la Gaceta de Barcelona, 1876).
75. Luzzatto, *La mummia della Repubblica*.
76. George Lorimer, speech in the Music Hall, Edinburgh, *The Caledonian Mercury*, June 28, 1865. See also: report of the meeting of the National Reform Union, *Reynolds's Newspaper*, May 19, 1867; speech of William Lloyd Garrison in the Victoria Hall in Leeds, *Leeds Mercury*, October 22, 1867. On the idea of America in the debates leading up to the 1867 Reform Act see also, Keith McClelland, "England's Greatness: The Working Man," in *Defining the Victorian Nation*, ed. Hall, McClelland, Rendell, 90.
77. *Lloyd's Weekly*, January 20, 1886, cited in Biagini, *Liberty, Retrenchment and Reform*, 80.
78. *The British Workman*, July 1, 1865; Biagini, *Liberty, Retrenchment and Reform*,
79. On the continuing power of Lincoln's image to define political cleavages some years after the Civil War ended, see *Reynolds's Newspaper*, April 10, 1881.
80. D. F. Sarmiento, *Vida de Abran Lincoln, décimo sesto presidente de los Estados Unidos* (New York: D. Appleton & Co., 2nd edn., 1866), The book was substantially plagiarized from two US biographies.
80. Sarmiento, *Vida de Lincoln*, xliv.
81. Eduarda Mansilla de García, *Recuerdos de viaje* (Madrid: Ediciones El Viso, 1996, fasc. edn. of 1882 version published by Juan A. Alsina, Buenos Aires), 90–91.
82. Guerra y Sánchez et al., eds., *Historia de la nación cubana*, vol. IV, 31.

83. Emeterio Santovenia, "Lincoln, el precursor de la Buena Vecindad" in his *Estudios, biografías y ensayos*, (Havana: La Habana, 1958), 481–499, 490.
84. Santovenia, "Lincoln, el precursor...," 488.
85. Portell Vilá, *Historia de Cuba en sus relaciones con los Estados Unidos y España*, vol. II, 171.
86. José Martí, Letter to the editor of *La Nación* (Buenos Aires), August 15, 1889, New York, in *Obras completas*, vol. 12, 287–295, 294.
87. José Martí, "Roscoe Conkling" [1888], in *Obras completas*, vol. 13, 175–183, 181.
88. José Martí, "El General Logan" [1887], in *Obras completas*, vol. 13, 305–307, 306.
89. José Martí, "Congreso Internacional de Washington" [1889], in his *Nuestra América* (Barcelona: Lingkua, 2006), 79.
90. José Martí, "Nuestra América" [1891], in Ramos, *Divergent Modernities*, 296.
91. Cupertino del Campo, *Prohombres de América* (Buenos Aires: Asociación de Difusión Interamericana, 1943), no page numbers. Chile's main newspaper, *El Mercurio*, noted in 1959 that in many respects Lincoln was a product of his times, but "the unusual thing about him was his determination to teach himself." See "La memoria de Lincoln y la opinión universal," in *El Mercurio* (Santiago), February 13, 1959, 3.
92. "Il Ponte Americano sul Po," *Rivista Bolognese*, 1867, 385–391. On Excelsior: Luigi Manzotti, *Excelsior* (Milano: Ricordi, 1881). Carol Lee, *Ballet in Western Culture: A History of its Origins and Evolution* (New York and London: Routledge, 2002), 176. "Excelsior," in *The Encyclopedia of Dance and Ballet*, ed. Mary Clarke and David Vaughan (London: Pitman, 1977), 134; Alberto Testa, *Storia della danza e del balletto* (Roma: Gremese, 1994), 78. Jutta Toelle, *Bühne der Stadt. Mailand und das Teatro della Scala zwischen Risorgimento und Fin-De-Siècle* (Vienna: Böhlau/Oldenbourg, 2009), 120 sq.
93. J. C. Zenea, "The Literature of the United States," in *The Cuban Herald/El Heraldo Cubano* (Havana), March 30, 1862, vol. I, no. 2, 2.
94. *Bee-Hive*, July 8, 1876.
95. See James Epstein, "'America' in the Victorian Cultural Imagination," in *Anglo-American Attitudes*, ed. Leventhal and Quinault, 107–123.
96. Gladstone, "Kin Beyond Sea," 183.
97. Quoted in Pelling, *America and the British Left*, 45.
98. Rolle, *The Immigrant Upraised*, 28–29. On Turner see also Bender, "Historians, the Nation, and the Plenitude of Narratives," in *Rethinking American History in a Global Age*, ed. Bender, 1–22.
99. Biagini, *Liberty, Retrenchment and Reform*, 51. See also Thompson, *The Making of the English Working Class*, 105.
100. *Newcastle Weekly Chronicle*, July 1, 1876.
101. This continued stress on the land question explains the persistence of the myth of the "Norman Yoke" and reinforces the argument that in ideological terms Victorian working-class radicalism remained structured around Painite republican themes. Asa Briggs, "Saxons, Normans and Victorians,"

Collected Essays of Asa Briggs (Brighton: Harvester, 1985, 2 vols.), vol. 2, 215–235.
102. Liverpool Mercury, December 25, 1880.
103. Reynolds's Newspaper, May 17, 1887.
104. Ibid., October 24, 1886.
105. Ibid., April 24, 1887.
106. Glasgow Herald, June 3, 1867.
107. Review of an essay on American land laws by C. M. Fisher, in *Essays in the Systems of Land Tenures in Various Countries* (London: The Cobden Club, 1870), in *The Examiner*, January 15, 1870.
108. Elwood P. Lawrence, "Henry George's British Mission," *American Quarterly* 3 (1951).
109. Reynolds's Newspaper, October 24, 1886.
110. Ibid., August 17, 1851.
111. Ibid., November 25, 1900.
112. Ibid., November 8, 1896.
113. Ibid., November 8, 1896.
114. Ibid., October 14, 1900.
115. Istituto Centrale di Statistica, *Sommario di Statistiche Storiche dell'Italia, 1861–1975* (Rome: Istituto Centrale di Statistica, 1976), 34–35; Martellone, "Italian Mass Emigration to the United States, 1876–1930"; Pierattini, 'Vien via, si va in America, si parte', 59.
116. Carlo Levi, *Christ Stopped at Eboli*, trans. Frances Freneye (London: Penguin, 1963), 121.

2

A Model Republic

Kate Ferris

I say that we can affirm that all that is fundamental and effective that has been achieved in the Republic of the United States is the *work of man*; and therefore I say that all can be attempted and realized among other peoples, within the sense, currents, ideas and compromises of the contemporary Era, taking into account, as to how it is applied, the singular elements and very particular conditions of the locality, the environment and the exigencies of History.

Rafael María de Labra, La República de los Estados Unidos de América, *1897*

In the late nineteenth century the United States of America was habitually invoked by an epithet: in Spain it was the *gran república* or *república-modelo*; in Britain, the "great Republic of the West"; in Spanish America, *la gran república del Norte*. This image—of the United States as the model republic—was one of the most widely circulated in Europe and Latin America in the second half of the nineteenth century. The Constitution, the institutions, and the democratic practices of the United States lay at the core of contemporaries' understandings of what that country represented in its modernity. When outside observers debated aspects of the United States, whether it was the issue of slavery, the state of the economy, or striking railroad workers, more often than not the underlying subtext of these discussions was the opportunity that they provided for either lauding or discrediting the United States as a model or anti-model republic.

The political actors of nineteenth-century Europe and Latin America, especially reforming and radical liberals, operated within deeply cosmopolitan networks for the circulation and exchange of ideas.[1] Popular expressions of republicanism likewise drew upon an international vocabulary and set of symbols. After the revolution of 1868 in Spain, for example, when numerous towns and villages declared themselves "for the republic," a French traveler observed young republicans wearing "Garibaldian shirts," witnessed the symbolic planting of the US federal flag alongside the Spanish one, and heard shouts of "Viva la República francesa" to accompany the ubiquitous vivas "a la República Federal."[2] The ultimate symbol of international republicanism was Giuseppe Garibaldi, who had cultivated an iconic status as a romantic political hero since his exploits on behalf of Latin American independence movements in Europe and the Americas.[3] In the United States itself, Phrygian caps, habitually worn by Marianne, adorned the US national seal and featured in Washington Irving's *Rip van Winkle*, whose eponymous hero awakes to find be-capped Americans celebrating their new republic.

The place occupied by images of the republic in the United States among Europeans and Latin Americans must be located within this transnational circulation of people, texts, ideas, symbols, and practices concerned with democracy, liberalism, national unity, and independence. The United States often perceived itself as the originator of an exportable political model,[4] but it faced severe competition for the mantle of *república-modelo*. In the minds of both political reformers and grassroots republicans the political model of the United States jostled and competed with the models and symbols of French, Swiss, Italian, and classical republicanism as well as, in many cases, with a locally developed version of liberalism and/or republicanism. In addition, the British political system of constitutional monarchy was much admired for its liberal values, political tolerance, parliamentarianism, and cabinet decision making. Indeed the two—the British and the US political systems—were frequently conflated as originating from the same "Anglo-Saxon" political tradition. This was certainly the view taken in France, where among liberals it was rather a question of individual taste than of principled disagreement whether one looked across the Atlantic or across the Channel for political guidance. In Britain itself the "Anglo-Saxon" roots of American republican institutions were taken for granted, both by supporters and detractors.

While there may have been broad agreement that the US version of republicanism and democracy was at least one significant touchstone for anyone interested in developing more modern forms of government, there was little consensus as to how the founding documents, principles, and practices of the United States should be understood, or what exactly was the key to the seeming success of the US political system. The political model of the United States came to prominence in different countries in Europe and Latin America at different times, and was seized upon by different political groups—conservatives as well as liberals and radicals—with different interests in mind. Some were advocates of federalism (although that was variously understood), others of the expansion of individual rights and self-government, or the cultivation of local democratic cultures; others still pursued outcomes, such as increased centralization, that were precisely the antithesis of what the United States was seen to represent. The degree of interest in and understanding of US republicanism and democracy depended on national and partisan concerns that were both particular and contingent. This chapter explores how these images were refracted through domestic and national lenses and what such images tell us about how Europeans and Latin Americans took stock of their own political systems and their place in the modern world.

There is an extensive literature on the US Constitution of 1787 and its significance in debates about new constitutions in both Europe and Latin America during the Age of Revolution. Less attention has been paid, however, to the various revivals of interest in the US Constitution later in the nineteenth century, particularly in those countries that themselves sought to establish republics. By that time, it was possible to test how the principles had been applied in practice, which for many observers only increased the significance of the US experiment. Interest in US political institutions and practice was particularly great, at least at certain times, in the following countries: Argentina, which became a republic nominally in 1826, substantially in 1853, and fully in 1880; France, which was a republic from 1848 to 1851 and then again—the Third Republic—from 1870; Brazil, where a republic was declared in 1889, after nearly seven decades of postcolonial monarchy since independence from Portugal in 1822; Spain, which became a republic (albeit unratified by a constitution) from February 1873 for just 11 months, during the turbulent six years of the *sexenio revolucionario* or *democrático* from 1868 to 1874; and Cuba, which remained a Spanish colony until 1898, but where a struggle for independence had begun in 1868. In those countries that had constitutional monarchies, such as Britain and Italy, the United States tended to be seen and interpreted as the main modern alternative to their own system.

The chapter is divided into three sections. The first one focuses on the founding documents of the United States, particularly the Constitution, as the bearer of republican and democratic values. The second section analyzes how the US political system was seen in practice by asking which of its aspects observers chose to highlight as crucial to understanding its success (or otherwise). The final section explores the limits of imaginaries of the United States as a model republic, particularly the challenges posed to admirers by the Civil War and the political corruption of the so-called Gilded Age. The accumulated evidence of this chapter suggests that the US example was imagined mainly as a repository of republican and democratic experience that could be mined for evidence of how these could and might work in practice rather than as a universal blueprint for an ideal modern republic.

A Model Constitution: Panacea or Chimera?

The political workings of the United States were familiar to the radical politicians and intellectuals brought to power or to prominence by the 1868 September revolution in Spain. Some of the revolutionary leaders and new deputies, including General Prim, the "sword" of the military intervention, had visited the United States.[5] Books and pamphlets were published on various aspects of the US Constitution and democratic system during the late 1860s and 1870s, with Tocqueville in particular enjoying a revival.[6] A new Spanish translation of the US Constitution was published in 1868 with the express purpose of disseminating ideas and information "indispensable [to] the period we are currently experiencing."[7] Equally, at the close of the *sexenio*, when the liberals' failure to secure their modernizing reforms had become all too apparent, the liberal *Nueva Prensa* pointedly published an account of the "young" and "truly free" peoples of the United States and Australia in order to "seek ... the solution to the problems" that Spain had been unable to resolve.[8]

Spanish liberals had a strong constitutionalist tradition of their own that inclined them to take a particular interest in the founding order of the United States. The Cádiz Constitution of 1812 had in many respects been conceived as an alternative to the US Constitution: although creating a constitutional monarchy rather than a republic, it enshrined the principle of national sovereignty, established universal male suffrage, and committed the state to preserving liberal freedoms of contract and expression. When the politicians of the revolutionary *sexenio* came together to draw up a new constitution for Spain, first in 1869 and then again after the First Republic was declared in February 1873, they looked not only to their own constitutional tradition but also to that most enduring of constitutions—in reality a set of disparate documents—that of the United States. Spain's 1869 Constitution in particular owed much to the US Constitution. The republican deputy to the Constituent Cortes, Manuel Palanca, declared the preamble to the 1869 Constitution to be "so similar that it could almost be said that it is a translation of the United States' constitution."[9] Despite their differences, the new politicians had all become familiar with the vocabulary of "inalienable rights" and "self-government"; the former term, apparently untranslatable at midcentury, was now rendered easily into Spanish as *los derechos ilegislables* while *self-government* had simply been adopted in the original and no longer required explanation.[10] The first article of the 1869 Constitution granted Spaniards, for the first time, their rights as individuals to associate, assemble, petition, practice a religion (or not), publish, and from 1873, for Spanish males, to vote. During the 1873 constituent assembly discussions, the veteran republican deputy José María Orense went so far as to suggest that the nascent republic's best course of action would be to simply translate the US Constitution word for word and disseminate it as the Spanish.[11]

In Argentina, as is well known, the example of the United States featured prominently at the constitutional convention of 1853, and it remained the most significant external point of reference in Argentine political debates into the late nineteenth century. It was scarcely possible for an Argentine politician or commentator—at least not one who wished to claim liberal credentials—to make any point about Argentine institutions without making the obligatory comparison with the United States. However, many and varied were the interpretations of US experience that Argentines of varying liberal hues drew upon to support their arguments. The most authoritative contributor to the 1853 convention was undoubtedly Domingo Faustino Sarmiento, who was well known for his admiration of the United States, dating back to his travelogue of 1847, *Viajes por Europa, Africa y Estados Unidos*, which was a standard source of images of the United States for Latin Americans for several decades after its publication. Sarmiento, who tended to see political disunity in the River Plate from the late colonial period onward, maintained that the United States provided a valid comparison of a united federal nation forged out of previously independent, separate states. For him, a sense of Argentine nationality had emerged only during the independence period, when it was confined to an educated minority, mainly from Buenos Aires. The attempts of this first generation of liberals to impose their vision through a unitarian Constitution in 1826 had foundered on the resistance of conservative regional interests, and it had taken over three decades for a liberal approach to nation building to triumph. Sarmiento's view was that the success or otherwise of a modern republic was determined not by any particular organization of the state—"whether it is unitarian or federal is simply an administrative matter"—but by the capacity of its people to enact the rights granted to them, which was mainly a question of education. Nevertheless, he wanted to see the Argentine Constitution of 1853 as an adoption of the US Constitution of 1787 because he hoped that it would come to be a comparable balm for Argentine ills: "The Constitution could come to be, then, [...] like those tisanes that come in bottles with instructions for use wrapped around them."[12] For Sarmiento, the US Constitution was significant to Argentina not so much for its content as for what it symbolized, namely, the hope that Argentina, like the United States (in Sarmiento's eyes), would become suffused with the values of good democratic practice.

Alongside the Argentine Sarmiento it was among French liberals that the importance of educating citizens to create liberal democracy was most loudly expressed. The American constitution had served as a reference point for the constitution writers of the 1848 Republic and did so again in 1875: in debating the proposed constitutional laws, the Duc de Noailles asserted the legitimacy of the US Constitution as a prototype that deserved to be studied for what it might illuminate in the French case.

> In the present state of France, should we not first of all focus our careful attention on America? Where could we study the conditions and the consequences of our new institutions more profitably than in the living body of a vigorous and prosperous republic, a republic, in short that has never been equalled. Without question, it is a model of its kind and sets a lasting standard, a superior and unique prototype to which we would do well to refer.[13]

However, even Edouard Laboulaye, surely the Third Republic's greatest *américophile,* while admiring of the US Constitution and founding principles, insisted that these were not yet perfected. In defiance of European constitutionalism, he questioned the ability of founding documents and principles per se to bring about the democratic, political and social transformations required of a liberal, bourgeois revolution. In his vision, the US Constitution was no panacea; on the contrary, Laboulaye asserted, "a charter is only a piece of paper [...] even the constitution that is the most perfect and free is no more than a dangerous chimera."[14]

The chasing of constitutional paper dragons was perhaps folly, but where the US Constitution might still act as something of an exemplar was in the recognition of its imperfect, evolving nature, which was written into the Constitution through the provision for amendments. This, then, was a different reading of the relationship between America, modernity, and the future. To many the United States afforded a glimpse of a utopian future already realized in the present—"the country whose present is the dreamed of future of other countries"[15]—but for others, perhaps more astute, the vision of the United States as the epitome and exemplar of modernity had not yet been attained. It was portrayed not in the present, but in the future tense. In the midst of the US Civil War, Laboulaye maintained that "America is the future of civilization; America is the future of liberty," and only with the abolition of slavery and the enlargement of its population "will [its system of government], with irresistible force, draw the whole world to follow the example."[16] Laboulaye was not alone in this view. In a different context, driven this time not by dismay at the conflict in the United States that revealed that country's imperfection all too clearly, but by disappointment in Spanish domestic affairs, Gumersindo de Azcárate insisted on the necessity of "the principle of revision." Writing in 1877, after the restoration of the Bourbon monarchy, the Krausist academic and political actor of the democratic *sexenio* argued that constitutions must be both revisable and disputable as were, he noted, the contemporary constitutions of Austria, Belgium, Switzerland, Germany, the Netherlands, Russia, Norway, Portugal, and the United States. By insisting on "unreformability" Cánovas' conservatives had introduced dogma into the restoration Constitution (1876).[17] Gladstone, too, shared this view of the American republic as a work in progress, its significance lying in what it would become rather than what it had already achieved. "When a young politician came to him for advice as to the political studies that he should choose," Gladstone always, he said, "advised him to study the political history of the United States [because] the destinies of America loomed so large that the mere thought of what was contained in them became almost overwhelming."[18]

There was not simply a dichotomy between those, like Laboulaye and Gladstone, who believed the US system of government was a work in progress and those, like Manuel Palanca, who advocated the (near) wholesale exporting of the New World Constitution to the Old, word for word. For the most part, all saw its utility as an experiment in practice, not as a universal model or blueprint: as the Duc de Noailles acknowledged, the United States was a "living body"—living and therefore evolving.[19] Manuel Palanca may well have asserted that the preamble to the 1869 Spanish constitution was so similar to that of the United States that it could have been lifted word for word, but this is to overlook the significant differences between the two constitutions and also to ignore the influence of long-standing and "homegrown" liberal values in Spain since 1812. The US Constitution begins, of course, with "we the People..." enshrining the notion of popular sovereignty; in the Spanish document sovereignty is entrusted not to the people but to the Spanish nation—a result, perhaps, of the most obvious distinction between the US and Spanish documents, the one republican, the other monarchical. Nor did the Spanish Constitution provide very easily for the addition of amendments, reflecting, perhaps, the view that if the Constitution was a panacea, it could hardly be an evolving document in need of revisiting. The 1869 Constitution also lacked one of the crucial checks on executive power provided by the US document—impeachment—which perhaps helps explain the number of newspaper inches in the Spanish press expressing amazement and admiration at the trial in office of President Johnson or the "harmonious and peaceable" disbanding of the armies at the end of the US Civil War. That the head of state could be impeached without violence or military intervention or that soldiers could seamlessly return to civilian life without "the slightest turmoil" was—in the words of one satirical journal—"perfectly logical" in the United States.[20] It was, however, unthinkable in "this land of black sheep" where the intervention of the army in politics had become a ritualized mechanism for changing the political guard; military interventions brought both the revolutionary *sexenio* into being in 1868 and the first republic to an end in 1874.

In its enshrining of national rather than popular sovereignty, the 1869 Spanish Constitution was rooted in the founding moment and document of European liberalism and constitutionalism—from which the term "liberal" in its modern political sense originates—the 1812 Constitution of Cádiz (which had been inspired more by Britain than the United States). The constitutional arrangements put forward in 1812, like those of 1869, included the defense of national sovereignty, separation of powers, universal male suffrage, the continuation of the monarchy and of Catholicism as the official religion of Spain. National political traditions were hardly brushed aside during the *sexenio* in favor of the wholesale adoption of the US constitutional model. Instead, domestic political values and traditions blended with ideas and concepts from abroad where these were seen to have been proven in practice. As Gumersindo de Azcárate noted, the founding documents and principles of the United States had been "put to the test" not just of time but of "difficult times": part of the appeal of the US model, after 1865, was that it had emerged "exceed[ing] [...] the intentions of its authors" from the "great tempest" of the American Revolution and, surely the greatest test, the Civil War.[21] As such, Azcárate subscribed to the prevalent US interpretation of the war—that it had provided a kind of ultimate test of the United States' political system and values, from which it had emerged not only intact but strengthened. This was a crucial aspect of the United States' appeal: in comparison to the French experience of "nine changes of government, eleven constitutions for a fourteen-centuries-old and therefore more mature people" and Spain's seven constitutions in one century, the single Constitution and regular, democratic transferal of power across the Atlantic must have seemed enviably stable.[22] It was this political stability that prompted Claudio Jannet to compare the US Constitution with the role of a monarch, in its embodiment of political permanence and timelessness.[23]

British conservatives' reappraisals of the American Constitution in the light of the Civil War reveal similar tropes of experience and practice. The endurance of American institutions through the Civil War had a significant impact on the way republicanism was viewed in Britain. In the early years of the twentieth century, Gladstone's friend and biographer, John Morley, recalling Macaulay's pre – Civil War observation that the American Constitution was "all sail and no anchor" concluded "yet amid fierce storm and flood for fifty the years since Macaulay wrote, the American anchor has proved itself no mere kedge."[24] Searching for reassurance that the democratization (or, as it was often dubbed, the "Americanisation") of the British Constitution would not undermine the foundations of political stability and respect for property, Liberals and conservatives alike in the post – Civil War era showed great interest in the role of the Supreme Court and the Senate as bulwarks against the threat of revolution. The English-born Civil War general Matthew M. Trumbull, writing in the August 1885 issue of *The Nineteenth Century*, dryly observed that "the Toryism of the American Supreme Court would comfort the soul of Lord Eldon."[25] This view was elaborated at greatest length in James Bryce's influential work, *The American Commonwealth*, which constituted a watershed in British images of the "Great Republic of the West." In a direct riposte to Tocqueville, the European interpreter of America with whom Bryce was so often compared, Bryce argued that the United States should be studied and understood on its own terms, not as a genus to be examined for its utility as a model or a warning. Furthermore, Tocqueville had been wrong to worry about the tyranny of the majority (he had failed to understand the bulwarks created against this) and, most of all, Tocqueville had simply overestimated the potency of democracy "in the moral and social sphere." Again and again in *The American Commonwealth*, Bryce insisted that there was nothing truly revolutionary or unprecedented about the American republic. Indeed, the emphasis on the Revolutionary moment and the genius of the Founding Fathers missed the point. In Bryce's deeply Whiggish view, the resilience of American republican institutions was due to their having evolved slowly from English precedents. "There is little in that Constitution that is absolutely new," he declared. "There is much that is as old as Magna Carta."[26]

The Secret of the United States' Success

There was no consensus among European and Latin American observers as to which aspect(s) of the "great republic" provided the key to understanding its apparent success. Was a republic essential to democracy or did a constitutional monarchy have the potential to be as democratic as a republic? Was the success of the United States attributable to its federalism, the flexibility of its system of government, or the capillary networks of political activism and grassroots democracy that constituted its civil society? Was its secret even American at all, or did the US model simply distill values and ideals developed in the Old World, specifically Britain?

The answers to such questions were shaped by changing national circumstances, political allegiances, and European and Latin American perceptions of their own present and future circumstances. This section traces three themes that were salient in debates about the tenacity and promise of the US republic: federalism; an "Anglo-Saxon" tradition of liberty; and democratic practice.

Federalism

While in Italy federalism was no longer an option after the failure of the 1848 revolution, in Spain, Argentina, Brazil, and even in Britain federal republicanism was a feature of the United States that attracted great interest. The majority of Spanish republicans—at least of the elite variety— were federalists, starting with the Republican Party leader, Francisco Pi y Margall, who argued that a federal state would provide unity without losing variety and was compatible with nationhood. Thus, it is little surprising that the most significant aspect of the US political system from the Spanish perspective was its federalism, not least during the period of the first Spanish republic in 1873. With the introduction of the republic, the rhetoric of mutual respect between the "first" and the "youngest" of modern republics increased. The US government had been the first to acknowledge the legitimacy of the provisional government following the September revolution in 1868, and was again the first to recognize the new republic. The declaration in return made by Estanislao Figueras— the first of the republic's four presidents—underlined Spanish republicans' sense of obligation to the United States. He painted the transatlantic transfer of federalist ideas and practices as the repayment of a historic favor: Spain had exported "civilization" to the Americas and it was now importing federal republican principles in return.[27] This was not simply ceremonial rhetoric. The Constitution of 1873—formulated but never ratified—was federalist, taking its cues very clearly from the United States. The Spanish federation would comprise 17 states, each of which would be free to compose its own constitution, legislative, executive, and judicial organs, provided these respected the division of federal and state powers laid down by the constitution and remained true to its democratic underpinnings. The US version of federalism also resonated strongly with the dissident cantonalist republicans, who rebelled against the vacillating First Republic during the summer of 1873. One breakaway dissident group in Cartagena asked to join the US federation. Its leader, Roque Barcia, a Cortes deputy as well as author of a history of the United States, wrote on December 16, 1873, to the US ambassador in Spain requesting permission to raise "a glorious federal standard, observed throughout the north [...]

the standard which fluttered in Philadelphia" on their ships, castles, and bastions.[28]

Before 1873 (and after), successive Spanish governments had ruled from the center, largely ignoring the territory's regional diversity, so it was perhaps inevitable that Spanish federalists should look abroad, and especially to the United States, for guidance. What particularly concerned them was the compatibility of a federal system with the idea of the nation-state. They found reassurance in the experience of the United States. the Spanish-Cuban republican deputy, lawyer and academic, Rafael de Labra determined that "federalism in America [...] served only to unite" and demonstrated that liberty, nation, and republic were mutually reinforcing.[29] This compatibility was crucial for the radical Spanish liberals seeking to both recognize and overcome the tensions between territorial and political homogeneity on the one hand and regionalism, cultural difference, and loyalty to the *patria chica* on the other. In his defense of federalism, *Las Nacionalidades*, published in 1877, three years after the failure of the federalist republican experiment in Spain, Pi y Margall weighed up a number of potential political models, including the cantonalist confederation of Switzerland, but repeatedly returned to the United States for evidence of the practicability and efficacy of federalism, which he found in its jurisdictional balance of federal and state law, in its devolved system of customs and duties, and in its organization of the armed forces and state militia.[30] He was by no means alone in conveniently overlooking the enormous and bloody cost at which the United States' federal system had been confirmed.

Following unification (1859–70), the Italian state was constructed according to decidedly centralist principles. Although Garibaldi had traveled to the United States in the early 1850s and Mazzini included Young Americans in his transnational republican movement, both advocated unitarian republics and seemed little interested in drawing positive lessons from any example it may have set.[31] There were some Risorgimento patriots who did look to the federal system of the United States as a possible model.[32] However, the coincidence of Italian unification and state building with civil war in the United States served to irrevocably tarnish the "model" of its republic in Italian eyes, now associated with internal conflict, barbarism, and the absence of civilization.[33]

The image of the United States as a federal republic was perhaps most central to Argentine debates where its federal "model" was deployed by diverse participants in the post-independence power plays between the center and the regions. Again, the Constitution provided a key site for the contestation of power. It was Sarmiento's interpretation of Argentine history—the independence movement of 1810 as the incarnation of Argentina's true spirit as a modern, united nation, with the provinces as retrograde outposts of selfish local interests defensible only by the violence of *caudillismo*—that was elaborated and documented by Bartolomé Mitre and Vicente Fidel López, the founders of Argentine historiography, disseminated in schools and dominant well into the twentieth century. In this liberal historiography, it became conventional wisdom that the US Constitution had served as a model for the Argentine Constitution of 1853.[34] In practice, if you set the two side by side, as was done by an Argentine lawyer to make the case in 1875,[35] there are notable correspondences, but there are also significant divergences; whether similarities or differences were emphasized mainly depended on what the observer wished to argue. Most early Latin American constitutions drew to a notable extent on the US Constitution, which was widely deemed to be "the most finished model of a representative democratic republic."[36] It was only in Argentina, however, that the question of the relationship between the two documents became so politically charged.

By contrast, another great Argentine intellectual of the era, Juan Bautista Alberdi, who played an important role in drafting the 1853 Constitution, had a very different perspective. He saw the Vice-Royalty of the River Plate as *politically* and culturally united, divided into provinces only for economic and administrative reasons; for him, "while in the United States of North America union was artificial, in Argentina it was decentralisation that was artificial." He therefore argued that comparison with the United States was inappropriate and irrelevant to an understanding of the Argentine Constitution and that studying US constitutional practice, as became standard fare in Argentine universities from the 1850s onward, would do little to help resolve Argentina's problems of national consolidation.[37] For Sarmiento, then, Argentine federalism had been born of Argentine experience of disunity, but it behooved Argentines to learn from a more successful example of balancing tensions between unity and diversity. For Alberdi, federalism was an unnatural import into Argentina, and Argentines had little to gain by studying the US experience. Thus the man who saw Argentine problems as created by Argentine conditions advocated finding the solution in a foreign model; the man who saw Argentine problems as created by a misguided attempt to introduce foreign models advocated Argentine solutions. Both positions were perfectly coherent in their own terms; what they had in common was the external referent.

The argument was played out, with variations, in subsequent generations. The first professor of constitutional law at the University of Buenos Aires, a Colombian called Florentino González, appointed in 1868, took the United States as a constant reference point. He reprinted the US and the Argentine Constitutions together and included lengthy citations from US legal writings in his influential textbook, particularly Joseph Story's commentaries on the US Constitution (1833), George Ticknor Curtis's

1854 historical account of it, and Frederick Grimke's *Considerations upon the Nature and Tendency of Free Institutions* (1848).[38] González paid little attention, however, to US federalism; instead, his main interest—like Sarmiento's—lay in the US example of democratic practice and its institutional framework for guaranteeing public freedoms. His successor, José Manuel Estrada, echoed Alberdi in emphasizing the differences between Argentina and the United States, arguing that in Argentina there had historically been a people that was organically united, preceding any provincial divisions, therefore the US example had little to teach Argentina, which had not copied nor even imitated the US Constitution. In yet one more twist in the tale of Argentine appropriations of images of the United States, it was in reaction *against* the liberal version of history that members of the subsequent generation, who led a political movement against oligarchic liberalism during the 1890s, turned once again to the example of the United States. In his essay "Argentine Federalism" (1889), Francisco Ramos Mejía argued that a united Argentina had been created not by the liberals of the independence generation but instead by agreements between the provinces in 1852, 1859, and 1860, and he identified the roots of the Argentine federal system in imperial Spain. The logic of his argument was that "The Argentine Republic thus has not been [...] a decentralised unity as has been claimed, but rather a union of entities that were previously independent, which was constituted in the same way as the United States, with which we can compare the origin and formation of our nationhood."[39] Ramos Mejía upheld the validity of the comparison between the United States and Argentina, but pointed to one difference that he deemed to be crucial, namely, that in the United States the separate states had formally relinquished their sovereignty in dissolving themselves to create simultaneously the nation and its constituent states. This fiction enabled the preamble to the US Constitution to refer, credibly, to "We the representatives of the Union" and to invest the new federal state with legitimacy. In Argentina, by contrast, the preamble emphasized the agency of the provinces in creating the nation, thereby leaving an unresolved tension as to where sovereignty lay, which was reflected in the widespread tendency to refer to "the United Provinces" whereas in the United States it was usually "the Union."[40]

As Chiaramonte and Buchbinder noted, a similar argument was adopted by Leandro Alem, an influential politician who was strongly against the centralization of power in Argentina. He made his name in a famous speech opposing the federalization of Buenos Aires as the national capital in 1880 and later went on to become the leader of the first significant political movement against liberal oligarchic rule, the UCR (Radical Civic Union, founded in 1891). Arguing against Vicente Fidel López in the Chamber of Deputies, Alem said that he agreed with him that the United States had gone from diversity to unity while Argentina had moved in the opposite direction, from unity to diversity, but he drew different conclusions from this argument, namely, that more, not less, autonomy should be granted to the states. For him, the crucial distinction between the United States and Argentina was that in the United States the advocates of union—Washington and Hamilton—were not pure centralizers, but had merely sought to counter autonomist tendencies by securing sufficient powers to ensure preservation of the Union. In Argentina, by contrast and regrettably, unitarianism had been dogmatic and extreme, "a nefarious tendency which has been the origin and the cause [...] of the major part of our misfortunes." Thus, in his version of history, in the United States a pragmatic, accommodating centralism had achieved a balanced situation in which the states had used their powers responsibly, whereas in Argentina a visionary, overbearing centralism had resulted in the provinces resisting and behaving like petulant children.[41]

Anglo-Saxon Liberty

The University College London historian Professor E. S. Beesly may have considered the US republic "a standing rebuke to England," but for many it was not so easy to distinguish between the assumed political ideals of the two Anglo-Saxon countries.[42] Indeed, their values were very often elided and conflated. Praise for the US Constitution and political values often seemed a proxy for those of the British parliamentary system. As Gumersindo de Azcárate told his illustrious audience at a Columbine anniversary conference in 1892, the citizen of the United States was not "an entirely new national type" who had constructed "a substantially different civilization" across the Atlantic. Any distinctions between the political order of the New and Old World were of scale rather than of essence:

> Even in the political order, which appears the most original, it is easy to see the entire anglo-saxon tradition in the North American Constitution, despite the distance which at first glance appears to exist between a unitary monarchy, with an aristocracy and an official religion and a democratic and federal republic, in which the churches are absolutely independent of the state.[43]

Azcárate's opinion was widely shared. Adolphe de Chambrun saw the origins of US political institutions in the Magna Carta and "infinitely more analogy between the republican form of government of the United States and the English monarchy [...] than between the same republican form of government and the Republic such as it exists at this moment in France," while Bryce considered the United States "an improved England."[44] In this view, what was key to understanding the United States was the ideal of liberty. According to Rafael de Labra, Britain invented political liberty; the importance of the United States came insofar as it acted as a conduit for transforming the peculiar and contingent vision of liberty infused within British institutions and ideals, which had arisen more by historical accident than design, into a political principle or theory and in putting that principle into practice. "It was necessary," he said, "that the English spirit passed through America."[45] Such pronouncements only confirmed what many Englishmen thought they knew. In a famous essay, "Kin beyond Sea," published in the *North American Review* in 1878, Gladstone argued that while American liberties had English origins, the institutions created after the Revolution could not be exactly replicated in Europe because the circumstances in the New World were so radically different. "Passing from a narrow island to a continent almost without bounds, the colonists at once and vitally altered their conditions of thought, as well as of existence," he wrote. This did not diminish the Constitution—he praised it as "the most wonderful work ever struck off at a given time by the brain and purpose of man"—but it did put it into perspective, turning it from a model to be emulated, to an exhibit to be admired with a detachment secure in the knowledge of the equal, if very different, genius of the British Constitution.[46]

It was not only that US political values and institutions were understood as the distillation of British antecedents. Many of these European and Latin American "Americophiles" saw in British institutions principles and practices that rivaled, or even surpassed, those in the United States. For example, the moderation of executive power by the presence of ministers and, particularly, by a parliament was "the height of progress," claimed Spanish republican Labra.[47] Even for assured republicans like Labra and Laboulaye, the fact that Britain was ruled by a monarch did not diminish the lessons it too could provide for state building. Indeed, Laboulaye, though certainly a (conservative) republican by inclination, insisted that the actual form of government mattered less than certain institutions—that is, two chambers and a strong executive—and a vibrant civil society. It was in relation to the powers accorded to the head of state that Gumersindo de Azcárate found much to praise in the British system. Convinced of the need to address the topic in his 1878 lecture to the *Instituto* by the recent political crisis in Paris, Azcárate undertook a comparison of the powers and checks accorded to heads of state in Britain, France, and the United States.[48] This comparison was valid, he maintained, given that there was little difference between a constitutional monarchy and a republic. According to Azcárate, it was in Britain that the greatest degree of separation of power had been achieved: executive power lay with the cabinet, the legislative with the parliament, the judicial with the courts, and the power to nominate ministers and dissolve parliament, with the monarch. As the head of the executive branch, the French president could intervene at will in the legislative to propose laws, to use the suspending veto, and, with the agreement of the Senate, to dissolve the Chamber of Deputies. In the United States, he suggested, the president's power resided almost exclusively in the executive branch, with authority to intervene in the legislative only to use the suspending veto and to address the house but not to propose laws or to dissolve the legislative chamber.

In Azcárate's comparative exercise the power of the US president emerged not as the absolute-monarch-in-disguise that many contemporaries suggested he was but as the head of state subject to the greatest checks. The impeachment of Andrew Johnson had demonstrated that the president "is responsible, just like any other official."[49] Indeed, it was the distrust of presidential authority that had paradoxically led, according to Azcárate, to the associations between the power of the US president and that of a king because the prevention of the president from intervening and debating with the legislative branch ensured that US presidents made use of the sole method of intervention open to them, that of the veto. Such had been the case with President Johnson, who, "far from considering himself simply an adjudicator of the legislative power, assumed a supremacy [which he could] infer from *written law*."[50] Though all three systems came in for criticism by Azcárate, the one that appeared most satisfactory was the one founded upon constitutional monarchy.

> You will agree [with me] that Queen Victoria, even if she wished to, could not in England today place herself in a posture similar to that in which Johnson in 1867 in the United States, and Marshal Mac-Mahon in France in 1877, placed themselves. This, then, is because there [in England] the ultimate consequences of the principle of *self-government* have been deduced, the parliamentary regime has been fully developed and, consequently, the role and power of the head of state has continued to be contained within its proper limits, within those limits which the head of state ought to be contained in monarchies, just as in republics.[51]

Democratic Practice

Not all observers of the United States focused on the political principles and values enshrined in America's founding documents or institutions as they tried to unravel the secret of the United States' apparent success. For Sarmiento, as for Laboulaye and others, what cemented America's modernity had to be sought in its political processes and practices: how its democracy was made, not constituted. What was worthy of note—and perhaps of emulation—was its political culture, how its people were educated politically and how they made politics work. The images of the United States as a vibrant political culture recur throughout Europe and Latin America, albeit most strongly in France, Brazil, and Argentina. Given that Argentina's Constitution was often compared to that of the United States, the question arose of why, considering the similarity of their institutions, the United States appeared to be implementing self-government more effectively. The editorial of the first issue of *Ambas Américas*, the journal founded by Sarmiento in New York in 1867 to disseminate information about the United States throughout Spanish-speaking America, stated:

> Governments could do nothing for themselves, if society did not help them with effective cooperation. In the United States it was the people, not the government, that created public education: eminent citizens, voluntary associations formed the opinion that sustained it, and also prepared the systems that made it effective.[52]

For many admirers of the United States, including Laboulaye and the Brazilian conservative Viscount of Uruguai, their interest in US civil society was intimately connected to their insistence that liberal democracy could not be legislated into existence through constitutions or laws. "Self government," the Viscount argued, was "not a talisman which could be used by anybody [but] a habit, an education, a custom. It is in the tradition, in the race, and when these conditions are absent, it cannot be established by laws."[53] Unpersuaded of the capacity of values and principles set out on paper to effect real change, and convinced that these values and principles had to be learned, where they did view the United States as a potential model was in its democratic practices, lively civil society, and protection of civil liberties. Both Laboulaye and Viscount Uruguai's interest in US democracy took their cues from Tocqueville's discussion of the US custom of "for ever forming associations."[54]

If Argentines pointed to process because of the perceived similarity between their political institutions and those of the United States, then the French (and some Brazilians) did so because of their insistence on the difference between their country and the United States. In the French liberal interpretation, the United States had been a "democratic" society, reigned by a spirit of liberty, already well before independent statehood. The American Revolution had thus been a solely political and formal transformation. It reflected the already long-practiced freedom and equality of American society: it did not have to create them. The French Revolution, by contrast, had been a social revolution that had brought about totally new conditions and social relations, which had not yet been brought to an end. From the Brazilian perspective, their compatriots lacked "the dogma of the sovereignty of the people" and civil society remained a "powerful stranger."[55] What was contested was what action Brazilian rulers should take in response: continued or increased centralized monarchical government, as Uruguai insisted, given what he saw as Brazil's unpreparedness for self-rule, or Tavares Bastos's solution, the teaching of democratic practice through greater decentralization and universal suffrage just as "the North-American people [...] are teaching the ideal government of the future."[56]

What particularly impressed both Europeans and Latin Americans of the second half of the nineteenth century, echoing and reviving Tocqueville, was the way in which democracy was practiced locally. Images abounded of the United States as a place where democratic practices were firmly rooted in communities, where sheriffs and other office holders were elected by their neighbors, where local government was effective, where men and women formed networks of associations and pressure groups, where newspapers proliferated, most notably around election time, and where philanthropists—often women—directed their wealth and energy toward the "public good."[57] Laboulaye's fictional New England town, "Paris, Massachussetts," the setting of his transnational best seller, *Paris en Amérique*, was characterized by a flurry of such activity. Indeed, the whole novel was rich in images of the vibrancy of local life and the strength of civil society in the United States: a not particularly subtle but effective illustration of Laboulaye's mantra that the secret of the success of the American republic was to be found in its democratic practices—and not in its Constitution per se.[58] For Sarmiento, coming from a country in which he perceived a great gulf between the life of the capital and of the provinces, even the urban areas, the extent to which an active civil society, with powerful local loyalties, was developed throughout the United States, even in remote places, was remarkable.

> The bank, the newspaper, the post, the railway are attracted to each village [...]; and the traveller is astonished to see the same level of civilisation in every place in the territory, the same factories, the same good taste, and even luxury and elegance in buildings in recently populated areas, hundreds of miles away from the coast.[59]

Echoing Sarmiento's frustration at the perceived absence of local manifestations of national democracy and "public good" at home, Spanish liberals concluded gloomily that "we have to consider American municipal organisation [...] as a dream as golden as it is unattainable."[60] *Caciquismo*, the practice of negotiating power and privilege between the political center and the locality through clientelist networks mediated by *caciques* (local bosses), endured through the revolutionary *sexenio* and well into the twentieth century in Spain. "Everywhere," the *Nueva Prensa* lamented, could be felt "the fatal influence of a politics that corrupts and poisons everything." Eyeing the "unattainable" American municipal dream, it observed,

> There will be hardly a Spaniard who can conceive the possibility that political change does not profoundly influence the municipality: ask any of those influential men in the localities who are richer in ambition than patriotism and await their turn to *mandar* [command] (as they themselves put it) in the office of mayor or town councillor or manipulator of municipal business, whether they find it just that personal politics be represented in the mayoralty, and whether they would be content for such a thing to be placed in doubt. Because for them it is clear that the mayor should be shaped by the minister, and the town hall should be a political representation.[61]

The process of electioneering and voting in the United States appeared carnivalesque, made up of parades, party colors, and celebratory public meetings. Spanish forestry engineer José Jordana y Morera, for example, witnessed one well-attended, "festive" Republican reunion in Middlebury, which led him to observe that "North Americans are very fond of political meetings."[62] That said, the perception of the theatricalities of US democracy was not always complimentary. The pageantry and commercialism of US elections—the financial resources needed to mobilize support for candidates across such a large territory and the employment of modern business practices to "advertise" candidates as if they were products—could also appear vulgar.[63] Besides the distasteful "selling" of politics, there were several aspects of the processes and functioning of US democracy that struck Europeans and Latin Americans as far from exemplary. Those who professed admiration for the US republic had to somehow reconcile what they had to admit were malfunctioning or corrupt democratic practices with their insistence on the advanced nature of American politics, while those who were opposed to the modernity that the United States was deemed to embody could seize upon the corruption of its democratic culture as evidence that the United States was more anti-model than exemplar. The following section sets out the contours of the limits of the United States as a political model for modern democracy.

The Limits of the United States as a Political Model

It was evident not only to Mark Twain and Charles Dudley Warner that in practice American politics often fell short of its lofty ideals. The political scandals of the "Gilded Age"—the spoils system, "carpetbagging," political patronage, vote rigging, and corruption, epitomized most infamously by the "political machine" at Tammany Hall in New York City—were closely followed in Europe and Latin America.[64] Responses to news of US corruption scandals in many ways mirrored responses to news of the Civil War. For example, the moderate Italian prime minister (1863–4 and 1873–6) Marco Minghetti described political corruption in the United States as *grandissima e notoria* and noted the vast changes the country had gone through since De Tocqueville wrote his own observations.[65] While some commentators had managed either to ignore the Civil War or followed the US line that the war had proved to be the ultimate test that had been triumphantly met, it was certainly difficult for observers of the United States not to acknowledge and address the imperfections in the "great republic's" democratic system. Conservatives opposed to republicanism and greater democracy at home made sure of that. Indeed, they delighted in these imperfections for the ammunition they provided to indict the "model republic." The Spanish satirical journal, *Gil Blas,* imagined such "blessed men, [...] clapping their hands [at] the most insignificant disruption" to US political life, and exclaiming:

> There you have it, this *enlightened people* as the *liberalescos* tell us, this country which the *ingobernables* present as a model, is destroying itself, annihilating itself in civil struggles which before long will bring it to a premature death.[66]

Those European and Latin American liberals and radicals who looked to the United States as a paragon of modern democratic practice had somehow to counter such views. Many did so by recasting the narrative of electoral fraud and corruption in a similar way to their interpretation of the Civil War, viewing all such problems as a national trial or test, which, as in the case of the Civil War, "showed that fearful ordeals can be passed unscathed."[67]

The contested election of 1876, fought between Democrat Samuel J. Tilden and Republican Rutherford B. Hayes, was a key moment of political disillusionment in the United States as a model political culture. US elections were occasions when "the nation en masse throws itself into the political arena with great enthusiasm," but they were also more "venal and despicable there than in few other places."[68] In Spain, the 1876 election and the Compromise of 1877 between republicans and southern Democrats, which allowed Hayes to win the US presidency despite not having won the popular vote and effectively brought an end to Reconstruction, was used to remind Spaniards that even "the first and greatest" democracy in the modern world was not immune to the kinds of political corruption and *caciquismo* that blighted their own political forms. The *Ilustracion Española y Americana* reported in 1876 that Hayes's election victory had been violent and "truly grotesque"; the spectacle of suspected illegal voters in New York imprisoned in "Davenport's cage" for the duration of election day, as the accompanying illustration demonstrated, was enough to set "Heraclitus and Democritus weeping and laughing."[69] Gumersindo de Azcárate noted that political parties in the United States were stronger and more influential than in any other country, a viewpoint formed in light of the restoration of the Bourbon monarchy to the Spanish throne and the establishment of the *turno pacífico*, the illusorily democratic, yet stable political system whereby the conservative and liberal parties alternated periods in power.[70] In France Noailles, Boutmy, Chambrun, and Cucheval-Clarigny understood the 1876 presidential election through the paradigm of the national trial, successfully passed, but were nonplussed by the lack of differentiation between US political parties that the 1877 Compromise appeared to reveal. Here, the Duc de Noailles observed, were "two right wings, one in power and one in opposition, and taking turns."[71] Nor were they impressed by the caliber of US politicians (since Lincoln); the political parties were run by a "class of unenlightened men without morality," who sought only personal advancement through politics.[72] The idea that politicians should represent the people—rather than guide them—and should come from the same social strata, and look, dress, and behave like the people they represent was far removed from the elitist view of the role and place of the politician held by French political figures from across the spectrum.[73] But what apparently most surprised the French "Americanists" about the 1876 presidential elections was that the election fraud had been met with such calm acceptance and not the violence and riots they were sure would have ensued in France.[74]

Fears about the "Americanisation" of British politics focused not so much on the franchise per se but on the mechanisms of mass political organization that, it was claimed, gave inordinate power to demagogues at the expense of rational debate. Joseph Chamberlain's Birmingham "caucus" was attacked on precisely these grounds, as was Gladstone's "whistle-stop" Midlothian campaign. Even *Lloyd's Weekly*, a moderate Liberal paper, rebuked Chamberlain for "importing" the caucus system and attacked the American "prototype" on which it was based for undermining the people's liberties.[75] Even so fervent an admirer of the American system of government as Goldwin Smith warned in 1877 that "in the United States the masters of the party machine have every-where taken the representation out of the hands of the people; you are practically not at liberty to vote for anyone but their nominees; and the Republican horse, to vanquish the Democratic stag, becomes absolutely the slave of its rider."[76] It should be noted that Smith's intervention was part of a transatlantic liberal discourse about the impact of party machines on democratic processes in the "Gilded Age", and he was in no way renouncing his commitment to the ideal, even if not always the reality, of American democratic government.[77] Even so, Smith's criticisms fuelled the perception of a political system that was being run in the interests of plutocrats, not the people. It became commonplace to read reports in the British press of the disillusionment of radicals—ex-Chartists and the like—who had emigrated to America in the hope that it would be a model of all that they had strived for in their home country. One such radical reported on a visit to the United States in the *Newcastle Chronicle* in the 1880s:

> It was a curious (and to me an almost unaccountable) circumstance that many of the friends I met, who had in earlier years been intimately identified with the popular movements of the old country, were inclined rather to disparage than to praise the political forces of the Republic. One of them, who had suffered in the Chartist cause, remarked that America would be a good place to live in "if it were not for the politicians and the newspapers". Another, who had played a prominent part in Newcastle some forty years ago, was still more emphatic in his condemnation of the politicians. Speaking of one of the great parties, he paused in his argument to explain—"They call themselves Democrats, but they are all thieves!"[78]

News of US corruption scandals could have important implications for the position of foreign admirers of the US political model domestically. After the disputed presidential election of 1876, Sarmiento himself expressed deep disillusionment, not only—as hitherto—with Argentina's capacity to absorb the best of the United States, but also with the United States' own capacity to live up to its ideals.[79] Those members of the new generations who were increasingly critical of the template for modernization represented by Sarmiento latched on to his criticisms of the United States to attack him, contriving to associate thinking about the United States with a limited—indeed, an "anti-patriotic"—way of thinking about Argentina. His enemies turned his own arguments against him: the great admirer of the United States had, "in practice, done the opposite of what they did [there]. The United States became great through individual initiative, but Sarmiento dreams only of the absorption of everything by his government."[80]

The most notorious example of political corruption in the United States was without doubt that associated with the so-called Tammany ring in New York in the 1860s and early 1870s. The name of William Tweed, the "boss" of Tammany Hall infamously caricatured by Thomas Nast, would be recognized by any literate Madrileño or Parisian who read the postings to the larger dailies by foreign correspondents based in New York and Washington. Spanish and French conservatives jumped at this chance to highlight the failings of democratic practice in the United States. In Madrid, for example, the leading newspaper, *La Epoca*, regularly covered the internecine working of the party machines, especially those of the "Tammany Club, made so famous by Tweed" and seized the opportunity to ridicule the idea of the United States as a model republic.[81] Claudio Jannet denounced the corruption of the American cities, exemplified by Tweed, "as proof of the iniquity of democracy."[82] The curious manner of Tweed's recapture in Galicia in the autumn of 1876, following his escape from jail some months earlier, served to increase his notoriety in Spain and hints at the diffusion of American political caricature, especially Thomas Nast's work for *Harpers Weekly*, throughout the peninsula. Tweed was apprehended in Vigo, identified by the Spanish officer who recognized him thanks to Thomas Nast's depiction of Tweed as a thief all too willing to punish two young "lesser" thieves in his caricature "Tweed-le-dee and Tilden-dum" published in June 1876. That a Spanish officer at the peninsula's edge, far from the political centre of Madrid, was familiar with Nast's caricature of Tweed, suggests a wider circulation of images of the contemporary United States than simply among the political cognoscenti and intellectual elites of the capital. However, Nast's cartoon, which the secretary of the American Legation in Madrid, Alvey A. Adee, later told Nast "made you famous in Madrid," was not "read" entirely as had been intended. The first report of Tweed's arrest stated that a certain "Twid" had been captured in Vigo for the crime of "kidnapping two American children." The arresting Spanish officer was familiar enough with the cartoon to recognize the man from his caricature but apparently unable to understand its explanatory annotations. He interpreted the cartoon literally and thus presumed Tweed to be guilty of child abduction, seemingly ignorant of the accusations of political corruption.[83]

Political corruption was tied to images of money making, rampant capitalism, and individualism. In Britain, the "corrupt politician" character epitomized by Boss Tweed fed into the long-standing Arnoldian imagery of American materialism and vulgarity.[84] Similar ideas were aired in Argentina to suggest that democratic culture was undermined by an obsession with making wealth: abstention rates were high in US elections because "*It does not pay*" (orig. English) "Don Dinero" (Mr Moneybags) to vote.⁸⁵ Since the 1860s, members of the Argentine elite expressed fears about what democracy combined with industrialization could mean for culture—uniformity, mediocrity—which they projected onto the United States; the ethos of industrial production would be transferred to culture, it was argued. To see this, one need only look at the United States, which produced quantities of "journalism, illustrated textbooks, monographs," but no poetry, either lyric or epic.⁸⁶ An explicit contrast was drawn with Britain, which Argentines constructed as an image of gentlemanly modernity, retaining some sense of the finer things in life; lack of corruption in political life; and good taste in manners and customs. Such images are exemplified in the "Letter from Lord Chesterfield to His Son," originally cited by Bolívar, which was repeatedly invoked throughout the nineteenth century; it was one of the very few translations (besides Milton) included in Juan María Gutiérrez's compilation of required reading, *El lector americano*, 1874. In this view, English and American political values and practices were not conflated into an Anglo-Saxon whole. Rather, it propagated the idea that the "civilized" aspects of the United States—secular law and constitutional practice—came from England, whereas the barbaric, corrupt ones had been made in the United States. These intertwined images of America as a place of political corruption and capitalist greed can be found in all the countries surveyed here and provided important counterweights to the positive perceptions of impeccable political institutions and empowered local communities flexing their individual and federal freedoms. Both are explored further in chapters 1 and 4.

Conclusion

The European and Latin American liberals who were most vocal and unstinting in their praise for the US political model tended to be identified by their contemporaries as "Americanists," a label that was not always used approvingly. For example, in France Laboulaye and Boutmy, both moderate-to-conservative republicans, were thrown together with more rightist and more peripheral Third Republic political figures such as the monarchists Jannet and the Duc de Noailles.⁸⁷ The Spanish liberals brought to power by the September revolution were so effusive in their positive references to the United States in Cortes debates, as one exasperated deputy lamented, that it is hardly surprising that the restoration politicians looked elsewhere for their political models, namely, Britain, despite Cánovas considering the United States a "distinguished democracy."⁸⁸ In Argentina, the figure of Sarmiento loomed large in Argentine politics for decades and the association of his name with a pro-US position was so automatic that an attack on Sarmiento would imply—could be taken as shorthand for—an attack on the United States and vice versa. But the apparently easy labeling of these politicians and intellectuals as Americophiles belies the disparities in their political thought and the relative sophistication with which they imagined and interpreted the "model republic." Not all foreign admirers of the United States agreed on the political lessons they wished to draw from its example: Constitution, democratic culture, federalism, self-government, liberty. Nor were they (all) blind to the limits to the United States' ability to serve as an exportable political model, set by the brutality of the Civil War and difficulties of its aftermath, the political scandals and corruption of the Reconstruction era, and, of course, by the particular contours of their own domestic debates and contexts.

The national circumstances of each country, and within them the particular domestic debates of the day, shaped the way in which the constitutional arrangements, institutions, and practices of the United States were imagined: what was focused upon; what was dismissed; what was conflated or "misunderstood"; what was seen as the secret of success. While some identified the United States' founding documents—the Declaration of Independence, Constitution, and Bill of Rights—and thus its codification of modern, liberal political principles as paramount, others looked to the vibrancy of its civil society and democratic culture—the strength and extent of political parties, rallies, and associationalism—and thus its revelation of how democracy operated at a local, even individual, level. While some pointed to federalism or individual rights, others were more interested in the enshrinement of religious tolerance *and* the separation of church and state, the role of the president, and checks on presidential power or, indeed, the political corruption and vote rigging that dogged many US elections of the "Gilded Age". In these multiple ways, the United States was viewed and interpreted through the prism of domestic concerns.

It makes little sense, therefore, to see the place of the United States in European and Latin American political discourse of the second half of the nineteenth century in terms of "influence," given that "the United States" signified so many different things to the various parties who imagined it, depending upon their partisan and national perspectives. Rather, the utility of the "model republic" was found in the evidence thrown up by its century of constitutional republicanism and democracy in practice. In words of the so-called father of Spain's September revolution, José María Orense, the United States was the place "in which our ideals are realised"; whether or not this was the course Spain wished to follow, the United States was a country worth examining.[89]

Notes

1. See Isabella, *Risorgimento in Exile* and Riall, *Garibaldi*.
2. *La Revista Blanca* (Madrid): March 1, 1932 "Impresiones de un viaje por España, por Eliás Reclus"; April 1, 1932 "Impresiones del Elías Reclus durante in viaje por España en días de revolución"; June 15, 1932 "Impresiones del Elías Reclus durante in viaje por España en días de revolución."
3. Riall, *Garibaldi*.
4. On the meeting of US self-perceptions and foreign observations of the United States as a political model see Gemme, *Domesticating Foreign Struggles*.
5. Oltra, "La visita del general Prim a los Estados Unidos"; and idem, *La influencia norteamericana en la Constitución Española de 1869*, 34.
6. B. Pérez Galdós, *España Tragica* (Barcelona: Circulo de Lectores, 1987 [1906]), 51; R. M. Labra, *La República de los Estados Unidos de América* (Madrid: Tipografía de Alfredo Alonso, 1897), 18.
7. *Constitutión de los Estados Unidos de America traducida del ingles con algunas notas y observaciones por Don Austin Santayana* (Avila: Imprenta D. P. Vaquero y Comp., 1868), preamble.
8. La Redacción de la Nueva Prensa, *Los Pueblos Jovenes. Estudio Histórico-Filosófico sobre los Estados-Unidos y la Australia* (Madrid: Victoriano Suárez, 1880), 3.
9. Cited in Oltra, *La influencia norteamericana en la Constitución Española de 1869*, 97–100.
10. Oltra, *La influencia norteamericana*.
11. Oltra, "Jefferson's Declaration of Independence," 1373.
12. D. F. Sarmiento, *Comentarios de la Constitución* (Buenos Aires: Luz del Día, 1948), vol. VIII of *Obras completas*, 29.
13. Noailles, "Les publicistes américains et la constitution des Etats-Unis," *Le Correspondant*, May 25, 1876, cited in Portes, *Fascination and Misgivings*, 168. See also Curtis, *The French Assembly of 1848 and the American Constitutional Doctrines*.
14. Laboulaye, *Histoire des Etats-Unis*, vol. 1, vii.
15. *La Ilustración Española y Americana*, January 30, 1878.
16. Laboulaye, *Histoire des Etats-Unis*, vol. 1, v.
17. G. Azcárate, *El self-government y la monarquia doctrinaria* (Madrid: J. Peña, 1877), 107–109.
18. *Times*, April 27, 1887.
19. Noailles "Les publicistes américains et la constitution des Etats-Unis," *Le Correspondant*, May 25, 1876. Cited in Jacques Portes, *Fascination and Misgivings*, 168.
20. *Gil Blas*, April 26, 1868, "Crónica política."
21. Azcárate, "Los Estados Unidos," 184.
22. Abbé Gagnol, *Histoire contemporaine de 1789 à nos jours* (Paris: Librarie Poulssiègue, 1889), xii; cited in Portes, *Fascination and Misgivings*, 167.
23. Portes, *Fascination and Misgivings*, 174.

24. John Morley "Democracy and Reaction," in *Critical Miscellanies* (London: Macmillan, 1908, 4 vols.), vol. 4, 325. On Macauley's criticism of the US Constitution, see *New York Times*, March 24, 1860.
25. Matthew M. Trumbull, "Aristocracy in America," *Nineteenth Century* (August 1885), 215. On Trumbull, see Boston, *British Chartists in America*, 29, 95–96.
26. James Bryce, *The American Commonwealth* (London: Macmillan, 1889 [1888], 2 vols.), vol. 1, 51. Similar views are expressed in Sir Henry Maine, *Popular Government: Four Essays* (London: John Murray, 1885), xii.
27. See "La felicitación de los Estados-Unidos á la República de España," *El Abolicionista*, May 23, 1873.
28. Oltra, *La influencia norteamericana*, 51.
29. R. M. Labra, *La Revolución Norte-americana del siglo XVIII* (Madrid: Imprenta de Aurelio J Alaria, 1881), 442–443.
30. F. Pi y Margall, *Las Nacionalidades* (Madrid: Imp. de Eduardo Martinez, 1877), 137–139.
31. On Garibaldi see Riall, *Garibaldi*, 109–114.
32. Cited in Rossi, *The Image of America*, 14. Marco Meriggi "Centralismo e federalismo in Italia. Le aspettative preunitarie," in *Centralismo e federalismo tra Otto e Novecento*, ed. Janz, Schiera, Siegrist, 49–63, 58. In particular Carlo Cattaneo was inspired by American federalism: Carlo Cattaneo, "Dell'insurrezione di Milano nel 1848 e della successiva guerra. Memorie," in idem., *Il 1848 in Italia* (Turin: Einaudi, 1972), 11–283, 271–272. But some of his writings reveal the extent to which he was aware of potential difficulties between the federal government and the member states of the Union: idem, "Notizia sulla questione delle tariffe daziarie negli Stati Uniti d'Amerca desunta da documenti officiali" (1833), in idem, *Scritti economici*, ed. Alberto Bertolino (Florence: Le Monnier, 1956), vol. 1, 11–55. On Cattaneo's view of the US see Filippo Sabetti, "Cattaneo e il modello americano: per una scienza politica nuova," in *Carlo Cattaneo: i temi e le sfide*, ed. Colombo, della Peruta, Lacaita, 345–366.
33. See Chapter 4.
34. For example, see the secondary school textbook by Joaquín V. González, *Manual de la Constitución Argentina* (Buenos Aires: Angel Estrada y Cía, 1951 [1897]), 38.
35. Pedro Scalabrini, *Concordancia del derecho público argentino con el derecho público norteamericano* (Paraná: Imprenta El Liberal, 1875).
36. Florentino González, *Lecciones de derecho constitucional* (Buenos Aires: Imprenta J. A. Bernheim, 1869), 479.
37. Juan Bautista Alberdi, *Estudios sobre la Constitución argentina de 1853* (Buenos Aires: Jackson, n.d.); and idem, *Bases* (Buenos Aires: Plus Ultra, 1982). For an excellent account of Argentine constitutional debates, see Chiaramonte and Buchbinder, "Provincias, caudillos, nación y la historiografía constitucionalista argentina," 93–119, esp. 95–97. Chiaramonte and Buchbinder documented the development of a veritable industry of translating and disseminating US texts on constitutional law (96). On that, see also Francisco Ramos Mejía,

El federalismo argentino (Buenos Aires: La Cultura Argentina, 1915 [1887]), 15–17.
38. González, *Lecciones de derecho constitucional.*
39. Ramos Mejía, *El federalismo argentino,* 276.
40. Ibid., 281 and 287.
41. Leandro Alem, "Anormalidad y violencia del centralismo," in *Cámara de Diputados de la Provincia de Buenos Aires,* September 15, 1879, in his *Autonomismo y centralismo* (Buenos Aires: Editorial Raigal, 1954), 1–25, 5 and 22.
42. *Bee-Hive,* April 29, 1865.
43. G. Azcárate, "Los Estados Unidos," *El Continente Americano* (Madrid: Establecimiento Tipográfico "Sucesores de Rivadeneyra," 1894), vol. 2, 43.
44. A. De Chambrun, *Droits et libertés aux Etats-Unis* (Paris: A. Thorin, 1891), 358; cited in Portes, *Fascination and Misgivings,* 175.
45. R. Labra, *La Revolucion Norte-americana del siglo XVIII* (Madrid: Imprenta de Aurelio J Alaria, 1881), 9–10.
46. James Bryce, *The American Commonwealth* (London: Macmillan, 1889, 2 vols.); Gladstone, "Kin Beyond Sea," 185.
47. Labra, *La Revolucion Norte-americana,* 394.
48. The Parisian crisis that prompted Azcárate's lecture was effectively a coup d'état, in which Mac-Mahon reasserted conservative republicanism in the face of what was seen as excessive anticlericalism. Republican newspapers were prosecuted and republican meeting places persecuted. Nevertheless, in the elections that followed in October 1877, the republicans retained their parliamentary majority by 317 seats to 199. See Tombs, *France,* 441.
49. G. de Azcárate, *El poder del jefe del estado en Francia, Inglaterra y los Estados-Unidos* (Madrid: Establecimiento Tipgráfico de J. C. Conde, 1878), 92.
50. Ibid., 99.
51. Ibid., 101.
52. *Ambas Américas, Revista de Educación, bibliografía i agricultura* (New York)I, no.1 (1867), 5.
53. Visconde de Uruguai, *Ensaio sobre o direato administrativo* (Rio de Janeiro: Typog. Nacional, 1862), 180.
54. Tocqueville, *Democracy in America,* vol. 2, 662.
55. Uruguai, *Ensaio,* 480.
56. Aureliano Cândido Tavares Bastos, "O governo americano e a descentralização," cited in Luiz Pinto, *Idéias e Pensamentos de Tavares Bastos* (Rio de Janeiro: Editora Minerva, 1943), 141–142.
57. See, for example, *Ambas Américas* 1, no. 2 (1868), 3–13. On US women philanthropists see Chapter 3.
58. Laboulaye, *Paris en Amérique.*
59. *Ambas Américas* I, no. 1, 6.
60. La Redacción de la Nueva Prensa, *Los Pueblos Jovenes,* 124.
61. Ibid.
62. J. Jordana y Morera, *Curiosidades Naturales y Carácter Social de los Estados Unidos* (Madrid: Tipografía de Manuel G Hernández, 1884), 159; A. Llanos, *El*

Gigante Americano Descripciones de los Estados Unidos de la América del Norte (Madrid: Tipográfico de Ricardo Fé, 1886), 96.
63. Portes, *Fascination and Misgivings*, 196.
64. On the political scandals of "the gilded age," see Summers, *The Era of Good Stealings*, passim or Cherney, *American Politics in the Gilded Age*, 54–56.
65. Marco Minghetti, *I partiti politici r la ingerenza loro nella giustizia e nell'amministrazione* (Bologna: Zanichelli, 1881). Quoted after idem, *Scritti Politici* (Roma: Presidenza del Consiglio dei Ministri, 1986), 655.
66. *Gil Blas,* May 17, 1868, "Crónica política."
67. M. Cucheval-Clarigny, "Les années de l'histoire des Etats-Unis. L'administration de M. Hayes," *Revue des Deux Mondes,* February 15, 1881; cited in Portes, *Fascination and Misgivings,* 174.
68. A. Llanos, *El Gigante Americano,* 14–15.
69. *La Ilustración Española y Americana,* December 8, 1876, "Nueva York: Votantes ilegales detenidos en la nueva Casa de Correos."
70. Azcárate, *El self-government y la monarquia doctrinaria,* 4–40.
71. Noailles, "Le centenaire d'une constitution," *Revue des Deux Mondes,* April 15, 1889; cited in Portes, *Fascination and Misgivings,* 189.
72. A. Gigot, "La présidence d'A. Jackson," *Revue des Deux Mondes,* March 1, 1884; cited in Portes, *Fascination and Misgivings,* 203.
73. Portes, *Fascination and Misgivings,* 204.
74. Ibid., 173–174.
75. *Lloyd's Weekly,* February 25, 1877.
76. Goldwin Smith, "The Decline of Party Government," *Macmillan's Magazine* xxxvi (August 1877), 302. For more conservative reactions to the corruption issue, see *Spectator,* April 27, 1876; *Economist,* January 13, 1872.
77. On transatlantic liberalism, see Butler, *Critical Americans.*
78. W. E. Adams, *Our American Cousins: Being Personal Impressions of the People and Institutions of the United States* (London: Walter Scott, 1887), 122.
79. *La Tribuna* (Buenos Aires), 1877.
80. Lucio V. Mansilla, *Una huaca* (Montevideo: Imprenta de *El Siglo,* 1877), 14 and 10.
81. See *La Epoca,* July 22, 1877, "Cartas de los Estados-Unidos."
82. Portes, *Fascination and Misgivings,* 199.
83. For an account of the improbable circumstances of Tweed's apprehension in Spain thanks to Nast's caricatures, see A. B. Paine, *Thomas Nast. His Period and his Pictures* (New York and London: Harper Brothers, 1904), 336–337 or Summers, *The Era of Good Stealings,* 11–14.
84. Arnold, "A Word about America" and "A Word More about America."
85. Lucio V. Mansilla, *En vísperas* (Paris: Libreros-Editores, 1903), 85.
86. Lucio V. Mansilla, *El diario de mi vida ó sean estudios morales* (Buenos Aires: Imprenta Tribuna Nacional, 1888), 102–103, citation from 1863.
87. Portes, *Fascination and Misgivings,* 165–166.
88. See Oltra, *La influencia norteamericana,* 43.
89. *Gil Blas,* May 17, 1868, "Crónica política."

3

Liberty, Lipstick, and Lobsters

Nicola Miller

The greatest discovery of the century is the discovery of woman. We have emancipated her, and are opening countless opportunities for our girls outside of marriage. This freedom is one of the greatest glories of the nineteenth century.

> Orison Swett Marden, Pushing to the Front, or Success under Difficulties, *1894*

The emancipation of women was a vital element in the United States' self-image as the ultimate progressive nation, as illustrated by the above quotation from a self-help book that became an early "best seller" in Latin America.[1] To a significant extent, the United States was accepted abroad as the society of the most advanced debates about the role of women and as a testing ground for radical policies toward them.[2] Correspondingly, observers of the United States, both sympathetic and unsympathetic, tended to regard US women both as a cultural signifier for the country at large and as the embodiment of what the future might hold for their own societies. Both Europeans and Latin Americans who encountered US women either at home or abroad expressed astonishment and not a little bemusement at the combination of their beauty and their boldness. Tocqueville had already made much of the fact that US women were educated and that relations between the sexes were much freer than in Europe.[3] Was it possible that all this independence for women, "the most absolute choice allowed them, of where they will go, and what they shall do and say—[could] tend to the happiness, or the best development of the species?"[4] Images of US women, US domestic life, and US manners and mores featured prominently in coverage of the United States.

The Cuban newspaper column of 1877 that brought together vignettes of an unconstrained woman (a young Miss obliged to become Mrs. with somewhat undue haste), an invention (the telephone), and a quack cure (Dr. Pleasonton's pane of blue glass, supposed to relieve rheumatism) under the heading "Things About the United States" captured what was popularly seen as characteristic about US modernity.[5] Women were widely deemed to be particularly susceptible to inventions of all kinds, so the wonders of US household gadgets and appliances, or beauty potions and remedies, were often refracted through images of women.

This chapter explores three aspects of images of US gender. The first section, "Calibrating Modernity," focuses specifically on images of women, as the potential "receptors" of modernizing policies such as political reform, primary education, and paid employment.[6] In Argentina, for example, women were explicitly made the measure of modernization when the towering figure of Domingo Sarmiento, liberal reformer and admirer of the United States, declared: "A nation's level of civilization can be judged by the social position of its women."[7] The Italian Republicans, a relatively small and sectarian, yet influential, opposition group, explicitly linked an idealized image of women to a utopian vision of the United States: "America wants its wives, its maidens, its mothers, to be fervent for liberty, so that husbands, fathers and sons will never lose that holy love. The most logical of all nations, wishing to be free, it began by emancipating its women. And on the bosoms of these mothers are formed and educated generous souls that have faith in justice and defend liberty. With such souls a great people is formed, and therein lies the greatness of America."[8] American women, particularly young women—vigorously striding through the streets, venturing anywhere and everywhere without a chaperone—were widely perceived to be symbolic of the allure of US liberty—and of the dangers it posed. Women were taken to represent the moral standing of the society: onto their bodies were projected a range of debates and opinions about the relationship between the proclaimed idealism of the United States and the perceived materialism of its way of life.

The second part of this chapter, "Domesticity and Domestication," takes as its starting point Amy Kaplan's analysis of the extent to which the US nation was imagined from within in domestic terms—as a home—during an era of expansionism involving "violent confrontations with Indians, Mexicans, and European empires." An ideology of "Manifest domesticity," she argued, allowed the United States to represent itself as taming the wilderness, establishing "the conditions of domesticity [as] markers that distinguish civilization from savagery."[9] Building on Kaplan's compelling arguments about the dependence of US constructions of a sense of "at home-ness" upon its growing urge to conquer the territory and resources of other peoples, this section asks to what extent such reassuring images of "Republican motherhood," domestic bliss, and domestication were accepted abroad, or whether wholly different images were being generated. The third part of the chapter starts from the premise that, as feminist historians have long argued, modernity itself is represented in gendered ways, and analyzes the gendering of images of US modernity during the late nineteenth century.[10]

As has been the case for the other themes explored in this book, the nature and prominence of images of US gender (and gendered images) varied both within and between countries and over time. Among the diversity of images specifically of US women, however, it is evident that two stereotypes stand out, which can be characterized as "philanthropic woman" and "cosmetic woman." These two, from opposite ends of an index of moral worth, were vividly depicted by the great Cuban chronicler of the United States, José Martí, in 1886. The first, the strong self-sufficient woman, was represented as a direct descendant of the Puritans, "for whom passion is morally wrong, duty is fundamental and falling short is impossible":[11]

> These women have a sober majesty, which could be compared with ancient Greek statues: their feet are broad, a base of common sense; their hands are long and as if dipped in balm, like those of a race attaining perfection; on their white necks they wear their well-turned hair, which is no invitation to sin, only to respect. They are never seen in strong colours: black seems to be their natural dress. They know a great deal about elevated, theological matters, and about American and English literature; little about art; little about shameless and hateful greed.

Such women were industrious even in their piety and embodied the US ideal of disinterested public service. In stark contrast, at the other end of the spectrum from idealism to materialism, was the second type: "the modern New York girl, who is like one of those [...] puppets with little bells inside: when you tap her she sounds only of money." These flibbertigibbet *misses* (who were customarily demarcated thus in "Latin" cultures, in distancing italicized English), "polished off [...] in Paris, with no more soul than a silk purse," were the outward manifestation of what many people saw as the vacuity and superficiality of a US society that was parasitically dependent upon old Europe for any patina of culture. Whereas philanthropic women were usually represented as particular named individuals, such as the imposing figure of Harriet Beecher Stowe, cosmetic women tended to remain anonymous, as if they came off a production line (prefiguring Stepford Wives and Barbie dolls).

The majority of images of US women conformed to one of these alternatives of miss or matron, which was of course restricted by race, class, and region: it was a typology of women who were white and well off, and who were the products of New England (above all, Massachusetts) in the case of philanthropic woman, and, in the case of cosmetic woman, of New York or California. There were relatively few images of black, Creole, indigenous, immigrant, indigent, or criminal women, which lent especial significance to the exceptions, examples of which will be discussed in the second section below.

Calibrating Modernity

The first prominent example to resonate abroad of the benefits of educating women was Harriet Beecher Stowe, "the most internationally visible American writer of her time."[12] Commentary on *Uncle Tom's Cabin* (1852, available in French, Italian, Spanish, and Portuguese editions by 1854) drew attention not only to the problem of slavery, but also to the role that intelligent and educated women like Beecher Stowe could play in public affairs in the United States.[13] She was heralded as the perfect combination of a warm heart, a cool head, and an elevated soul, all marshaled in the great cause of freedom.[14] By having made such a significant intervention in the campaign to purge the great moral stain on the US republic, she was seen as the personification of all that was most idealistic about the United States. Comparable figures were Mary Peabody Mann or Julia Ward Howe, who lived both in Cuba, where she felt compelled to "rush in amongst" the heavily powdered Cuban women "with a feather duster, and lay about [them] a little,"[15] and in Florence, where she was half-mockingly, half-admiringly classified as "one of those women from New England," fired up by abolitionist literature and "full of faith in the destiny of humanity."[16]

Such images of the strong, stalwart woman, selflessly dedicated to the common good, were reinforced in some countries by reports of the role of women in the US Civil War. This feature of the conflict attracted attention and approval in Latin America and Spain, although it was scarcely noticed in France or—more surprisingly—Britain.[17] In the River Plate republics, which had already experienced several civil wars of their own, awe and admiration was expressed for the "indefatigable constancy, self-denial and boundless charity" of the women who tended wounded soldiers on the battlefields; "in times of crisis," it was claimed, "the mettle of American women has proved stronger than Toledan steel."[18] In Spain, there was one particular female figure from the Civil War era who resonated with the (relatively few) exponents of greater female emancipation. The struggle for women's emancipation was at times conflated by Spanish liberals with the struggle for emancipation from slavery, even if in the United States itself the relationship between the two could be difficult and divisive. The person who—to Spanish minds—embodied the two forms of emancipation was Miss Anna Carroll of Maryland, whose story was picked up by Spain's noted early feminists, Concepción Arenal and Emilia Pardo Bazán, and by the women's journal *La Ilustración de la Mujer*. To them, Carroll represented both the emancipation of women and of slaves, not only because she had freed her own slaves in 1860 but, more importantly, because she counseled Abraham Lincoln on the constitutional issues surrounding emancipation, wrote pamphlets defending the Unionist position, and—this is the contribution most often flagged up by her Spanish admirers—reputedly gave the Unionist military leaders important and effective strategic advice on military operations in Tennessee. Thus the 1850s and 1860s saw the creation of an ideal type of philanthropic US woman, the power of which seemed to stem at least partly from the fact that her role in public life was based less on legal rights than on moral conviction and sheer force of character.

During the period covered in this book, in most countries formal political rights were deemed to be less important to the cause of women's emancipation—or further beyond reach—than access to education, employment, and public debate. The US campaign for women's suffrage attracted attention in Britain, Cuba, and Spain, where there were comparable movements, but was not yet a significant talking point elsewhere. In Britain, some interest—by no means all of it approving—was aroused by the enfranchisement of some women in the West soon after the Civil War,[19] but it was not until the 1890s, when the United Kingdom's own campaign gathered momentum, that there was extensive newspaper coverage of the US campaign for female suffrage.[20] In colonial Cuba, the potential role of women in a future Cuban nation came to the fore during the first war of independence, known as the Ten Years' War (1868–78), in which many women participated: couples went to fight together, often taking their children along. Women's rights remained a lively topic of debate in Cuba throughout the rest of our period, as the independence struggle, defeated in 1878, reemerged in the 1890s, leading to the second war of independence (1895–8). From the 1870s onward, both supporters and opponents of women's suffrage in Cuba drew upon US ideas. Cuban women militants, especially those exiled to the United States during the Ten Years' War, introduced the arguments of US women's movements in support of their own, while their opponents noted dryly that even in the United States, where democratic principles were applied more extensively than anywhere else, women still had not been granted the right to vote.[21]

But the cause of suffrage remained less important to Cuban reformists than access to education and the right to work.

The focus was similar in Spain, where education was seen as a prerequisite to gaining the vote, but there was no suggestion that Spanish women should be granted suffrage anytime soon. Even the liberal reformer Rafael de Labra, who went the furthest in championing female emancipation, declared that full political emancipation would surely come to Spain— "eventually." It was common to argue, as the feminist Arenal did in 1869, that women would be better off without the vote because they lacked the education to use it judiciously. She wrote scathingly of the political sphere as a "field of confusion, lies, and often iniquity," doubting that women would prove a moralizing force in politics and worrying instead that they would become contaminated by such a corrupt and disreputable business. By 1883, however, she had changed her mind, apparently as a result of reading a report issued in June 1882 by a US Senate Committee charged with evaluating a possible constitutional amendment extending the vote to women. The testimonial evidence gathered in this document convinced Arenal that she had been mistaken: the US experience had demonstrated that women could have a civilizing impact on the world of politics. While this pioneering feminist still felt the question of female suffrage in Spain to be one for the future, it was "facts gathered in North America" that persuaded her that "the day can and will arrive when universal suffrage will be both a reality and a great advantage."[22]

Education policy was debated throughout Europe and Latin America during the nineteenth century and several countries, notably Britain and France, supplied models and manuals that circulated widely. In the mélange of ideas from which most policymakers drew, the United States became associated above all with women in education, both as pupils and teachers. Observers often highlighted the contrast between the social acceptance of educated women in the United States and the stigmatizing of them elsewhere. "In Europe," one Italian commentator observed in 1868, "above all on the Continent, a woman who occupies herself with literature and science is considered to be a wayward star that has fallen out of its own orbit. It is not so in the United States."[23] Male educational reformers in Latin America critically compared their own women, who "worried only about looking pretty and pleasing visitors, and perhaps managing to sing a little," with the US women who could "contemplate and philosophize" like men.[24] The possible effects of coeducational institutions were much debated, especially in France, where they were unknown.[25] Everywhere, there were images of female US schoolteachers as capable, powerful women, who could run schools without much, if any, help from men. In Spain, there was a local example in Alice Gordon Gulick, a teacher from the United States, who created the "Mount Holyoke of Spain" in the International Institute for Girls, founded in 1892 in San Sebastián. Her pupils were taught science and physical education alongside the more traditional female subjects; she employed "new North American methods," emphasizing direct, practical ways of learning, and recruited female teachers for the east coast colleges to implement them. At its height her school had 100 day pupils and 50 boarders and her pupils regularly outperformed the boys at the local institution (which caused some friction).[26]

That the United States was in the vanguard of women's education was widely accepted in a general way, but even in those countries where US educational models were most influential, namely Cuba and Argentina, very different images came to the fore, depending on the interests and orientations of those who disseminated them. One feature that was common to both countries was physical education. In Cuba, this dated back to as early as 1833, when the great educator and intellectual José de la Luz y Caballero, who spent several years in the United States, mainly in Philadelphia, proposed a program of girls' education. His overall program merged elements from several European and US sources, the most important of which was Victor Cousin,[27] but his emphasis on regular exercise for schoolgirls was specifically drawn from the United States. Likewise Sarmiento, who saw the United States as having revived the ancient Greek emphasis on gymnastics, held that physical education would help to emancipate Argentine young women from a "sedentary life behind the walls of [a] dimly-lit home."[28]

Beyond a shared commitment to exercise, however, educators in Cuba and Argentina focused on different images from the United States. In colonial Cuba, virtually no public provision for elementary education was made by the Spanish authorities, but during the Ten Years' War women of all classes who spent time in the United States found that they could earn an independent living there and, on returning to Cuba, spread the idea that it was indeed a land of opportunity for women. Many of these returning migrants joined the Asociación de Amigos de la Educación Popular (Association of Friends of Popular Education), founded in 1874 to promote education for artisans and women. As a result, the more radical proposals about what women should learn had greater appeal. One pioneering figure was María Luisa Dolz y Arango, the first Cuban woman to obtain a doctorate in natural sciences (from the University of Havana in 1898). She took over a private Catholic school in Havana and added scientific topics, along with physical education, to "the obligatory dogmatic subjects." As happened in the United States, she encouraged women to teach and many of her pupils became teachers at other schools for women in Havana.[29]

A far less radical vision of women's education was promoted by Argentine president Sarmiento, who recruited 65 American teachers, all but four of whom were women, to start normal schools (for teacher training) throughout Argentina during the 1870s and 1880s. It is worth emphasizing that Sarmiento's purpose in importing US women teachers was neither Americanization nor the introduction of education for girls, which dated back to the 1820s in Argentina compared with the 1840s in the United States, as Argentine educationalists could rarely resist pointing out. Instead, Sarmiento's scheme was designed to provide role models that would encourage Argentine women to challenge the social conventions and become professional teachers themselves. His policy was intended as a transitional one, which aimed to break down the high level of resistance among Argentine elite women to working outside the home. He therefore drew upon relatively conservative images of US women schoolteachers in an attempt to promote their acceptability: "In the presence of women, says an American educationalist, the School is no longer that gloomy prison which saddens and discourages children; under their gentle influence it becomes an extension of the home. Their very grace and beauty lend a secret enchantment to their lessons."[30] Apparently, with the help of Mary Mann, Sarmiento endeavored to ensure that the women selected to go to Argentina were indeed handsome and elegant, with irreproachable manners and morals, in order to reassure the upper-class Argentine women that he sought to attract into teaching.[31] The US teachers who went to Argentina also tended to be relatively moderate in their views on the kind of education desirable for women, supporting Catherine Beecher's vision of practical, domestic education rather than the science-based curriculum that would have qualified them for a wide range of jobs.

The level of hostility and criticism expressed in Argentina toward the US women teachers suggests that caution was justified. Why not Germans, it was argued, who cost less? Sarmiento responded that German teachers taught pupils to accept, not to question, whereas in the United States the individuality of each child was respected. Why women? Sarmiento argued that "the prosperity, happiness, intelligence and kindliness" he encountered in the United States could be attributed to "the excellent free grade school system, where most of the teachers were women,"[32] but his views were not widely accepted. Argentine teachers "bitterly resented what seemed to them the fabulous salaries paid to the gringos,"[33] although the gringos did not always actually get paid, it transpired. Mary Gorman, for example, almost went home in dismay and despair at such difficulties. The Argentine educationalist Juana Manso (1817–79) befriended many of the US women when they first arrived, but there are indications that she was herself deeply ambivalent about their presence. In the periodical she edited,

Los Anales de la Educación, she offered her own explanation for why Mary had not been paid: "First, because she is a gringo; secondly, because she is the apple of my eye—and they hate me—against me it is war without truce. Many times have I seen poor Miss Gorman, pale and dejected, but with angelic resignation, with this heavy weight of sadness on her heart, maltreated and disregarded."[34] The magazine carried a succession of tragic stories, such as that of Fanny Wood, who left Buenos Aires in 1871 to escape the yellow fever epidemic, but returned to nurse the American family with whom she had lived when she first arrived, "meeting death in the fulfilment of her Christian duty."[35] In Manso's articles, the US teachers were represented as noble and long suffering, but profoundly disempowered by the Argentine context in which they found themselves. However, there were also images of achievement: one later researcher found that mos Argentine parents who encountered the US women were grateful and admiring of their work, as were many of those who had been taught by them, although the former pupils also recalled that they "had to make considerable effort to figure out what the Bostonians were saying."[36] By 1910, all but two of the US teachers had retired, having trained hundreds of Argentine teachers. Overall, the presence of these teachers reinforced an image of American women as stalwart, good-hearted, self-sacrificial, and disciplined—but there was also the impression created that the force of the "philanthropic woman" was diminished when she was transplanted outside of the United States.

Images abounded of pioneering US women who had proved to be highly capable in various professional roles, beyond teaching. The prestigious Cuban periodical *La Habana Elegante* highlighted the story of "Isabel" (Elizabeth) Blackwell and her sister "Emilia" (Emily), the first women to qualify as medical doctors in New York, who went on to found the Women's Medical College. In this article, the careers of these two women were inaccurately represented as unproblematic examples of the inevitability of progress, which, in time, would be experienced in "South America" as well as in "North America."[37] The Blackwell sisters actually had a difficult time working in the United States: they devoted their energies to promoting education mainly because they found it virtually impossible to practice medicine in New York on account of the prejudice against them, and Elizabeth returned in 1875 to her native England. Further examples of young women who were represented in Cuba as being just as capable as men were: a famous Texas telegraph operator, Ella Brown, who was only seven years old; the indomitable daughter Bessie (no age specified, but "a schoolgirl") of an engineer, George Bauman, who could apparently fix a train as well as anyone; and the wife of "Roebelin" (Emily Warren Roebling, 1843–1903), builder of the Brooklyn Bridge, who learned engineering when her husband, Washington, became paralyzed and helped him to finish the work, all the while refusing to take public credit.[38] Cubans and Argentines, particularly, were also familiar with the phenomenon of women journalists and *reporters*.[39] In Spain, images of US women working as doctors, nurses, ships' captains, architects, and lawyers provided inspiration and also ammunition for feminist arguments that a life solely of domesticity was incompatible with being a modern people "that is or is hoping to become free."[40]

Not everyone shared the view that giving women such opportunities was a good idea—indeed, throughout the period there continued to be echoes of the 1854 lament from *Household Words*: "Oh Transatlantic Utopians leave nature's work alone! Let women have their rights, in Heaven's name, but do not thrust them into places which they cannot fulfill, and give them functions which they cannot perform, except to their own disadvantage."[41] But it was widely perceived that such opportunities were real and that they constituted a defining aspect of US modernity.

Of all the freedoms enjoyed by US women, perhaps the one that most frequently attracted attention abroad was their freedom of movement, particularly in relation to social contact with men. The French and the British seemed to be as fascinated by this phenomenon as were the Spaniards and the Latin Americans. However, it was among the latter that the contrast between their native lands and the United States was drawn particularly sharply. Juana Manso, who visited the United States with her husband, noted as early as 1854: "in Buenos Aires they do not allow a married woman to do what she can do in Boston, New York or Philadelphia: namely to put on her hat and coat and spend the whole day in the street if she deems it necessary to her interests or her wishes."[42] Men noticed it, too: the Chilean writer Benjamín Vicuña Mackenna, visiting around the same time, marveled that a woman was "mistress of herself here," unlike in "Spanish countries," where "we have robbed women of all their social dignity and destroyed the importance of their saviour role among peoples."[43]

One widely shared perception of US women was that the degree of freedom they were allowed in no way diminished the respect in which they were held: indeed, if anything, the opposite was the case. French and Latin American sources particularly emphasized this aspect of women's experience. It was noted that for US women to walk the streets in no way compromised their morals; moreover, the public thoroughfares were seen as more generally respectable as a result of their presence: in downtown Manhattan, noted one male Argentine traveler in the early 1880s, there were none of those "repugnant solicitations that make it impossible for families to walk along the boulevards of Paris or certain streets in London."[44] Indeed, a woman was "a sacred being" on the street.[45] For one well-known French traveler, Thérèse Bentzon, the respect with which women were everywhere treated far outweighed any drawbacks she perceived in the American way of life: "for anyone who has tried life in the United States," she concluded, "it seems impossible anywhere else."[46] In being accorded both freedom and respect, US women symbolized what was seen by many as one of the most enviable aspects of US modernity: "It has been said that there are only two positions in life to which it is desirable to be born—Czar of all the Russians and an American woman."[47]

What many observers saw as the "serene confidence [...] peculiar to North American women,"[48] was often attributed, especially by Latin Americans, precisely to their freedom of movement.[49] US women—the Uruguayan intellectual José Pedro Varela wrote in 1867—moved smoothly and naturally through public spaces. He admired "the calm with which those charming creatures of fifteen walk alone through the streets, get onto the omnibus, go into theatres, mix with men and remain ever decorous and pure."[50] It was mainly this physical poise that accounted, in many depictions, for the remarkable beauty associated with US women: one French visitor spelled out that, for him, "their beauty had more to do with ease of movement than with the delicacy of their features or the perfection of their figures."[51] But the idea that American women, at least the young women, were unusually and distinctively beautiful—"perhaps the most beautiful and graceful in the world"— was widespread,[52] particularly in Latin America. The following excerpt from a male traveler's account is self-consciously exaggerated, but not atypical of Latin American representations from the mid-nineteenth century:

> Did Murillo and Rubens know about American women when they painted their divine creations? You would think so when you meet at every step of the way along the streets of New York either Murillo's ideal of beauty or the incomparable virgins of Rubens. [...] North American women are of such exquisite beauty, such enchanting grace, that it is impossible to imagine them without having seen them.[53]

Where American women were less often portrayed as beautiful was in Britain, where—in stark contrast to Latin America—the stereotype was that they were pretty but sickly and too thin, which was blamed on poor diet.[54] The elites of the former colonial power were perhaps reluctant to ascribe too much independent health and regenerative capacity to the United States, at a stage when US challenges to UK influence in the rest of the Americas were just beginning to be felt. In one of the many articles comparing English and US women, one commentator from 1870 ascribed far greater physical vigor to English women, who liked their "out-of-door sports as well as the men. They row, they ride, they have archery meetings and more than this, they walk out in every kind of weather." The prospects of American women living a long and vigorous life had been greatly improved, he continued, by the "introduction of English walking boots" consequent upon the opening of Central Park, but if they were ever to become as healthy as English women in general "they should wear warmer under-clothing, walk more in the open air, and take horseback exercise regularly."[55] By the 1890s, after the United States had seen three decades of economic expansion that had tripled the size of its economy, there were new British images of American women as sporty—especially in regard to the increase in athletics in the universities—marking a sharp differentiation from previous images of them as poor physical specimens.[56]

Beautiful, US women may have been, in the eyes of most of their foreign beholders, but fashionable they were not. If a US woman succeeded in being thought à la mode, it was attributed precisely to her susceptibility to Parisian style: "American women dress with more taste than Englishwomen," noted one male Cuban observer. "They owe it to the French."[57] More commonly, they were portrayed as resistant or indifferent to fashion, on practical or principled grounds. For benevolent observers, their lack of fashion sense was to their advantage, indicating their greater natural beauty and want of artifice, which was held to be a sign of their innate virtue and instinctive ability to exercise freedom without compromising morality. Those less favorably disposed toward the American way of life tended to depict young US women as frivolous and obsessed with acquiring extravagant ornamentation to attain the stylishness that their essential vulgarity denied them. One such critical observer was the Argentine writer Eduarda Mansilla de García (1834–92), who first went to the United States in 1861, traveling alone with her two children while she awaited the arrival of her diplomat husband from France; later, from 1868–72, she was based in Washington when her husband served as Argentina's representative. Her *Recuerdos de viaje* (1882), which was a composite account of both experiences, was serialized in a very popular Argentine newspaper column and then published as a best-selling book. Mansilla discreetly but unmistakably sought to establish her work as a rival—and a response—to Sarmiento and his widely read travelogue of the United States. In contrast to Sarmiento's evocations of dignified US women educators, Mansilla gave a running commentary on the self-indulgent frivolities of the "*miss*": love of presents, weakness for aristocrats, overuse of cosmetics, addiction to high heels and ostentatious jewelry.[58] In Britain, too, the idea that American women were hopelessly spoilt became a leitmotiv.[59]

The most significant drawback to the unchecked freedom enjoyed by young US women, even for many sympathetic observers, was their perceived lack of allure or sexuality. French male travelers commented particularly on "the sexual neutrality of such encounters." The waitresses in bars and restaurants came across as "a separate sex, neither embarrassed nor provoking, neither graceful nor clumsy, which corresponds to nothing known to us in France."[60] In the very different context of Argentina, where Britain played a neo-imperial role from the 1870s onward, images of asexual US women were often invoked in contrast with English women, who were typically represented as repressed but fundamentally passionate. Images of unnatural US women were deployed by critics of the technology-driven model of modernization implemented in Argentina during the 1870s and 1880s. Women writers and journalists of the 1880s wrote a succession of articles raising doubts about "materialist science, technology, and medical practice," proposing, instead, "an organic representation of self, at one with family and community."[61] Women who had visited the United States, notably Eduarda Mansilla, Juana Manso, and Juana Manuela Gorriti, played a leading role in developing these arguments and drew upon images of the United States to support them.

What fascinated observers above all was the perceived US addiction to flirtation, which, in most representations, was imagined as a desexualized practice that, in its indiscriminateness, diluted rather than enhanced the intensity of sexual attraction. One Spanish diplomat found the flirtatiousness of US women a potential minefield for any recently arrived European male. Flirtation was a "national pastime," he observed—"an American woman who does not flirt is not an American"—but also a "sweet illusion" for the European man who found himself the recipient of "a beautiful New York girl's smile." Although such a smile would be "very significant in other countries", in the United States such flirtations "never last more than a week" and were simply a local custom, not to be taken to heart.[62] Latin American visitors, their horizons of expectation perhaps shaped by Tocqueville's distinction between coquetry arising from passion and coquetry stemming from calculation,[63] expressed particular disquiet about the extent to which sexuality had been reduced to joyless flirtation in the United States. For example, Eduarda Mansilla presented the following scene, which is worth citing in full for the poignancy of its image of a society that has lost any sense of what matters in human relations:

> In the furthest corner of a small, rather solitary room, there is quite a narrow pouffe upon which two people have managed to fit by sitting close together. [...] What can be glimpsed is a charming blonde, very languid and beautiful, who boasts a crinoline of exaggerated proportions, over which a dress of blue tulle billows and puffs up like a globe, describing a vast circumference. Enveloped, entwined, imprisoned, hidden, among the folds of tulle,

a young man sits by her side, at least it seems so, judging from his fine fair moustache, and his sparkling eyes, which are all that I could make out among the nebulous confusion of the cerulean-coloured tulle. That is flirtation.[64]

In France the successful playwright Victorien Sardou based a whole play on the subject of "flirting." *L'Oncle Sam* (1875), written in the aftermath of France's defeat in the war with Prussia (1870–1), was an acerbic attack on the idealized image of the American "model republic," or "l'Amérique en sucre" (sugar-coated America), which had held such sway over the liberal political imagination during the Second Empire.[65] Yet, what was really at the center of his drama was not politics but US social and sexual mores. The young French protagonist visiting the United States was told on his way to New York that "America is a paradise for young women!"[66] His guide, however, emphasized the economic and demographic reasons underlying US "idolatry" of their "*misses*":

> Women are rare! So young women are very much in demand and men are very anxious to please (*très-offert*). First consequence: no concern about a dowry! [...] Second consequence: whereas in France it is the highly desirable man who speculates and marries the most money possible; [...] here, it is the woman who compares, calculates and arranges the whole business![67]

The contemporary reception of the play revealed how alien these American practices were to French audiences. Sardou's images of the vanity fair of New York high society served to underpin more general misgivings about the United States: "No-one can doubt that flirtation is one of the most complete expressions of American corruption."[68] While flirting was commonly condemned, it nonetheless fascinated French commentators. It was almost exclusively associated with the American Miss, who was deemed to be very much in control of her male compatriots.[69] Intriguingly, this notion of the American young woman as a singularly strong-willed and single-minded creature has proved remarkably long lasting: many decades later Jean-Paul Sartre still thought it worthwhile to write a report for *Le Figaro* about "a school in New York [that] gives a course for girls on how to get their boyfriends to propose to them."[70]

Other commentators suspected, however, that American women paid a high price for the "period of unchecked flirtation" they briefly enjoyed while young: "we are sure that in married life and middle life in America, women must pay a penalty of insignificance and loss of influence for the leading part they played when youth was all the pre-eminence they needed," observed one pious British observer, who concluded that flirtation was "an evil."[71] Even more graphically, Sarmiento wrote that after marriage "the woman has said goodbye for ever to the world whose pleasures she enjoyed for so long with complete liberty." Her lot henceforth was "a closed domestic asylum," where "roastbeef was her eternal torment" and "an uncivilised husband, although *good-natured*, sweats all day and snores all night."[72]

Just as the price of freedom for women was often represented as a loss of seductive power, so too were there many expressions of the view that women's participation in public life diminished the quality of home life. Martí lamented: "The influence of women in the jobs and manly affairs of the republic is growing markedly, even though the health of the home is visibly declining, as is the sanctity of existence. It makes one shudder to think of their souls."[73] One positive image in this respect was of American women marrying for love, a factor that was deemed to be particularly important in France. Edouard Laboulaye's fictional alter ego, Dr. Lefebvre, cannot stop marveling at how much more affectionate than his French wife his American wife, Jenny, is: she calls him "mon amour" and even kisses him in public.[74] In contrast, however, there were many images stoking the idea that the all too easy association of men and women in US society had the deplorable outcome of a general diminishing of respect for marriage. "Yankee" marriages "differed from those of the rest of the world" because the couple "considered the sacrament to be a friendly connection which carried no obligation and could be easily broken," noted one Spaniard disapprovingly.[75] In the United States, it was widely imagined, constant recourse was made to the courts to resolve personal matters, with frequent divorces, petitions for indemnities after the breaking off of engagements, and prosecutions for bigamy and polygamy. Lurid stories circulated from the US press of women marrying seven or eight times, even tying the knot by telephone—in a perfect illustration of the way in which anxiety about technological modernity was projected onto gender relations.[76] By the late 1870s, the issue of divorce in America started to emerge as a source of moral panic in Britain.[77]

California, above all, came to be represented as a location where women took an entirely prosaic approach to marriage, which is symptomatic of a general tendency to see the land of gold as the site of typical US features writ large. An Italian magazine reported in 1899 that a town on the West Coast was offering courses in kissing for young women, costing one dollar per session or four dollars for the entire course of six.[78] In 1887, *La Habana Elegante* dryly told the story of one Lilly Brown, an heiress, of course ("who isn't one in California?!"), beautiful, it went without saying ("all heiresses are beautiful"), but heartless. On consulting a widowed friend as to how best "to enjoy her fortune freely," she was told that as a young single woman, she would not be able to do so and the only way to secure control over her own affairs was to become a widow. She should therefore get married as soon as possible, "to a dying man," which she duly did to a man diagnosed with tuberculosis. It turned out, however, that the doctors were wrong: "The fellow did not have tuberculosis; what was wrong with him was hunger. Within a few days of being well fed he was a different person, and he duly went to visit his wife to claim his marital rights."[79]

Diverse images circulated, then, of the consequences of the liberty that was everywhere attributed to US women. Positively, it could result in an educated mind and a healthy body, fired by a loving and staunch spirit committed to charity at home and abroad. Negatively, it led to a calculating mind and a corrupt body, painted and falsified with cosmetics, degraded by selfishness and heartlessness. Increasingly, however, US women became associated abroad with the unwelcome idea that women had to choose between the cultivation of elegance and sensuality on the one hand and the enjoyment of education and employment on the other. Alternative images of how to be a "modern woman" suggested that it was possible to combine being womanly with being free. For example, the Spanish writer Eva Canel, who lived in Cuba for many years, proposed as an icon of modernity Adela de Dupuy de Lôme, wife of the Spanish diplomat who later became notorious for his letter disparaging President McKinley, which caused a scandal in the run-up to the Spanish-American War. Working in her office, scanning the newspapers, walking alone in public gardens, Adela might almost be "taken for a Yankee," wrote Canel, were it not for "her Spanish majesty" and "her elegance [derived from] courage and wit." She showed, Canel concluded, that "to be a woman of the nineteenth century and to be equal in worth to men, there is no need to vote at the polls or to want to be a minister or to be in the least mannish."[80] In short, there was no need to be American to become modern.

Domesticity and Domestication

There was widespread interest in the domestic arrangements of the Americans. In Cuba, where connections and exchanges of all types (people, goods, ideas) with the United States dated back to the early nineteenth century, it is striking how strong and persistent was the image of the US home as a place of extraordinary comfort and convenience. What was admired in Cuba, as was later the case in other parts of Latin America, was the US capacity to adapt European designs to their own materials and situations. US adaptations of European models of domesticity were imported into Cuba, at least into the north-western coastal areas where US residents congregated, from the 1820s onward. Alexander von Humboldt, visiting in 1827, noted that house designs were "ordered from the United States, as one would order any piece of furniture."[81] During the 1850s and 1860s, there circulated in Cuba a slim but highly detailed manual on how to design and build European-style houses and gardens.[82] Later, well-off Cuban families purchased wholly prefabricated wooden houses from the United States, complete with furniture and fittings and even clothes and medicines.[83] In the late 1880s, Raimundo Cabrera translated Andrew Carnegie's glowing account of the houses of the wealthy in the United States, with their numerous devices to ensure comfort and convenience in every possible respect—electric bells for summoning servants, dumb-waiters, telephones, and elevators—which in Europe could not be found even in the most sumptuous of palaces. Cabrera added that in general US housing and town planning were at a far more advanced level than in Cuba, so that even those who were not rich could live in light, bright, clean, and airy buildings, with access to parks and gardens; he drew the contrast very sharply with the deplorable conditions he saw in Havana, which were described in a discourse of decadence as "disused tenements where the tropical vegetation appears stained by the putrefying waste of the masses."[84]

Intriguingly, virtually the opposite image of the state of US urban areas circulated in imperial Spain. A notorious example arose when planning the Madrid *ensanche* (suburban development) to the north and east of the old city in the 1850s. In developing his plan for lower density housing, the designer, Carlos María de Castro, researched various models, including the grid plan of New York, as well as London, Paris, and Barcelona. He found that New York did not compare at all favorably with European cities in terms of the circulation of air and light around buildings. Concluding that the traditional Spanish plaza or the new urban models of London suburbs or Parisian boulevards allowed for far better living conditions, Castro based his proposals for the *ensanche* on Hausmann's Paris and Cerdá's Barcelona.[85]

When Cubans traveled to the United States, they tended to go to the most rapidly modernizing US cities—New York, Boston, Philadelphia, and Baltimore, Charleston and New Orleans, later Tampa and Cayo Hueso in Florida—so they were particularly au fait with the latest inventions. US products, welcomed as symbols of modernity to counter the hold on Cuba of "backward" colonial Spain, displaced European goods among Cuban elites far earlier than elsewhere in Latin America, where British and French imports dominated until the First World War. There was an abundance of household and personal goods from the United States: kerosene lamps, washing machines, sewing machines, toys, albums—and guns. "For the young men we have the latest pistol from Smith and Wesson," proclaimed a newspaper advertisement proudly, a weapon that "for its safety, convenience and elegance is considered to be the best pistol invented this century."[86] The Cuban writer Aurelia Castillo de González's account of her visit to the Chicago World Fair of 1893, which would have been familiar to any educated Cuban, dwelt upon US ingenuity in applying technology to the domestic sphere: she was particularly struck, unsurprisingly, given Havana's climate, by electric fans and other ventilation devices; she was also captivated by the ingenious intricacy of hooks-and-eyes.[87] Even Martí, who was generally skeptical of US materialism, was greatly enamored of inventions and gadgets, writing many accounts of them.[88]

Cuba's utopian picture of US domestic life was not widely shared, however. The Argentine Eduarda Mansilla rather mockingly dwelt upon what she saw as the US preoccupation with "*comfort*" (again, the English word was used) in their homes, but she attributed it mainly to English influence.[89] It was therefore surprising to find, from the 1870s onward, many advertisements for US household goods even in Argentina, notoriously the Latin American country most resistant to them. It is also striking that at Argentina's National Exhibition, held at Córdoba in 1870, the United States was the second largest exhibitor after England, with a far greater presence than Germany or France.[90] Agricultural machinery was the most valuable US export to Argentina during the late nineteenth century, but domestic and personal items were also widely advertised. It is worth noting that some of them—washing machines, sewing machines, purpose-built furniture, cleaning brushes, tinned foodstuffs, and travel goods—succeeded in carving out a niche, while acknowledging that French and English domestic goods retained a high level of prestige in the Argentine market until well into the twentieth century. As early as 1873, an advertisement carried in the national newspaper *La Prensa* throughout the run-up to Christmas depicted three teapots engaged in a fight, with the English one prostrate on the floor, the French one falling down, and the "Yankee" one triumphant.[91] In continental Europe, there was far less interest in US home comforts. Elite French visitors were taken aback by the lack of servants; in French illustrated magazines and newspapers there were very few advertisements for US goods even at the end of the period. In Spain, there was a flurry of interest in US cosmetics and sewing machines around the time of the Centennial Exhibition and the Chicago World Fair, but little visibility for US goods at any other time. Italians admired US engineering but remained almost wholly resistant to the lure of other US products during this period.

One of the most ubiquitous of all images of the United States, especially in Latin America, was that the comfort of home life had been carried over into the experience of travel. From the 1840s onward the United States was represented as a society perpetually, easily, and comfortably on the move. As Sarmiento wrote, the "yankie [*sic*] might have been born to travel."[92]

For Sarmiento, movement was intimately linked to modernity: "The stationary peoples like Spain and its former colonies have no need of a hotel, for the domestic hearth is enough for them [but] for the active peoples, who are living life in the present with a sense of the future, a hotel will be far superior to any other public building," a monument in itself to modern convenience.[93] Even Eduarda Mansilla, who (as described in Chapter 4) represented her disembarkation at the New York quayside as a descent into hell, expressed heartfelt appreciation of the company that efficiently delivered her luggage from the ship to the hotel. She was even prepared to say that in this respect the United States was superior to France (usually, for her, beyond compare).[94] Hotel life in the United States—at least in New York and other East Coast cities—was portrayed by travelers (usually of some means) as incomparable, with all manner of home comforts for the traveler.[95] The exceptions were Italian travelers, who came themselves from the first country in Europe to experience tourism and occasionally tended to see US hotel conditions as comparatively primitive (see Chapter 4).

Widespread appreciation was also expressed of US railways and steamships. The famed US commitment to equality could be found on the railways (if nowhere else), Sarmiento argued, where there was just one class of accommodation for everybody, which was "always comfortable."[96] Above all, travelers waxed lyrical about the steamboats, especially those that plied the Mississippi, as "floating palaces" with "all the comforts that travelers have become accustomed to in the hotels on land," despite being "fabulously cheap."[97] Even though "English manufacturing or Parisian food and fashion" reigned supreme among the Latin American elites of the late nineteenth century,[98] the United States acquired an unrivalled reputation for the superiority of its transportation.

Other public spaces in the United States were often represented far more negatively than those connected with travel, however. An association was created in the imagination of many critics of the United States between women's preoccupation with employment, their resulting failure to create quality leisure time for their families, and the public spectacle of leisure as empty time. If work was often held to represent US ideals, how US families—particularly the young women—spent their leisure time was sometimes portrayed as emblematic of its debasements. For Eduarda Mansilla, US leisure entailed consumption: it was not possible, she claimed, to "pasear" (stroll about in public spaces) in New York, as everyone did in Paris, Vienna, Madrid, or Buenos Aires, people-watching and window-shopping, "without spending a cent." In New York, "you are compelled to spend, and to spend a lot, at the theatre or at spectacles of one kind or another, if you do not wish to die of boredom or of indigestion from too many ice-creams or *sherri-cobler,* which are the passion of the Americans and their beautiful daughters."⁹⁹ In many Latin American accounts of the American way of life, parks and leisure areas generated particularly contested images—they were conceived as spaces where liberty, in all its different meanings, was enacted, and they were often compared disadvantageously with Spanish American leisure places and practices. The Mexican liberal Ignacio Altamirano compared Sundays in Mexico, full of warmth and happiness on the streets, with the bleak housebound dourness of the Protestant Sunday.¹⁰⁰ Martí built an entire critique of the US social hierarchy on a description of a summer's day on Coney Island: US manners, mores, and consumption habits were all on display there.¹⁰¹ Women could move freely, but there was no shortage of hostile images of their behavior in public. Their leisure time was associated with vacuity and pointlessness and by implication so was that of the whole society.

The ideal American woman was widely imagined, then, as healthy, wealthy, virtuous, and white. It is perhaps not surprising that it was a visitor from Brazil, where the founding of a republic in 1889 had been closely bound up with the campaign for the abolition of slavery, who made this explicit. The distinguished young Brazilian novelist Adolfo Caminha was an admirer of the United States who spent a few months there and published an account of his trip, *No País dos Ianques (In the land of the Yankees)*, in 1894.¹⁰² Like so many other visitors, he marveled at the "proverbial self-assurance" of US women and compared it favorably with the reticence of women in Brazil, "where ladies are eternally forbidden to compete with the other sex in public life."¹⁰³ Where Caminha differed from other visitors was in his frankness about the extent to which his idealized image of US womanhood was racialized: it was the "blonde" and "blue-eyed" women of the Northern states, particularly of New England, who epitomized the "true American woman," whom he contrasted with the *Creole* (orig. italics) female population of a place such as New Orleans, with their "dark complexion" and "very dark eyes." Unlike the Northern women, who were characterized by their independence of mind, what best defined these Creoles from the South was the "voluptuous sensations" that they evoked in him.

Thus images of US women tended to be images of safely domesticated, educated, respectable women, their sexuality—and any other threatening instincts—neutered by the civilizing drive of US modernity. One exceptional image of a white American woman consumed by passion reveals what was at stake in preserving the unwritten rule. It was published in a Cuban illustrated magazine as a chronicle of one Mary Young, the daughter of a wealthy Chicago pork-butcher, who, scandalously, ran away to marry a Native American. The article opened with a graphic account of the "modern" method of slaughter developed by the butcher—"great knives open up the quadrupeds, passing rapidly and bloodlessly over the surface like a legion of dead fish. [...] Next they go into a laboratory." In the next paragraph, immediately following on from this image of clinical violence, Mary was depicted as "an enchanting and spiritual blue-stocking: she adores all things graceful and flaccid, all manner of sweets and sweetmeats." She was lost in romantic dreams from reading Chateaubriand's novel *Atala, ou les amours de deux sauvages dans le désert* (1801), in which the Indian warrior Chactas is taken prisoner by an enemy tribe but then rescued by a young Indian woman, Atala, who has been converted to Christianity. Mary's father, finding her in tears, inquired what the matter was, only to be told that she was in love. Delighted, he tried to guess who it might be—"With luck it's the banker's son Patrick, the most gallant young man in the whole of Illinois"—but was rebuffed by the inconsolable Mary, who sobbed out that she was "dying of love for an ideal." The scene switched abruptly to a train stopped outside "a reservation of barbarous Indians," on the way from Kansas to Yuma; on being shaken awake by her elderly "Saxon" companion to be told that "we are among savages," Mary "rose up on her knees, her enormous blue eyes opening gradually wider, and [...] let escape her first sigh of love." She promptly hurled herself upon "the herculean breast of a wild chiricahna" and the next anyone heard of her was a short notice in the *Chicago Times* announcing her marriage to "an Indian of the most ferocious and bloodthirsty tribe," a ceremony that happened to be witnessed by two Cubans working in the area as an anthropologist and an archaelogist.[104] This story was told in a Cuban response to a piece in the *New York World* arguing that Cuba could not become a state of the Union because its ideas and traditions were too different from those of the United States. Elite Cubans regularly read US newspapers and were therefore perfectly well aware that for an influential strand of opinion in the United States, Cubans were likely to prove "as resistant to Yankee culture as the Sioux Indians."[105]

The curtailed range of images of American women that we found suggests that, to some degree, the United States' own image of itself as a domesticated and domesticating society won acceptance abroad. The idealization of the United States as a dynamic yet unthreatening society as embodied in its women is encapsulated in the following excerpt from *Reynolds's Newspaper* (1892):

> What is the one thing in America that strikes an Englishman as most unlike what he finds at home? According to the Duke of Marlborough it is the American woman. She has a natural quickness for appreciating the characters of the men around her [...]. Maternity does not seem to crush every-thing else out of them as it does with all classes in England. The bright

cheery girl remains the gay, carefully-dressed married woman who is always trying to show herself off quietly to the best advantage; and she understands the art perfectly, among all classes of the people. In middle age and even later in life she seems to preserve a perennial interest in everything around her: she does not grow old mentally as so many Englishwomen do. The tendency to nagging and gossip-mongering of an ill-natured character, moreover, seems rarer in that country.[106]

Here is a (male) model of how to resolve the dilemmas of modern life: the American woman, as depicted in this passage, is both intelligent and emotionally astute; she is committed to the private sphere of home and family yet remains interested in the social sphere; she knows how to use modern artifice to look her best yet she retains a naturalness of manner and appearance. She radiates health and vitality; she is attractive, maybe even beautiful, but she is not seductive and she is definitely not dangerous. She has banished the dark side of modernity and she enacts its dream of remaining perpetually youthful. She *is* Enlightenment, safely contained within an elegant, French-style dress. She represents the ideals, the promise—and the self-image—of US modernity. There were, however, images circulating that challenged such an interpretation, casting doubt on the persuasive power of the United States and highlighting its latent coercive force. Among the significant examples were Lombroso's influential descriptions of degenerate criminal women from the United States, and the graphic portraits of starving immigrant women published in Italian newspapers, some of which were reproduced in the working-class press in Argentina. Such images, which are discussed in Chapter 4, were constellations of concern about the willingness, let alone the capacity, of US modernity to domesticate either at home or abroad.

The Gendering of US Modernity

If images of women calibrate the measure and the moral legitimacy of modernity, then images of men are saturated with perceptions of its character and potency. The relationship between images of gender and debates about modernity will be illustrated here by focusing on developments in Latin America, where, it will be argued, there was a detectable shift from the middle of the nineteenth century to its end. At the start of the period, in the Civil War era, images of US men assumed predominantly the utopian forms of disinterested statesmen and idealist intellectuals. Washington, as the great hero of independence, remained a constant reference point for Latin American statesmen; Franklin was significant, particularly in the first half of the century; in the later part, Lincoln came to be seen, increasingly, as the last noble statesman produced by the United States. Latin American diplomats and travelers, themselves educated men, disseminated images of brilliant but, above all, benevolent US intellectuals, particularly those with a specialist interest in Latin America, such as historian William H. Prescott, whom Vicuña Mackenna described, after their meeting in the 1850s, as "the classical and amiable genius who has painted the epic of our conquest with such artistry,"[107] or George Ticknor, the pioneering critic of Spanish and Spanish-American literature. Of course, there were negative images circulating in the 1850s, particularly of filibusters such as William Walker, although even he was represented (not without plausibility) more as a misguided idealist than as a ruthless adventurer. And, to be sure, images of the average American male portrayed him as ripe for mockery, as embodying a certain casual self-satisfaction that did not appeal. Sarmiento, in an oft-cited image from his *Viajes en los Estados Unidos,* painted a vivid tableau of male physical informality:

> I saw seven Yankee dandies in friendly discussion, sitting like this: two with their feet on the table; one with them on the cushion of an adjacent chair; another with a leg slung over his arm on the edge of [...] his own chair, as if he were propping up his beard between his two knees; another with his arms or legs around the back of his chair.[108]

Contrasts were drawn between the physical grace of American women and the corresponding uncouthness of the men—the same quality of lack of artifice was thought to lead to naturalness in women but coarseness in men.[109] In the main, however, even those Latin Americans who, from the Mexican-American War of 1846–8 onward, were concerned about the expansionist tendencies of the United States, disseminated images of US maleness as noble and idealistic during this era.

At this stage, even US entrepreneurs tended to be depicted as morally superior, for example, the engineer William Wheelwright, who built railways in South America and established a steamship line to Chile. He was the subject of a hagiography by the Argentine intellectual Juan Bautista Alberdi, who had acted as his lawyer for a time in Chile. Alberdi portrayed Wheelwright as embodying the virtues he associated with the best of the United States—initiative, ingenuity, and integrity applied to public service—"sterling manhood in the service of humanity," following in the footsteps of Washington and Franklin.[110] In Alberdi's view, Wheelwright demonstrated "how a foreigner can sometimes be more of a national hero than a patriot," because he could distance himself from national politics.[111] The United States was doing more for Latin America through men like Wheelwright, argued Alberdi, than through the model of its written laws, which, he argued, were often misunderstood and misapplied in Latin America.¹¹² Alberdi emphasized that Wheelwright was from the North, indeed from Massachusetts, which Alberdi referred to as "the new England, or better said, the old England"—and therefore an exceptional part of the United States (a claim that he buttressed by citing Tocqueville).¹¹³ Significantly, Wheelwright was portrayed by Alberdi as a domesticated man, who preserved civilized habits even in the wilderness:

> His round, open and noble face was sympathetic in the extreme, and instilled trust at first sight. In any encounter, [...] his attitude was simple, serious and dignified. He had that effortless, restrained courtesy that comes from kindness and honesty of heart. [...] He did not smoke in public. He drank very little and slept even less. His habitual mode of dress was simple, formal and respectable.¹¹⁴

The Argentine liberals who ruled the country from 1853 to 1880 did not see themselves as being exploited by US entrepreneurs, but rather as willing participants in a shared endeavor of modernization. They felt it to be a privilege and a source of national pride to be capable of presenting challenges that noble spirits such as Wheelwright deemed to be worthy. At a banquet in Wheelwright's honor, government minister Nicolás Avellaneda proclaimed that a far greater challenge than anything in Chile was presented by the Argentine pampas, which therefore attracted Wheelwright to carry out "the supreme seduction of their conquest."¹¹⁵ Argentina is gendered female here, but at this stage that was not necessarily felt as a sign of weakness: in 1871, the year of the Argentine National Exhibition at Córdoba, Avellaneda portrayed his country as ripe for the adventure of becoming modern—"a new and immense theatre for human endeavour"—and in a position to demand a worthy partner.¹¹⁶ Like US women, the Argentine leaders felt that they knew how to maximize the advantages of being sought after, and that if anyone had to be wary, it was the suitor not the sought.

As disillusionment with the United States increased in Latin America during the 1870s and 1880s, however, hostile images of US men began to circulate far more widely, displacing the idealistic figures of the past and ultimately acquiring a grotesque aspect. In Mexico, the change in perspective was captured neatly in a newspaper chronicle of 1869, which took the opportunity of William Seward's visit, at the age of 74, to draw a contrast between him as "the personification of the spirit of the North American people: steady, positive, progressive and powerful" and the light-weight young American "dandies." Whereas men like Seward compared favorably with European visitors, "whose frivolous and mistaken opinions about our affairs [...] make us cringe," the self-absorbed youngsters represented a diminished version of masculinity, thinking only of clothes and food (*el buffet*).[117] A high-profile example of the new breed of US male was James Blaine, architect of the first Pan-American Conference, held in 1889 in Washington, after which José Martí famously and presciently warned Latin Americans to be wary of the economic ambition of the United States.[118] The Chilean writer and diplomat Benjamín Vicuña Mackenna wrote in 1884 about "Gin" Blaine, whom he portrayed as the coming man, or one of Emerson's "representative men," highlighting the extent to which he had taken advantage of political wheeler-dealing and the corrupt "whisky rings." He cited Henry Adams's book *Democracy, an American Novel* (1880), in which it was claimed that the United States would soon be more corrupt than Rome under Caligula; in so doing, Vicuña Mackenna built up an image of Blaine as a crude, aggressive politician riding roughshod over anything he perceived to stand in his way.[119] By the 1890s, the ubiquitous image of US men was of rapacious, ruthless capitalists—the bluff tycoons, puffed up with their own importance, throwing their weight around in a bullying way—the unforgettable "buffalo with silver teeth" conjured up by Darío in his notorious article denouncing US materialism, "The Triumph of Caliban" (1898).[120] The idealism associated with the United States had been eroded by the urge to "go ahead" and to "make money," terms that, in a wide range of Latin American sources, were cited in English to create instant caricatural pen-portraits of the pushy Yankee, who wanted to be "the greatest in the world" and to "break the record."[121] An example felt particularly acutely was of male tourists in Cuba (one of the earliest destinations for US men to buy abroad the gratification that they were unable to obtain at home): Cuban newspapers and magazines of the 1880s and 1890s carried many cartoons of fat, ugly American males brandishing ignorance and insensitivity along with their dollars, such as the caricature of a complacent male US tourist, "Mr E. C. T. Shops," from Ohio, who was on his third visit to Havana, yet able to spot "only one novelty: the colour of the lions in the Park."[122]

As was the case with US women, images of US men were both race and class bound. Black or Native American men were most often represented in stereotypical or romanticized images of laziness, malevolence, or stoic suffering, and the exceptions did not show the United States in a good light. For example, Eduarda Mansilla republished her account of life in the United States in 1882, shortly after the first major campaign of Argentina's War of the Desert (1879–80) had wiped out most of the nomadic indigenous tribes of the pampas, primarily in order to register a protest about the modernization policies of the Argentine elite. However, her powerful evocation of dignified Native American chieftains who had suffered from the "go ahead, destroying, pillaging and annexing" of "men who profess a religion of equality and meekness, but who nevertheless do not practice the first of their principles: fraternity" also conveyed a poignant sense of US idealism having been comprehensively defeated.[123] The only US man apart from Lincoln about whom Mansilla wrote admiringly as "a consistent example of virtue" was William Penn, founder of Pennsylvania, who made treaties with Native Americans.[124]

By the end of the century, virtually the only positive images of US men still circulating in Latin America were of statesmen of the past—Washington and Lincoln—and of idealist intellectuals—Longfellow, whose *Evangeline* (1847, translated into Spanish in 1871) was evoked in the 1890s by those expressing disillusionment with a cosmopolitan, technology-driven model of modernity;[125] Emerson, who was widely published in Latin American periodicals, although book-length translations of his works were a product of the twentieth century;[126] and Whitman, who was evoked in the widely read poetry of Darío as "the grand old man, beautiful as a patriarch, [remaining] serene and saintly [...] in his land of iron."[127] All of these visionaries lacked successors, it was lamented, as did William Prescott and Harriet Beecher Stowe.[128] Perhaps the ultimate symbol of the decline of US ideals was the fate of Edgar Allan Poe (1809–49). Accounts of his tragic decline into alcoholism and death from delirium, little known in Latin America at the time, began to circulate increasingly toward the end of the century, when there was a good deal of fascination with his life and work.[129]

Toward the end of our period, images began to feature in Latin America conveying the view that the best of the United States—even the only aspect that was worthy of an outsider's attention—was concentrated in its women. "The women aside," wrote the Argentine visitor Miguel Cané, "you can walk around the whole of New York without finding anything that awakens elevated ideas."[130] The Cuban Raimundo Cabrera, who used his translation of Andrew Carnegie's *Triumphant Democracy* to highlight the contrast between the certain progress to be achieved under republican self-government and the inevitable decadence of continued rule by Spain (see Chapter 2), echoed Carnegie's depiction of the US work ethic as incarnated, not in a rugged railroadman, but in a fair young woman:

> A young and beautiful American woman asked a lord who was visiting the United States how the aristocratic classes of Europe spent their time. Oh, he replied, they go from one house to another and enjoy themselves! They don't do any kind of work. Ah, she replied, in a natural way, we have people like that here—we call them tramps.

What is intriguing about this translation is that the phrase *con naturalidad* (in a natural way) was inserted by Cabrera, presumably specifically in order to draw attention to the innate goodness of the American woman.[131] Rubén Darío, writing about the Paris Exhibition of 1900, brought out the perceived contrast between US men and women even more starkly in the following two images:

> In the French section of the exhibition, in the palace of fine arts, a young fair woman, of fascinating elegance and fine beauty [...] stands before Gustave Moreau's Salomé. [...] Her gaze, her concentration on the pictorial music and her passionate admiration for it, show a very subtle and cultivated mind. The crowds go by and cluster around [paintings of soldiers or flowers]. [...] That young woman reveals her aristocracy of spirit and before the artist she stands a princess in her own right. That young woman is a citizen of the United States. [...]
>
> In an elegant bar: a man comes in who is red and robust, very robust, with a huge rose on the lapel of his jacket, a huge diamond and a huge ring, and a huge cigar in his huge mouth. [...] The strong fellow, a great drinker [...] and a great eater, orders sandwiches, orders port, orders champagne and it all disappears into his immense person. He looks at the whole world as if from a pedestal. [...] That is a male citizen of the United States.[132]

Yet it is worth pausing on these fin de siècle images of "good" US womanhood, which are very different from Civil War – era images of strong women actively involved in the cause of liberty, countering the violence and the exclusions of modernity with their moral force. It is noteworthy how much ideas about the agency of American women, as a force for social good, had been diluted by the end of the century. This point can be illustrated by looking at images of one of the relatively few US women who became icons of modernity during the 1890s, namely, Frances Folsom, who in 1886 married—aged 21—Grover Cleveland (president 1885–9 and 1893–7). Mrs. Cleveland was represented as the embodiment of the precious element of femininity that most US women were deemed to have lost, namely, the art of tender loving care for their men and families. One of her most valued attributes was that "her marriage was a true love match."[133] Martí noted that in the United States itself working women were compared unfavorably with Mrs. Cleveland: "Here there are women bankers, railway workers, opera impresarios. [...] But none of these women awakens the affection shown everywhere to the President's young wife, who rather than trying to work like a man chooses the more useful and arduous task of consoling him." Martí's own image of her was highly romantic: "Her eyes are of clear blue, and her thoughts are equally luminous." At a New Year's reception at the White House, at which she presided, "she was surrounded by beautiful women [...] but as the most tender and affectionate, she was the most beautiful of them all."¹³⁴ Thus, the image of Mrs. Cleveland that resonated, especially in Latin America, depicted a woman with far less force of character than a crusading Harriet Beecher Stowe, who had made an active intervention into the public sphere. Mrs. Cleveland's virtues were those of classic femininity, confined mainly to the home, only having the most discreet and indirect of effects on the public sphere through her gentle influence on her husband. Offered freedom, she has quietly shunned it for the alleged benefits of benign captivity.

Furthermore, Americans of both sexes were often represented by Latin Americans as autonomous, unresponsive to, and uninterested in the other. If the English were customarily portrayed as sexually inhibited and repressed, their American progeny were seen as having sublimated all erotic desire to the lust for material wealth and success. In such images, Latin Americans, who were increasingly on the receiving end of US expansionist tendencies, conveyed that far from being seduced, they could only be taken by force. Martí, fearful of the results of what he saw as the effeminacy of Cuba, called for all Latin Americans to be virile and steadfast in resisting the advances of the United States.¹³⁵ A comparison of images of the British in Brazil is revealing about the varying Latin American responses to the British and US ways of doing business. Historian Louise Guenther concluded, after an extensive analysis of nineteenth-century Brazilian images of the British, that they were widely depicted as engaged not in "violent conquest," but rather in "worldly wise seduction."¹³⁶ Seduction, she noted, of course involves manipulation but it has to be carried out with a degree of sensitivity. Moreover, it assumes that the object of desire knows the score, too—otherwise the seduction could lead to entrapment and even emasculation. It was such sensitivity, based on a fundamentally shared—if differently expressed—passion, that many Latin American images associated with the British but not the Americans.

To an extent, the Latin American sense of increasing distance from Americans was related to changes in US images of Latin America. By the mid-nineteenth century, there were many US images of Latin Americans as effeminate, irrational, and inferior—not manly and rational.¹³⁷ By the 1890s—as the US role became increasingly neo-imperial—the most common US image of Latin Americans depicted them as children (such images were prevalent *before,* not only after, the Spanish-Cuban-American War). Latin Americans began by representing the people of the United States as brothers in the struggle for liberty; the image of decent, manly men was revived during the Civil War with Lincoln and Seward, that is, people with whom they might be prepared to establish a respectable alliance. As images of US contempt for Latin Americans spread, Latin Americans, realizing that their calls for brotherhood were falling on deaf ears, responded with images of gross men and desexed women. Eduarda Mansilla, one of the earliest Latin American critics of the United States, noted bitterly: "We call them [...] our northern brothers, while they are unaware of our very existence."[138] Even in Cuba, where it is probably fair to say that idealistic images predominated until the end of the century, the United States was perceived as a neighbor to keep at a distance rather than a partner to embrace. "Ties of singular intimacy" have often been claimed in Cuba's relations with the United States—but proximity does not necessarily mean closeness. Even when Latin American republics refused to recognize the Cuban independence movement, leaving the United States as the only possible source of aid to fight the war launched in 1895, the independence leader Máximo Gómez declared, in a letter to his wife of 1896,

> In vain the Yankees, with their powerful mercantilism and their territorial ambitions, try to take advantage of Cuba's conflicts to make Cuba fall in love with them. Cuba will be free; it will courteously return US favours but it won't throw itself into US arms.[139]

On the eve of the Spanish-Cuban-American War of 1898, the United States was still sometimes symbolized by "a statue of a good-hearted woman."[140] More often than not, however, it was depicted as an overweight middle-aged man with huge teeth and a cigar, or a lanky elderly man, with glasses, a top hat, and beard—the sinister figure of Uncle Sam (that is, *not* a father, a man who was powerful but not potent). The United States was quite widely seen as an ultimately sterile society, in which sexuality had been displaced by materialism. The grossest images were associated with men, but women were certainly not seen as immune from the disease of excess consumption. Young American women "eat and drink like the heroes in Homer," noted Mansilla, who could not get out of her mind the repellant vision of them indelicately gobbling up seafood—"an elegant girl of 18 years old, devouring half a lobster, sucking even at the antennae, with a delight that was eloquently expressed on her perfectly beautiful face."[141] For Martí, "the violent, overweening zeal for prosperity" had robbed rich American women of all their beauty, leaving them in a state of physical degeneration with "discoloured complexions, shrunken profiles, or hump backs."[142] Images proliferated of the bodily distortions of overconsumption as Americans were depicted as engaged in an orgy of mastication, swallowing, digestion, and disgorgement, as reified in Darío's "The Triumph of Caliban." Perhaps the ultimate metaphor of alienation was an imagined eating machine, supposedly Edison's latest invention: "a machine to manufacture artificial foodstuffs identical to those produced by Mother Nature." Why not, demanded the Cuban writer of this article, given that "we have machines for sewing, writing, counting, reading, moving around, hearing and speaking"?[143]

By the end of our period, US modernity was no longer so often imagined, in contexts where once it had been, as an ideal. For some of its critics, the United States had become bestial and depraved; for others, mechanistic and dehumanized. The connection between material and moral progress— "the natural effect of material improvement is the elevation of the moral and intellectual level of the country"—that had been taken for granted by Latin American liberals in the 1870s could no longer be assumed.[144] There was a growing sense that not only women, but US society in general, had paid too high a price for its much-vaunted freedoms, and that there must be a better route to modernity. It was no coincidence that after the Spanish-Cuban-American War, the archetype of Latinity represented by José Enrique Rodó in his influential essay, *Ariel* (1900), was the ephebe—the ancient Greek citizen-warrior, lithe and virtuous, combining the strengths of a man with the integrity of a woman, and the ultimate rejection of the all-conquering, crudely materialistic US male.

Conclusion

It has been argued that, as a twentieth-century hegemon, the United States often sought to achieve its aims by "soft power," assuming that people across the world would consume its principles along with its products. Victoria La Grazia has vividly described it as having "the outlook of a great emporium."[145] The idea of imperialism by persuasion was built upon the images of a glowingly domesticated United States that were widely consumed abroad during the mid-late nineteenth century. Images of generous, capable women, dedicating themselves to their communities while running a home, crossing the supposed divide between public and private, remained in circulation during the 1890s. However, by then there were few contemporary US women who were thought to live up to the idealized image of philanthropic woman, and many of the images produced toward the end of the century suggested that US women with such aspirations had become intrusive and/or absurd. The zeal for charitable works, which had already been "taken to the level of neurosis by English women," had mutated into "caricature through the zealous imitation of North American women," sneered the Spanish writer Eva Canel, writing from Cuba, who went on to mock and disparage the busybody "Lady Managers" who had designed the women's pavilion at the Chicago Fair.[146] For some observers, US women still represented what the best of modernity could be: free, happy, virtuous, equal, and autonomous.[147] Yet the limits of such possibilities can also be detected in the many images that were circulating of neutralized sexuality, sentimental domesticity, gross consumption habits, and degeneracy. It was primarily through images of gender that doubts about US modernity emerged and crystallized. Such images were affected not only by class and race, which are significant in all of the themes of this book, but also by nationalism. The nationalist dimension was most visible in Latin America, as this chapter has illustrated, but it was also there in Europe. US goods might have been imagined as irresistible, but its people—at least not those who came to be known as WASPs—certainly were not. Even before the United States' rise to economic dominance, its way of life was widely seen—to give the last word to an Argentine woman—as having the capacity "to surprise but not to seduce."[148]

Notes

1. Orison Swett Marden, *Pushing to the Front, or Success under Difficulties* (Boston: Houghton and Mifflin, 1894), 101; a Spanish translation was published as *¡Siempre Adelante!* (Barcelona: Editorial Parera, 1913).
2. See, for example, from Italy: Gerolamo Boccardo, "I diritti politici delle donne," *L'Universo Illustrato*, IV:38 (1870: June), 631. From Britain: *Westminster Review*, 122:243 (1884: July), 185–213.
3. Tocqueville, *Democracy in America*.
4. F. Verney, "The Americans Painted by Themselves," *Contemporary Review*, 46 (1884: Oct.), 543–56, 546.
5. "Cosas de los Estados Unidos," *La Sombra* (Havana), April 8, 1877, 214.
6. For the term "calibrating modernity," see Davies, "On Englishmen, Women, Indians and Slaves," 316.
7. Domingo Faustino Sarmiento, *Educación Popular* (Buenos Aires: Editorial Juan Roldán, 1915), 120.
8. *Almanacco Repubblicano*, 1871, Enrico Bignami, ed. (Lodi: Società Cooperativo-Tipografica, 1870), 67ff.
9. Amy Kaplan, "Manifest Domesticity," in Davidson and Hatcher, eds., *No More Separate Spheres!*, 183–207, esp. 184–5.
10. In a large literature, a good starting point is Felski, *The Gender of Modernity*.
11. All citations in this paragraph are from José Martí, "Letter to *La Nación* (Buenos Aires)," May 2, 1886, New York, in *Obras completas*, vol. 10, 427–33, esp. 428–9.
12. *Transatlantic Stowe*, Kohn, Meer, Todd, eds., xi.
13. See, for example, the preface to the Italian edition: Enrichetta Beecher Stowe, *La capanna dello zio Tomaso o la schiavitù* (Milano: Borroni e Scotti, 1852), vol. 1.
14. Aurelia Castillo de González, *Un paseo por América* (Havana: Imprenta La Constancia, 1895), 85.

15. Julia Ward Howe, *A Trip to Cuba* (Boston: Ticknor and Fields, 1860), 146.
16. S. Frenfanelli Cibo, "Del progresso intellettuale degli Stati Uniti di America," in *Rivista Bolognese* (Bologna) vol. II, nos. 9–10 (1868), 852–61, 852.
17. An extensive search of the main newspapers and journals yielded only one article: "The Sick and Wounded of the Army of the United States," *Good Words*, 4 (1863: Jan.), 814.
18. José Pedro Varela, *Impresiones de viaje en Europa y América* (Montevideo: Ministerio de Instrucción Pública, 1945), 105. These "Letters" from the 1860s were first published in the Montevideo newspaper *El Siglo*, which was also read in Buenos Aires.
19. *Saturday Review of Politics, Literature, Science and Art*, 27:688 (1869: Jan. 2), 20; *London Review of Politics, Society, Literature, Art, and Science*, 14:342 (1867: Jan. 19), 80–1; *St. James's Magazine*, n.s. 1 (1868: Apr.), 288–96; *Westminster Review*, 34:2 (1868: Oct.), 437–62; *Saturday Review of Politics, Literature, Science and Art*, 27:693 (1869: Feb. 6), 176.
20. The United States granted national voting rights to women with the 19th Amendment in 1920, compared with 1918 in the United Kingdom (for women over 30) or 1928 (for everyone over 21).
21. González Pagés, *En busca de un espacio*, 30.
22. Concepcíon Arenal, *La Mujer del Porvenir. La Mujer de la Casa* (Barcelona: Ediciones Orbis, 1889), 61–2, 152–3; (*La Mujer del Porvenir* was first published in 1870; *La Mujer de su Casa* in 1883). Emilia Pardo Bazán, in *Nuevo Teatro Crítico* (Madrid), February 3, 1893.
23. Frenfanelli Cibo, "Del progresso," 852.
24. Varela, *Impresiones*, 104.
25. Portes, *Fascination and Misgivings*, 247–53.
26. Zululeta, *Misioneras, feministas, educadoras* and Scally Grigas, *Mission to Spain*.
27. José de la Luz y Caballero, *Obras*, vol. II, *Escritos educativos* (Havana: Ediciones Imagen Contemporánea, 2001).
28. Luiggi, *65 Valiants*, 18; reference to Sarmiento's letter to Aurelia Vélez Saarsfield, October 15, 1865, in Alberto Palcos, ed., *Sarmiento: Páginas confidenciales* (Buenos Aires: Editorial Elevación, 1944). See also Crespo, *Las maestras de Sarmiento*.
29. González Pagés, *En busca de un espacio*, 31–3 and 40–1.
30. "Indicaciones del Ministro de Instrucción Pública en su memoria al Honorable Congreso en 1869," in *Ley y decretos para la creación y organización de la Escuela Normal Nacional del Paraná* (Buenos Aires: Imprenta de La Tribuna, 1870), 1–5, 2–3.
31. Luiggi, *65 Valiants*, 18.
32. Ibid., 26.
33. Ibid., 52.
34. Ibid., 41.
35. Ibid., 47.
36. Ibid., 65.

37. *La Habana Elegante*, Año 5, no. 12, March 20, 1887, 4.
38. *La Habana Elegante*, Año 5, no. 36, September 6, 1885, 12.
39. Eduarda Mansilla de García, *Recuerdos de viaje* (Madrid: Ediciones El Viso, 1996, fasc. edn. of 1882 version published by Juan A. Alsina, Buenos Aires), 120–2.
40. Arenal, *La mujer de su casa*, 90.
41. *Household Words: Conducted by Charles Dickens*, 9:210 (1854: Apr. 1), 158.
42. *Album de Señoritas* (Buenos Aires), January 1, 1854, 7, cited in Davies, Brewster, and Owen, *South American Independence*, 246.
43. Benjamín Vicuña Mackenna, *Páginas de mi diario durante tres años de viaje 1853–4–5* (Santiago: Universidad de Chile, 2 vols., 1936).
44. Miguel Cané, *En viaje 1881–1882* (Buenos Aires: Ediciones Estrada, 1949), 415.
45. Vicuña Mackenna, *Páginas*, 155.
46. Portes, *Fascination*, 158.
47. A Woman, "The Effects of Civilization Upon Women," *National Review* (London), 9:49 (1887: Mar.), 26–39.
48. Mansilla, *Recuerdos*, 43.
49. Cané, *En viaje*, 415.
50. Varela, *Impresiones*, 103.
51. Portes, *Fascination*, 256–7.
52. José Jordana y Morera, *Curiosidades naturales y carácter social de los Estados Unidos* (Madrid: Tipografía de Manuel G. Hernández, 1884), chapter 3.
53. Varela, *Impresiones*, 102.
54. For example, "Female Beauty in Old England and New England," *Chambers's Journal of Popular Literature, Science and Arts*, 2 (1854: Jan. 14), 24.
55. "Mrs Beecher Ward, English and American Ladies," *Bow Bells*, 13:331 (1870: Nov. 30), 452–3.
56. *Saturday Review of Politics, Literature, Science and Art*, 70:1820 (1890:Sept. 13), 320.
57. Raimundo Cabrera, *Los Estados Unidos. Reducción de la obra "Triumphant Democracy" de Mr. Andrew Carnegie, con notas, aplicaciones y comentarios* (Havana: Ricardo Veloso Editor, 3rd edn., 1889), 50.
58. Mansilla, *Recuerdos*, 92–3, 101, 125–6, 132, 175 and 178.
59. J. G. Kohl, "American Young Ladyism," *Bentley's Miscellany* (London), 50 (1861: July), 317; C. De Thierry [an Australasian], "American Women, from a Colonial Point of View," *Contemporary Review* (London), 70 (1896: Oct.), 516–26.
60. Roger, *The American Enemy*, 190.
61. Masiello, *Between Civilization and Barbarism*, 7.
62. J. Bustamante y Campuzano, *Del Atlántico al Pacifico. Apuntes y Impresiones de un viaje á través de los Estados Unidos* (Madrid: Victor Saíz, 1885), 57–9. Jordana y Morera, *Curiosidades*, 48.
63. The Chilean publicist Benjamín Vicuña Mackenna explicitly evoked Tocqueville on US women, Mrs. Trollope on US men, and Chateaubriand

on the general frivolity of US social relations. *Diez meses de misión a los Estados Unidos de North América como ajente confidencial de Chile* (Santiago: Imprenta de la Libertad, 1867), 394–5.
64. Mansilla, *Recuerdos*, 179.
65. Victorien Sardou, *L'Oncle Sam, Comédie en 4 actes, en prose* (Paris: Michel Lévy frères, 1875), 10. On the controversy surrounding its initial staging see Albert Wolff, *Victorien Sardou et l'Oncle Sam, avec les Documents Relatifs à la Suppression de la Pièce* (Paris: Librairie nouvelle, 1874). See also Roger, *The American Enemy*, 99
66. Sardou, *L'Oncle Sam*, 16.
67. Ibid., 16–17.
68. Wolff, *Victorien Sardou*, 138.
69. Portes, *Fascination*, 258–60.
70. Cited in Roger, *The American Enemy*, 190.
71. ART. III.-Civilized America, *Christian Remembrancer*, 37:104 (1859: Apr.), 317.
72. Sarmiento, *Viajes*, 84–5.
73. Martí, "Letter to *La Nación*," Jan. 3, 1887, New York, in *Obras completas*, vol. 11, 133–6, 134.
74. Édouard Laboulaye [René Lefebvre], *Paris en Amérique*.
75. A. Llanos, *El Gigante Americano. Descripciones de los Estados Unidos de la America del Norte* (Madrid 1886), 30–2.
76. Carlos Pellegrini, "Desde los Estados Unidos (Seis cartas a La Nación)" [1904], in his *La nación en marcha (Discursos y escritos políticos)* (New York and Buenos Aires: W. M. Jackson, Inc., 1938), 215–20. Pellegrini was comparing his experiences of the United States in 1904 with those from a visit made 20 years earlier.
77. John C. Hutcheson, "Marriage à la Mode in the Land of Freedom," *Belgravia: a London Magazine*, 6 (1875: Apr.), 191–8.
78. Dall'Osso, *Voglia d'America*, 58.
79. M. Bolet Peraza, "Carta de Nueva York," *La Habana Elegante*, Año 5, no. 23, June 5, 1887, 4.
80. Eva Canel, "Crónicas de la Exposición de Chicago" (Chicago, September 1893), *Boletín de la Cámara de Comercio* [Havana], no. 48, October 31, 1893, 183–205, 196.
81. Alexander Humboldt, *The Island of Cuba*, translated (from a Spanish translation of the original French) by J. S. Thrasher (New York: Derby and Jackson, 1856), 110.
82. Andrew Jackson Downing, *Cottage Residences, or a Series of Designs for Rural Cottages and Cottage Villas, and their Gardens and Grounds adapted to North America* (New York: John Wiley & Sons, 4th revised edition, 1865 [1842]).
83. Vega Suñol, *Norteamericanos*, 140.
84. Cabrera, *Los Estados Unidos*, 89–90.
85. C. M. de Castro, *Memoria Descriptiva de Ante-Proyecto de Ensanche de Madrid* (Madrid, 1853), 84 and 163.

86. "Novedades! Novedades! Novedades!," *El Siglo* [Havana], Año 3, no. 213, October 20, 1864, 4; "Aviso. Casas de Nueva York especialmente recomendidas á los cubanos," *La Conciliación* [Havana], Año 2, no. 2, February 23, 1879, 2; "Máquinas de coser de la Comp. de Singer," *La Conciliación*, Año 2, no. 64, May 30, 1879, 4.
87. Mansilla, *Un paseo*, 61–2.
88. See González Stephan, "Martí, invenciones tecnológicas y Exposiciones Universales," 25–43. Martí, *Obras completas*, vol. 8.
89. Mansilla, *Recuerdos*, 18 and 36.
90. *Boletín de la Exposición Nacional en Córdoba (Publicación oficial)* (Buenos Aires: Imprenta de J. A. Bernheim, 7 vols., 1869). The table of exhibition space shows England with 322 square meters; the USA 227, Germany 110, France 38, Italy 38, Chile 28, Paraguay 28, Bolivia 58, and Brazil 37 (vol. II, 425). Vol. IV gives a full list of US exhibits (227–40), plus there are additional items listed in the supplement, *Suplemento al Catálogo General de la Exposición Nacional en Córdoba*, October 15, 1871 (Imprenta de Pedro Rivas, 1871), 63–4.
91. "Para Navidad y año nuevo," *La Prensa*, advertisement section, December 10, 1873 and every issue until Christmas Day 1873.
92. Sarmiento, *Viajes*, 85.
93. Ibid., 91.
94. Mansilla, *Recuerdos*, 41–2.
95. Ibid., 43; Giuseppe Giacosa (a major Italian dramatist and the librettist of, for example, Puccini's *La Bohème*), *Impressioni d'America* [1898]. Padova: Franco Muzzio, 1994.
96. Sarmiento, *Viajes*, 81.
97. Vicuña Mackenna, *Páginas*, 120–2. Sarmiento, whom Vicuña Mackenna had certainly read, also referred (in Spanish) to "floating palaces," *Viajes*, 81.
98. Bauer, *Goods, Power, History*, 154.
99. Mansilla, *Recuerdos*, 41.
100. Ignacio M. Altamirano, *Crónicas de la semana* (Mexico City: Instituto Nacional de Bellas Artes, 1978), January 23, 1869, 43–4.
101. José Martí, "Coney Island" [1881], in *Obras completas*, vol. 9, 121–8.
102. Adolfo Caminha, *No País dos Yankees* (Rio de Janeiro: Domingos de Magalhães, 1894).
103. Caminha, *No País*, 42 and 31. All remaining quotations in this paragraph, 40.
104. Adolfo Carrillo, "Los ideales de Mary," *La Habana Elegante*, Año 6, no. 12, March 18, 1888, 6.
105. "Desde New York," *La Habana Elegante*, Año 9, no. 11, March 22, 1893, 8.
106. "English and American Women. The Duke of Marlborough's Opinion," *Reynolds's Newspaper*, January 10, 1892.
107. Vicuña Mackenna, *Páginas*, 159.
108. Sarmiento, *Viajes*, 97.
109. See, for example, Varela, *Impresiones*, 103.
110. J. B. Alberdi, *La vida y los trabajos industriales de William Wheelwright en la América del Sud* (Paris: Librería de Garnier Hermanos, 1876), 3; translated as

The Life and Industrial Labors of William Wheelwright in South America, with Additional Memoranda (Boston: A. Williams & Co., 1877).
111. Alberdi, *La vida y los trabajos industriales de William Wheelwright*, 1 and 17.
112. Ibid., 22.
113. Ibid., 26, 35 and 37.
114. Ibid., 308–9.
115. Nicolás Avellaneda, "Banquete en honor del señor Wheelwright," Buenos Aires, 1869, in his *Discursos, Oraciones cívicas* (Buenos Aires: Librería La Facultad de Juan Roldán, 1928), 37–41, 38.
116. Avellaneda, "Exposición nacional de Córdoba," October 15, 1871, in *Discursos*, 53–9, 54.
117. Ignacio Altamirano, *Crónicas*, December 4, 1869, 277ff.
118. José Martí, "El Congreso Pan-americano de Washington" [1889], *Obras completas*, vol. 6.
119. Benjamín Vicuña Mackenna, *Blaine* (Santiago: Imprenta Victoria, 1884).
120. Rubén Darío, "El triunfo de Calibán," *Escritos inéditos*, E. K. Mapes, ed. (New York: Instituto de las Españas, 1938). There was a similar typology in France: see Simon Jeune, De F. T. Graindorge, and A. O. Barnabooth, *Les Types Américains dans le Roman et le Théâtre français, 1861–1917* (Paris: Didier, 1963).
121. Pellegrini, *La nación en marcha*, 162–3.
122. *La Política* [Havana], Año 1, no. 6, December 31, 1894, 4.
123. Mansilla, *Recuerdos*, 63. In 1869 she had published a novel, written in French and advocating a more respectful and peaceable approach to the indigenous people, *Pablo, ou la vie dans les pampas*. It was translated by her brother Lucio V. Mansilla and serialized in the Argentine newspaper *La Tribuna* (Buenos Aires). See Eduarda de Mansilla, *Pablo, o, La vida en las pampas*, María Gabriela Mizraje, ed. (Buenos Aires: Biblioteca Nacional, 2007).
124. Mansilla, *Recuerdos*, 109.
125. Rafael Obligado, letter to Joaquín V. González, April 5, 1892, Buenos Aires, in J. V. González, *Mis montañas*, Félix Lajouane, Buenos Aires, 1893, v–xxxvi, xiii.
126. Englekirk, *Bibliografía*, 51 (Longfellow) and 34 (Emerson).
127. Rubén Darío, "Walt Whitman" (1890), from the collection *Azul*, in *Poesía*, Fondo de Cultura Económica, Mexico City, 1952, 180.
128. Salvador Camacho Roldán, *Notas de viaje*, vol. II, 334.
129. Edgar Allan Poe, *El Kuerbo*, trans. J. A. Pérez Bonalde, Editorial Franzisko Enrríkez, Balparaíso [sic], 1895. The "Advertencia" mentions a second edition published in Buenos Aires in 1888 (p. 7). Italians also knew Poe well and various translations were available, contributing to degenerate images of the United States. Gustavo Tirinelli, "Edgardo Allan Poe," in *Nuova Antologia, seconda serie*, vol. IV, no. 4 (April 1877), 731–62.
130. Cané, *En viaje*, 416–7.
131. Cabrera, *Los Estados Unidos*, 105; Carnegie, *Triumphant Democracy*, 90.
132. Rubén Darío, "Los anglosajones" [Paris, 1900], in his *Peregrinaciones, Obras completas*, vol. XII, Editorial Mundo Latino, Madrid, 1918, 51–68, 64–5.

133. "Mrs. Cleveland," *La Habana Elegante*, Año 7, no. 12, May 24, 1889, 6.
134. Martí, *Obras Completas*, vol. 11, 133–6, 135.
135. Ibid., vol. 8, p. 121.
136. Louise Guenther, "The Artful Seductions of Informal Empire," in Brown, ed., *Informal Empire in Latin America*, 211.
137. O'Brien, *Making the Americas*, 5.
138. Mansilla, *Recuerdos*, 68.
139. Máximo Gómez, "Odisea del general José Maceo," July 27, 1896, in Gómez's *Obras escogidas* (Havana: Editorial Letras Cubanas, 1979), 88–100.
140. Hanan al-Shaykh, in "What We Think of America," *Granta* (London), 77 (Spring 2002), 13.
141. Mansilla, *Recuerdos*, 46–8.
142. Martí, "Un gran baile en Nueva York," February 7, 1888, *Obras completas*, vol. 11, 392–8.
143. *La Habana Elegante*, Año 5, no. 9, February 27, 1887, 6.
144. Alberdi, *La vida y los trabajos industriales de William Wheelwright*, 7.
145. De Grazia, *Irresistible Empire*, 3.
146. Canel, "Crónicas," 397.
147. For example, Castillo, *Un paseo*, 63.
148. Mansilla, *Recuerdos*, 34.

Il piccolo Beniamino nella fabbrica di suo padre.

Young Benjamin [Franklin] in his father's factory

Capture: The life of Benjamin Franklin was a popular topic for European periodicals throughout the nineteenth century.
Source: *L'Illustrazione Popolare*, November 1, 1874.

Machine to make Yankees

Capture: Spaniards were both fascinated and horrified by US mechanical inventions. This late nineteenth-century image of a Machine to Make Yankees notes that the materials needed to produce prefabricated American males—sawdust, lard, bits of cork, garbage, potato peelings, et cetera—were cheaply available, which explains why the population of the United States was increasing at such an extraordinary rate.
Source: *Blanco y Negro* (Madrid), April 11, 1896, p. 20.

Harriet Beecher Stowe, ca. 1870s–1880s

Capture: The author of *Uncle Tom's Cabin* became the ultimate philanthropic woman throughout Europe and Latin America.
Source: US National Archives & Records Administration.

Karl May's *Winnetou*, first edition in book format (Freiburg im Breisgau: Verlag Friedrich Ernst Fehsenfeld, 1893)
Capture: Karl May (1842–1912) wrote about Winnetou from 1875 onward.
Source: Courtesy of Karl-May-Verlag.

Uncle Tom at the whipping post. Scene from a stage production, ca.1901.
No capture.
Source: Library of Congress. Prints and Photographs Online Catalogue.

 BRASIL E ESTADOS UNIDOS
OU OS DOUS IRMÃOS...... CAIM E ABEL

Brazil and the United States

Caption: This image from a Brazilian illustrated magazine of 1868, *A Vida Fluminense* (Rio de Janeiro), highlights both the perceived parallels and differences between the United States and Brazil. The reference to Cain and Abel, juxtaposed with the depiction of the two indigenous figures, suggests not only Brazilian perceptions of the threat posed by the United States, but also the idea that the two countries were fatally locked together in a struggle over what forms "civilization" and "barbarism" might take.

Source: "Brasil e Estados Unidos. Ou os dous irmãos...Caim e Abel", July 14 1868, *A Vida Fluminense* (Rio de Janeiro), no. 28, p. 328, Biblioteca Nacional, Rio de Janeiro.

4

Barbarous America

Axel Körner

L'America a ci acconza e a ci uasta!
(America accommodates some and ruins others!)
Proverb from Basilicata, Southern Italy[1]

Beyond the Model Republic

Alongside established images of the United States as the epitome of a positively defined modernity, a model republic, and a land of opportunities, America was also seen as a barbarous country, the very negation of European cultural values. In these images barbarism could take the form of the sheer brutality associated with life in the United States, but it also appeared, perhaps more often, as an absence of civilization. Claims in the existing historiography about the prevalence of positive images of America are often based on the notion of people "voting with their feet," whereby patterns of migration are read as proof of widespread admiration for the United States.[2] This chapter takes a typical emigrant society—Italy—as a starting point to challenge such accounts and, through a comparative analysis of images, to demonstrate that there were many people throughout Europe and Latin America who rejected the United States as a model, instead stigmatizing it as a barbarous repudiation of everything that mattered in the Old World.

Claims about the universal appeal of the United States tend to be based on evidence drawn mainly from the twentieth century. The Americanization of daily life, the "cultural colonization" in terms of language, habits, and aesthetics, started in the late nineteenth century in Europe and in much of Latin America, at a time when large numbers of Europeans arrived in the United States not just as emigrants, but also as travelers with the specific aim of experiencing the modernity of the New World. Through travel writing and journalism they permeated the Old World's cultural sphere with their mostly positive impressions of the American way of life, which contrasted sharply with Frances Trollope's caustic international best seller of 1832, *Domestic Manners of the Americans*.[3] While Mrs. Trollope had been appalled by the lack of refinement she encountered in the United States, from the late nineteenth century onward Americans displayed a lifestyle of gracious ease and comfort, based on luxury goods and readily available commodities, that deeply impressed many Europeans and Latin Americans. However, historians have paid insufficient attention to what happened in the decades between the publication of Mrs. Trollope in 1832 and the foundation of *Vogue* magazine in 1892. Interest in the *Homo Americanus* started long before the *fin-de-siècle* fascination with US consumer culture, and throughout most of the nineteenth century discourse about America was not necessarily focused on consumption and material progress, but more on ideals and values. The American Constitution, the War of Independence, also slavery, the Civil War, and the political compromises of the Reconstruction period, all provoked great interest but also critical assessment in intellectual and political circles. As mentioned in the introduction Paola Gemme even argues that the idea of America as a model for Italian patriots was at least partly an American projection. Although Europeans and Latin Americans certainly demonstrated a great deal of interest in the social, political, and cultural development of the United States, it was to a large extent the Americans themselves who liked to think of themselves as a model for the rest of the world.[4]

Even during the later part of the nineteenth century, when illustrated magazines and the world fairs were displaying all manner of US inventions and gadgets, the development of a new national identity in France, after the defeat in the Franco-Prussian war, and Italy's intellectual embrace of German Idealism both drew upon contrasts with the perceived crude materialism and positivism of the United States and the supposed grossness and vulgarity of its citizens. The heirs of German Romanticism, with its idea of organically grown communities, were unable to countenance the rationalizing impulse they saw behind the American Revolution and the society it had generated.[5] Images of the United States as the incarnation of grossness became increasingly common in Latin America toward the end of the nineteenth century. Many of them originated from Argentina, where Anglophile and/or Francophile elites saw themselves as rival modernizers who wanted—and plausibly believed to be within their grasp—the prosperity of the United States without its vulgarity. In England, too, there was an important and long-established discourse that viewed the United States as the epitome of vulgarity, running from Dickens's *Martin*

Chuzzlewit (1843–4), to Thomas Carlyle's claim that America's supreme achievement was to have "begotten with a rapidity beyond recorded example, eighteen Millions of the greatest bores ever seen in this world before,"[6] to John Ruskin's indictment of the Americans' "total ignorance of the finer and higher arts."[7] It culminated in Matthew Arnold's essay on *Civilization in the United States* (1888), which articulated the by-then widespread view that there was no such thing as civilization across the Atlantic.[8]

Such disillusionment about the United States among the elites, especially artists and writers, is a well-known and well-studied phenomenon. The main focus of this chapter, therefore, will be on images of American barbarism—in both senses—beyond the elites. One of the most revealing sources of such images is theater, from the privileged private boxes at La Scala to the open-air performances of Buffalo Bill.

Staging American Slavery: Uncle Tom in Europe

In 1853 the Teatro alla Scala in Milan staged what was to become not only one of the greatest success stories in the history of Italian ballet but also one of the most powerful Italian images of America on stage: *Bianchi e Neri*, Giuseppe Rota's adaptation of Harriet Beecher Stowe's epochal novel, *Uncle Tom's Cabin* (1852).[9] Although a rather free adaptation, abridged to six or seven scenes, the ballet depicts the dehumanizing brutality of a slave-holding society in unfailing clarity, making a deep impression on Italians imagining life in the New World. Unlike the British, French, or Spanish, who were fully aware of slavery and had participated in debates about abolition for several decades, contemporary Italians had very limited experience of colonization, the slave trade, or the slave economy. Although in 1846 Giuseppe Mazzini had expressed his hopes that the American Republic would put an end to the evil of slavery, for Italians the issue was largely associated with Ancient Rome or discussed in orientalizing images of non-European societies.[10] As a review of *Bianchi e Neri* in a Milanese literary journal argued in 1853, slavery is "a crime of remote countries, and has nothing to do with us, where before the law everybody is the same."[11] However, in no small part due to the remarkable success of *Bianchi e Neri*, which enjoyed long runs in Genoa, Rome, Turin, Bologna, and Naples during the years leading up to the US Civil War,[12] Italian awareness of the problem of slavery changed dramatically, with striking effects on the ways in which Italians discussed American politics and society.

The ballet's reception changed markedly according to the specific context of its performances: for example, in 1863, at the height of the American Civil War, the ballet had a great impact on Milanese audiences as a direct commentary on the great issue of international politics—emancipation—that was closely covered in the newspapers. Ten years earlier, however, in the context of the Italian Risorgimento, Italian audiences had interpreted the ballet as a story about liberation. For the scene of the slave rebellion Rota had asked his composer to introduce four bars of the French anthem into the score. Because the audience regularly exploded into applause during this scene, the Austrian police suspended performances after just four evenings.[13] Hence, from the very beginning, *Bianchi e Neri* was read politically. In the reception of Rota's ballet America was compared to and put on equal terms with the despotism of the Ancien Régime and the Habsburgs' rule in Italy.

The first Italian translation of the novel itself had appeared in the year of the original American publication, 1852. By the end of 1853 cheap editions were available in all Italian capitals, with the noticeable exception of Rome, where the book of the militant Protestant Beecher Stowe was censored by the Papal administration.[14] Countless newspapers reviewed the book and, with the exception of the Catholic press, articles all over Italy featured portraits of its author, elevating her to an almost saint-like status.[15] *Uncle Tom* became a household name for Italians, regularly referred to in illustrated magazines, academic treatises on slavery, and general commentaries on the United States. The fact that in 1858, for the second round of stagings, Rota's ballet was performed as *La Capanna di Tom*, suggests that the book was by then widely known. The Italian reception of the novel set the scene for the subsequent coverage of the excesses of the Civil War as well as the uncivilized nature of American society.

Across Europe, as early as 1854, there were already countless translations and adaptations of *Uncle Tom's Cabin*, including those into "minor languages" such as Armenian, Slovenian, and Welsh.[16] In Cuba even the slaves themselves knew about Uncle Tom. Stage adaptations of *Uncle Tom* are as old as the novel itself and represent a well-studied aspect of the Beecher Stowe phenomenon.[17] American newspapers dubbed the traveling shows the "U.T.C. companies" (Uncle Tom's Cabin Companies).[18] They were generally regarded as mediocre by critics, but that did not stop them from attracting even more people than the later Buffalo Bill shows. On the Old Continent, toward the end of the century, Uncle Tom shows reached regions as remote as Lower Lusatia in the borderlands of Saxony and Prussia, where they were performed by Sorbes singing in their own Slavonic language.[19] As Henry James noted, "the fate of Mrs Stowe's picture was conclusive: it simply sat down wherever it lighted and made itself, so to speak, at home."[20] Arguably, the novel and its various staged versions had a more significant impact on images of the United States than Tocqueville's writings or even those of Karl May or James Fenimore Cooper.

Although there were some Uncle Tom shows that adopted a pro-slavery position,[21] in the main *Uncle Tom* became the focus for a general critique of American society. In Britain, for example, the introduction to a stage adaptation for the London Metropolitan Theatre declared that the "star-spangled banner" was stained by slavery and the preface to Routledge's sixth edition of *Uncle Tom* (1852) maintained, "it is vain to assert for the republic of the United States greatness, or any share of progress in the world. Commercial greatness we are willing to allow her; but prosperous infamy is not palliated infamy, and cruelty imbibes no virtue from purple and fine linen."[22] As the authors of a study on "transatlantic Stowe" argue, "Uncle Tom's Cabin in its British context is framed by discussions of American failings and backwardness and English superiority and progress."[23]

The commercial success of the book—150,000 copies of the American edition sold in the first three months after publication; four English editions of 100,000 rapidly exhausted; ten different translations on the market in Paris—in itself created negative associations in some quarters. Publishing for the masses on an industrial scale had started in the United States during the 1840s, a development of which Europe became increasingly aware.[24] French publishers showed themselves so eager to sate public demand for *Uncle Tom* and to maximize profits in the same way as their US rivals that they attracted ridicule. The satirical newspaper *Le Charivari*, for example, published a parody of a group of needy publishers' efforts to secure a special preface by the celebrated author herself for their respective editions.[25] In this piece, Beecher Stowe's breakfast is repeatedly interrupted by the arrival of a succession of pleading letters from publishers, resorting to melodramatic threats and emotional blackmail: "This preface will be my fortune. If you refuse it to me, I will kill myself. Consider whether you would want to have this on your conscience."[26] The book did indeed prove to be a goldmine for publishers across Europe. Yet notwithstanding its undeniable popular success and the undoubted appeal of the abolitionist message, it was arguably these frantic publishing activities and the air of commercialization surrounding the book that made *Uncle Tom* appear to be just another example of the materialistic "American way of life." The influential *Revue des Deux Mondes* argued that "this unprecedented success of a book by an average talent"[27] diminished its credentials as a landmark of a new and exciting American culture. *Uncle Tom* had become more akin to an industrial object than a work of art.

In colonial societies, or in societies that practiced slavery, the novel played a different role than in countries such as Italy or the German-speaking lands, where slavery was largely unknown. In France the novel appeared just after the abolition of slavery by the Second Republic.[28]

As in Italy, its success increased when *l'Oncle Tom* was dramatized for the stage: an eight-act-play *La case de l'Oncle Tom*, adapted by Dumanoir and Denenry for the Théâtre de l'Ambigu-Comique,[29] and a version with five acts and 12 *tableaux* by Edmond Texier and de Wailly[30] at the Théâtre de la Gaîté. "One comes from far away [...], dying to know what this *Uncle Tom* book is all about! What a strange success and what an incredible fortune!" a French theater periodical reported.[31] Other dramatizations were put on around the country and proved to be a memorable experience for many, among them the young Georges Clemenceau, who was moved to tears watching the play.[32]

In Spain *Uncle Tom's Cabin* was first published in translation in December 1852 and immediately flew off the booksellers' shelves. In 1853 it was retranslated and republished more quickly than any other foreign novel ever before, and it was serialized in several of the most important national papers. It was also converted into stage plays, such as *Haley, ó, el traficante de negros*, staged in Cádiz in October 1853, which transferred the action to a Spanish colonial context. These various editions and stagings of *Tío Tom* put forward—and reflected—a range of Spanish attitudes toward slavery and abolition in Spain's Antillean colonies of Cuba and Puerto Rico, from demands for the immediate abolition of slavery to the tacit acceptance of the need to continue the practice, essential for the continued economic and political grip of the Spanish metropole over its colonies.[33] The stage play *Haley* is not so much abolitionist as reformist. By focusing on the slave trader, who repents at the end—of the play and of his life—the writers are able to suggest a way forward for Spain and the Antillean colonies that would not jeopardize the metropole-colony relationship and would not risk a much feared Haitian-style race war or US-style civil war.

In Argentina slavery was not legally abolished until the liberal Constitution of 1853, just after *Uncle Tom* made it into the journals and bookshops. The dictator defeated in 1852, Juan Manuel de Rosas, had encouraged Afro-Argentine culture as part of his bid for popular support. As a consequence, liberal intellectuals, embarking on a precarious modernizing project, preferred to say as little as possible about slavery, not least because the legal situation of some former slaves remained unclear until 1860. The influential liberal intellectual Sarmiento, who became president of Argentina in 1868, hardly mentions slavery in his writings about the United States and even in his biography of Lincoln, published in 1865, he referred to emancipation only briefly and in highly gendered terms as a "great cry of redemption" emanating "from the entrails" of "Mrs Beecher Stowe."[34] He identified with Lincoln mainly as a nation builder. Thus, in the fraught context of the Argentine elite's reluctance to face up to their own society's slavery, elite interest in the international phenomenon of *Uncle Tom's*

Cabin was directed mainly at Beecher Stowe herself, who was seized upon by both supporters and opponents of women's rights as an icon of virtuous civic motherhood, which fitted in with the education-for-citizenship policies advocated by Sarmiento and others.[35] Emphasizing Beecher Stowe as a beacon of general human benevolence allowed the Argentine liberal elites to elide her views on race and the position of blacks in society, just as they were ignoring the appalling living conditions endured by their own black population after abolition.

As discussed in Chapter 6, Brazil took much longer to abolish slavery. Here the novel was first serialized in *A Redenção (The Redemption)*, the newspaper of the national runaway movement, the Caifazes. Subsequently, when the cause of abolition was gaining ground during the 1880s, the novel was banned, demonstrating how closely it was read in connection with domestic issues.

Most editions of the novel presented the story of Uncle Tom as more than just a piece of compassionate literature. A widely reproduced commentary by the French critic Jean Lemoine drew readers' attention to the role that women like Beecher Stowe played in American debates on slavery. Moreover, the novel itself made it clear that it offered an authentic account of contemporary America. In the last chapter of the final volume Beecher Stowe explains the background to the plot and the extent to which it is based on a careful character study of people living in a slaveholder society, either as victims or as perpetrators. Quoting the original description of the person who became the model for the slave trader Legrée, her epilogue underlines once more the barbarity of the slave economy: "He actually made me feel of his fist, which was like a blacksmith's hammer, or a nodule of iron, telling me that it was *calloused with knocking down niggers*," the author explains. Situating the narrative in a realistic account of social life in the United States, she continues, confirms "that the tragical fate of Tom, also, has too many times had its parallel, there are living witnesses, all over our land, to testify." Thus readers encountered plenty of material linking the narrative of *Uncle Tom* to a general analysis of the ways in which American society was affected by the institution of slavery. It was this kind of information, rather than the plot itself, that was picked up by references to the novel in the periodical press.

The most influential commentary was probably Beecher Stowe's own two-volume *Key to Uncle Tom's Cabin* (1853), reconstructing the facts on which her work was based, which was translated and circulated widely in Europe and Latin America.[36] These detailed and well-documented volumes offered proof that the novel was more than a piece of fiction, that it delivered what was intended to be an authentic image of American society. While in America itself the publication of the *Key* became an instrument in the political confrontation between North and South, between abolitionists and supporters of slavery, in many parts of Europe it opened a window onto a still largely unknown society, perceived as profoundly different from anything known at home. With its rich quotations from original documents, correspondence, legislation, newspaper clips, and "oral histories" Beecher Stowe's *Key to Uncle Tom's Cabin* became one of the first social-anthropological studies of American life accessible to European readers in their own language.

Compared with Britain, which enjoyed a close relationship to the United States and a wide range of information readily available via periodicals, in Italy the documentary passages of the novel had a more important impact on the construction of an image of America, because economic and diplomatic relations with the United States still played only a minor role, with the consequence that the circulation of information about the United States was still rather limited.[37] Stowe became a star in Italy and was well known beyond circles of educated Italians. Sojourning in Rome in 1857, she visited the workshop of the brothers Castellani and observed one of them carving the head of an Egyptian slave in onyx. Recognized, she was greeted with the words: "Madam, we know what you have been to the poor slave. We ourselves are but poor slaves still in Italy; you feel for us; will you keep this gem as a small token of recognition for what you have done?"[38] As inappropriate as the comparison between American slaves and Italians in the Papal States might seem, one of the reasons for Uncle Tom's popularity was the fact that Italians were able to assimilate their own fate to that of the oppressed slaves. In 1859, on her second visit to Italy, Beecher Stowe attended the meeting of the Tuscan Assembly at which the adherence to Piedmont was declared, which gave rise to the unification of Italy.[39]

Despite the novel's important role in Italian debates on the United States, one should not overemphasize possible political readings of theatrical representations of America. What many of these works depicted was the despotism and cruelty of uncivilized or non-enlightened cultures, often in the form of humorist parody for the carnival season. Their emphasis was on the humanism of Western civilization, contrasting with the character of the noble savage of the New World, as in Donizetti's cantata *Cristoforo Colombo o sia la scoperta dell'America*.[40] A modern version of this genre was Franchetti's opera *Cristoforo Colombo*, commissioned by the city of Genoa in 1892 and performed two years later in Treviso and Bologna under Toscanini. Within this genre America was not just a New World, but also a different world, treated in a rather undifferentiated fashion, which emphasized its perceived exotic otherness.[41] Reading *Bianchi e Neri* within the context of other stage works on American themes, it is striking that Rota's America seemed to lack the values and the culture that characterized the

Europe of the Enlightenment.⁴² Beecher Stowe's America was a particularly brutalized form of what many Europeans saw as the negation of their own civilization.

In his best-selling *History of Europe*, published more than half a century after the end of the American Civil War, the great liberal philosopher and historian Benedetto Croce still identified the legacies of slavery as the one issue that set the United States apart from Europe. The United States had once been "the typical country of democracy," but then it became paralyzed by "the conflict between advocates and opponents of slavery," an issue Europe had overcome "a millennium and a half ago" and that it was now "rooting out in her colonies." As a consequence of what was basically a conflict of economic interests, the United States had fallen out of step with the great struggle for liberalism and democracy that characterized progress in Europe.⁴³ For Croce, the conflict over slavery explained why US politics and society were so different from Europe and why the Old World had little to learn from the United States.

Beyond the "Model Republic" in Italy

As demonstrated in the previous chapters of this book, when *Bianchi e Neri* toured Italy slavery represented only one among many images of America circulating in nineteenth-century Europe and Latin America. These images were largely determined by the particular circumstances and the (national) perspective of the observer. Here the Italian example seems particularly striking. The American War of Independence coincided with the awakening of national sentiment in Italy. However, as Suzanne Stewart-Steinberg has recently argued,⁴⁴ more than in other nations the positive sense of the new associated with nation making also resulted in a political and cultural anxiety that was fundamental to Italy's experience of modernity. This made it almost compulsory for Italian patriots to look across the Atlantic for lessons. When Beecher Stowe pointed to the Christian motives behind her battle this seemed to confirm that freedom of religion, as practiced in the United States, encouraged political liberation. This could not go unnoticed in Italy, where national liberation was also understood as liberation from Papal dominion and as the end of a theocratic system of government. Meanwhile, the fact that Beecher Stowe was praised as a Protestant writer and activist obviously alarmed the Catholic Church.⁴⁵ As a matter of fact, the republican almanac *Friend of the People* saw no difference "between the Jews in the Papal States and the Negroes in America."⁴⁶ Apart from her admiration for the Catholic Church's symbolism and authentic spirituality, Beecher Stowe echoed the condemnation of "Catholic tyranny" by Italian patriots and made the Pope's "perverted religion" the topic of her

Italian novel, *Agnes of Sorrento*.⁴⁷ The Italian anticlericals found a willing supporter in the first American minister to the Kingdom of Italy, George Perkins Marsh, who regarded the Catholic Church as an institutionalization of "tyranny, reaction and superstition."⁴⁸ This image was so persuasive that the Catholic press in Italy made particular efforts to counter such impressions.⁴⁹

Meanwhile, European revolutionaries knew that public opinion in the United States was not unanimous in its support for their uprisings, that many Americans feared the negative consequences of revolution for their business relations with the old continent. Despite the fact that a number of American envoys to Italy supported the process of unification, officially the government of the United States adopted a policy of strict neutrality.⁵⁰ Catholic Americans condemned the revolutionaries for their treatment of the Pope.⁵¹ Meanwhile, the widely read accounts of Garibaldi's life did not present a rosy picture of his experiences of the United States, despite the fact that his arrival had been greeted with a great deal of anticipation and he was often compared to General Washington. Even for Garibaldi making a living in New York turned out to be difficult.⁵² When the German 1848er Friedrich Hecker wrote about the splendid welcome he had received in New York, it should be noticed that this warm reception was largely the work of German Americans.⁵³ One of the first Italian novels of emigration, published by the Mazzinian Antonio Caccia just after 1848, presented the unpleasant image of an American nativist, who resented "the daily arrival of hungry Europeans."⁵⁴ All this was known to Italian observers and influenced the construction of a rather ambivalent image of the United States.

Many Italians read Carlo Botta's *History of the War of Independence* (1820–1) as a model for the liberation of Italy, and for some time the United States' federal Constitution seemed to offer a blueprint for the political unification of the peninsula, and likewise for German democrats and for the suppressed Poles.⁵⁵ However, for others there was something fundamentally wrong with the American understanding of freedom. Mazzini criticized its republican thought for stifling "the principle of association under the omnipotence of the individual [...] and enthroned selfish interests, materialism, and contradiction," and as early as 1838 he confessed his "cordial antipathy for the very name of that country."⁵⁶ Even the Duke of Orléans and future king Louis Philippe considered the American Constitution acceptable.⁵⁷ How could that be a model for a true European democrat? While, for instance, in Spain and Brazil most republicans were federalists (see Chapter 2), Mazzini, the advocate of a strongly centralized and unitarian Italy, considered the federal model a great risk for the future of his movement, favoring instead the republican centralism of the French revolutionary tradition.⁵⁸ Regarding the place of the United

States in these debates, the fact that it was the federal character of the Constitution that gave slaveholders the ability to oppose abolition seemed to confirm Mazzini's fears. A generation later the experience of the Civil War seemed to vindicate those voices who had questioned the practicality of federalism altogether.

As Leonardo Buonomo has pointed out, in Italy "notions about the United States were mostly dim or extravagant, and not merely among the lower and middle classes but also among the nobility and even, sometimes, the heads of state. What is more, for a surprisingly large number of people, America was a non-entity. Its citizens were commonly called *inglesi* [English], a frequent cause of irritation for many US travellers and an actual disadvantage: among all foreign visitors of Italy, the least popular were precisely those from England."[59] For many Italians even the distinction between the United States and South America was far from obvious, and frequently one notices their confusion about which territories of the New World actually formed part of the new Republic. As mentioned earlier, this was also because ideas of America were often based on a very limited acquaintance with literature on the New World. Even a fervent reader such as Mazzini knew hardly more than the works of James Fenimore Cooper, in whom he recognized an American Walter Scott: a historian, but also a mythmaker.[60] Only after the American Civil War did Italian periodicals start to write regularly and in more detail about events and political developments across the Atlantic, then presenting a shockingly brutal image of life in the war-torn society. The 1860s were also the years in which literary works about life and travel in America became increasingly popular and were translated into Italian, often transmitting the idea of a rather primitive lifestyle.[61] Although certainly not prejudiced against Americans, Giovanni Capellini, the Bolognese geologist and future rector of the university, included in his travel account numerous episodes illustrating the contrasting manners of the New and the Old World. He was shocked by the cultural consequences of a society that denied the natural distinction between social classes. Especially, the hotels did not offer what Capellini expected. Not only was he tortured by the feeling that most of the time he had to keep his Colt revolver under his pillow, mice danced on his blanket and scurried happily over his face![62] Even for a traveler with ample experience of the Italian South, the North American Republic was hard to take in. For this passionate supporter of Italian unification, the United States provided no model to follow.

Lincoln became president of the United States ten days before Vittorio Emanuele was proclaimed king of Italy and the United States was the first country to recognize the Kingdom of Italy. Despite the recent secession of the Union, Americans continued to follow events in Italy and in December

1860 *La Nazione* reported a meeting in New York bringing together more than 3,000 people in support of Garibaldi.[63] Likewise, although Italians had reason enough to concentrate on their own civil war in the South, they followed the news about the escalating conflict across the Atlantic closely. When Baron Ricasoli, Cavour's successor as Italian prime minister, expressed his strong support for the constitutional authorities of the North, he did this also in the awareness of secessionist hopes among Papal and Southern legitimists of the Italian peninsula.

Many Italian patriots saw the struggles for unification and for the abolition of slavery in the United States as "one single cause."[64] Historically, the Italian democrats had close relations with the Democratic Party in the United States and they were hesitant to declare themselves in favor of Lincoln. However, they were sympathetic toward the abolitionists and their official attitude to Lincoln changed after the Emancipation Declaration. As an international champion of freedom Mazzini was popular in American antislavery circles and his concern over the dangers of the federal system was to some extent shared by the American republicans.[65] Henry Ward Beecher, Harriet Beecher Stowe's brother and the most famous Congregationalist preacher of his time, supported Italian republicans in exile such as Jessie White Mario, and Lincoln offered Garibaldi a commission as major general in the Union Army. A Garibaldi Brigade of 350 men, of which about 50 were Italians, fought for the North. Many individual units included experienced Italian officers, including the later director of the Metropolitan Museum, Luigi Palma di Cesnola. However, there were also about 500 Italians fighting for the South. The American administration saw the Redshirts largely as a wild bunch of adventurers seeking US-paid transport to the New World.[66] The decision not to recognize the Confederacy, despite the fact that the Italian cotton mills depended on raw material from the South, was one of the few issues on which Italian democrats and moderates were able to agree.

The policy of the Holy See was in this respect less clear and the South tried to gain legitimacy from the fact that the Pope maintained correspondence with the Confederate president, Jefferson Davis.[67] The Catholic Church questioned the legitimacy of the United States on the same basis as it questioned the Kingdom of Italy: "While Italy constitutes itself as one, which it has never been, [...] in the United States they dissolve their union, because for some of them unity is such an unbearable condition that a war seems justified."[68] The impact of the church on the formation of an Italian image of America is not to be neglected. In terms of readership, *Civiltà Cattolica* was still the peninsula's most influential periodical and even in Piedmont, where it counted as an antigovernmental publication, it had more subscribers than any of the liberal periodicals.[69] However, even the church was unable to defend the slave economy in the South. Although not against slavery in principle, it took the view that under the paternal protection of the church "the master becomes father, and the slave almost a son. But in America things are different: there slavery results in tyranny, a monstrosity..."[70] As explained in more detail in Chapter 6, supporters of slavery in Spain and some Latin American countries took a similar view when they described US slavery as much harsher than in the Spanish Antilles or Brazil.

Despite a widespread enthusiasm for the North's cause, what Italians followed more closely and with growing consternation was the unimaginable brutality of the bloodshed. The liberal Capellini described the conflict as the "devil's war," showing particular concern over the circulation of weapons among the civil population.[71] *La Nazione*, the influential newspaper from Florence, used the term "terrorism" to describe the policies of the Confederacy, but it also shed doubts on Lincoln's own integrity: "for him the negroes are no more than a means to go to war against the whites."[72] Although this sort of attack against the US president was rare in the Italian press, it seemed to echo the personalized campaigns of the pro-Southern members of the British parliament around Alexander Beresford-Hope and the *Saturday Review*, which caricatured Lincoln as a rude frontiersman, a great "rail-splitter, bargee, and country attorney," the opposite of Jefferson Davis' image of "an able administrator and calm statesman."[73] As early as September 1861 *Civiltà Cattolica* described the "degeneration" of the "civil fractures" into "fervent warfare," calling the fate of the thousands of victims a human "catastrophe."[74] For the Catholic press Washington's regime during the Civil War was "a kind of military dictatorship" and comparable to the political situation of "occupied" Sicily. Suddenly discovering a concern for the treatment of prisoners and the freedom of the press, the Catholic paper noted that the regime no longer respected the law of *habea corpus*. Numerous newspapers were banned, "following exactly the same practice as the Neapolitan Garibaldini in the service of Piedmont."[75] While Catholic papers questioned the motives of the Union, the liberal press pointed to the desperate actions of the Confederates, "burning their own cities, devastating their fields, prepared to suffer deprivations of any kind."[76] Irrespective of their political sympathies, Italian liberals and Catholics seemed to have agreed that "a lot of blood and violence could be spared. A war pursued with such levels of *accanimento* has to have most horrific consequences."[77]

Confronted with these impressions of the Civil War and the political realities of the United States, the former model republic increasingly lost its appeal for Italians, and in the view of many its political development could not even be compared to the conditions in Europe.[78] As a commentator for the liberal *Nuova Antologia* maintained in 1867, political life in the

United States "had become extremely corrupted and violent. If one were to transmit this model of society and government onto one of our states, it would collapse within a week."[79] The example of the United States served as a proof for anybody who feared the negative consequences of democratic advances without the progress of political education:

> [In the American South,] the honest, virtuous and well-off classes retire from political life, feeling unable to give direction or to influence decisions. They leave matters to the country's least educated and least distinguished strata. Thus, democracy seems to be ochlocracy, where the government of the people becomes the government of the plebs. The Congress of the United States has today the reputation of being the most corrupted assembly in the entire world.[80]

In assessing the views of this influential periodical it is interesting to note that, originally, *Antologia* had advocated the federalization of Italy, but experience taught America's former supporters a different lesson. As they observed political developments across the Atlantic many Italians became increasingly disenchanted with republicanism in general. While some radical democrats continued to see a link between prosperity and republicanism (see Chapter 1), the Italian liberals compared developments in the United States and Britain, which seemed to illustrate that opportunities did not depend on the form of government.[81] What kind of country was it where elections were won "by means of tumultuous meetings and the use of Colt revolvers?" commented liberal as well as Catholic papers in Italy.[82] News about Johnson's conflict with Congress seemed to confirm that the American Constitution simply did not provide the stability that was needed to steer the country out of its self-incurred crisis.[83]

Europe, American Theater, and Buffalo Bill

Alongside images of the United States as a failed political model, there emerged a view of it as culturally barren. A powerful Franco-Italian image of America appears in Stendhal's novel *La Charteuse de Parme* (1839), when Fabrizio del Dongo speaks about his plans to emigrate to New York, but is warned by his aunt of a sad life without elegance, music, theater, or love, dominated by the cult of the dollar. Another influential source, in particular for the assessment of America's cultural scene, were the memoirs of Mozart's librettist Lorenzo Da Ponte, who had left for the United States in 1805. Widely discussed in literary circles throughout most of the nineteenth century, his three volumes, modeled on the popular memoirs of his friend Casanova, made it clear to European readers that in the New

World "Italian language and literature were [...] about as well known as Turkish or Chinese."[84] This was at a time when in most major European cities Italian opera theaters were at the center of cultural life, a trend Latin America was keen to catch up with. In fact, a good deal of opera was performed in the United States; for example, since the 1820s Spontini's and Bellini's works had been staged in New Orleans. The Astor in New York City specialized in the performance of Italian repertoire, although the theatre was a commercial failure. The Metropolitan Opera House, which opened in 1883, included 65 musicians from Venice and Naples.[85] Even so, theater in the United States was commonly perceived by Europeans to be different from that of the Old World. News of the violent reactions against British Shakespearean actors in New York in 1849, which left dozens of people dead, spread all over Europe and did nothing to improve America's reputation as a land of the arts.[86] Spanish travelers suggested that US theater suffered from the American obsession with creating something new and distinct, to distinguish itself from the Old World.

> The Yankees have no gift for the beautiful, and with their thirst for innovating and for separating themselves from old molds, searching for something new which corresponds to the idiosyncrasies of new societies, they digress and lose themselves in a sea of strange lines and forms, the scope of which it is impossible to gauge [or rather it's impossible to gauge where they're going with what they do].[87]

French commentators went beyond these condemnations, attesting to a general absence of aesthetic feelings as the root of America's alleged lack of culture:

> Although they are very intelligent, the biggest obstacle that the Americans will have to overcome if they are to understand a work of art [...], is that excessive confidence in themselves, this exaggerated pride in their own merit which will always prevent them from looking with that naivety, that suspicion of tenderness, which is half of what intuition and genius are [...] and which showed itself in an intimate manner in Raphael and Mozart, those sublime children of candour, so full of modesty and love.[88]

The Americans were deemed to be too sure of themselves, too lacking in sensitivity and feeling to produce (or even to appreciate) great art. That said, US theaters were "full of spectators" and their plays full of "explosions, shipwrecks and rifle and revolver shots [which] often produce great effect among the popular classes."[89] In sum, while theater in nineteenth-century Europe was strongly influenced by Schiller's concept of aesthetic education and his lofty notion of *Nationaltheater* as a moral school for the nation, European perceptions were that US theater was reduced to a commercial enterprise. In every aspect American theater seemed the opposite of Europe's classicist and idealist tradition, contributing to the idea of America as a profoundly uncivilized country.

And then came Buffalo Bill. Although there is a large literature on William Cody's popular shows, it is still difficult to know what Europeans really made of the phenomenon. Undoubtedly, the European tour of the late 1880s became a major attraction. The English were particularly keen. The show toured London and several provincial towns, and Thomas Cook even organized trips for British tourists to attend performances at the Paris *Exposition Universelle*.[90] Traveling shows on exotic themes were by no means new to Europeans. Native American artifacts were regularly on display—even provincial Italian cities such as Bologna housed permanent collections of them—and popular fiction such as Thomas Mayne Reid's came with lavish illustrations of daily life on the frontier. It was probably the sheer scale of the Buffalo Bill shows that most impressed the audiences of the Old World, and the amount of business they generated. Some newspapers reported profits of one million dollars for the London show alone, despite the fact that much of the money seemed to vanish as quickly as it arrived in the till.[91] Enormous sums of money went into publicity. As a consequence, our image of Buffalo Bill's success in Europe is to a large extent the product of these (American) advertising campaigns rather than of the Europeans' own impressions at the time.

However, the significance of Buffalo Bill in Europe goes beyond the entertainment factor. During the first visit to England, in 1887, William Gladstone attended the show and used the occasion to speak "in the warmest terms of America." As Cody's sister recorded in her memoirs, Gladstone thanked Will for the good he was doing in presenting to the English public a picture of the wild life of the Western continent, which served to illustrate the difficulties encountered by "a sister nation on its onward march of civilization."[92] Gladstone was being diplomatic here, which encouraged Cody's sister to ennoble her brother in her memoirs to the status of catalyst of the "special relationship." When during a later performance the American flag was borne in front of the royal box, the Queen, to the astonishment of everyone present, rose and saluted it with a bow, followed in her gesture by the entire court party. As Cody's press agent noted, "for the first time in history, since the Declaration of Independence, a sovereign of Great Britain had saluted the star spangled banner, and that banner was carried by a member of Buffalo Bill's Wild West."[93] When, subsequently, members of the cast broke with royal etiquette, cordially shaking hands with the Princess of Wales, the court had to pretend that this was a pleasing variation on the established custom of saluting royalty; likewise when Great Chief Red Shirt made use of his "Indian gift of oratory," talking to the prince about "the Great White Chief and his beautiful squaw."[94] While the Americans were sure of their interpretation of the event's diplomatic significance, according to some historians the queen understood her saluting of the flag to be part of the performance, displaying a sense of irony that American observers and the press might not have immediately caught. As Warren reports, the scene was accompanied by "Yankee Doodle," which was originally a British song deriding rebel foolishness at the outset of the American Revolution. Only later was it adopted by the Americans as a patriotic tune. The scene offers in fact multiple readings. Raising the flag in honor of the queen could be understood as the American visitors recognizing their debt to Her Majesty for attending the show. The rumor that Buffalo Bill was the first show the queen had attended since the death of Prince Albert, some 30 years earlier, is a myth. While she did not show a great interest in theater, "she was an ardent circus fan," and shortly before Buffalo Bill she had attended a performance of the Paris Hippodrome on tour in London.[95] Whether Britain understood Buffalo Bill as a celebration of Anglo-Saxonism in the Wild West, as Warren suggests, also remains questionable.[96] Although the continental Europeans frequently made racial connections between Britain and the United States, from a British perspective this suggestion seemed less flattering or convincing. With travel writing fashioned by colorful accounts of German, Italian, and even Chinese immigration, some members of the British establishment did not accept that there was a pure Anglo-Saxon race on the other side of the Atlantic.

At the 1889 Paris exhibition President Carnot and several members of his cabinet saw Buffalo Bill in the company of the American ambassador. One of the ministers who remained particularly impressed by Cody's shows was Général Boulanger. His personal ambition would soon lead to one of the Third Republic's most serious constitutional crises. Press comment on the encounter was that Buffalo Bill seemed to be Boulanger in disguise. The fact that they described the general as a showman says as much about Boulanger as it does about Cody, who was certainly not seen as a man of great culture.[97] Other visitors to the show included Queen Isabella II of Spain, the Shah of Persia, Paul Gauguin, and Edvard Munch. Subsequently, Buffalo Bill toured Spain, Italy, Austria, Germany, and the Low Countries.[98] Not everywhere did the show go as smoothly as in London and Paris. In Barcelona, the city was quarantined for typhoid and the show's compère, as well as several Native American actors, died during the stay. In Rome the entire company attended the ceremonies for the anniversary of the coronation of Pope Leo XIII, a crucial moment of the church's international mobilization and the new cult of the papacy.[99] A member of the cast recorded these impressions: "In full war paint and all the panoply the war chest afforded, the Wild West lined up along the corridor down which the Pope would pass. Cody, in dress coat with his long hair flowing over his shoulders—perhaps the only man who could ever wear such a combination without being ludicrous, towered a full head above the rest. His Holiness gazed intently at the great hero, and spread his hands in blessing"—perhaps a diplomatic gesture toward Catholic America.[100] In Verona, Cody staged a special show in the Roman arena and liked the idea that this was supposed to be the largest building in the world, just appropriate for a man like him.[101] Giacomo Puccini remained impressed by the show: "In eleven days they drew 120,000 lire!"—[102] a comment that seemed to confirm prejudices that he himself was somewhat vulgar.[103] Nevertheless, the inspiration for his opera *La Fanciulla del West* did not in fact come from Buffalo Bill, as is sometimes suggested, but from Belasco's play *The Girl of the Golden West*, which he saw many years later in New York. Moreover, the reinvention of Buffalo Bill as melodrama was not an Italian, but an American, idea.[104]

In Germany, Cody's show toured at least 13 cities, from Munich to Hamburg and Dresden to Düsseldorf. The most lasting effect Buffalo Bill had in Germany was its impact on the author Karl May, the popularity of whose 80 volumes of fiction about life on the American frontier reached well beyond the educated reader across most of Central Europe.[105] However, while Cody certainly sparked May's imagination and inspired several of his books, May's most popular story, *Winnetou*, had its debut as early as 1875 and many of his later novels were an explicit critique of the white man's mission for which Cody himself stood. Karl May gave literary expression to a widespread sympathy for Native Americans, on whose fate the European press had reported with growing concern since the 1840s, contributing to a rather gloomy image of America and the Americans. Even radical 1848-ers and pro-American republicans, such as Ferdinand Freiligrath, criticized the so-called model republic for the brutality with which it eliminated its native population.[106] In May's epic novels the German hero Karl, renamed Old Shatterhand, saves the life of Winnetou and is invited to perform the ritual of blood brotherhood, thus becoming one and the same with the chief of the Apaches. The tale of this friendship ends with the Apache throwing himself in front of the bullet of a brutal frontiersman to save Old Shatterhand's life. He dies in the arms of his friend and to the tune of an *Ave Maria*, his last words confirming that he believes in Christ.[107] Winnetou gives his life for the sins of humanity and civilization, exposing the moral corruption and brutality of American expansion through Christian symbolism. May's novels become a widely admired version of German *Zivilisationskritik*, popularized all over the world, and in particular in those countries of Europe that at the time did not have Westerns of their own.[108]

Apparently less critical of the white man's Western mission were the armed forces in Germany, which allegedly took an interest in Cody's ability to move several hundreds of actors, cattle, and horses from city to city in a special railway train. Allegedly, 40 Prussian army officers interviewed the organizers and took notes.[109] The story is recorded by Cody's sister, who might have liked the idea that the Prussian army learned its logistical skills from Buffalo Bill. What impressed the Germans more were the stories about one of Cody's actors, a veteran Indian of the famous battle of Little Big Horn, Standing Bear, who became romantically entangled with his Austrian nurse after he was wounded during the show's performance in Vienna. The episode perfectly fitted continental imaginations nurtured by May, in particular the account of the love between the German Old Shatterhand and Winnetou's sister Ntscho-Tschi, who was killed by white bandits on the way to a boarding school on the East Coast. In 1892 the Lutheran nurse Louise Rieneck and Cody's Standing Bear got married and settled with the bride's parents and other relatives in Pine Bridge.[110] Louise set up a Lakota Sioux household and nursed her new kin in the reservation, where poverty and disease took a heavy toll. She also taught the community basic carpentry, in particular how to make coffins and to bury their dead in the earth. Again, given European sympathies for Native Americans the accounts of her story did not necessarily contribute to a positive image of the United States. The end of the European Buffalo Bill tour was overshadowed by rumors that Cody had mistreated the Native Americans among his cast and the company had to face an official investigation by the Bureau of Indian Affairs. Highly successful as the shows had been, they were regarded by Europeans as entertainment,[111] not culture, and vulgar entertainment at that, thereby compounding the impression that the United States was barbarous both in its brutality and in its lack of culture.

Buffalo Bill shows did not feature in Latin America (although Cuban independence fighters were incorporated into the show in 1897), partly because it had its own distinctive equivalents of frontier culture. In Latin American countries representations of the North American genocide of Native Americans were inflected by their own policies toward native populations. In Argentina, both the ruling elites and those from the professional classes who, by the 1890s, were beginning to challenge them politically, shared a commitment to the scientific modernization of Argentina. With few exceptions, they supported the Conquest of the Desert (1879–80), a ruthless military campaign to clear the indigenous people off the pampas, in which many of them were slaughtered, as a supposedly necessary stage of that modernization. In the words of Juan B. Justo (a medical doctor, social reformer, and founder of the Argentine socialist party): "we can't leave the pampas in the hands of Indian chiefs."¹¹² Justo, in 1895, presented a wholly unenchanted vision of William Penn's treaty with the Indians, noting that "the only Indians left in Pennsylvania were those in bronze on Philadelphia town hall. Even if the North Americans thought that was a treaty of justice and liberty, the Indians certainly did not feel it to be so."¹¹³ The Argentine labor movement, particularly the socialist and anarchist press of the 1890s, popularized utopian images of stateless societies among the Native Americans of the United States, in which everyone lived in fraternal freedom and equality, focusing especially on the Iroquoi.¹¹⁴

For nineteenth-century Europeans, the frontier of savagery and civilization was not just the Wild West but the whole of America itself. Perhaps the organizers of the Chicago World Fair, in 1893, sensed these feelings toward American culture when they banned Buffalo Bill from the spectacular Columbian Exposition. While outside the gates Buffalo Bill became one of Chicago's main attractions, the exhibition planners "defined art as the statuary and painting of an elite European tradition."¹¹⁵ But even those attempts to identify with European culture usually met with contempt. The modish Cuban magazine *La Habana Elegante* remarked, ironically, in 1895, "oh, there is art in New York, as confirmed by the sumptuous copies of Pisano's pulpit from the Cathedral in Siena; the Japanese altar, whose gold and lacquework engage the soul; the windows of a house from Cairo; [...] Renaissance furniture; a Buddhist temple from China; [...] always presented with the name of the donor inscribed with golden letters on a plaque."¹¹⁶ As America had no culture of its own, it could only buy it in from elsewhere.

Or did it have a culture of its own? For Charles Baudelaire, if culture existed in the United States it had emerged in opposition to the peculiar conditions and values of American society, a phenomenon exemplified most notably by the poet Edgar Allan Poe.¹¹⁷ While unremittingly critical of the United States, Baudelaire was nonetheless in awe of Poe, whom he saw as an exceptional artist from a country he derided for its "utilitarian movement, which wishes to bring poetry into line like all other things."¹¹⁸ According to Baudelaire, Poe stood out because he, unlike other American writers, did not lend himself, or his works, readily to ulterior interpretations or political purposes. With his devotion to style and his Romantic conception of art, as it commonly existed only in Europe, Poe was a singular figure among American poets. Baudelaire charged the latter with being just as utilitarian as the society that had borne them: American poets were not artists, motivated by a desire to create *l'art pour l'art*, but rather campaigning writers, "poets of universal suffrage, abolitionist poets, poets of corn laws."[119] For Baudelaire, then, Poe had succeeded in becoming a great artist in spite of his surroundings, which his French champion likened to "a vast cage, a large accountancy firm."[120]

Corruption and Crime

Although England generally had a much more positive idea of American life, even here there were continuing concerns that the "best men" were excluded from positions of power. While increasing numbers of establishment figures gained a new appreciation of the conservatism of the US political system in the late nineteenth century (see Chapter 1), there were fears that the absence of the "best men" resulted in a degeneration of the whole standard of government, symbolized by the "caucus" system, which in turn threatened representative democracy. In the late 1870s, the innovation of the local party "caucus," notably the liberal organization of Joseph Chamberlain in Birmingham, was attacked as the "Americanising" of British politics. Even the Americanophile Goldwin Smith voiced fears about the dangers of importing American partisan practices into the United Kingdom. "In the United States," he wrote, "the masters of the party machine have every-where taken the representation out of the hands of the people; you are practically not at liberty to vote for anyone but their nominees; and the Republican horse, to vanquish the Democratic stag, becomes absolutely the slave of its rider."[121]

In Spain the 1876 elections and the subsequent machinations of the Grant administration were closely followed in the national press and provided additional fodder for the conservative argument that the United States represented an anti-model republic. Political corruption and violence were all too familiar to Spaniards, who had their own political bosses, known as *caciques,* to stitch up elections on the basis of favor, money, and patronage. Thus, while liberal Spaniards were undoubtedly disappointed by news of the serious imperfections in US-style democracy, they were at least able to observe that in the United States "the moment arrives when laziness or indifference is shaken off" and *gran caciques* like William Tweed are brought to justice.[122]

Other issues also shocked European readers. From the 1880s popular magazines wrote a lot about modern nervousness as a typical product of American civilization, which was imagined as increasingly spreading into Europe.[123] Illustrated magazines carried stories about the excesses of gambling and the violence related to this particularly crude form of making money.[124] Organized crime was another topic that occupied the press. While commentators agreed that the US authorities had to stamp out such phenomena, they were also concerned about the frequent application of the death penalty and the fact that different states did not apply it in the same way.[125] The Spanish-based (and distributed widely in Latin America) journal *La Ilustración Española y Americana* declared itself little surprised that "the electric spark" was to become "the new agent of death"—the modern method of capital punishment—given that "the modern man expects everything from this fluid [sic] and wants it to intervene in everything." Although the world's first state-sanctioned death by electrocution did not take place until four years after this article was written, in New York in 1890, the journal took the opportunity to mark the passing of "the age of burning at the stake" and its replacement by "the age of burning at the wire." The electric chair, it declared, would deliver death at the touch of a button. But even this, it had to admit, was a form of progress: "Just a few years ago, in order to execute somebody electrically it would have been necessary to take the convicted offender out onto a terrace with a lightning rod at his neck."[126]

The European press widely reported the practice of lynching. While Spanish commentators abhorred lynching, their repugnance was sometimes based more on what they thought it signified about American disregard for the rule of law than on any feelings of empathy or sympathy with the black population. It was seen as the sign of an uncivilized people who sought to bypass their courts, rather than being particularly related to the politics of race. The conservative paper *La Epoca* published an article relating the story of John Lynch and his eponymous law, and the postbellum origins of the Ku Klux Klan and the Know-Nothing party. The less than subtle implication of the article was that the United States had no moral authority to intervene in Spanish colonial affairs (in Cuba) and still less should it be exalted as a model that Spain should emulate. Indeed, *La Epoca*'s ire was directed principally at Spanish Americophiles:

> These facts [the Lynch Law and Ku Klux Klan] help to form an idea of the authority with which the United States seeks to impose on the Spanish colonies, Christian and Catholic—and therefore humane and gentle towards the slaves—a heartfelt love for the blacks, against whom they invented the practice of hanging from a tree, streetlamp or railing, without informing anyone as to the motive; assassination by secret society decree; and almost permanent popular tumults and unrest in order to protect whites' jobs and prevent Africans from prospering.[127]

While the Italian press was alarmed by the activities of the Ku Klux Klan,[128] questions were also raised about "a policy which results in allowing

Negroes to occupy the same level in the administration of the State as Whites, who become the servants of their former slaves."[129] Even provincial papers such as the *Giornale di Sicilia* reported tensions between white soldiers and black volunteers, and protests against black suffrage.[130] In 1867 *L'Universo Illustrato* maintained that most Negroes "never proved to possess any of the virtues for which they were praised in *Uncle Tom's Cabin*."[131] Cesare Lombroso, the father of criminal anthropology, maintained that "race shapes criminal organisations" and was convinced that the emancipation of slaves had not helped the United States to improve its conditions.[132] Between the 1870s and the 1890s, America, along with the Italian South, became the basis for his ideas about degeneration and his theory of the "born criminal." These views were widely shared across Europe and Lombroso enjoyed influence well beyond criminologists. As Otto Weininger maintained in his book *Sex and Character*, which was dedicated to Lombroso, "there has probably never been a genius among Negroes, and their morality is generally so low that the Americans ... are beginning to fear that it was an ill-considered move to emancipate them."[133] Similar concerns were raised regarding the capacity of East Asian immigrants to assimilate.[134] This new form of biologically informed racism contributed considerably to negative views of the United States and seemed to offer an explanation for its high levels of crime.

From Civil War to Class War and Imperialism

The assassination of Garfield in 1881 offered an opportunity to reflect again on the assassination of Lincoln, and was still explained as the consequence of the country's material and moral devastation during the Civil War.[135] What affected Europeans even more, and Italians in particular, was the fact that numerous anarchists, including the assassin of the Italian king Umberto I, seemed to have learned their trade in the United States.[136] The anarchist Errico Malatesta explained their actions as a consequence of the "infamous persecutions" and the "social injustice" they had to endure. The Italians in particular, Malatesta claimed, were treated as "an inferior race just a little above the negroes," and the fact that they were Catholics made their situation even more difficult.[137] A labor periodical from Bahía Blanca, a port city just south of Buenos Aires that was a key hub for produce from the pampas, contained the following story of an Italian anarchist in the United States, driven to violence by the unbearable suffering to which he has been subjected. Having been expelled from his job and his home for being an anarchist, he took recourse in a job on an Italian ship, but ended up on trial for assault back in Genoa, where after three months in prison he was acquitted on condition of deportation back to the United States. As he prepared to reenter the United States, he observed bitterly:

> From the ship, people cried "America, America." [...] Poor wretches, "America," they cried, yes, America, the irony of the word!

On making his way back to where he had left his family eight months earlier, the man found that his wife had been obliged to prostitute herself to try to support the children, one of whom had died even so. The story culminated in the narrator, incensed by rage and grief, murdering the man he held responsible for the cruel fate of his family. His denunciation of US society could hardly be more damning: "It's made up of a few wicked people, who live from bullying [*prepotenze*], who've made themselves masters of everything that there is under the sun for us to share, who [...] have enslaved and subjected the people like a flock of sheep, who devour and oppress everything, claiming to be the instrument of the people itself, but serving instead as soldier, policeman, spy, executioner."[138]

During the 1890s, the Argentine anarchist press, in which Italian immigrants played an important role, reproduced many lurid stories of corruption, lawlessness, and state violence against workers, citing local US newspapers as their sources. For example, *L'Avvenire*'s round up of US news in one edition of 1896 included a claim that the Republican Party had spent 8 million dollars buying votes at the last election ("Oh, the integrity of universal suffrage!"); a story that at Bellefontaine, Ohio, all the prisoners had been released because the local authority lacked the funds either to feed them or to pay the guards ("Oh happy country!"); and, just in case any reader was in any doubt about "the truth" that lay behind the image of the United States as "a model republic," a grim note that in Landville, Colorado, troops with cannons had been marshaled to protect the mines against strikers. The only positively represented item in the column was the announcement of an anarchist congress.[139] A labor periodical from Argentina's third city, Rosario, even claimed that the US Ministry of War, seeking to test out a new way of feeding troops, had ordered a company of 50 men to go on a 3-hour forced march through Colorado, nourished only by "tablets of coffee and a condensed soup." As the condensed food began to condense in the men's stomachs, most of them became mortally ill. However, when "the company doctors telegraphed the ministry to revoke the barbaric order, they received the reply that the march should continue, whether the soldiers were dead or alive." The item concluded, "What a marvel is the efficiency of bourgeois rule, when so much stupidity and savage ignorance govern your military laws!"[140]

Leaders of emerging workers' movements in Latin America used images of the United States as barbarous in order to criticize their own ruling elites for pursuing a similar model. Statesmen, such as the Argentine Roque Sáenz Peña, represented the United States as barbarous in order to undermine its pretensions to hegemony and to assert Argentine claims to influence by portraying it as the more civilized country. It was part of the same strategy that they tended to emphasize that their country had abolished slavery earlier, despite the often rather sad fate of their own former slaves. US expansionism undoubtedly played its part in undermining the image of the model republic, in particular in Latin America. Even the pro-US Domingo Sarmiento was warning the distinguished members of the Rhode Island Historical Society, in 1865, that such policies could be potentially lethal not only abroad but also at home. "It is dangerous," he intoned, "to convert the Federal System into an invading republic, swallowing ever, without being able to digest." He conjured up a compelling image of the United States as Cyclops, a bloated, blundering monster that did not know itself or its own power, which blundered about consuming others and ultimately gorging itself to death.[141] A quarter of a century later, José Martí, the political leader of Cuba's second war of independence, famously declared, after many years in the United States, that he had lived in the belly of the monster. Although his statement of 1891 was certainly the most famous Latin American depiction of the United States as monstrous, both at the time and subsequently, it was by no means the first. Such images can be found even in the works of the midcentury generations of supposedly pro-US Argentine and Chilean liberals. In 1856, fearing US expansionism—"first Texas, then the North of Mexico and the Pacific coast greeted a new master," followed by the filibustering of the 1850s—the Chilean intellectual Francisco Bilbao evoked the United States as a "boa constrictor." Acknowledging that it was "mesmerising," he conjured up a vivid image of other parts of the Americas falling into its "Saxon jaws" and being crushed in its "winding coils."[142]

For very different reasons, then, a variety of Latin American actors reinforced images of the United States as grotesque. One famous expression of this view was the short essay "The Triumph of Caliban," published in Buenos Aires about a month after the outbreak of the Spanish-Cuban-American War, by *modernista* poet Rubén Darío.[143] Originally from Nicaragua, Darío spent several years in a rapidly modernizing Buenos Aires during the late 1880s and early 1890s, and was a well-known figure of great stature throughout Spain and Spanish America. His widely disseminated work was a litany of metaphors of monstrosity: the United States was a Goliath, a Behemoth, "a land of Cyclopses," who devoured raw meat, inhabited "houses big enough for mastodons," and "charged through the streets pushing and shoving like animals, in the hunt for dollars." And he was in no doubt about what such gross consumption habits would mean for Latin America: "under the guise of helping the longed-for Pearl [of Cuba], the monster is swallowing it up, oyster and all." Even before the Spanish-Cuban-American-War, images of the United States as the epitome of barbarism had become common in Latin America; after 1898, they were enshrined in a lasting opposition between Anglo-Saxonness and Latinity that found its most influential expression in the Uruguayan writer José Enrique Rodó's famous essay of 1900, *Ariel.*

Mass Emigration

By the late nineteenth century, images of the United States as a violent land, lacking in history, culture, or ideals, overshadowed myths about the so-called land of opportunity that might offer a solution to the difficult fate of Italian peasants and workers at home. As the proverb from Basilicata goes, *L'America a ci acconza e a ci uasta* (America accommodates some and ruins others); similarly popular was the simple phrase *Managgia l'America!* (Damn America!); and in the Habsburg lands of Bohemia *Geh af Amerika!* meant "Go to hell!"[144] While parts of the radical Left, like the Italian republicans, continued to praise the United States as a country of great promise, the liberal majority had long broken with the Risorgimento's glorification of the United States.

Nevertheless, the new century brought a new wave of mass migration to the United States and for the first time Italian migration to the United States outnumbered other destinations.[145] As the work of Emilio Franzina has demonstrated *la febbre o la smania di andarsene*, especially among village people, became a contagious folly.[146] In 1901 the mayor of a small town in Carlo Levi's Lucania presented the Italian prime minister with "the greetings of 8,000 citizens, 3,000 of which are in America, soon to be followed by the remaining 5,000."[147] Depressing social, economic, and political conditions at home, combined with persistent reports of the United States' material prosperity, convinced hundred thousands of Europeans to cross the Atlantic permanently. But judging from the way the press, literature, and political debate depicted life in the United States there cannot be much doubt that many of the emigrants would have been fully aware that the land they sought had little in common with the idealized image of the model republic held up by the revolutionaries of the 1830s and 1840s. A famous investigation among working-class readers of the *Società Bibliografica Italiana* of 1906 revealed that at least 49 out of 459 had read De Amicis' classic emigration novel, *Sull'Oceano,* which depicted the fate of migrants with a grim realism.[148] Recent immigrants in particular seemed to become the victims of organized crime, as the illustration of a popular magazine in 1891 revealed, depicting a group of greenhorns during an attack by bandits on the road to Santa Fe.[149]

Moreover, the political circumstances in Europe had changed completely, and workers in the United States did not necessarily enjoy more freedom than workers in Germany, France, or Italy. The first major industrial conflict in the United States was the railroad workers' strike of 1877. Based on the compromise between Republicans and Democrats after the disputed election of 1876, industrial capitalists and political leaders had forged an alliance that helped the advance of industrial capitalism on the back of the working class. For the first time railroad workers met the brutal force of the state on an unprecedented scale, leaving a deep impression on European observers, most prominently Karl Marx.[150] The Civil War seemed to have given way to class war. As discussed in Chapter 1, the Haymarket hangings sent shockwaves through Europe and Latin America alike. Increasingly, class conflict was perceived as a distinctive feature of American political life and its industrial development.[151] However, what emigration seemed to offer was an economic opportunity. At least the United States was able to offer work. Therefore, the decision to cross the Atlantic to New York was less the fulfillment of a dream than the outcome of a sober calculation of the risks involved in going or staying. For the majority of emigrants only the desperate situation at home made them accept these conditions. And many returned after having taken a closer look, especially once steamships lowered the cost of transatlantic travel: 70 percent of immigrants from the Balkans, 62 percent of Greeks, and 58 percent of Italians came back, usually after they had made enough money to buy land at home.[152]

According to widely accessible images, life in the US part of the New World was characterized by a brutality that remained foreign to Europeans. It seemed that the trauma of the Civil War had left Americans in a state of moral decline, which affected society as a whole—men, women, and even children. Despite their admiration for the country's material wealth and their attraction to it as a place to work, Italians never fully recovered from the shock they received from the reports on the excesses of slavery and the Civil War. Although the fact that the Civil War had resolved the issue of slavery was generally seen as a positive development,[153] this gigantic conflict had demonstrated that the United States had little in common with the political and social values of the Old World. While the conflict in the Italian South was often described as a civil war in its own right, the idea of a war between fellow citizens that cost the lives of 600,000 men remained simply inconceivable for a nation that had constructed the idea of its own national resurgence on the concepts of brotherhood and kinship.[154]

The *fratelli d'Italia*, which the Italian anthem praised, and on which the Italian nation was based, did not seem to have an equivalent across the Atlantic.

Notes

Some of the material in this chapter is also discussed in Körner, "Uncle Tom on the Ballet Stage: Italy's Barbarous America, 1850–1900."

1. La Sorte, *Images of Italian Greenhorn Experience*, 195.
2. Friedman, "Beyond 'voting with the feet'."
3. Dall'Osso, *Voglia D'America.*
4. Gemme, *Domesticating Foreign Struggles.*
5. Diner, *Verkehrte Welten*, 38.
6. Thomas Carlyle, *Latter-Day Pamphlets* (London, 1850), 21.
7. John Ruskin, in *Munera Pulveris* (1863), reprinted in *Works*, vol. II (Orpington, Kent, 1872), 130.
8. Arnold, "A Word About America"; Idem., "A Word More About America."
9. Giuseppe Rota (music by Paolo Giorza), *Bianchi e Neri* (Milano: Teatro alla Scala, 1853): New York Public Library (NYPL), Walter Toscanini Collection, Libretti da Ballo, nos. 809 and 939. The ballet was also performed under the titles *La Capanna di Tom* (Bologna) or *I Bianchi e I Negri* (Torino).
10. See Giuseppe Mazzini's "Prière a Dieu pour les planteurs par un exilé," reprinted in Leopoldo Ramanzini, *Una lettera di Garibaldi ad Abramo Lincoln* (Vincenza: Neri Pozza, 1970), 10.
11. *La Fama del 1853. Rassegna di Scienze, Lettere, Arti, Industria e Teatri*, November 14, 1853.
12. G. B. Valebona, *Il Teatro Carlo Felice. Cronistoria di un secolo, 1828–1928* (Genova: Cooperativa Fascista Poligrafici, 1928), 348–57. On the three versions in Naples in 1853, one in local dialect, see Rossi, "Uncle Tom's Cabin and Protestantism in Italy," 418. The fact that many of Italy's smaller theaters did not stage the piece had more to do with the fact that its cast of several hundred participants was too expensive for the smaller houses than with any lack of public interest. Carlo Gatti, *Il Teatro alla Scala nella Storia e nell'arte. Cronologia* (Milano: Ricordi, 1964), 195, 200; Carlo Marinelli Roscioni, ed., *Il Teatro di San Carlo* (Napoli: Guida, 1988), Vol. 2, 361.
13. Note by Walter Toscanini, son of the conductor Arturo Toscanini, in: NYPL, Walter Toscanini Collection, Libretti da Ballo, no. 809.
14. *La capanna dello zio Tomaso o la schiavitù* (4 vols.) (Milano: Borroni e Scotti, 1852); Rossi, "Uncle Tom's Cabin and Protestantism in Italy," 418.
15. For a detailed analysis of press reactions see Jackson, "Uncle Tom's Cabin in Italy" and Rossi, "Uncle Tom's Cabin and Protestantism in Italy," 419. Articles about Beecher Stowe continued to feature in the popular press long after the publication of the novel. See, for instance, *L'Universo Illustrato* 1, no. 23

(March 1867), 303. In Berlin a popular beer garden, established in 1885, was named after *Uncle Tom's Cabin*.
16. John MacKay, "The First Years of Uncle Tom's Cabin in Russia," in *Transatlantic Stowe*, Kohn, Meer, Todd, eds., 67–88, 69.
17. Stowe's other abolitionist and more radical novel, *Dred*, was also dramatized. See Judie Newman, "Staging Black Insurrection: Dred on Stage," in *The Cambridge Companion to Harriet Beecher Stowe*, Weinstein, ed., 113–30.
18. Harry Birdoff, *The World's Greatest Hit: Uncle Tom's Cabin* (New York: Vanni, 1947), 6.
19. Erwin Strittmatter, *Der Laden* (Berlin and Weimar: Aufbau, 1984), 189.
20. Quoted in: Williams, *Playing the Race Card*, 45.
21. Robbins, *The Cambridge Introduction to Harriet Beecher Stowe*, 78–9.
22. Quoted ibid., XX-XXI. On this issue see also Robbins, *The Cambridge Introduction to Harriet Beecher Stowe*, 115.
23. Kohn, Meer and Todd, "Reading Stowe as a Transatlantic Writer," XX.
24. Rydell and Kroes, *Buffalo Bill in Bologna*, 34ff.
25. Clément Caraguel, "Un préface pour *l'Oncle Tom*," *Le Charivari* (January 4, 1853).
26. Ibid. See also *Le Charivari*'s caricature mocking "Tom Manie," which depicts a couple being awakened in the middle of the night by a man showing them the order: "Lisez *Oncle Tom!*" *Le Charivari* (June 21, 1853). Reprinted in Kohn, Meer, and Todd, "Reading Stowe as a Transatlantic Writer," XIX.
27. Emile Montégut, "Le roman abolitionniste en Amérique: Uncle Tom's Cabin de Harriett Beecher Stowe," *Revue des Deux Mondes* (October-December 1852), 161.
28. Jennings, *French Anti-Slavery*.
29. Dumanoir and Adolphe D'Ennery, *La case de l'Oncle Tom. Drame en huite actes* (Paris: Michel Lévy, 1853).
30. Edmond Texier and Léon de Wailly, *L'Oncle Tom. Drame en cinq actes et neuf tableaux* (Paris: Michel Lévy, 1853).
31. "La Semaine Dramatique," *Le Journal des débats politiques et littéraires*, January 24, 1853.
32. Sancton, *America in the Eyes of the French Left*, 29.
33. Surwillo "Representing the Slave Trader."
34. D. F. Sarmiento, *Viajes en Europa, Africa y América* (Buenos Aires: no publisher given, 1854), xxviii.
35. See Frederick, "Harriet Beecher Stowe and the Virtuous Mother."
36. For the Italian translation see *La chiave della capanna dello zio Tomaso contenente I fatti e I documenti originali sopra cui è fonadato il romanzo colle note giustificative* (Milano: Borroni e Scotti, 1853). Here also the translation of Lemoine's commentary.
37. The United States established diplomatic relations with the Kingdom of the Two Sicilies in 1816, with Sardinia in 1840, and with the Papal States in 1848.
38. Quoted in Wyck Brooks, *The Dream of Arcadia*, 129.
39. Wright, *American Novelists in Italy*, 88–9.

40. Paologiovanni Maione and Francesca Seller, "Cristoforo Colombo o sia la scoperta dell'America di Donizetti," *Studi Musicali* 34, no. 2 (2005), 421–49. For on overview of operas on the New World see Polzonetti, *Italian Opera*. Heck, "Toward a Bibliography of Operas on Columbus." Idem., "The Operatic Christopher Columbus."
41. For American themes in ballet see also Raimondo Fidanza's *Colombo, ossia La Scoperta del Nuovo Mondo* (Genoa, 1802): Selma Jeanne Cohen, "Feme di Gelosia! Italian Ballet Librettos, 1766–1865," *Bulletin of the New York Public Library* 67, no. 9 (November 1963), 555–64, 558.
42. In Russia *Uncle Tom* was read exactly in this context, comparing Russian serfdom, abolished by Tsar Alexander II in 1861, with slavery in the United States: John MacKay, "The First Years of Uncle Tom's Cabin in Russia," in *Transatlantic Stowe*, 67–88, 68–9.
43. Croce, *History of Europe in the Nineteenth Century*, 146–7, 152–3.
44. Stewart-Steinberg, *The Pinocchio Effect*, passim.
45. Rossi, "Uncle Tom's Cabin and Protestantism in Italy," 421.
46. *L'Amico di Casa. Almanacco Popolare Illustrato. 1863* (Torino: Stamperia dell'Unione Tipografico-Editrice, 1862).
47. The novel was written during her second visit to Italy in the winter of 1859–60. Vance, *America's Rome*, vol. 2, 22. Wright, *American Novelists in Italy*, 88, 90–103.
48. Trauth, *Italo-American Diplomatic Relations*, XV. It should be noted that the author writes as a Sister of Notre Dame and a student of the Catholic University of America. The book's weakest point is the complete lack of references to Italian historiography or to Italian primary sources.
49. See, for instance, "Il liberalismo e gli Stati Uniti di America," *Civiltà Cattolica* (January 1876), 272–86.
50. Daniele Fiorentino, "La politica estera degli Stati Uniti e l'unità d'Italia," in *Gli Stati Uniti e l'unità d'Italia*, Fiorentino and Sanfilippo, eds., 45–81.
51. Giuseppe Monsagrati, "Gli intellettuali americani e il processo di unificazione italiana," in *Gli Stati Uniti e l'unità d'Italia*, Fiorentino and Sanfilippo, eds., 18. Vance, *America's Rome*, vol. 2, 122ff., 129. See also Buonomo, *Backward Glances* as well as the essays in Martin and Person, eds., *Roman Holidays*.
52. The fact that he writes so very briefly about his period in New York speaks for itself. Giuseppe Garibaldi, *Memorie Autobiografiche* (Firenze: Barbèra, 1888), 264.
53. Freitag, *Friedrich Hecker*, 147.
54. Antonio Caccia, *Europa ed America* (1850). The two protagonists of the novel were surprised how little interest Americans had in their revolution. Franzina, *Dall'Arcadia in America*, 43. On criminalizing Southern Italians in America see also Margavio, "The Reaction of the Press to the Italian-American in New Orleans."
55. Sarti, "La democrazia radicale," 137. On Botta and America see Canfora and Cardinale, eds., *Il Giacobino Pentito*. On Polish images of America see Adam

Krzeminski, "Amerika und Polen," in *Amerika und Europa*, von Thadden and Escudier, eds., 165–71, 167–8.
56. Quoted in Rossi, *The Image of America*, 5, 14. See also Denis Mack Smith, *Italy. A Modern History* (New edition. Ann Arbor: The University of Michigan Press, 1969), 13–14.
57. See in this context also the monarchical-federal pamphlet by Alessandro Luigi Bargani, *Progetto di costituzione dei Regni Uniti d'Italia offerto ai circoli politici e federativi degli Stati italiani da un cittadino degli Stati Uniti d'America*. (Turin, 1848).
58. Rossi, *The Image of America*, 6–7. Sarti, "La democrazia radicale," 139, 147.
59. Buonomo, *Backward Glances*, 18.
60. Rossi, *The Image of America*, 2–3. On the appeal of Cooper to emigrants from Europe also Rolle, *The Immigrant Upraised*, 26, 59.
61. Franzina, *Dall'Arcadia in America*, 76.
62. Giovanni Capellini, *Ricordi di un viaggio scientifico nell'America settentrionale nel 1863* (Bologna: Vitali, 1867), 20–1.
63. *La Nazione*, January 10, 1861. See for similar campaigns Riall, *Garibaldi*, 296.
64. Enrico Dal Lago, "Radicalism and Nationalism: Northern 'Liberators' and Southern Labourers in the USA and Italy, 1830–60," in *The American South and the Italian Mezzogiorno*, Dal Lago and Halpern, eds., 197–214. 197. Sarti, "La democrazia radicale," 145–8. Ramanzini, *Una lettera di Garibaldi*. Also Richards, *Italian American*, 118.
65. Timothy M. Roberts, "The Relevance of Giuseppe Mazzini's Ideas of Insurgency to the American Slavery Crisis of the 1850s," in Bayly and Biagini, eds., *Giuseppe Mazzini and the Globalisation of Democratic Nationalism*, 311–22. In 1872 Lincoln's *esequie ferroviarie* and his embalming became the model for Mazzini's funeral: Luzzatto, *La mummia della repubblica*, 35–6.
66. Rossi, *The Image of America*, 162. Trauth, *Italo-American Diplomatic Relations*, 8–34. See also Belfiglio, "Italians and the American Civil War."
67. See for its ambiguous position "Il concetto morale della schiavitù," in *Civiltà Cattolica*, February 1865, 427–45. Jordan and Pratt, *Europe and the American Civil War*, 194. Later, however, the Papal States fully collaborated with the prosecution of one of the alleged accomplices in Lincoln's assassination. Trauth, *Italo-American Diplomatic Relations*, 36. For a recent study of the problem see Sanfilippo, *L'affermazione del cattolicesimo*, 97 sq.
68. "La Disunione negli Stati Uniti," *Civiltà Cattolica*, February 1861, 312.
69. See "La stampa cattolica in Italia," in *Civiltà Cattolica*, January 1865, 44.
70. "La Disunione negli Stati Uniti," *Civiltà Cattolica*, February 1861, 322.
71. Capellini, *Ricordi di un viaggio scientifico*, 72, 144.
72. *La Nazione*, May 11, 1861 and October 13, 1862.
73. Quoted in Boritt, Neely Jr., Holzer, "The European Image of Abraham Lincoln," 153.
74. "Cronaca Contemporanea," *Civiltà Cattolica*, September 1861, 630.
75. "Cronaca Contemporanea," *Civiltà Cattolica*, October 1861, 249–56.
76. *Monitore di Bologna*, April 28, 1865.

77. *Gazzetta delle Romagne,* March 12, 1865.
78. See, for instance, the review of *Histoire de la guerre civile en Amérique,* par M. le Comte de Paris, *Nuova Antologia,* March 1876, 703–04. This assessment was shared by the Catholic press: "La Disunione negli Stati Uniti," *Civiltà Cattolica,* February 1861, 312–24. For a much more positive evaluation of the United States after the Civil War see Aurelio Saffi, "Lezioni d'oltre l'Atlantico," (1865), in *Ricordi e Scritti di Aurelio Saffi,* Municipio di Forlì, ed. (Firenze: Barbèra, 1902), vol. 3, 213–302.
79. "Rassegna Politica," *Nuova Antologia,* August 1867, 840.
80. Idem. The article partly follows Mazzini's argument that it was for geographical differences that the American federal model was not applicable to Italy. Rossi, *The Image of America,* 10.
81. *Almanacco Repubblicano. 1871,* Enrico Bignami, ed. (Lodi: Società Cooperativo-Tipografica, 1870). "Rassegna Politica," *Nuova Antologia,* January 1866, 200–01. Also "Rassegna Politica," *Nuova Antologia,* June 1868, 433–4.
82. *Civiltà Cattolica,* August 1868, 502. Also *L'Universo Illustrato,* October 1868, 20.
83. "Rassegna Politica," *Nuova Antologia,* December 1866, 846. *Civiltà Cattolica,* August 1868, 498–512.
84. Quoted from the American edition Da Ponte, *Memoirs,* 345. For the Italian edition see Lorenzo Da Ponte, *Memorie di Lorenzo da Ponte da Ceneda in tre volumi scritti da esso* (2nd. ampl. ed.) (New York: Gray and Bunce, 1829–30).
85. Rolle, *The Immigrant Upraised,* 55. Stanislao G. Pugliese, "The Italian American Experience, 1492–1998," in *The Italian American Heritage,* D'Acierno, ed., 691–702, 694–5.
86. Thaller, *Studien zum europäischen Amerikabild,* vol. 1, 22.
87. Rafael Puig y Valls, *Viaje á América* (Barcelona, 1894), 210; Juan Bustamante y Campuzano, *Del Atlántico al Pacífico. Apuntes e impresiones de un viaje a través de los Estados Unidos* (Madrid, 1885), 76–7.
88. Antoine Etex, *Essai d'une revue synthétique sur l'Exposition Universelle de 1855 suivi d'un coup d'oeil jeté sur l'état des beaux-arts aux Etats-Unis* (Paris: Chez l'auteur/Martinet, 1856), 90.
89. Henri Tresca, *Visite à l'Exposition Universelle de Paris de 1855* (Paris: Hachette, 1855), 132.
90. Rosa and May, *Buffalo Bill and his Wild West,* 143.
91. Warren, *Buffalo Bill's America,* 346.
92. Cody Wetmore and Grey, *Buffalo Bill,* 182.
93. Quoted in Warren, *Buffalo Bill's America,* 283–4.
94. Ibid.
95. Ibid., 286–7, 321–2, 286.
96. Ibid., 317.
97. Ibid., 348. Snyder Yost, *Buffalo Bill,* 221–2.
98. Unfortunately, we do not have Cody's own account of the experience. His autobiography ends before the trip to Europe. Cody, *The Life of Buffalo Bill.*

99. On the new cult of the papacy see Papenheim, "Il pontificato di Pio IX e la mobilitazione dei cattolici in Europa."
100. Quoted in: Snyder Yost, *Buffalo Bill*, 224. By the 1880s there were 10 million Catholics in the United States, served by 82 archbishops and bishops. Pollard, *Money and the Rise of the Modern Papacy*, 73.
101. Cody Wetmore and Grey, *Buffalo Bill*, 193–4.
102. Quoted in: Snyder Yost, *Buffalo Bill*, 224.
103. Wilson, *The Puccini Problem*, passim.
104. Sagala, *Buffalo Bill on Stage*.
105. On Karl May's image of America see Berger, *Amerika im XIX. Jahrhundert*, 78ff.
106. These debates date back to the 1840s and included reports in the conservative press: see Thaller, *Studien zum europäischen Amerikabild*, 29, 46, 56. Popular magazines played on the theme of Indians as an aspect of the Wild West. See, for instance, the adventures of Baron Wogan in *L'Universo Illustrato* 1, no. 41 (July 1867).
107. The "Lied von der Königin des Himmels" is sung by the freed settlers and was composed by Karl May himself (included in his *Ernste Klänge* of 1898). We are grateful to Annette Fischer for sharing her expertise.
108. This is not to imply that for Karl May all Native Americans were good. Throughout most of his novels Comanches are represented as bad, mostly as the consequence of corruption through contacts with European traders. France produced very successful "homegrown" Westerns, for example, those by Gustave Aimard, published in the 1850s and 1860s. Villerbu, *La conquête de l'Ouest*, passim.
109. Snyder Yost, *Buffalo Bill*, 231. Cody Wetmore and Grey, *Buffalo Bill*, 199.
110. Warren, *Buffalo Bill's America*, 390–1.
111. John G. Blair correctly uses the term in his "First Steps toward Globalization: Nineteenth-Century Exports of American Entertainment Forms," in *"Here, There and Everywhere,"* Wagnleitner, Tyler May, eds., 17–33. The bombastic Buffalo Bill show of 1906 in Florence was perceived by the local avant-garde as symbolic of the city's cultural decline: Adamson, *Avant-Garde Florence*, 112.
112. Quoted in Pan, *Juan B. Justo y su tiempo*, 57.
113. Juan B. Justo, *En los Estados Unidos. Apuntes escritos en 1895 para un periódico obrero* (Buenos Aires: Imprenta Jacobo Peuser, 1898), 64.
114. For example, Gabriel Deville, "La sociedad sin estado," *La Montaña. Periódico socialista revolucionario* 1, no. 1 (April 1, 1897), 12–16 (facsimile edition, Universidad Nacional de Quilmes, Buenos Aires, 2nd edn. 1998).
115. Rosenberg, *Spreading the American Dream*, 6.
116. *La Habana Elegante*, 11, no. 27 (July 28, 1895), 13.
117. Charles Baudelaire, *Edgar Allan Poe: sa vie et ses ouvrages*, Constantin Tacou and Stéphanie de La Rochefoucauld, eds. (Collection Confidences; Paris: La Herne, 1994).
118. Ibid., 34.
119. Ibid., 34 and 56.

120. Ibid., 12.
121. Goldwin Smith, "The Decline of Party Government," *Macmillan's Magazine*, xxxvi (August 1877), 302.
122. Gumersindo de Azcárate, "Los Estados Unidos," *El Continente Americano* (Madrid, 1894), 35–6.
123. Dall'Osso, *Voglia d'America*, 67 sq.
124. *L'Universo Illustrato*, November 1866, 122ff.
125. "La Pena di Morte," *Gazetta delle Romagne*, March 7, 1865.
126. *La Ilustración Española y Americana*, April 30, 1886, "Crónica general."
127. Bustamante y Campuzano, *Dal Atlantico al Pacifico*, 272. *La Epoca*, January 8, 1873.
128. "Rassegna Politica," *Nuova Antologia*, October 1868, 413–27.
129. "Rassegna Politica," *Nuova Antologia*, October 1866, 421–32, 431.
130. *Giornale di Sicilia*, August 22, 1865.
131. *L'Universo Illustrato*, March 1867, 303.
132. Cesare Lombroso, *Criminal Man* (1876–97) (Durham: Duke University Press, 2006), 90, 128.
133. Otto Weininger, *Sex and Character: An Investigation of Fundamental Principles* (1901/1903) (Bloomington: Indiana University Press, 2005), 273.
134. See, for instance, Gaetano Mosca, *The Ruling Class. Elementi di Scienza Politica* (New York: McGraw-Hill, 1939), 477.
135. G. Boglietti, "Il Presidente Garfield," *Nuova Antologia*, October 1881, 181–207.
136. According to Bologna's *Resto del Carlino*, anarchist circles in the United States had spent months preparing the assassination of the Italian king: *Resto del Carlino*, August 1, 1900. See also Cesare Causa, *Giovanni Passanante condannato a morte per avere attentato alla vita di S.M.Umberto I Re d'Italia* (Firenze: Adriano Salani, 1879). Lombroso argued that crime rates in the United States were particularly high in cities with an elevated rate of Italian and Irish immigration: Lombroso, *Criminal Man*, 317–18. On the connection between Italian and American anarchism see in particular Pernicone, "Luigi Galleani and Italian Anarchist Terrorism in the United States."
137. Errico Malatesta, "Anarchia e Violenza," in *Pensiero e volonta. Scritti*, idem. (1936) (Ginevra: Risveglio, 1975), vol. 3, 108. Idem, "Gli Italiani all'estero," in ibid., vol. 1, 251.
138. *I° de Mayo* (Bahía Blanca), March 18, 1898 (no page nos. given).
139. "Dal Nord America," *L'Avvenire. L'anarchia e l'avvenire dell'umanità* (Buenos Aires), Anno II, no. 15, November 22, 1896, 4.
140. *La libre iniciativa* (Rosario), I, 6, April 10, 1896, 3.
141. Domingo F. Sarmiento, "North and South America," A speech given to the "Rhode Island Historical Society," 1865.
142. Francisco Bilbao, « Iniciativa de la América. Idea de un Congreso Federal de las repúblicas » (1856), in *Obras completas*, Manuel Bilbao, ed. (Buenos Aires: Imprenta de Buenos Aires, 1866), vol. I, 285–304, esp. 289–90.
143. Rubén Darío, "El triunfo de Calibán," in *Escritos inéditos*, E. K. Mapes, ed. (New York: Instituto de las Españas, 1938), 160–2. Darío had been calling

the United States Caliban since the early 1890s: see, for example, "Polilogia Yankee," *La Habana Elegante*, Año 9, no. 31, August 6, 1893, 5–7.
144. La Sorte, *Images of Italian Greenhorn Experience*, 195. Rolle, *The Italian Americans*, 29. Friedman, "Beyond 'voting with the feet,'" 562. On images of America among migrant communities see Franzina, *L'immaginario degli emigrant*, passim.
145. During the first decade of the twentieth century 232, 945 Italians emigrated to the United States: Istituto Centrale di Statistica, *Sommario di Statistiche Storiche dell'Italia, 1861–1975* (Rome: Istituto Centrale di Statistica, 1976), 34–5.
146. Franzia, *Dall'Arcadia in America*, 69.
147. Quoted in Margariti, *America! America!*, 5.
148. Franzina, *L'immaginario degli emigranti*, 30 sq, 81.
149. *Giornale illustrato dei viaggi e delle avventure di terra e di mare* (1891), reprinted in Franzia, *Dall'Arcadia in America*, 94.
150. The strikes of 1877 were a gift for Spanish conservatives, who insisted on the United States being an anti-model. The conservative *La Epoca* wasted little time in declaring, on July 26 and 27, the strikes to be nothing short of social revolution, the United States' "1789" and the beginning of the end of the *república modelo*.
151. Czaja, *Die USA und ihr Aufstieg zur Weltmacht*, 73.
152. Friedman, "Beyond 'Voting with the Feet,'" 558 (figures for the years after 1908).
153. See, for instance, Giovanni Boglietti, "Repubblicani e Democratici negli Stati-Uniti d'America," in *Nuova Antologia*, August 1868, 766–88.
154. Banti, *La nazione del Risorgimento*, passim.

5

A World Apart, a Race Apart?

Maike Thier

The two branches [of Europe], Latin and German, are reproduced in the New World. South America is Latin and Catholic like Southern Europe. North America belongs to a Protestant and Anglo-Saxon population.

Michel Chevalier, Lettres sur l'Amérique du Nord, *1836*[1]

During the course of the twentieth century, the discourse of "Anti-Americanism" became the dominant mode of articulating difference from or even outright opposition to the United States and the "American way of life."[2] The standard French dictionary of the late nineteenth century, however, did not even recognize the term "Anti-Americanism." It offered only "Americanist: partisan of the Americans; someone who loves, who affects their manners, their customs" and "*Américomanie*: affected, ridiculous admiration for everything associated with America."[3] It does not follow, however, that nineteenth-century images of the United States were wholly or mainly positive, either in France or elsewhere. While a handful of individuals might have been infected by *Américomanie*, more often than not the US experiment was examined rather more critically. In general, however, the nineteenth-century discourse on the pros and cons of the American way life relied on a different terminology from the one we are familiar with today. Designations such as "le frère Jonathan," "Uncle Sam," or "el yanqui" were popular colloquialisms. Yet, when it came to explaining American society or identifying its particularities, such labels proved insufficient. More commonly, both Europeans and Latin Americans applied the binary concepts of "Anglo-Saxonism" and "Latinity" to make sense of the "American way of life" and to explain its distinctiveness from their own societies: the United States was imagined in terms of a conception of cultural and historical difference as determined by a society's "racial" properties.

This chapter discusses how these notions of "Anglo-Saxonism" and "Latinity" shaped European and Latin American debates on the United States and, in a second step, also analyzes the construction of distinct national and regional identities vis-à-vis the US "Other." The first intellectual formulations of "Anglo-Saxonness" and "Latinity" were produced in France, as early as the 1830s. These ideas remained central to French debates about identity throughout the nineteenth century and, because of the international prestige of French culture and the imperial ambition of Napoleon III (who sent troops into Mexico during the 1860s), also had ramifications for other European and Latin American countries. Indeed, "Latin America" is the only term from this discourse that is still current (although, as noted below, the reasons for that lie more in the twentieth century than in the nineteenth). This conceptualization of a transatlantic space divided between "Anglo-Saxon" and "Latin" cultures shaped the context from which discourses of Americanism and anti-Americanism emerged. When analyzing European perspectives on the United States in his Adorno Lectures, given in Frankfurt in 2004, the German sociologist Claus Offe explained the meaning and the relevance of such images in a way that is also valid for Latin America:

> America provokes a question that is nonsensical with regard to Africa or Asia. It is the question of whether we will become like them over time, or whether they will become like us, and if neither comes true, how we can explain and evaluate continuing differences. We cannot describe America without describing us as America—be it as more or less similar variants of the "Western" civilisation, be it as the configuration of contrasts. The examination of the American social experiment has always also been an occasion for reflection and self-interpretation of European identity.[4]

In this vein, the construction of "Latin" and "Anglo-Saxon" identities in the analysis of the United States in nineteenth-century Europe and Latin America is just one chapter in the still evolving history of the global fascination with the "American way of life."

A Racial Distinction?

Using "race" as a means of constructing difference was, of course, ubiquitous in the nineteenth century. The "racializing" both of society at the time and of historical developments took many forms: one that became particularly important and that had fateful consequences was biological racism with its resort to pseudoscientific methodologies, for example, in the form of phrenology. Undoubtedly, the legacy of this kind of discourse was to be disastrous: it served to justify the brutal and inhumane practices of European colonialism abroad. Closer to home, it was used to rationalize the stigmatization of minorities such as Jews or immigrants.[5] "Race," however, was not only used as a marker of physical difference, but also became a category to describe and establish cultural difference, less catastrophic in its consequences, yet also problematic. In the French case, Ernest Renan, Hippolyte Taine, and Gustave Le Bon are probably the most prominent representatives of the practice of employing the concept of "race" in analyses of culture and society—past and present.[6] While acknowledging other factors that shape a people's history, namely, "moment" and "milieu," Taine, for example, deemed "race" to be "the first and richest source of [a people's] masterly faculties from which historical events derive."[7] Likewise, there was a tradition of thinking about the history of France itself as one of a racial duality of Franks and Gauls, revived and elaborated in the first half of the century by Augustin Thierry.[8]

The boundaries between "biological" and cultural interpretations of race were rather fluid in practice. The works of Arthur de Gobineau, surely the most infamous French racialist nowadays, are especially revealing about how blurred such the distinctions could be.[9] Obsessed with purity of blood, Gobineau argued that the mixing of races, especially that of "superior" and "inferior" ones, had brought about a decline of civilization.[10] In America, therefore, "Anglo-Saxons, being the last to carry the banner of Aryanism [were] already infected by all the corrosive fruits of modernity. [...] They [were] modern barbarians."[11] Such direct links, however, were rarely made between biology and the idea of "Latin" and "Anglo-Saxon" races. In France, Henri de Ferron did attempt to connect the theory of Latinity and Anglo-Saxonism to his reading of Darwin.[12] Similarly in Italy, the founding father of criminal anthropology, Cesare Lombroso, drew on American examples for his work on "born criminals."[13] Yet these were exceptions. More commonly, the construction of a racial antagonism between "Latin" and "Anglo-Saxon" appeared in subtler forms—without any crude references to pseudoscience, but instead resorting to the idea of innately different civilizations. In Latin America, particularly, religion, rather than race, was often seen as the crucial marker of difference. Hence, one should be aware that in spite of "Latinity" and "Anglo-Saxonism" often being paired with "race," most commonly this was an association free from biological underpinnings but, rather, a way of conceptualizing cultural difference.

Meanings of Anglo-Saxonism and Latinity

In both Europe and Latin America there was widespread agreement that the United States was an "Anglo-Saxon" nation—together with Britain part of the *stripe anglo-sassone,* as an Italian journal put it.[14] In the non-English-speaking countries, feelings about these "two great nations of the Anglo-Saxon race" were ambivalent and, in Europe at least, conflated. In France the fascination with everything "Anglo-Saxon," be it "le style anglais" or "le free trade," became a tradition, which, one might say, extends to the present day. It is an ambiguous attitude characterized by the juxtaposition of attraction and disdain, enthrallment and mockery.[15] More often than not, it has been the English incarnation of "Anglo-Saxonism" that has been the focus of attention. The French poet-politician Alphonse de Lamartine captured this ambivalence perfectly: "One cannot love the English, but it is impossible not to admire them."[16] The historian Jules Michelet, however, was more forthright in declaring England to be the "anti-France."[17] It might be argued that it was exactly this perceived sense of being opposites, intensified by the concrete and long-lasting political rivalry between the two European powers, that underpinned the ambivalent yet always strong allure of the English for the French. In the case of France the obsession with the strictly British facet of Anglo-Saxonism—like the actual relations between the two countries—has a long history. Arguably, it was this engagement with the immediate neighbor *outre-manche* that was to remain a more formative influence than that of the United States throughout the nineteenth century, notwithstanding the very different picture that emerged during the twentieth century, especially after 1945.[18]

Even so, French stereotypes of the English strongly colored French thinking about the Americans. Throughout the nineteenth century, the United States was explained primarily in relation to its *mère-patrie,* thereby implicitly confirming a British vision of a transatlantic Anglo-Saxon community (see below). To all intents and purposes, views on the two Anglophone countries and their inhabitants tended to be conflated in debates on France's role in the world. In this vein Philippe Roger, for example, has claimed that the root cause of Talleyrand's desolation during his years in exile in the United States was that "he discovered the Englishman hiding inside the American."[19] In Spain images of the United States and Britain were similarly conflated—particularly in relation to political values such as liberty and democracy. The early feminist Concepción Arenal routinely referred to "the Anglo-North American woman," while the noted academic Gumersindo de Azcárate spoke of "the Anglo-American state."[20]

In 1851 the French writer Émile Montégut even went so far as to identify a *génie de la race-Anglo-Saxonne*, specifying certain characteristics common to both Americans and Britons.[21] Contrasting them not so much with the Latin race but rather with the Slavic peoples, Montégut showed himself in awe of the Anglo-Saxons, whom he saw as "pioneers of civilisation *par excellence*":[22] "What a race! What a destiny! Its force and the basis of its power make it absolutely necessary in the order of the world!"[23] Anticipating future conflict between the Anglo-Saxon and the Slavic people, Montégut wrote, "On the one side, there is the genius of liberty, on the other, the genius of authority. Without fear of being accused of partiality or blind admiration for foreign peoples, we wanted to describe the character of a race that has always believed in itself, that has always had an invincible faith in the individual."[24] This love of liberty and the individual and the corresponding distrust of authority and centralization made "Anglo-Saxonism" attractive for many Europeans striving for democratization and liberalization in their own societies.

Actively embraced by the Americans themselves,[25] the "Anglo-Saxon" identity of the young republic on the other side of the Atlantic was first explicitly established in Europe, however, by Alexis de Tocqueville and Michel Chevalier in the 1830s—with the former focusing on politics and society, the latter more closely on the economy. Tocqueville was most insistent that in order to understand the American Republic it was crucial to understand its English roots: programmatically, one of his first chapters was entitled "On the origin of the Anglo-Americans and its importance for their future."[26] In it, Tocqueville underlined the centrality of a common language, English, as a bond between these first immigrants.[27] The French liberal Edouard de Laboulaye would pick up on this idea, explaining American liberty as an expression of English liberty, which had been able to flourish on the other side of the Atlantic without the fetters of aristocracy or "gothic forms."[28]

The Saint-Simonian Chevalier, by contrast, was more impressed by the economic development and industrial energy of the United States, which, next to a love for liberty, was the key characteristic commonly associated with the "Anglo-Saxon" peoples. Chevalier made use of the racial paradigm more explicitly than Tocqueville ever did, as the epigraph to this chapter illustrates, but the differences he perceived between Anglo-Saxons and Latins were not limited to religion or language: rather, the divide was reinforced by dramatically different levels of economic and material achievement. For Chevalier, however, these differences did not limit themselves to religion or language; rather, the Latin/Anglo-Saxon-divide was one of dramatically different stages of economic and material achievement.

Chevalier was widely read in Latin America during the 1850s.[29] His work first appeared in Spanish in 1853, when a translation of his introduction to *Lettres sur l'Amérique de Nord* was published in the Madrid-based *Revista Española de Ambos Mundos*, which had been founded by a Uruguayan writer in emulation of the Parisian *Revue des Deux Mondes*.[30] But many Latin American intellectuals of that era read French, regarded French publications as their main source of ideas and spent time in Paris, so the fact that Chevalier's concept of Latinity became current in the 1850s, rather than any earlier, can only be explained by developments far beyond the greater availability of his work at that time. There is, of course, a long history of perceived cultural differences between British America and Spanish or Portuguese America, but it was not until the 1840s that those cultural differences came to be widely perceived as more significant than a shared political commitment to modern republican values. In 1844, for example, the Argentine intellectual Juan Bautista Alberdi, stating his opposition to US involvement in any initiative toward union in the Americas, argued,

> I am one of those who think that only Republics of Spanish origin should participate in the General [American] Congress. I see the elements of their [...] unity less in community of soil than in *the moral terms that form their sociability*. If unity of soil might make us form a common political system, [...] why should Russia be excluded [...], since it possesses three times as much territory in the Americas as Chile? [...] I consider frivolous our pretensions to form a common family with the English republicans of North America. [...] If their political principles are what call us to community, then why not the Swiss [...]? Certainly the North Americans have never refused us celebratory toasts [...], but I do not recall that they have fired one cannon shot in our defence.[31]

At this stage, US sins, for Latin Americans, were mainly ones of omission: failing to live up to the Monroe Doctrine's implicit commitment to defend Spanish American republics from the marauding expeditions of European powers (for example, the British seizure of Las Malvinas—renamed the Falkland Islands—from Argentina in 1833). President James Monroe's famous assertion of 1823 that the United States government would consider any European attempt to establish further colonies in the Americas as "dangerous" to its own "peace and safety" has so long been interpreted, in the light of twentieth-century US interventionism in Latin America, as a threat, that it is often forgotten that for much of the nineteenth century Monroe's statement was perceived by many Latin American leaders as a *promise* to defend republicanism in the New World. Latin American disillusionment with the United States arose initially not because they did intervene, but because they did not.

Attitudes changed markedly, however, in response to the US expansionism of the late 1840s, particularly the Mexican-American War (1846–8), as a result of which Mexico ceded over a third of its territory to the United States, including Upper California (where the Gold Rush began in 1849). Filibustering, too, caused great alarm among Latin American intellectuals and statesmen, who interpreted it as further evidence of US lack of respect for them. President Pierce's recognition of William Walker's "government" in Nicaragua in May 1856 was received in Latin America as confirmation that filibustering was not merely an aberration carried out by lawless individuals but a highly threatening policy supported at the highest levels of US society. During the 1850s, a series of meetings among Spanish American leaders called for unity not *with* the United States, as had been the main emphasis of earlier discourses of *americanismo*, but explicitly *against* it. Images of the United States as hostile, aggressive, and therefore fundamentally "other" began to proliferate during this period, and it was in this context of a shift in Latin American perceptions of the United States from admired model to feared monster that the mutually reinforcing contrast between Anglo-Saxonism and Latinity began to take hold. In most parts of Latin America, however, particularly toward the end of the nineteenth century, there was a tendency to separate out images of England from those of Anglo-America, identifying England as the upholder of all the admirable qualities of Anglo-Saxonness and seeing all the bad bits—"Yankee individualism"—as made in the United States,[32] as if Anglo-Saxonness had somehow been corrupted as it crossed the Atlantic. This distinction between the two Anglo-Saxon powers was particularly apparent in Argentina, where pro-Britishness did not begin to diminish markedly until well into the twentieth century, but it is fair to claim that throughout the region the opposition was expressed not so much as Anglo-Saxon versus Latin as Yankee versus Latin. Moreover, the overriding characteristic of the Yankee was seen as the capacity to prevail and to eclipse other identities. Recalling her visit to San Francisco in the era of the Gold Rush, the Argentine educator Juana Manuela Gorriti noted that even "in that cosmopolitan emporium of nationalities, the Yankee element was always dominant."[33]

In Spain, Italy, and France, as in Latin America, commentators drew contrasts between the Anglo-Saxon civilization, distinguished by its love of liberty and its material progress, and their own societies. This discourse of "Latin decadence" and "Anglo-Saxon progress" was to shape debates about national identity in these countries for much of the nineteenth century.[34] While "decadence" was not necessarily interpreted as something negative, the sweeping comparison of civilizations on both sides of the Atlantic was linked to the more general concerns about decline and degeneration that dominated so much of Europe's cultural and intellectual history in this period.[35] Writing on the origins of the *Action française*, Victor Nguyen pointedly spoke of "decadence" as the *mythe majeur* of the French nineteenth century.[36] Yet while this inferiority complex affected many of the writings on America, it was not always tantamount to defeatism or a sense of doom. Chevalier, for one, thought that there was nothing providential in Anglo-Saxon progress: he argued that the Anglo-Saxon peoples, and in particular the Americans, at this point in time far in advance of the Latin nations, distinguished themselves especially by their efficient organization of labor and their use of new production techniques.[37] Hence he identified not "race" as such but acquirable skills and plain effort as the keys to such success. Not least because Chevalier himself played a key role in its administration, the modernizing impetus of the Second Empire, exemplified in the adoption of a policy of free trade and the staging of the World Exhibitions in Paris, arguably epitomized this desire to emulate the industrial progress of the Anglo-Saxon peoples.[38]

Philarète Chasles, a professor at the *Collège de France*, did much to introduce the French to English literature in the nineteenth century—also to that of "the Americans of the United States, the last-born of the great Anglo-Saxon race."[39] Chasles, too, explained his interest in America as at least partially a result of the apparent contrast between France and the United States. Writing in 1851, he made this explicit in his preface: "I have juxtaposed our moral feebleness, our weakness of action with the energetic life of the United States."[40] His introductory remarks are again exemplary of a more general preoccupation with decline, degeneration and disintegration. "With profound sorrow," Chasles diagnosed his country—"the most beautiful of Europe and its most unfortunate"—to be in a state of decay: suffering from "vices," "intrigue," "envy" and "stagnation," literally "devouring itself." The contrast with America could not have been more starkly evident: "the United States, remarkable and grandiose in so many ways, is essentially modern; her genius is material and mechanical; her force rests in her good sense, in the patience of her observation and her industry." Yet, he adds, somewhat patronizingly, "it is a country without imagination because it does not have any memories."[41] While he was not especially complimentary about the literary achievements of the Americans (for all intents and purposes, his declared subject matter), Chasles' examination of American culture and society more broadly defined is a further example of how the "Anglo-Saxon" United States came to be used as a symbol of the very qualities France was deemed to be missing: a practical spirit, an entrepreneurial drive and a desire for progress and expansion.

Similar opinions were aired in Spain: in its opening editorial, the scientific journal *El Progreso* declared, "we are more poets, they are more practical." This was a judgment that accorded natural spheres of interests and character traits to each race. Yet, while these "separate spheres" of Latin and Anglo-Saxon aptitudes were not necessarily adjudged unequal, it was the Anglo-Saxon race—as *El Progreso* lamented—that was better equipped to face the challenges of the modern world: "We create literary academies, they (create) schools; we paint beautiful pictures, they design crude machines, which carry out beautiful works; we trust that the fertility of the earth will meet our needs, and they trust their intelligence and study the invention of mechanical means to overcome the relative sterility of their territories."[42] The Spanish press in Cuba, seeking to counter the pro-US tendencies of some sectors of political opinion opposed to Spanish rule, published lurid visions of a "war of races" in which "wherever the Anglo-Saxon has prevailed, the Spaniards and their descendants have been despoiled and driven out."[43] Images of the poetical Latins versus the practical Anglo-Saxons became prominent in other parts of Latin America during the 1850s: for example, Chilean Juan Manuel Carrasco Albano characterized the Latin race as "the heart of humanity," while the Germanic race was its "arm"; "the first represents poetry, enthusiasm, abnegation; the latter, material progress, industry, commerce." By then, of course, Latin Americans had already had bitter experience of the likely outcome of the struggle between the "Germanic race [...] in all its vigour" and "the vegetating Latin race"; when predicting which was best placed to dominate the future: "Texas and California answer us eloquently."[44] By the end of the century, as the gap in economic prosperity between the United States and Latin America became ever more glaring, a mutually reinforcing cycle of self-criticism of "Latin" traits and criticism of "Anglo-Saxon" ones had set in, as exemplified in the following passage published in a magazine for the emerging consumer class by a Cuban writer in 1895: "Our noble race lacks practical sense. It lacks, if you will, the vice of the age, that feverish ambition that together with the sweat of the brow brings about marvels. It lacks, if you will, that hard necessity of this century, which has made numbers its emblem and calculation its lever."[45]

Interestingly enough the constant stream of immigrants of very different origins into the United States had little impact on European and Latin American notions of "Anglo-Saxonism" as the defining characteristic of the expanding American nation. To be sure, these changes were acknowledged and at times even interpreted as problematic and dangerous for the future of the United States. An Italian commentator, for example, stated that "on the old island the Anglo-Saxon tribe, isolated and pure, demonstrates more clearly its vigour and its political temperance than in the far away Republic of the United States, where every single day it gets mixed up with new elements."[46] In France, people also pondered the consequences of immigration for the development of American democracy: while New England had retained its original democratic culture, so Edouard Laboulaye argued, the immigrant influence was in the course of transforming the *moeurs* (customs) of the populations of the newer territories to the West of the United States.[47] Émile Montégut even diagnosed the United States to be descending into "semi-barbarism," in which "the Anglo-Saxon character changes and deforms; [...] the English character disappears; an American character, exclusively American, forms itself and manifests itself gradually."[48] Yet, when it came to sweeping comparisons between different cultures, more often not than the Anglo-Saxon roots of the United States were accorded more weight than its later, evolving population mix. In Latin America, it was often precisely the United States's capacity to absorb "all civilization's elements, [...] the Spanish, Dutch and French races" into a greater unity that prompted admiration and rueful comparison with their own countries, where political instability and economic stagnation made it difficult to attract immigrants.[49] There was a widespread consensus among Latin American elites that Anglo-Saxons (a category in which they included the Germans as well as the English) were the most desirable immigrants. However, other, more negative images of Anglo-Saxons taking people in but then refusing to mix with them led to claims that Latin Americans would manage immigration far better than the United States once the obstacles had been overcome: one Brazilian intellectual, for example, argued that in Brazil Anglo-Saxons and Latins would fuse together to give birth to a perfect racial synthesis.[50]

The conception of transnational "civilizations," which was at the basis of the images of "Latinity" and "Anglo-Saxonism," also lends itself to reverse effects: if "race" was a signifier of American "otherness" in both Latin America and on the European mainland, it played exactly the opposite role across the Channel. In Britain, the United States was increasingly seen not as a truly foreign place, but as part of the extended "Anglo-Saxon family"; while the exoticism of America was constantly explored, much of the political power and salience of images of America in mid to late nineteenth-century Britain derived from the assumption of common "kinship." The press sometimes even used the term "the Greater Britain of the United States," taking its inspiration from the best-selling account of his travels around the English-speaking world by Sir Charles Dilke.[51] As the historian James Epstein has put it, America was a "place to be dreamed of, a reference point whose significance for Victorians was that it was an extension of, or a reflection of themselves."[52]

Ultimately, the degree of emphasis placed on the singularity of the Americans was dependent on the political beliefs and aspirations of the observer. While republicans and liberals across Europe and Latin America viewed the United States as a "Model Republic"—albeit not without qualifications—there were many others who remained fiercely opposed to a democratic system of government, or at least to its American incarnation. In France these political fault lines became particularly apparent in the middle decades of the century: after the failure of the Second Republic and the coup d'état of Louis Napoléon in 1851, republicanism in France was yet again on the defensive.[53] For the defeated it was a time of soul searching and retreat, or even exile in many cases; some, like Edouard Laboulaye, liberal publicist and professor at the Collège de France, turned to the United States in their disillusionment with French politics, wanting to learn from the apparent success story of the American democratic system.[54] Laboulaye was utterly convinced that, in spite of their tumultuous history ever since the Revolution, the French were capable of drawing on the American experience and adopting the fundamentals of a stable and lasting democracy. He did not, however, ignore potential differences of character or mentality: in fact, he stressed the peculiarities of the "American race with its love of order and its habits of liberty"—thereby also resorting to a terminology of race.[55] Nevertheless, Laboulaye emphasized the basic transferability of the key to the American success story: not the Constitution per se, but distinct features of American life such as the local organization of militias, education, and government, which Laboulaye thought to be at the heart of the American experience. Much like Tocqueville before him, Laboulaye was impressed by democratic practice in the United States. Hence, intriguingly, the legal scholar was apparently less interested in the constitutional setup than he was in American *moeurs,* which, in his eyes, made possible a vibrant civil society of active and responsible citizens.[56] Likewise, many German 1848ers, especially the "professors of the Paulskirche," turned to America as an example of "democracy in practice." In fact, their knowledge about the American political system as such remained patchy and relatively superficial throughout the nineteenth century.[57]

Laboulaye saw the character of a people as well as its political system as the product of historical experience. In his view, then, certain properties or tendencies were not innate to a people but acquired, and therefore they were malleable and receptive to new influences. While Laboulaye shied away from spelling out the practicalities such a learning process might entail, his belief in the Enlightenment values of the fundamental human faculty for rationality and understanding separates his favorable analysis of the American way of life from the more essentialist view of human nature presented by skeptical voices in the debates on the American example.

In Spain this acknowledgment that "racial" characteristics were not innate found its most eloquent expression in the writings of Rafael María de Labra, the noted politician, academic, and reformer and—in his attitude toward the United States—something of a Spanish Laboulaye. A man of his time in many respects, Labra used "race" as a paradigm through which to understand national differences and historical developments. For him, though, the Latin and Anglo-Saxon races were cultural and contingent constructions. Therefore, the apparent ascendancy of the United States in commercial and technological fields could hardly be ascribed to race. "Such exaggerations," which he regretted, presently enjoyed much influence in "national education," must be countered by "the truth of history, the vigour and force of principles." Progress and liberty "can and does live in all latitudes and in the bosom of all societies"; they were not reserved for one race alone. In order to emulate the modernity, prosperity and political "advances" of the United States, one simply needed "the will to aspire, the will to work, the will to study and to make the most of examples, the will to persevere and to insist until success is achieved."[58] In Latin America, the quality most often singled out as the crucial factor differentiating its history from that of the United States was unity. If only the Spanish American republics could unite in the same way as the 13 colonies had done, it was repeatedly claimed, they would be able to overcome all obstacles. In imperial Brazil, however, where the monarchy was widely seen as a source of unity, the United States was perceived to be the only successful republic in the Americas, an achievement that was customarily attributed to its embrace of Anglo-Saxon institutions. It was only later, when Brazil had itself become a republic, that hostile images of the "Anglo-Saxon" United States acquired greater currency.[59]

In Britain, the pervasive sense that America was fundamentally part of the same community came to the surface most explicitly, as one might expect, at times when American affairs prompted outpourings of sympathy, notably the extraordinarily passionate responses to the assassinations of Lincoln in 1865 and Garfield in 1881.[60] Speaking to a public meeting in Newcastle to express sympathy with the American people after the death of Lincoln, the Rev. J. C. Street echoed countless speeches and newspaper editorials: "It was not an assassination that had taken place in some foreign country," he said, "but it was an assassination in a land kindred to our own, speaking the same language, moved by the same impulses, and animated by the same principles."[61] Even in less heightened moments, though, the discourse of Anglo-Saxonism was central to the imagined relationship between Victorian Britain and America. The very ubiquity of paeans to Anglo-American racial unity, especially from the 1880s onward made it seem almost platitudinous. The language can be heard not just on formal occasions, such as the visit to Britain in 1877 of former President Grant, but also in more apparently spontaneous, if incongruous, encounters. One example occurred when W. E. Gladstone was introduced to "Red Shirt," one of the Indians accompanying Buffalo Bill's Wild West Show to London in 1887, mentioned in the previous chapter. The conversation had to take place through an interpreter since apparently "Red Shirt" spoke no English, yet, after an introductory enquiry about the weather, the Prime Minister's next gambit was to ask the Indian chief if "he thought there was that cordial relationship between the two great sections of the English-speaking race—the people of England and of the United States—that there ought to be between two nations that were so much akin." "Red Shirt," in reply, muttered that he "did not know much about that."[62]

By the end of the nineteenth century, British ideas about Anglo-Saxonism were increasingly connected to pseudoscientific notions of physical difference, but, even then, appeals to the idea of an Anglo-Saxon racial community generally drew heavily on cultural notions of the character of a "people" being the product of a shared history and way of life, ideas that echoed Laboulaye's analysis in France. Liberals and radicals were as likely as conservatives to use the language of Anglo-Saxonism in Victorian Britain; indeed, until the 1880s, perhaps more likely. This was because one of the principal characteristics of the Anglo-Saxon people was imagined to be their commitment to liberal ideas, symbolized, from the 1830s onward, by opposition to slavery. The abolition of slavery in the wake of the American Civil War was, therefore, a critical moment in the evolution of the idea of a transatlantic Anglo Saxon community. The London-based labor newspaper the *Bee-Hive* welcomed the moral as well as the material progress of the United States that the ending of slavery signified, while a speaker at a meeting in Newcastle to mourn the death of Lincoln predicted, to "loud cheers and applause" that "after that Cain-like mark of slavery—that black cloud on the majestic brow of America—shall be obliterated, and some more radiant feature shall take its place... the two great nations of the Anglo-Saxon race will go on together in the race of liberty and prosperity."[63]

In France, interpretations were shaped by very different domestic concerns. Yet, here too, the Civil War provided an occasion for members of the French opposition to align themselves with a struggle that was deemed to transcend national boundaries.[64] Nonetheless, even in this discourse rivalries between "Latins" and "Anglo-Saxons" played a certain role. Laboulaye spent all his energies on pitching the cause of the Union to the French public: to the end of advocating French neutrality, he not only defended the cause of the North as just but also highlighted how much it was in France's own interest to ensure the existence of a strong United States in order to counterbalance the commercial and political power of England: "For the whole of Europe, the unity and independence of America, the only maritime power that can equal England, is the only guarantee of the liberty of the seas and world peace for the whole of Europe."[65]

While tactically also bringing Franco-British rivalry into play, Laboulaye's plea for French neutrality rested on the one common denominator of the very diverse French opposition: in light of the government's not so secret sympathies for the Confederate states, siding with the North had a double significance. Support for American democracy as represented by the North was an affirmation of the very principles it stood for, and thereby also an oblique attack on the then French government, which denied such liberties to its own citizens. While there were distinct divisions between the various advocates of the Union cause in France, party lines between radical republicans and moderate liberals were blurred in the common initiatives to combine transatlantic solidarity and domestic opposition.

Comparing European and Latin American Conceptions of Latinity

It was exactly these moments, when the United States was at the centre of international attention and even domestic politics, which provoked a more adversarial discourse, paving the way for constructions of "Latins" as antagonists of "Anglo-Saxons." It is also at such moments that sharp differences were revealed between European and Latin American perspectives. US claims on Latin America had, as noted above, already provoked opposition in the region itself two decades earlier, with the Mexican-American War. From the 1850s onward, although many positive images of the United States continued to circulate in Latin America, there was a proliferation of negative images that reflected growing fears about US intentions and hostility toward its policies. The emphasis became increasingly weighted toward what separated Latin Americans from the United States rather than what brought them together. One claim, which was to become a staple of Latin American identity discourses in the twentieth century, was that the indigenous peoples of Latin America had been treated far better than those of the United States. For example, a Cuban cartoon from 1877 shows the "system of Spanish colonisation of the Indians of the United States of Mexico" as a beautiful young woman proffering a crucifix to some peaceable Indians, while the image of "Yankee colonisation of the Indians of the United States of America" shows six Indians impaled on a sword, with others dying on the ground around them.[66] In general, the originally benign features of "Uncle Sam" were increasingly depicted as twisted by greed and cruelty. The culmination of this trend was the famous image of the United States as Caliban to Latin America's Ariel, which became so prevalent throughout Latin America during the early twentieth century (see

Chapter 4). Thus Latinity was repackaged as a route to the differentiation of a shared culture in a region that was increasingly impelled toward cultivating common cause against the threat of US interventionism.

In contrast to Latin American experiences, in Europe the idea of "Latinity" was not always or even usually associated with a discourse on the United States.[67] Focusing only on Europe, one could justifiably tell the story of the concept of a "Latin" community without reference to the United States. Certainly, to interpret the notion of "Latinity" as deriving exclusively or even mainly from the examination of the Anglo-American "Other" would be to gloss over many other contacts with more immediate European neighbors that were arguably stronger and informed the construction of national identities more decisively. The French, for example, tended to define themselves against the British or the Germans.[68] For Gustave Flaubert, the French surrender to the Prussians at Sedan in 1870 meant "the end of the Latin world."[69] It is important not to lose sight of these profound and lasting European rivalries. Again the distinctiveness of the nineteenth century from the twentieth century in this regard has to be emphasized. In fact, in France, during the nineteenth century the "American enemy"[70] made a strong appearance only at the specific juncture of the 1860s, when the United States, in its very essence—Protestant and republican—at odds with the French imperial order, posed a concrete threat to French imperial ambitions in Mexico.

The idea of a "Latin" community has its roots in Romantic, and thus largely linguistic, conceptions of the nation. Madame de Staël, for example, divided Europe into three blocs in her famous reflections from exile, *De l'Allemagne* [1813]: Germanic, Slavic and Latin.[71] We have seen how two decades later Michel Chevalier extended this conceptualization to the New World, making use of the racial paradigm by comparing the religious, cultural and linguistic differences of North and South America to those of Northern and Southern Europe. While Chevalier is thus commonly credited with being the inventor of the concept of a "Latin" America and is often referred to as such in the specialist literature, the importance of the antagonism with the "Northern" and "Anglo-Saxon" United States in the creation of this label tends to be ignored.[72] Yet Chevalier was no exception: generally, French images of the United States were shaped by an interest in the dynamics of the New World as a whole and in the contrasts between "North" and "South."

However, while it was certainly stimulated by the triangular relationship between Europe, the United States and the former Iberian colonies, the discourse on "Latinity" and "Anglo-Saxonism" was not wholly dependent upon it. In order to appreciate fully the role of constructions of "Latinity" in images of America, it is important to bear in mind that this concept was also explored in a different context altogether. While our interest in this chapter mainly lies in the role of "Latinity" in discourse on international affairs, it is worth bearing in mind how central such a notion was to become to nascent regionalist and federalist movements in France, for example those originating in the *Midi*, the French South. "The chief proponents of Latinism," among them Frédéric Mistral, were concerned with the promotion of micro-nationalisms in an attempt to break down what was seen as "the overbearingly hegemonic attitude of the modern nation-state."[73] This concern about centralization might be considered an especially French preoccupation, yet these regionalists were keen to establish links with similar movements across Europe, in Catalonia or in the Ukraine, for example, thereby foreshadowing today's emphasis on a "Europe of regions." "Latinity," moreover, was also a way of binding nations together: speaking for the Extreme Left in the Italian parliament after the assassination of the French President Carnot by an Italian anarchist, Felice Cavalotti lamented that the murderer Caserio had wounded the "Latin brotherhood" between France and Italy.[74] In fact, such notions of a *fratellanza latina* proved to be so enduring in Italy that they still influenced the debate on intervention in 1914–15.[75] Similarly, in Spain, Emilio Castelar, the Spanish historian and politician, fresh from Garibaldi's Congress of Peace and Freedom, at which the notion of a "United States of Europe" had been raised, and invigorated by Spain's "glorious" Revolution of 1868, seriously agitated for a "Republican Latin Union," led by Spain, and encompassing France, Italy, and Portugal.[76]

In the mid-to-late nineteenth century, then, there were thus at least two strands to European versions of Latinity: one of more or less sophisticated reflection on culture and language, and one of (proto) activism, which promoted a particular interpretation of "Latinity" and the interests of a defined "Latin" community—be it regional or transnational. The notion of "Latinity" developed in the context of French thinking on the United States arguably incorporates elements of both. The evocations of a community of "Latin" nations in this context, and thus the use of the idea as a political tool, however, are particularly intriguing as evidence of how a supposedly inclusive and merely descriptive concept such as "Latinity" could be instrumentalized for the benefit of nationalist aims. Internationally, the promotion and proclamation of France as the embodiment and leader of *Latinité*, in opposition to both Britain and the United States, was the reflection of renewed assertiveness both political—that of a "Great Power" with certain claims on the international order—and cultural—confidence in one's superiority over other countries. Arguably, Latinity was an expression of the distinctively French idea of a *mission civilisatrice* in the broadest sense. So while Félibrige activists were concerned with strengthening regionalism (not necessarily in antagonism to the national state; more often, in fact, as an integral element of French nationalism), many French invocations of a Latin community vis-à-vis an Anglo-Saxon, or specifically American, one were linked to international designs and visions of French grandeur.

While Alan Pitt has argued that the French preoccupation with the "Anglo-Saxon myth," particularly in its American incarnation, only reached its peak at the end of the century, one can make a good case that in France it was actually the 1860s that were particularly marked by a stylized polarization between the Anglo-Saxon and the Latin races.[77] French views of the United States became more partisan in the context of the American Civil War, but it was mainly due to the intervention of the French themselves in neighboring Mexico—with the intent of installing the Habsburg prince Maximilian as emperor—that events in the Americas took centre stage.[78] The stakes in both conflicts were high and—in spite of French neutrality in the Civil War—interpreted as symbolic of the domestic battle. Apart from two fundamental antagonisms of slavery, or oppression in the wider sense, versus the yearning for liberty and, more relevant in Mexico, of monarchy and republicanism, other questions that came to the fore concerned the role of religion and the future order of the world.

Whilst opposition figures such as Laboulaye lobbied French opinion in support for the North and interpreted the struggle against slavery as a metaphor for their own fight for greater freedom,[79] and while many ordinary Frenchmen were simply exasperated by the material costs of the Mexican adventure,[80] opinion makers close to the government sought to convince the public of the immediate relevance of the events in the Americas. With turgid prose, American "Anglo-Saxonism," supposedly epitomized by the Unionist campaign, was stylized as a threat to French interests. One pamphlet from 1863, for example, calling for an end to French neutrality and support for the Southern States, gave this verdict: "the Anglo-Saxon element has effaced or strives to efface all others [. . .], it is on its way to absorb all the varieties of the white race."[81] Yet even supposedly objective studies such as one on emigration from France expatiated on the Americans' "profound disdain for other races."[82] The Americans were represented as expansionist aggressors, which was an expedient image not only in light of French sentimental attachment to its old territories in the South but also with a view to justifying its own interference in Mexico. While any direct or official partisanship against the Federation was out of the question, there was still scope to express opposition—and a more general unease with the American model. Hence there was a flurry of saber rattling and rhetorical posturing, which centered on the idea of a struggle between the "Latin" and the "Anglo-Saxon" races on a global scale.

By the time of the US Civil War, French fears of the United States already went back several decades. Even after the French had begun to concentrate their imperial efforts in other parts of the world, developments in the Americas were still able to cause them considerable anxiety.[83] The expansion of the United States on the continent was interpreted by French commentators of all political persuasions as a threat to French interests—both concrete and abstract. Even "Americanists" like Laboulaye remarked on "this drive to colonisation, which distinguishes the Anglo-Saxons."[84] With an eye on this "power of the first order," the pro-government newspaper *Le Constitutionnel* not only voiced such fears over American imperialism, but even called for action as early as 1852. In light of the huge territorial expansion of the United States as a result of its victory in the war against Mexico, the paper predicted that Canada would become the next country to be absorbed by the United States, turning the latter not only into the master of the Americas but more generally into a truly powerful international force. At the same time, *Le Constitutionnel* lamented the decline of the Latin races, with France, Italy and Spain having "renounced all outside expansion," "withdraw[ing] into themselves and spend[ing] all their energies on fighting the symptoms of interior dissolution." The paper concluded this slightly hyperbolic analysis with a call for the European governments, and particularly its own, to intervene in order to control this expansion of the Anglo-Saxon race, "which—advancing via the two Indies on the one side and the Pacific Ocean on the other—is about to reunite the two heads of the columns, the English and the American, in the waters and ports of China."[85] Interestingly, "American" and "English" were distinguished, yet seen as a whole: "John Bull" and "le frère Jonathan" were pulling on the same rope. Joined by their common "Anglo-Saxon" heritage, they were represented as conspiring to rule the world—while the "Latin" races were paralyzed and in decay.

Launched in 1857, the aptly entitled *Revue des Races Latines* saw its mission, indeed its very raison d'être, as being to remedy this bleak situation.[86] It took the stylized polarization of a global "racial" struggle to an extreme. While Pascal Ory has made a convincing case against the explanatory power of the concept of "anti-Americanism" by claiming that "hostility was never organised in the sense of motivating the formation of a specific group or association, or the creation of a journal," the *Revue* comes quite close to fulfilling his criteria.[87] It depicted the Americas as the central combat zone of an international struggle between the forces of good and of evil. The *Revue*'s founder and editor, Gustave Hugelmann, justified his publication's singular obsession with denouncing the United States in a grandiloquent editorial: "If Yankeeism triumphs, hell will have won."[88]

The *Revue* epitomizes the mid-nineteenth-century politicization of the idea of a "Latinity" vis-à-vis the perceived threat to French interests coming from the United States; its bias can be explained by the international context elaborated above and by the circumstances of its creation: after his involvement in the revolution of 1848, the founder Hugelmann had spent a number of years in exile in Spain, where he discovered his passion for "Latin" culture. At the same time, the former revolutionary reassessed his political beliefs and priorities: following a secret trip to Paris and a meeting with the Minister of the Interior, Hugelmann was made a French agent with the task of spreading Bonapartist propaganda in Spain. Finally pardoned officially in 1856, he returned to Paris to devote himself to the task of establishing the *Revue des Races Latines*—the new medium for these propaganda activities.[89] It is not surprising that these efforts were supported by substantial subsidies from the French imperial government.[90] In the very first issue, Hugelmann proclaimed the intention of introducing his French readership to the cultural riches of neighboring Spain, the country that had welcomed him "like a brother."[91] While the *Revue* celebrated the Roman tradition in Europe as a whole in the following issues, French civilization was singled out as its "definitive" or most "progressive" expression.[92] With this special role of French culture established, Hugelmann claimed his publication to be the "champion of (all) Latin races and ideas."[93]

Mirroring the transatlantic dimension of Napoléon III's initiatives, the *Revue*'s appraisals of the cultural riches created by Latin peoples did not limit itself to those of Europe. Instead its manifest ambition was to claim also the New World, or at least its Southern half, for "Latinity": to this end, it featured, for example, articles on Mexican literature.[94] In a subsequent issue more than 50 pages were devoted to a long essay on the history of Cuba.[95] Supplementing the many essays on history and culture of South and Central America, the *Revue* offered a regular news roundup from South America, the *Courrier de l'Amérique du Sud*, from its seventh issue onward—as part of which it featured an especially detailed *Courrier du Mexique*.[96] The *Revue* did not trouble to hide its own agenda for Mexico's future. Hugelmann contributed an epilogue to a more than fifty-page long feature on the history of Mexico,[97] in which he made it very clear that the country's stability and progress were dependent on "monarchical organisation" as envisaged by Napoleon III.[98] Yet it was not only in the context of Mexico that monarchism was celebrated: Hugelmann himself waxed lyrically about the Brazilian emperor and composed a poem in honor of his newborn son.[99]

Linked to this special interest in Central and South America—and arguably an integral aspect of it—was a veritable campaign of promoting emigration to the continent.[100] The *Revue* did not limit its activities to mere information and advertisement; in fact, Hugelmann declared the paper's offices to be "an international agency" in the service of facilitating contacts between French business and Spain, Portugal and South America.[101] In this context, albeit with specific reference to the Central American territories, one of the *Revue*'s other writers lamented the fact that France had so far been ignorant of these opportunities—all the more so as "frère Jonathan" and "John Bull," the twin faces of the "race anglo-saxonne," had been keeping an eye on this region for a while already.[102] Interestingly, the *Revue* never offered any analysis of the relationship or the differences between "John Bull" and "le frère Jonathan." It sufficed to underline again and again that both, albeit to differing degrees, belonged to the opponents of the "Latin race."

The policy of promoting French initiatives in South America went hand in hand, then, with open disapproval of US claims in the region. In reference to the latest change of title, which honored also the *races hispano-américaine et brésilienne*, Hugelmann proclaimed, "We declare clearly that we place ourselves on the side of the adversaries of the United States."[103] Why did the *Revue* deem it necessary to "come clean" about its antagonism toward the United States? Hugelmann and his fellow writers felt that the New World had become the most important stage for a global struggle between "Anglo-Saxonism" and "Latinity." Comparing the shape of the Americas to two mirrored pears, another contributor called attention to the fact that Anglo-Saxon North America had already succeeded in wrongly claiming the name "America" exclusively for itself. According to him, this was not merely a question of geographical terminology but had to be taken seriously as a statement of intent.[104] Hence the *Revue*'s battle cry: "Latin races, let us defend ourselves!"[105] In South America, the United States' act of terminological appropriation was seen as closely related to its much-resented ignorance of any other country of the Americas:

> For [someone from the United States], *American* means citizen of North America; he knows no America other than the Union; he takes no account of the rest; the educated disdain them, the ignorant are ignorant about them. They know something of Mexico, because they have steadily been appropriating pieces of the ancient empire of Moctezuma; [...] but of South America [...] oh, how little they know. And what's more, they don't care in the slightest.[106]

In the face of such bellicose rhetoric and the actual involvement in Mexico, the French foreign minister Drouyn de Lhuys thought it necessary to reassure the American representative in Paris, John Bigelow, that such ideas were "rather designed for home than foreign consumption, and (were) rather an assertion of the right of the Latin race to expand, than that the Anglo-Saxon race should not." Indeed, the Emperor's minister further played down Napoléon III's initiative in this matter because "the doctrine of the equilibrium between the Anglo-Saxon and the Latin races in Mexico" had been "first formulated" in the course of an exchange in the French Chambers between François Guizot and and Adolphe Thiers, who were both known to be enemies of the Emperor, in the wake of the annexation of Texas.[107] Rather than a project of imperial vanity, the Mexican intervention, claimed Drouyn de Lhuys, was a long-standing project supported by all Frenchmen. While this particular claim about French policy was not granted much credence, the fundamental motivations for the French involvement in Mexico were well appreciated in Italy. Writing in the wake of the assassination of the Emperor Maximilian and thus when the total failure of the French expedition had become clear, the *Nuova Antologica* reasoned that it had been "in order to stop and contain the expansion of the Anglo-Saxon race, as well as to return to the Latin race some space in the New World, [that] the Emperor of the French got involved in the Mexican enterprise."[108]

The poet and statesman Lamartine, by then a bitter old man, who had made peace with the Emperor he had previously despised, gave his support to the "generous and eminently civilising purpose which has directed Imperial policy" in Mexico. Writing in *La France,* he judged the cultural achievements of the Aztecs to be superior to "the purely utilitarian structures of the Americans of the North." Moreover, Lamartine accused the United States of being motivated only by selfishness: "Their liberty, which is entirely personal, has always in it something hostile to someone else." With a direct reference to one of the key figures of American foreign policy, Lamartine closed his damning verdict: "Such is this people to whom Mr. Monroe, one of its flatterers, said in order to gain its applause: 'the time has come when you must not permit Europe to interfere in the affairs of America, but when you must henceforth assert your preponderance in the affairs of Europe'."[109] Lamartine thus saw the French intervention in Mexico almost as a preemptive strike against American imperialism.

As it transpired, the French intervention in Mexico turned first into travesty, and then into tragedy. With the fall of Napoléon III, the Franco-Prussian War, and the Commune, moreover, there was a dramatic shift in the parameters of domestic debates.[110] Similarly, the Third Republic's imperialist ventures in Africa and Asia refueled a racial discourse of an altogether different kind from the ambiguous love-hate relationship that always characterized the "Latin" perspective on the "Anglo-Saxons." While the framework of the debates changed toward the end of the century, this way of conceptualizing the United States survived. Speaking at the inauguration of the Statue of Liberty in New York in 1886, Ferdinand de Lesseps, the man behind the Panama Canal, for example, confirmed the longevity of French claims on the New World:

> It is a joy for me to talk to you with an open heart and to know that my speech will be received like that of a real friend. Soon, Gentlemen, we will come together to celebrate a new Pacific conquest. We will see each other again in Panama where the pavilion of the thirty-eight stars of North America will flutter next to the banners of the independent states of South America and will form in the new world for the good of humanity the peaceful and fruitful alliance of the Franco-Latin race and the Anglo-Saxon race.[111]

While the rhetoric would become more bellicose again in the commentaries on the Spanish-Cuban-American-War, de Lesseps' proclamation reflects a new ease and contrasts with earlier battle-cries against *le Yankéeisme*. De Lesseps asserted French confidence in the equal aptitude of the "Latins" for "progress" and technical skills: following him and thanks to his own industrial initiative, the French were able to look the Americans in the eye. Furthermore what has shaped the French engagement with the United States so profoundly has found a resolution: while de Lesseps's grand designs for the canal would eventually fail and trigger a domestic political crisis,[112] at this point the Panama Canal project promised to fulfill the French desire for a stake in the affairs of the New World. In light of this particular French obsession, it can be considered an irony of history that, following the bankruptcy of the French *Compagnie du Canal de Panama* in 1888, this venture was completed under American leadership.

The meeting between Thomas Edison and Gustave Eiffel—the world-famous "Anglo-Saxon" inventor and the "Latin" star engineer respectively—by contrast, provided a more lasting symbol of parity between the two peoples' achievements. Crowned by a solemn handshake on top of the Eiffel tower, the showpiece of the World Exhibition of 1889, it was staged as a coming—together of equals—both embodying their nation's genius.[113] Again, however, this is indicative of a development toward a more level-headed, albeit just as serious, perspective on the construction of a rivalry between "Latins" and "Anglo-Saxons": from a preoccupation with American expansion and a debate of principle on the very desirability of "modernity" in France, by the end of the nineteenth century this discourse on "Latinity" and "Anglo-Saxonism" had been transformed into a competition over who was more "modern": the "Latin" French or the "Anglo-Saxon" Americans.[114] Similarly in Spain, *El Progreso* used its inaugural issue to send out a rallying cry to Spaniards to direct their learning and expertise away from the arts and toward science, engineering, and commerce, precisely in order to compete with the United States.[115]

Conclusion

Ideas of "Anglo-Saxonism" and "Latinity" helped to shape nineteenth-century perceptions of the United States in both Europe and Latin America. Exactly because of their vague and malleable nature, "Latinity" and "Anglo-Saxonism" became handy catch-all designations in the quest to make sense of the modern world: both were almost equally, at different times and in different places, shorthand for "progress" and "decadence," "civilization" and "barbarism." As such, they offer a window into the processes and debates surrounding the construction of national identities.

This vagueness, of course, creates a major problem for the historian. One might legitimately question to what extent this antagonistic pairing of contested labels really is a promising path toward an understanding of the meaning of images of America. Quite apart from the complexity of "Latin/Anglo-Saxon" discourse, it is clear that from the European perspective, the United States was still seen as the junior "Anglo-Saxon" power—at the very least until the Spanish-American War at the close of the century—and from a continental point of view, "Anglo-Saxonism" could be found closer to home, just across the channel. The picture looked rather different from the Western hemisphere, but at least in South America the British still loomed large, and Cubans were unusual in their tendency to see the United States as the ideal model of self-government and the epitome of modernity. It should also be borne in mind that there existed a genuine fascination and interest in the American Republic that went beyond such stereotypes and found expression in much more sophisticated and nuanced forms. An analysis of constructions of "Latinity" and "Anglo-Saxonism" in representations of the United States is thus certainly just one among many conceivable angles on the topic.

Even so, notwithstanding all these reservations and problems, the usage of "Latin" and "Anglo-Saxon" as categories of description is a meaningful indicator of "ways of seeing" European and Latin American selves in relation to the US other. It is precisely the limitations of this conceptual pairing that make it so attractive: due to the implicit polarization between the two "races" expressed by these signifiers, they lead us to the fundamental issue at stake in the debates on America—that of evaluation. Categories such as "anti-Americanism" or "Americanism" are certainly problematic and—especially if one loses sight of the process and context of the creation of such attitudes—somewhat inadequate. Yet in the end it is this question of evaluation that determines the relevance of these images and their interest to the historian as a source. The United States was rarely looked at disinterestedly: as a symbol of democracy and modernity, its representations were never value free. Irrespective of the particular contexts of their creation and reception, images of the United States always reflected contemporary attitudes regarding the desirability of the "idea of America." It is from this perspective that the question of being "Latin" or "Anglo-Saxon" must be analyzed.

Notes

Some ideas feeding into this chapter have been discussed in Thier, "The View from Paris"

1. Michel Chevalier, *Lettres sur l'Amérique du Nord* (Paris: Ch. Gosselin, 1836). I.x.
2. For references, see Note 11 of the Introduction.
3. Pierre Larousse, *Grand Dictionnaire Universel du XIXe siècle,* 17 vols. (Paris: Larousse, 1866–76).
4. Offe, *Selbstbetrachtungen aus der Ferne,* 10.
5. On this topic more generally see Liauzu, *La société française face au racisme.*
6. On all three see Todorov, *Nous et les Autres;* and his "'Race', Writing and Culture."
7. Hippolyte Taine, *Histoire de la littérature anglaise* (Paris: Hachette, 1863), vol. 1, xxv.
8. On this theme see especially: Nicolet, *La Fabrique d'une nation,* 107–138; also, Martin Thom, "Tribes within Nations: The Ancient Germans and the History of Modern France," in *Nation and Narration,* ed. Homi K. Bhahba, 23–43.
9. Arthur de Gobineau, *Essai sur l'inégalité des races humaines,* 4 vols. (Paris: Firmin Didot Frères, 1853–55).
10. It is interesting to note that Gobineau's old friend, Alexis de Tocqueville, was among the harshest critics of this work: Brogan, *Alexis de Tocqueville,* 545–546.
11. Ceaser, *Reconstructing America,* 87–105, esp. 102.
12. Henri de Ferron, *Théorie du progress* (Rennes: A. Leroy, 1867), discussed in Swart, *The Sense of Decadence in Nineteenth-Century France,* 96–97.
13. Cesare Lombroso, *Criminal Man,* first published 1876–1897, trans. and ed. Mary Gibson and Nicole Hahn Rafter (Durham: Duke University Press, 2006). Cesare Lombroso and Guglielmo Ferrero, *Criminal Woman, the Prostitute and Normal Woman,* first published 1893, trans. and ed. Mary Gibson and Nicole Hahn Rafter (Durham: Duke University Press, 2004).
14. "Rassegna Politica," *Nuova Antologia,* Vol. VIII, May 5, 1868, 197–212, 207.
15. See, for example, Tombs and Tombs, *That Sweet Enemy;* Crouzet, *Britain Ascendant;* and Jennings, "Conceptions of England and its Constitution."
16. Crouzet, "Problèmes de la communication franco-britannique," 119.

17. Pitt, "A Changing Anglo-Saxon Myth," 153.
18. Different not only in the sense that the United States became more important, but also socially: what was an essentially elitist discourse on political models and ideals in the nineteenth century has arguably been overshadowed by the centrality of American products in modern consumer culture in the twentieth century. Kuisel, *Seducing the French*. For overviews of research see: "Special Issue: Beyond 'Americanization'—Rethinking Anglo-American Cultural Exchange between the Wars," *Social and Cultural History* 4, no. 4 (2007) and "Special Issue: Americanization in Europe in the Twentieth Century," *European Review of History/Revue Européenne d'histoire* 15, no. 4 (2008).
19. Roger, *L'ennemi américain*, 69.
20. Concepcíon Arenal, *La Mujer del Porvenir. La Mujer de la Casa* (Barcelona: Ediciones Orbis, 1889); Gumersindo de Azcárate, *El poder del jefe del estado en Francia, Inglaterra y los Estados-Unidos* (Madrid: Establecimiento Tipográfico de J. C. Conde, 1878), 101.
21. Émile Montégut, "Du génie de la race anglo-saxonne et de ses déstinées," *Revue des deux mondes*, July-September 1851, 1027–1045.
22. Ibid., 1035.
23. Ibid., 1029.
24. Ibid., 1045.
25. See Horsman, *Race and Manifest Destiny*.
26. Tocqueville, *De la démocratie en Amérique*, vol. I, 69.
27. Ibid., 71.
28. Laboulaye, *Histoire des Etats-Unis*, vii.
29. On the influence of this idea in Latin America see: Ardao, *Génesis de la idea y el nombre de América Latina*; Frank Ibold, "Die Erfindung Lateinamerikas: Die Idee der Latinité im Frankreich des Neunzehnten Jahrhunderts und ihre Auswirkungen auf die Eigenwahrnehmung des Südlichen Amerika," in *Transatlantische Perzeptionen*, ed. König and Rinke, 77–98.
30. Ardao, *Génesis*, 67.
31. Juan Bautista Alberdi, "Memoria sobre la conveniencia i objetos de un congreso jeneral americano," in his *La unidad de América Latina*, 37–63, esp. 59–60 (our emphasis).
32. Francisco Bilbao, "Iniciativa de la América. Idea de un Congreso Federal de las repúblicas," in his *Obras completas*, vol. I, 285–304, 286.
33. Juana Manuela Gorriti, "Un viaje al país del oro," in her *Panamoras de la vida* (Buenos Aires: Imprenta y Librerías de Mayo, 2 vols., 1876), vol. II, 149–249.
34. See especially: Swart, *The Sense of Decadence in Nineteenth-Century France*. The influence of this discourse on notions of health and masculinity and particularly in the development of a culture of sport in France is discussed in: Pierre Guillaume, "L'hygiène et le corps," in *Histoire des Droites en France. Volume 3: Sensibilités*, ed. Jean-François Sirinelli (Paris: Gallimard, 1992), 509–577.
35. See, for example, Max Nordau, *Degeneration* (New York: D. Appleton, 1897).
36. Nguyen, *Aux origines de l'Action française*, 33.

37. Chevalier, *Lettres sur l'Amérique du Nord*, xiv.
38. Furet, *La Révolution Française.*, vol. 2, 347; Plessis, *The Rise and Fall*, 58ff. On Chevalier's life and career see Walch, *Michel Chevalier*.
39. Philarète Chasles, *Etudes sur la littérature et les moeurs des Anglo-Américains au XIXe siècle* (Paris: Amyot, 1851), 1.
40. Ibid., iv.
41. Ibid., 9.
42. *El Progreso*, Vol. 1, No. 1, January 1884, 1.
43. J. S. Thrasher, "Preliminary Essay," in Alexander Humboldt, *The Island of Cuba*, trans. J. S. Thrasher (New York: Derby and Jackson, 1856), 13–95, 42.
44. Juan Manuel Carrasco Albano, "Report presented before the Faculty of Laws of the University of Chile . . . on the Necessity and Aims of a South American Congress," Santiago, March 1855, in Burr and Hussey, *Documents on Inter-American Cooperation*, vol. I, 110–16, quotation at 110–11.
45. N. Bolet Peraza, "La 'influencia' americana," *La Habana Elegante* [Havana], September 1, 1895, 8.
46. "Rassegna Politica," *Nuova Antologica*, Vol. VIII, June 6, 1868, 421–440, 432.
47. Laboulaye, *Histoire des États-Unis*, 315–317.
48. Montégut, "Du génie," 1041.
49. Carrasco Albano, "Report," 111.
50. Nicolau Joaquim Moreira, *Relatório sobre a Imigração nos Estados Unidos da América* (Rio de Janeiro, 1877).
51. *Reynolds's Newspaper*, September 11, 1887; Charles Dilke, *Greater Britain* (London: Macmillan, 1868). Duncan Bell has explored this theme at length in his *The Idea of Greater Britain*.
52. James Epstein, "'America' in the Victorian Cultural Imagination," in Leventhal and Quinault, eds., *Anglo-American Attitudes*, 107–123.
53. Furet, *La Révolution Française*, vol. 2, 335–340.
54. Gray, *Interpreting American Democracy in France*.
55. Laboulaye, *Histoire des États-Unis*, 17.
56. In a sly reference to Laboulaye's very vocal obsession with this aspect of the American system, Gustave Flaubert closed his entry on "Amérique" with the following lines: "L'exalter quand même, surtout on n'y a pas été. Faire une tirade sur le self-gouvernement." Gustave Flaubert, *Dictionnaire des idées reçues* (Paris: Aubier, 1978), 21.
57. Lerg, *Amerika als Argument*, passim.
58. Rafael María de Labra, *La República de los Estados Unidos de América* (Madrid: Tipografía de Alfredo Alonso, 1897), 354–355.
59. See the influential essay by Eduardo Prado, *A Ilusão Americana* (Paris: Armand Colin, 2nd edn., 1895).
60. On the British response to the assassination of Garfield see Sewell, "All the English-Speaking Race is in Mourning."
61. *Newcastle Daily Chronicle*, May 5, 1865.
62. *Times*, April 27, 1887.
63. *Bee-Hive*, July 8, 1876; *Newcastle Weekly Chronicle*, May 5, 1865.

64. Gavronsky, *The French Liberal Opposition and the American Civil War.*
65. Laboulaye, *Les États-Unis et la France,* 5.
66. *La Sombra* (Havana), III, no. 45, August 6, 1877, 356.
67. Surprisingly little work has been done on the concept of "Latinity" and its uses in European political discourses. A notable exception and a good introduction is: Panick, *La Race Latine.*
68. For a general introduction see Jacques Portes, "L'épreuve de l'étranger," in *Histoire des Droites en France. Volume 3: Sensibilités,* ed. Jean-François Sirinelli (Paris: Gallimard, 1992), 165–201; also Digeon, *La crise allemande de la pensée française* and Zeldin, *A History of French Passions,* vol. 2, esp. 86–138.
69. "Nous assistons à la fin du monde latin," Gustave Flaubert, *Correspondance,* 4 vols. (Paris, 1884–92), Vol. VI, quoted in: Swart, *The Sense of Decadence in Nineteenth-Century France,* 123. Swart discusses such interpretations of *"l'année terrible"* at length, see, 123–138. See also Schivelbusch, *Die Kultur der Niederlage,* 125–220.
70. Roger, *L'ennemi américain.*
71. Madame (Anne-Louise Germaine) de Staël, *De l'Allemagne* (Paris: Flammarion, 1968), 45.
72. An exception is Ibold, "Die Erfindung Lateinamerikas."
73. Clark and Wright, "Regionalism and the State in France and in Prussia," 280. See also Wright, *The Regionalist Movement in France;* Thiesse, *Ecrire la France;* and Gildea, *The Past in French History,* 166–213.
74. Della Peruta, "Il mito del Risorgimento e l'estrema sinistra," 5.
75. Mario Isenghi, "La grande Guerra," in *I luoghi della memoria. Strutture ed eventi,* ed. idem, 273–309, 279.
76. Hennessy, *The Federal Republic in Spain.* See also "El Pacto de los pueblos latinos," *La Igualdad,* 15 August and September 29, 1870.
77. Pitt, "A Changing Anglo-Saxon Myth," 154. Admittedly, Pitt is rather more concerned with the positive interpretation of the "Anglo-Saxon" model by establishment liberal elites than with the use of "Anglo-Saxon" in more heated political discourse.
78. Cunningham, *Mexico and the Foreign Policy of Napoleon III.* On the expedition itself: Edison, "Conquest Unrequited." On the more general background see: Nichols Barker, *The French Experience in Mexico.*
79. Gavronsky, *The French Liberal Opposition and the American Civil War.*
80. Case, ed., *French Opinion on the United States and Mexico,* esp. 309–435.
81. Alfred Mercier, *Du Panlatinisme* (Paris: 1863), 9–10.
82. A. Legoyt, *L'émigration européenne: son importance, ses causes, ses effets* (Paris: Guillaumin, 1861),123.
83. For a general survey on French imperialism see Aldrich, *Greater France.*
84. Jean-Frédéric Astié, *Histoire de la République des États-Unis depuis l'établissement des premières colonies jusqu'à L'élection du Président Lincoln (1620–1860), Précédée d'une préface par M. Ed. Laboulaye, de l'Institut,* 2 vols. (Paris: Grasset, 1865), x.

85. *Le Constitutionnel,* June 5, 1852.
86. Founded as the *Revue Espagnole et Portugaise* at the beginning of 1857, it changed its name to *Revue Espagnole, Portugaise, Brésilienne et Hispano-Américaine* in June of that year and finally to *Revue des Races Latines (Française, Espagnole, Italienne, Portugaise, Belge, Autrichienne, Brésilienne et Hispano-Américaine)* with the May-Issue in 1858. Irrespective of these changes of title, I will henceforth only refer to *Revue des Races Latines (RDRL).* At its high-point in the early 1860s, it had up to 3,000 subscriptions.
87. Pascal Ory, "From Baudelaire to Duhamel: An Unlikely Antipathy," in *The Rise and Fall of Anti-Americanism,* ed. Lacorne, Rupnik, Toinet, 42–54, 42.
88. Gustave Hugelman, "A nos lecteurs," *Revue des Races Latines,* Vol. 3, No. 9, June 1857, 8.
89. On Hugelmann's colorful life and career see Emile Témime, "Un journaliste d'affaires: Gabriel Hugelmann, propagandiste au service de Napoléon III et homme de confiance de Thiers," *Revue d'Histoire Moderne et Contemporaine* 18, no. 4 (1971).
90. The two historians, Käthe Panick and Emile Témime, who have studied the *Revue,* both make this claim: Panick, *La Race Latine,* 176, referring back to Témime, who is quite adamant in stressing Hugelmann's position as a agent and propagandist (Témime, "Un journaliste d'affaires," 617). I have been unable to verify this information from archival sources but, judging from the gist of most articles contained in the *Revue,* there is no reason to question it.
91. Gabriel Hugelmann, "*Introduction,*" *RDRL,* Vol. 1, No.1, February 1857, 5.
92. Hugelmann, "*Discours sur l'histoire,*" *RDRL,* Vol. 1, No. 1, February 1857, 44.
93. Hugelmann, "*Nos intentions,*" *RDRL,* Vol. 8, No. 23, May 1858, 5.
94. *RDRL,* Vol. 2, No. 8, June 1857, 668–677.
95. Altève Aumont, *Histoire de l'Ile du Cuba, RDRL,* Vol. 7, No. 21, March 1858, 29–80.
96. Aumont, *Histoire de l'Ile du Cuba,* 491–495, 496–503.
97. Eugène Muller, "Histoire du Mexique," *RDRL,* Vol. 8, No. 23, May 1858, 56–118.
98. Muller, "Histoire du Mexique," 116.
99. Hugelmann, "*A son excellence, le Général Prim, comte de Reus,*" *RDRL,* Vol. 6, No. 20, February 1858, 444–446.
100. Introducing a feature on the agreements between the Brazilian government and a Société centrale de colonisation, Hugelmann praised the advantages of emigration to Brazil. "A son excellence," 293.
101. Hugelmann, "*A nos abonnés,*" *RDRL,* Vol. 5, November 1857, 2.
102. Théodore Casaubon, "*Amérique centrale,*" *RDRL,* Vol. 4, No. 15, September 1857, 439.
103. Hugelmann, "Avis Important," *RDRL,* Vol. 2, No. 6, May 1857, p.181.
104. A. Hernández, "*Courrier de l'Amérique du Sud,*" *RDRL,* Vol. 7, No. 21, March 1858, 247.
105. Hugelmann, "*Nos intentions,*" 16–17.

106. Eduarda Mansilla, *Recuerdos de viaje* [1882] (Buenos Aires: Ediciones El Viso, 1996), 80.
107. *Bigelow to Seward,* November 30, 1865, *Consular Correspondence and Papers,* Vol. 12, John Bigelow Papers (Mss, Col. 301), Archives and Manuscripts Division, New York Public Library (henceforth, "JBP")
108. "Rassegna Politica," *Nuova Antologica,* Vol. II, No. 8, August 1867, 840.
109. Quoted in *Bigelow to Seward,* November 21, 1865, JBP.
110. Schivelbusch, *Die Kultur der Niederlage,* 125–220; Swart, *The Sense of Decadence in Nineteenth-Century France,* 123–138.
111. *Journal des Débats,* October 30, 1886 (*Petit Journal,* 31 October 1886).
112. Agulhon, *The French Republic,* 51–2; Matsuda, *Empire of Love,* 57.
113. Trocmé, "Les Etats-Unis et l'Exposition Universelle de 1889," 293.
114. Agulhon suggests that it was actually in these early years of the Third Republic that France and the United States were closest in spirit—with the French government's entrepreneurial and expansionist initiatives mirroring "American" ideas of progress, individualism, and imperialism. Agulhon, *The French Republic,* 46.
115. *El Progreso,* Vol. 1, No. 1, January 1884, 1.

6

Slavery and Abolition

Natalia Bas, Kate Ferris, and Nicola Miller

Advance, Lincoln, advance, you are our deliverance.
Song heard on Cuban plantations during the US Civil War[1]

Abraham Lincoln has been widely hailed as "immortal," but historians have only recently charted how sharply the reasons for his attributed status in eternity varied in different places and at different times.[2] This was the case worldwide, but it was particularly so in those societies where slavery persisted after 1865. For many people in the Empire of Brazil, the colony of Cuba, and the imperial monarchy of Spain, Lincoln had nobly fulfilled the founding ideals of the US Republic, purging its "great stain" and restoring its claim to be the model of all human emancipation. For others, he was a dangerous idealist whose irresponsibility had caused untold and unnecessary bloodshed—an enduring example of precisely how *not* to pursue the path to progress. In these three slave-holding societies, unlike in those places where abolition was not an immediate issue, the meaning of Lincoln's image was shaped by the overshadowing questions of how and when to bring slavery to an end. While virtually everyone agreed that Lincoln and the US Civil War had made abolition elsewhere inevitable at some point, beyond that there was very little consensus about what else the US experience implied for other countries.

In Brazil, where slavery lasted the longest, its demise was a long drawn out process that became bound up with the politics of the transition from empire to republic. An abolition law was finally passed in 1888, followed in the next year by the overthrow of the monarchy and the founding of the Republic of the United States of Brazil, which adopted a Constitution drawing substantially on the US version. The Brazilian abolitionist movement had two main phases: the first in the 1860s, when it was almost exclusively an elite debate; the second in the 1880s, when it developed a popular base. In both phases, images of emancipation in the US underpinned the arguments of both sides to a far greater extent than has hitherto been recognized in a historiography dominated by discussion of the British presence.[3] In Cuba, slavery lasted almost as long as in Brazil, and it is harder to pinpoint the actual moment of its demise: the Spanish parliament passed an Abolition Law in 1880, but slavery was not finally ended until 1886, when a royal decree released former slaves from the eight-year period of *patronato* (indentured labor) mandated by the 1880 legislation. The US Civil War not only affected debates on slavery and abolition in Cuba, but also—unlike any other country apart from Mexico—in itself decisively shaped the country's political dynamic, most obviously by removing the possibility of Cuba being annexed to the United States to create a common sugar economy based on slave labor. US experiences were exhaustively mined by all parties to the debates in Cuba, particularly during the three years between the ending of the US Civil War and the beginning of Cuba's first war of independence, known as the Ten Years' War (1868–78). There is no shortage of valuable works illustrating the significance of the United States in Cuban history, but what this chapter hopes to add is an illustration of just how varied were the Cuban interpretations and appropriations of US ideas and practices, even—or perhaps especially—in such a crucial matter as abolition, thereby displaying the extent to which Cuban images of the United States were shaped and colored by their own experiences and concerns.

In Spain, too, this was a turbulent time politically: within days of the onset of the Ten Years' War in October 1868, a group of Spanish liberals, under the "sword" of General Prim, came to power in what became known as the "glorious" revolution. Their efforts to introduce a more modern political system, based on universal male suffrage, "inalienable rights"—a term borrowed directly from the United States—and freedom of the press, inevitably prompted questions about how all these estimable reforms could be reconciled with the continuing practice of slavery in the Antilles. Indeed, it was partly in response to such pressures that immediate abolition was decreed in 1873 for Puerto Rico, where slaves were only about 10 percent of the population, compared with over 25 percent in Cuba. The continuing colonial war in Cuba, however, which was Spain's most highly prized and profitable colony, complicated the liberals' attempts to bring about abolition there. Some saw the ending of slavery as a prerequisite to ending the war; others insisted that abolition could not be contemplated until the insurrection had been defeated. Ultimately, abolition was left unfulfilled by radical liberals as their experiment in modern democracy and republicanism imploded amid infighting, indecision, and internal civil conflict,[4] and it was under the restored Bourbon monarchy that the Spanish government eventually abolished slavery in Cuba.[5] Throughout the debates, all parties looked to the United States, its experience of abolition and its expectations of Cuba, when formulating their arguments and policies. The abolition of slavery undoubtedly had an impact upon images of the United States throughout Europe and Latin America, as has already been indicated in chapters 1 and 4. However, this chapter will focus upon those countries in which the institution of slavery was part of their own social structures: Spain, Cuba, and Brazil. The strategic manipulation of US images to suit specifically local purposes can perhaps be seen more starkly in relation to abolition than to any of our other themes. It therefore acts as a test case of how a set of specific US events affected the creation of images of the United States in other societies.

Spain

It had been clear even before the revolution of 1868 that abolition in the United States would have important repercussions for colonial Spain. After the Gettysburg Address (November 19, 1863), in which Lincoln affirmed the principles of equality, freedom, and democracy as values fundamental to the US nation, Spanish diplomats in Washington came to the conclusion that a victory for the Confederate South, which it was thought would have provided slave-holding Spanish Cuba and Puerto Rico with a political and moral ballast against international abolitionist pressure, was no longer realistic. Not only had the demise of slavery in the whole of the Americas become a question of when, rather than if, but Spanish officials feared that a victorious Union might seek to claim the moral high ground of abolitionism as a pretext for intervention in Cuba. At that stage, slave traders were still welcome in Cuban ports, although they had been barred from Puerto Rico in the 1840s and from Brazil in 1850. It was in this context that the Spanish minister in Washington, Gabriel Tassara, advised his government in July 1865 that it might be prudent to plan for the abolition of slavery in the Spanish Antilles, if only as a means of preempting greater US interference there.[6] In 1867, a Spanish Reform Commission recommended a series of liberalizing measures, including the ending of the slave trade and a plan for gradual abolition; the Spanish government's decision to ignore these recommendations precipitated both the liberal revolution in Spain and the war of independence in Cuba.

After the September revolution the question of abolition became one of the most debated topics not only in the Cortes (Spanish parliament) but also in the lecture halls, conferences, *tertulias* (literary soirées), and journals of the capital. The voices of abolitionists tended to prevail;[7] indeed, the prospects for the abolition of slavery in the Spanish Antilles seemed auspicious, given that many prominent figures supported it, including the first two ministers responsible for the colonies. Yet, although the second of these ministers, Segismundo Moret, oversaw immediate abolition in Puerto Rico, in 1873, his policy toward Cuba was more cautious. The Moret Law of 1870, freeing only certain categories of slave, set in train the gradual process of ending slavery in Cuba that was not fully completed until 1886. In the ensuing dismay about the failure to match reform at home with reform overseas, US examples came to the fore in the arguments of both the defenders of a gradual approach and the supporters of outright abolition.

Moret himself justified his law on the basis of the US experience. His moderation was informed by a desire, he told the Spanish parliament, to "prevent great evils such as the terrible war that cost the United States so much." After all, he added, even "the great Lincoln did not want to abolish slavery till 1900."[8] The path to abolition in the United States served as a lesson of precisely how *not* to move from slave labor to free labor for those Spaniards, many of whom also counted themselves as liberals, who argued, if not against abolition entirely, then certainly against a rapid decreeing of immediate abolition without compensation for slave holders.

The fears that abolition and war (race or civil war) were irrevocably linked were widely held.[9] Events in Haiti, which became the world's first "black republic" in 1804 after a successful slave-led revolution, during which white slave owners were violently murdered, were repeatedly invoked by Spanish colonialists—as by slave owners elsewhere—to warn against the danger of "race war," which was perceived to lie in all areas with a sizeable or majority black enslaved population.[10] In the US case, they argued, the decision to declare immediate abolition could not be separated out from the context of the Civil War, nor could such a policy be enacted without sparking or exacerbating a similarly fratricidal conflict in Spanish Cuba. The conservative Spanish daily *La Epoca*, habitually unstinting in both its criticism of proposals for abolition in the Spanish Antilles and its hostility to the "great Republic" across the Atlantic, published a front-page article pleading against the extension of the recently decreed abolition of slavery in Puerto Rico to Cuba.[11] Claiming to speak for "the Spanish nation," the author claimed that immediate and unconditional abolition would lead Spain away from its rightful position as "the august representative of European civilisation in America" and inexorably toward "ruin, inevitable infallible ruin" in the form of "the absorption of the American continent by the followers of Monroe." Colonial reform could only come, it was argued, after peace had been restored in Cuba. The clinching evidence for this argument was the negative experience offered by the recent history of the United States of America, which showed that immediate abolition would bring only economic, social, and political ruin.

For those who were in favor of outright abolition, such as the economist Gabriel Rodríguez, the US experience had proved the validity of Lincoln's "famous maxim" from the "House divided" speech of 1858: "a people cannot be half free and half slave [sic]," a "fundamental principle of the political order" that Spanish liberals, he argued in 1873, had ignored for too long.[12] In his concluding remarks to the Abolitionist Society conference the previous year, Rodríguez spelled out for his audience the two clear lessons that he thought could be drawn from the North American experience:

> First, certain social injustices cannot be tolerated. In certain cases, compromises and tolerance can avoid certain costs for a generation but the egoism of this increases the harm that will then weigh on the following generations. The second lesson tells us that immediate and radical abolition, besides being the only kind possible is the one that causes the least disruptions and losses. Laws of gradual abolition are either not fulfilled or, when they are fulfilled, give rise to violent conflicts, which said laws pretend to avoid.[13]

The first lesson was one that Rodríguez insisted was being played out there and then in the Ten Years' War, which he saw as "caused by our tolerance of slavery, sustained by our weakness with regard to slave owners and that will endure, in one form or another, until slavery disappears."[14]

The US Civil War did pose some problems, however, for radical Spanish abolitionists, who proposed the United States as a model that Spain would do well to emulate. How could the US experience of abolition be presented as an inspiration when it was so bound up with such a bloody, fratricidal conflict? Some of them dealt with the difficulty by presenting the war in polarized and simplistic terms as a crusade of the morally righteous North against a corrupt and cruel South, carried out with the express and sole purpose of bringing an end to the practice of slavery, with victory for the progressive Unionists always assured.[15] Others adopted the prevalent postwar US interpretation of the conflict as the ultimate test of US ideals and institutions, a necessary purging of its unmodernized and undemocratic aspects, from which the United States had emerged better and stronger. There were a few individuals, however, who did not shy away from addressing the complexities of the American Civil War and what it might mean for Spain. The most outstanding example is Rafael María de Labra, a Cuban lawyer who represented Puerto Rico in the Cortes, and perhaps was the greatest champion in Madrid of an immediate end to slavery.

Labra's understanding of the connection between civil war and slavery in the United States was informed by his liberal and Krausist convictions about free trade, education, and associational life as the reformist route toward a harmonious society.[16] For him, the reduction of the US Civil War to the sole question of an abolitionist North versus a pro-slavery South—even granted that "the separatists are precisely the slave-owners and those resisting abolition"—ignored the complexity of its causes.[17] Instead, Labra pursued a more subtle line of argument, namely, that, although during the course of the Civil War the question of the continuance of slavery in the South had become inextricably bound up with the question of Southern separatism, it did not follow either that the war resulted solely from the slavery debate or that when immediate abolition was finally decreed it was simply a wartime expedient. On his mind was the Ten Years' War in Cuba, then in its fifth year. Labra's concern was to demonstrate both that even a polarized debate on abolition would not necessarily end in fratricidal war and that immediate abolition had been in the United States—as he argued it should be for Spain and Cuba—a matter of principle rather than expediency.

For Labra the lesson that could be drawn from the United States was not simply that immediate action had to be taken. In his extensive writings on the abolition of slavery in an international context, US examples always featured prominently. In 1873 he devoted a whole book to the United States, with the express purpose of educating Spaniards on this model of abolition ahead of debates in the Cortes on slavery in Cuba.[18] The book was also serialized in the abolitionist society's newspaper from May 1873 onward. Labra's work is particularly interesting for having made a socioeconomic and political case for abolition. Feeling the moral case to be self-evident and unassailable, he concentrated his efforts on refuting and assuaging the fears of those who argued that abolition would bring economic ruin to Spain's most profitable colony. In so doing, he sought to rebut the argument that the opponents of abolition—who often had colonial economic interests themselves—saw as their strongest weapon. Thus, both in this work and the later *La Brutalidad de los Negros* (1876), Labra built an argument to counter the ubiquitous slave holder claims that immediate and unindemnified abolition would lead to high levels of absenteeism, crime, vagrancy, and poverty among the suddenly liberated and supposedly ill-prepared black population.[19] He turned to the US example for the evidence to support his case, claiming that it proved that the fears that emancipation led inevitably to a decrease in productivity—the presumption being that free men did not work as hard as their enslaved counterparts—were entirely unfounded. As he pointed out, far from harming production levels, the abolition of slavery had actually proved beneficial in terms of increasing profits and improving the US economy in general. Despite acknowledging the undesirable short-term effects of emancipation, such as increased vagrancy, which he attributed to the state of war, Labra's main evidence was designed to show that in the years since the end of the civil war, the production of cotton, tobacco, corn, and rice in the old slave-owning states, now produced using the labor of free men, had not only regained prewar levels but actually surpassed them. What's more, census figures revealed that the population of the cotton-producing states had increased by 83.4 percent since 1860, which Labra cited to refute the slave-holder argument that "with liberty and without the care of their masters, the slaves would become idle and dissolute, exposed to hunger and death such that their race would soon be exterminated."[20] Leaning as ever on the US model as well as on Krausist philosophy, Labra asserted that, with the essential help of educational and welfare organizations to help *libertos* manage the transition from enslaved to free status, Cuban ex-slaves would go on to make an invaluable contribution to society. Abolition was desirable for its economically and morally redistributive effects upon society, because it would fundamentally alter the conception of "work" through its elevation of the intrinsic value of labor.[21] This was a key element in the Spanish abolitionist debate, which mirrored and was heavily informed, both in terms of personnel and ideology, by earlier and concurrent debates relating to the freeing of economic markets and ending of protectionism in Spain's "second empire."[22] Abolition went hand in hand with the liberal principles of free trade, which required a free labor market.[23] Cuban slaves, like white working-class Spaniards had the right to sell their labor freely—indeed this was the basis of a harmonious liberal-capitalist society—although it was not expected that nonwhite Cubans would form anything other than an industrious, docile proletariat alongside a white Hispanic middle class.[24]

Beside the socioeconomic case for abolition provided by the US model, Labra also cited the political argument for emancipation, again finding in the United States an exemplar for Spanish political leaders to emulate. For him, slavery was simply incompatible with the US democratic system and therefore—since the United States represented the most progressive form of government, he believed—with democracy *per se*. After all, he observed, Jefferson had included in a draft version of the US Constitution a paragraph condemning the British king for having sanctioned slavery and used his veto to oppose the decision of the US assembly to halt the traffic of slaves, which was removed only at the insistence of the slave-owning states of Georgia and South Carolina. Thus, for Labra, sure of the incompatibility of modern democracy and slavery, the subsequent growth of the abolitionist movement in the United States during the course of the nineteenth century came as no surprise. If anything, what was more remarkable was the tenacity of the practice of slavery.²⁵ He explained the intransigence of the US anti-abolitionists as a protracted clash between conservatism and progress. Slavery was supported predominantly in the South, he elaborated, where the most traditional and conservative settlers were found, whereas in the more urbanized North, being more favorable toward industry, having a greater concentration of workers, and also having stronger puritan traditions and spirit of protest and liberty, not only did slavery quickly disappear, or indeed never arrived, but it also formed the heartland of organized antislavery movements.

Labra's notion of abolition as a prerequisite for progress and modernity was widely echoed in debates throughout these years, particularly during the months of expectancy generated by the proclamation of the First Republic in February 1873, but also as Spanish liberals looked back after the restoration of the Bourbon monarchy in 1875 and sought to understand how they had failed to create a lasting liberally reformed Spain. The reforming climate of the early 1870s not only provided ideal conditions for emancipation, but demanded it. Abolition was, Labra declared, "a requirement of the civilised world," a key to ending the colonial problem and the war in Cuba, and "a condition of the September revolution."²⁶ The failure to abolish slavery once and for all during the revolutionary *sexenio* remained an enduring source of national shame for Spanish abolitionists. The seeming paradox of an apparently enlightened and progressive republic, defender of the "inalienable rights of man," failing to abolish the practice of slavery in its colonies was not lost on Spanish abolitionists. Gabriel Rodríguez "tremble[d] at the thought of the troubles that this conduct [the continued practice of slavery] prepares for us."²⁷

The US experience of abolition was highly visible in Spain not only in debates but also in organizational terms. The Sociedad Abolicionista Española was founded in April 1865 by the recent Puerto Rican émigré to Madrid, Julio Vizcarrondo, and his American wife, Harriet Brewster.²⁸ From the start, the "American" influences on the organisation, or at least a perception of these, were evident. Vizcarrondo, the "soul" of the society, had evidently been converted to the abolitionist cause in the United States, where, like many such Puerto Ricans and Cubans from wealthy families, he had been sent to complete his education. In 1854 he returned to Puerto Rico from the United States, with his new American wife, immediately liberated his slaves and began working for the cause of emancipation. Fellow abolitionist Joaquín María Sanromá recalled the abolitionist zeal of the society's founder: "he began the movement, organized it, united us, encouraged us, he looked after the meetings and the publications of pamphlets and [newspaper] *El Abolicionista*, and he did all this with a zeal, a diligence, and a practical sense that betrayed his Anglo-American education."²⁹ Leading members of the society acknowledged the influence of current events in the United States—namely, the Civil War and emancipation—in "giving tremendous support to the hitherto isolated efforts of our abolitionists."³⁰

The Spanish abolitionists made extensive use of an international frame of reference in arguing their case for an immediate end to slavery in the colonies. The pages of *El Abolicionista* were filled with articles reporting on historical or contemporary emancipation processes from around the world, but no non-Spanish-governed nation prompted greater interest than the USA. In the years between 1872 and 1874, for example, the number of articles that discussed the processes, causes, problems, benefits, and outcomes of abolition in the United States were surpassed only by articles considering the situation in Spain's own colonies of Puerto Rico and Cuba. Indeed, of the three principal models of abolition to which Spain might have looked—Great Britain, France, and the United States—the interest of *El Abolicionista*, not only in the volume of words but also in the degree of admiration, lay predominantly in the US process. Thirteen articles directly recounted and evaluated US abolition and six others reported on American issues more widely, compared with eleven articles on British abolition and one more on other British news. There was not a single article on France or the complex process of abolition in the French colonies.

Thus the United States was perhaps the most important international point of reference for most members of the Spanish political elite at this time, preoccupied as they were by the issue of colonial reform and abolition in the Spanish Antilles, which divided not only liberals from conservatives, but also liberals from liberals as the exigencies of the war in Cuba collided with political and moral principles. Images of the United States were crucial to shaping their discussions and bolstering their arguments either for or against abolition. But whilst providing a variety of potential lessons for Spain to absorb, the United States also constituted a potential competitor whose economic interests in Cuba posed a considerable threat to Spanish sovereignty there. The degree of political and practical support, notably in the shape of the supply of arms, sent unofficially to the separatist rebels by US politicians and civilian associations, meant that the view from Spain of the United States was tinged by caution and, often, hostility. US attempts to intervene in the issues of slavery and Cuban independence were widely reported in the Spanish press, from President Ulysses Grant's messages urging the pacification of the island and emancipation of its slaves, to American Quakers' petitions to King Amadeus for the "complete and immediate abolition of slavery in all Spanish dominions," to the filibustering activity and plotting of Cuban exiles in New York and Florida.³¹ The *Liga contra las reformas ultramarinos* (League against colonial reform) and others in the upper echelons of Spanish political circles who were opposed to immediate abolition thus found cause for concern not only in the US experience of emancipation but also in its contemporary attitude toward slavery in Cuba and the position of the island more generally. Pronouncements emanating from the United States—especially those of the president—calling for the immediate end to the practice of slavery were interpreted as unwarranted interference and even an antecedent to belligerence.

So close was the intertwining of Spanish abolitionist debates, the Ten Years' War, fears of annexationism and the reality of US-based support and assistance for the Cuban separatist rebels, that the advocates of abolition in Madrid time and again felt compelled to protest their patriotism and opposition to Cuban independence. Not only were they vulnerable to the *Liga*'s argument that abolition "would divide the loyal colonial forces and its practice would disrupt the Cuban [sugar] refineries, depriving our cause of the economic resources necessary to sustain it against the enemy." Spanish abolitionists were also susceptible to the criticism that by putting forward the US experience as the model that Spain ought to follow, they were effectively supporting the country that was most vocally and directly intervening in what Spain saw as a colonial insurrection but which many people in the United States—and elsewhere—identified as a war of independence, if not a perfect opportunity for annexation.[32] In response to the League's biting accusations that Cuban independence would inevitably follow abolition—backed up by comments made by the American ambassador in Madrid, Daniel Sickles, a friend of several of the metropolitan abolitionists—the abolitionists indignantly affirmed their commitment to the "integrity of the *patria*" and to the continued ties between colony and metropole, calling upon the blood ties that were imagined to link peninsular Spaniards and the creole settlers in Cuba and Puerto Rico.[33]

Images of US abolition thus provided an ambiguous model for both Spanish abolitionists and those who opposed the ending of slavery and colonial reform in the Spanish Antilles. The Spanish Abolitionist Society took its cues largely from the United States: the nexus between abolition and modernity, the evidence that immediate abolition was the method that worked most effectively, and on a practical level, how to organize and fight for abolition were lessons gleaned from viewing and imagining the United States. So too, though, did those who opposed immediate abolition in colonial Spain, like the *Liga contra las reformas ultramarinas*, for whom the United States showed that abolition went hand in hand with war and—what was more—that it was the United States that was stoking the flames of Cuban insurrection. In this way, the United States furnished both a motive and a model for debates on colonial reforms in

Spain. Perceived US interference in the "Cuban question" helped to ensure that colonial reform remained a crucial but sticky issue for late-nineteenth-century Spanish politicians and that images of the process of abolition in the United States were contested, imagined variously as a model, lesson, and rival for colonial Spain.

Cuba

The questions of slavery, Spanish rule, and relations with the United States had become entangled in Cuba long before the US Civil War. During the 1840s, as British pressure to abolish slavery intensified, support for US annexation of Cuba grew among slave owners both on the island and in the American South, in the hope of creating a powerful monopoly of slave-based sugar production. A substantial minority of Cuban planters was attracted by the possibility of ridding themselves of Spanish interference in their affairs whilst securing the protection of US slave-owning interests against any potential mass uprising that might turn Cuba into another Haiti. A failed military expedition in 1850, financed by Southern slave owners, set back the annexationist cause, but it retained support in both Cuba and the United States until US emancipation made it unviable. It was the US Civil War, the effects of which were probably "felt more intensely in Cuba" than in any other country,[34] that entrenched an identification of Cuban politics with US politics that reached far beyond the annexationists. Cubans fought on both sides of the US conflict, mostly for the Confederacy, although the adventures of the brothers Adolfo and Federico Fernández Cavada on the Unionist side were closely followed in the Cuban press, which reported daily on what they referred to as the "Guerra de Secesión" (War of Secession).[35] On his return to Cuba in early 1865, Federico Fernández Cavada recorded (with surprise) the depth of Cuban fascination with US affairs.[36]

Spain, which was officially neutral in the US Civil War, in practice gave aid and succor to the Confederacy from Cuba, as was all too visible there, where the Confederate representative, Charles Helm, was openly courting support from October 1861 onward.[37] The twentieth-century history of US interventionism in Cuba tends to eclipse the fact that in the 1860s the United States was seen by many of the Cubans who sought greater control over their own affairs as a source of support against Spanish colonial rule. There was concern throughout Latin America, and Cuba was no exception, about the extent to which European powers took advantage of the US conflict to reassert their claims in the Americas, with Napoleon III invading Mexico and Spanish troops occupying the Dominican Republic and attacking Chile and Peru. Secretary of State William Seward's famous memorandum of April 1861, in which he declared that the United States would "demand explanations from Spain and France" about their renewed incursions into the Americas, was interpreted by at least some Cubans as a sign that the Monroe Doctrine could be applied to their advantage. Lincoln's explicit disavowal of annexationism was welcomed by Cuban patriots, as was his decision in 1862 that the United States should finally recognize Haitian independence. Nor did it escape their attention that although Lincoln and Seward never officially supported the Mexican liberal leader Benito Juárez's fight against the French forces, his eventual victory was due in no small measure to the fact that US authorities turned a blind eye to arms purchases across the border by the Mexican liberals.

The combination of events in the United States and elsewhere in the region, together with internal economic changes and an increasing desire for self-government, prompted the revival of reformism in Cuba among some of the more moderate planters. The Partido Reformista, founded in 1862, was distinguished from earlier Cuban reformist movements seeking greater control over their own affairs by its cautious advocacy of abolition (the previous one, from the 1830s, had sought only the ending of the slave trade). As in Spain, there was also a counter-organization of merchants and slavocrats, the Partido Incondicional Español, which supported the continuation of both Spanish rule and slavery. The main vehicle of expression for the reformists was the newspaper *El Siglo*, founded in April 1862, which was distributed throughout most of the island, under a relatively tolerant Captain-General;[38] that of their opponents was *El Diario de la Marina*, and the different positions can be traced through these two publications, both of which drew constantly upon US examples. *El Diario de la Marina* supported the Confederacy, *El Siglo* was Unionist, as was majority opinion (so far as it is possible to document), not least because it was anticipated that a Union victory would weaken Spain's position in Cuba. The logic of both arguments created automatic alignments: reformist/abolitionist/Unionist on the one hand, colonialist/pro-slavery/Confederate on the other.[39]

After Lincoln's Emancipation Proclamations of September 22, 1862 and January 1, 1863, it was no longer possible for Cuban planters to sustain the position that annexation to the United States was the best way to break free of the Spanish colonial yolk while preserving slavery. Indeed, it became widely accepted in Cuba, including among the planters themselves, that slavery in Cuba would not be able to endure for long after abolition in the United States. In 1865, the *Asociación contra la trata negra* (Association against the slave trade) was formed in Havana, through which many Cubans and some Spaniards committed themselves not to buy slaves and to campaign against sale of them. There were no voices raised in favour of immediate emancipation of those already enslaved, however, and nearly all abolitionists supported the payment of indemnities to slave holders. The Cuban reformists were all cautious abolitionists, who deployed the US example to illustrate how disastrous precipitate action could be and to advocate a legalistic approach that recognized the sanctity of property rights.[40] "Look at the example of the United States," argued Fermín Figuera, who proposed a 25-year plan for abolition, "A disastrous Civil War is not necessary. A plan of gradual emancipation with compensation is possible and much more intelligent."[41]

In this climate of cautious abolitionism, it was no coincidence that Lincoln, imagined by Cuban reformists as an example of both nobility and moderation, figured so prominently in public discussion. Prominence was given to the speeches in which Lincoln spoke of abolition in terms of "a plan of mutual concessions."[42] Shortly after the Gettysburg Address, *El Siglo* published an article containing stark images of an isolated Lincoln—a noble lone defender of what he believed to be right in the face of opposition: "that misunderstood man, vilified and ridiculed, who raised himself from a wood-cutter to occupy the first position in that great nation [...], every fibre of whose being was penetrated by the duties imposed upon him by his oath to preserve the Constitution and the Union, shut his eyes to any possibility that did not further those sacred objectives."[43] As was to become common in Latin America during the late nineteenth century, Cuban reformists credited Lincoln personally with saving the Union that Washington had founded.[44] In this grand nation-building endeavor, the role of emancipation tended to be played down: Sarmiento's biography of Lincoln, which represented abolition as a necessary tactic to defeat the separatists, sold particularly well in Cuba—a third edition was printed primarily to satisfy demand there. After Lincoln's assassination, it was not only the Spanish authorities who feared that US emancipation would trigger a "slackening of the links of obedience and respect which the coloured race should entertain for the white," as the Captain-General put it in a confidential circular of December 1866.[45] Most eulogies to Lincoln published at the time in Cuba did not mention his part in abolition, for fear of provoking a slave revolt.[46] It is impossible to reconstruct how well-founded such fears were, but there is evidence that Cuban slaves were well aware of events in the United States. In addition to the much-quoted image of Cuban slaves singing "Advance, Lincoln, advance, you are our deliverance," which was found in two US diplomatic reports of 1862 and 1863,[47] a later report from a Spanish representative noted anxiously that: "The blacks [in Havana] go to meet every boat that comes from [the United States], and they ask with great interest about the state of the war and the abolition of slavery, they talk about Mr Lincoln, and all his acts please them, as it is easy to understand."⁴⁸ Furthermore, it is documented that *El Siglo* was read aloud in Cuban cigar factories in the series of readings that, from 1866 onward, became an established feature of Cuban working-class life, despite being banned by the colonial authorities, and were introduced into the United States in 1870.⁴⁹ For the elites, Lincoln was a masterly political strategist; for Cuban laborers, whether enslaved or free, he was a man of the people who had used his power to benefit his own kind.

The campaign for gradual abolition in Cuba was orchestrated through several periodicals published in three locations: *El Siglo* in Havana, *La América* and *Revista Hispano-Americana* in Madrid, and *El Porvenir* in New York.⁵⁰ The editor of *El Porvenir*, Porfirio Valiente, produced one of the many plans for gradual abolition proposed at this time, with a preface by no less an authority than Edouard Laboulaye (head of the French Anti-Slavery Society) adducing an image of the horrors of the US experience: "the United States abolished slavery at the price of a bloody war and huge expense."⁵¹ Valiente also cited, at some length, the US Unitarian William Ellery Channing (1780–1842), who argued for the absolute right to freedom of all human beings, therefore spoke out against slavery, but who also maintained that slaves would be unable to cope with freedom, mainly for lack of education, and would therefore need to continue working under overseers even after emancipation. Toward the end of his life, having been reassured by the abolition of slavery in the British West Indies in 1834, he changed his mind in favor of immediate abolition, but it was only his earlier views on the importance of allowing a long period to prepare slaves for freedom that Valiente cited: "There is only one serious argument against immediate abolition: namely that a slave would be unable to support either himself or his children by honest labour; having always worked through force, he would do nothing without it; having always worked at the will of others, he would do nothing of his own volition. [...] Liberty would produce laziness; laziness, poverty; poverty, crime [...]." Had it not been for the Civil War, Valiente concluded, "the form of abolition in the United States would have never been other than that advised by the famous American socialist" (a description that would probably have startled Channing himself, let alone anyone who knew him).⁵²

Meanwhile, Cuban exiles in New York, many of whom desired full independence, were drawing upon different aspects of the US experience. They argued that slavery was an obstacle to the unity necessary to win independence. Members of the Republican Society of Cuba and Puerto Rico, founded in New York in April 1866, argued that they could not depend upon help from the United States to defeat Spain and that if they were to be thrown back upon their own resources then they would need the support of Cuban slaves and former slaves, which together made up nearly half of the population.[53] They therefore tended to highlight the contribution of emancipated slaves to Northern victories.[54] Encouraged by the triumph of the Union, the Mexican liberals' defeat of Maximilian and Spain's withdrawal of 1865 from the Dominican Republic, they called for revolution, and their periodical, *La Voz de América*, circulated widely in Cuba.[55] As noted above, however, the Spanish government refused to implement even gradual abolition, and armed uprising came to seem the only option for those Cuban creoles who sought greater control over their own affairs.

Once the struggle for independence was launched in October 1868, Cuban patriots expected and felt entitled to US support,[56] a position that was closely related to their perception of US abolition. They argued thus: "the American people finally gave freedom to their slaves; and Cuba, now sure that this noble people would never be hostile, and never take the side of Spain, still trading in Africa and the supreme supporter of slavery, threw itself into the struggle to expel the tyrants from its land."[57] Most of them had an optimistic view of US involvement as benign and all-powerful: they were convinced that if the US recognized their status as belligerents, thereby making it legal for them to purchase weapons in the United States, then they would soon win.[58] Initially the insurgent leaders, most of whom were themselves slave owners, and still hoping to win other planters over to their cause, tried to hold the line that abolition would follow victory. The Constituent Assembly in Guaimaro, Oriente, of April 1869 backed its approval of a republican liberal Constitution with a commitment to annexation by the United States once liberation from Spain had been won. Ignacio Mora, one of the patriot leaders, explained support for annexation as follows: "If Cuba has prospered more than other states of Spanish America it is because Cuba is more Americanised than them, because it shares more in the ideas, the education, the activity and the example of the North American people."[59] As US support proved elusive, however, the republic-in-arms announced formal abolition, with freedom offered to all slaves from other parts of the island who could reach "Cuba libre" (free Cuba).

In the event, among Grant's cabinet, only Secretary of War John Rawlins (who died in September 1869) argued in favor of recognizing the Cuban republican government. This made it relatively easy for Secretary of State Hamilton Fish to block formal US recognition of the Cuban insurgents, on the grounds that Cubans were not ready for self-government and in anticipation of the Spanish agreeing to sell the island to the United States after the war. In June 1869 Fish told José Morales Lemus, the representative of the independence movement, that Grant intended to offer his services as a mediator with Spain to bring the conflict to an end. As a result, it was the Spanish, not the Cubans, who were able to obtain weapons from the United States. There is no doubt that Grant's decision caused deep disillusionment in Cuba, and from that moment on images of the United States never again displayed the wholly idealistic hue with which many (although by no means all) Cuban patriots had hitherto imbued them. In January 1871 one independence supporter lamented, "Cuba, heroic Cuba... Forgotten by America, slandered by the president of the United States [...]."[60] Cartoonists were more savage in their indictments (although it is worth noting that at this stage representations of US figures were in the main still relatively benign—the grotesque images of Uncle Sam with features contorted by cruelty were products of the 1890s). In one example from 1874, the Cuban insurrection was depicted as a sickly child, seated on the knee of Uncle Sam, being force-fed "sympathy."[61] Another Cuban satirical magazine set out a dialogue between President Ulysses Grant and José Morales Lemus, representative of the provisional government to the United States, in order to illustrate "The Game of Forfeits played by the Cuban Junta. Three times yes, and three times no." It went, "Lemus: You'll let us buy arms, won't you?... Grant: Yes. Lemus: And will they arrive in Cuba?... Grant: No. Lemus: But we will be able to buy a steamship? Grant: Yes. Lemus: And you'll let it leave? Grant: No. Lemus: Will you recognise us? Grant: No. Lemus: Then we'll go to the devil? Grant: Yes."[62]

What did endure in Cuba through the change in US government policy, however, were images of US popular sympathy for the rebels. The US Congress passed a resolution in support of independence for Cuba, and some supplies were sent privately, although the Cuban rebel army was obliged to fight mainly with machetes.[63] Cuba was also a great object of concern for US abolitionists, who were advocating a boycott of Cuban products to force Spain's hand over slavery even before the end of the US Civil War.[64] It was not only in Cuba that comparisons were drawn: there was a lot of public interest in the United States in the Ten Years' War, especially after the declaration of abolition in 1869, "because we had abolished slavery by the war process, and the same work was done in Cuba in the same way, only that the slaves were more active than with us, in the use of arms to secure their freedom."[65] US black activists identified with the cause of Cuban independence, an interest that dated back to the Cuban slave revolts of 1843–4, which were referred to as *La Escalera* (the Ladder Conspiracy). One of the leaders of that uprising, a poet known as Plácido, was executed by the Spanish. His poetry became known among blacks in the United States and he featured in a novel by Martin Robinson Delany, widely seen as the first US black nationalist, called *Blake or the Huts of America: A Tale of the Mississippi Valley, the Southern United States and Cuba* (1859). With the outbreak of the independence war in 1868, Frederick Douglass expressed support for the insurgency; in 1872 a Cuban Antislavery Society was founded in New York, which collected 5,000 signatures for a petition to President Grant to support the cause of Cuban independence.[66]

As the Ten Years' War dragged on, with neither side able to prevail, and the monarchy was restored to Spain in 1874, those who resisted abolition continued to argue that the Moret Law of 1870 (freeing children born of slaves) would in time resolve the problem. Under such conditions, it was impossible for an organized popular abolitionist movement to develop, as happened in Brazil during the 1880s. However, slaves who escaped their masters to join the insurgent army were a continual reminder to the leaders of the independence movement that, in the absence of US support, they needed the former slaves to fight for the proposed Cuban republic. Even after the end of the Ten Years' War, there is evidence that slaves, knowing "that great changes had taken place and that more would be forthcoming," resisted attempts by their owners to enforce discipline and successfully negotiated for concessions.[67] In the absence at that stage of anyone resembling their own Lincoln, images of the US president continued to serve as a source of inspiration and hope for the enslaved.

Brazil

From Rio de Janeiro, the triumph of the US abolitionists was observed with great interest, but in a context very different from that of Cuba. Brazilian planters, in contrast to their divided Cuban counterparts, remained united in their resistance to abolition well after the end of the US Civil War. When Emperor Dom Pedro first presented a package of tentative reforms to his Council of State in September 1865, he met with flat refusal to discussion the question: "slavery is a wound which must not be touched."[68] Even two years later, when he finally tried to force the hand of the planters by going public in his Annual Speech from the Throne,[69] his words were felt "like a bolt of lighting in a cloudless sky," according to abolitionist leader Joaquim Nabuco, because slave owners still saw abolition as "a sort of historical sacrilege, of dynastic madness, of national suicide."[70] Nevertheless, among the highly restricted circles of Brazil's rulers, it was acknowledged that the ending of the other great slave system of the hemisphere could not but "have a long and great impact on the empire,"[71] not least because the persistence of slavery in the "model republic" had previously served Brazil's rulers as a powerful riposte to the campaigners abroad who tried to shame them into abolition by insisting that slavery was inappropriate in a modernizing country. US emancipation was directly influential in convincing the highest circle of imperial statesmen that the clock was ticking fast against the continuation of slavery, but it also had the indirect effect of making Brazil a renewed target for abolitionists elsewhere. The British government stepped up their pressure on the Brazilian monarchy to outlaw slavery once and for all; the Brazilian emperor even received a letter from French anarchists urging him to take personal moral responsibility for ending slavery.

The importance to Brazil's imperial statesmen of being recognized as leaders of a civilized nation should not be underestimated, but they were also highly reluctant to be seen to succumb to external pressure. Internal pressures were, therefore, equally if not more significant in accounting for the gradual build up of a moderate movement toward abolition. By the mid-1860s the consequences of the ending of the slave trade in 1850 were beginning to be felt in the increasing atrophy of Brazil's socioeconomic structure. A new generation of liberal professionals emerged, less committed to a seigniorial lifestyle and accepting if not embracing the need for Brazil to address the "servile question."[72] The most significant factor, however, was the Paraguayan War (1864–70), also known as the War of the Triple Alliance (Brazil, Argentina and Uruguay) or, in Paraguay itself, where the losses were by far the heaviest, the Great War. It was in the context of this disastrous war, when the Brazilian army's many deficiencies required the passing of extreme measures to enable it to sustain a supply of soldiers, that the idea of emancipation first took hold in official spheres. The vexed causes of this war need not concern us here, but it is important to draw attention to what is hardly known outside Latin America, namely the very high rates of mortality, affecting—at least in Paraguay—civilians as well as combatants. In short, this was no minor border squabble, but a prolonged and devastating conflict, which dominated press coverage and haunted the minds of all those involved. Thus, to many Brazilian leaders of the late 1860s, the undoubted horrors of the US Civil War, which to European minds seemed so exceptional, seemed to offer a pertinent—if discouraging—comparison with their own appalling experiences.

Brazil's abolition process is customarily divided into two periods. The first, during the 1860s and confined to parliamentary circles, culminated in a timid program of reforms, including the passing of a Law of the Free Womb in 1871. Abolitionism did not return in strength until the 1880s, the second phase, when it acquired a far deeper social reach, with abolitionist societies, newspapers and campaigns across the country. Images of the United States were prevalent during both periods, but in very different ways. During the first phase, they were mainly negative; during the second, mainly positive. Perhaps even more than was the case in Spain or Cuba, the US example gave rise to multiple interpretations in Brazil and lessons politicians drew from it were many, varied and changeable. The signifier "United States" had no fixed meaning, nor did its symbolic significance belong to either side of the political battlefield of abolition. On the contrary, the experience of the United States became a highly malleable rhetorical device that was readily adopted by both reformers and their opponents.

The deep-seated resistance to abolitionism in Brazil can be measured by the fact that positive images of the United States, such as there were in Brazil during the 1860s, were associated almost exclusively with the Confederates, both throughout the Civil War and, perhaps especially, in the aftermath of their defeat. Whereas in many parts of Latin America, the American South was portrayed as the microcosm of a declining aristocratic society—whether viewed critically or nostalgically—in Brazil it was represented quite differently, as a laboratory for modern agricultural techniques. Thus, rather than being seen as the defeated exponents of an exhausted way of life, disaffected Southerners were depicted as unfortunate, hardworking entrepreneurs, carriers of cutting-edge agricultural techniques, and agents of modernity who could bring about the historic replacement of the Brazilian hoe with the Anglo-Saxon plough.[73] In the words of Aureliano Cândido Tavares Bastos, a prominent liberal statesman who at this time was busy establishing direct steamship lines with the United States, ex-Confederates "already stand out for the...great contribution that they promise to the overall production of the country."[74]

In the context of the manpower crisis caused first by the end of the Atlantic slave trade and then the high losses incurred fighting against Paraguay, the Brazilian government was on the lookout for skilled, modern farmers who could help increase agricultural production. Of these, the US Southern states appeared to have a formidable stock. It was declared that Confederate migration to Brazil could be "very advantageous for the Empire,"[75] and the Brazilian government accordingly set up an emigration office in New York and a subsidiary division in New Orleans, with the specific aim of attracting disgruntled US Southern farmer families to Brazil. Nor was this a notional policy: some trouble was taken to attract them,[76] through an extensive advertising campaign and the promise of a whole set of material benefits, notably cheap steamship tickets and mortgages for the most fertile lands in Brazil.[77] Dom Pedro even went in person to welcome the first group of Confederates into the port of Rio de Janerio. In part, Brazil's policy of encouraging ex-Confederates to settle there can be understood as a manifestation of the Brazilian elite's wish not to be intimidated into abolition by pressure from abroad. The determination to resolve the slavery question in their own good time and in their own way provides the backdrop against which elite Brazilians, irrespective of their political allegiances, welcomed [Confederates] "to this land of hospitality."[78] However, this immediate postbellum attempt to develop an alternative model for reconciling slavery with modernity lost momentum because of the emergency created by the Paraguayan War.

The War had initially been expected to be brief, but Paraguay's stout resistance turned it into a five-year ordeal. In the context of the Brazilian army's exhaustion in the face of the guerrilla-style tactics of the Paraguayans, commanders began urging the central government to override the constitutional stipulation that only citizens should fight. In the Council of State debates preceding the government's decision of November 1866 to emancipate slaves who agreed to serve in the army, the example of the US Civil War was prominent in the contributions by both sides.[79] A close look at these deliberations reveals the extent to which Lincoln's recruitment practices during the US Civil War were in the minds of Brazilian politicians.

Supporters of the proposal to grant slaves their freedom in exchange for military service cited Greece and Rome as historical precedents and the United States as a compelling and positive recent example,[80] drawing attention to Lincoln's "proclamations of 22 September 1862 and 1 January 1863, [ordering...] that slaves with the necessary aptitude be admitted to the Army and Navy." Should Brazil adopt a similar policy, "the civilised nations would applaud this act which by serving the [Paraguayan] war, also serves the [cause of] emancipation."[81] Opponents of the idea took the same images and deployed them differently, arguing that "the civilised world" would not be likely to approve if the Empire of Brazil had recourse to emancipation only to strengthen its forces against "one of the smallest states of America." "What was practiced in the United States in the last civil war could not serve as a lesson to Brazil," continued the same councilor, because there was a fundamental difference between the United States and Brazil. For the federal government in the US Civil War, southern slaves were "natural helpers," who, in fighting for their own cause, would also help the cause of the Union.[82] In Brazil, by contrast, the "natural helpers" of the regime were not the slaves from any part of the country but their owners. Emulating Lincoln's policy in Brazil would risk more than social turmoil. It would also cement the paradox of making slaves fight in the name of a slave country and, more importantly, hit the very interests of the regime's main supporters, the coffee planters of Central-South Brazil where most of Brazil's slave population was located.

As debates about abolition gathered momentum from 1867 onward, images of the United States were introduced both in order to argue that Brazil could not afford to do nothing *and* to advocate that abolition should be gradual and controlled by parliament. For these cautious reformers, as for their opponents, what stood out about the United States were the sheer horrors of its Civil War, the unprepared for and imposed character of its abolition—carried out by sudden proclamation in the heat of war—and the terrifying parallels of its North-South divide with the Brazilian situation. The US Civil War was represented in the Brazilian press as an apocalyptic event, a struggle between "barbarism and ambition," as the newspaper of the ruling elite, the *Diário do Rio de Janeiro*, put it.[83] It was invoked—even by an advocate of republicanism—"as a providential warning to show Brazil the need to bide our time, and not as a reason to emancipate."[84] The Brazilian Republican Party, founded in 1870, was progressive in some respects, but–unlike republicans in Cuba—its manifesto made no formal commitment to abolition.[85] Elite Brazilians of varying political views tended to agree that the dreadful experience of ending the slave regime in the United States was attributable to the regrettable radicalization of the Unionists rather than to the obstinacy of the planters in rejecting reform. These cautious voices also promoted the already widespread myth of the benign character of slavery in Brazil compared with slavery in the antebellum US South: there could be no special rush to liberate slaves in Brazil, given that they were treated so much better than in the United States.[86] Only because of its great wealth had the United States been able to withstand such a "colossal" struggle between "formidable titans" crossing "fratricidal swords,"[87] therefore Brazil, lacking such wealth, was obliged to be far more cautious. Thus, alarmist images of the US Civil War were invoked to argue that abolition should only be introduced gradually, if at all.

The nimbleness with which these reluctant abolitionists deployed images of the United States is vividly illustrated by the twists and turns of the conservative prime minister from 1865 to 1871, the Viscount of Rio Branco, in the Council of State, which first began tentatively exploring a schedule for abolition in 1867.[88] During the course of the debates, Rio Branco dismissed comparisons with French or British experiences of abolition, arguing that in their territories "slaves were not as numerous [as in Brazil], nor did private fortunes and the country's productive work depend so profoundly on slave labour."[89] For him, the only appropriate comparison was the United States, where, as in Brazil, a significant section of the country had recently experienced the heyday of the slave mode of production.[90] Yet his view of the United States was intriguingly flexible. First, he turned to the US case for a prominent example to counter the arguments of that sector of the imperial political elite who were minded to concede emancipation, mainly to placate demands from abroad. Later on, however, he would employ the US example differently, in order to convince intransigent slavocrats to accept a gradual abolitionist reform dictated by the state.

In 1867, Rio Branco selected images of the success of the slave economy in the American South to argue that the time was not ripe for abolition in

Brazil because slavery was still at the peak of its commercial profitability. The viscount also noted, in support of his case, that there was no popular demand for abolition in Brazil, no distinctive political party like the anti-slavery US Republicans devoted to the cause.[91] The other main respect in which he saw a critical lesson to be learned was that US abolition had been "a solution imposed by the force of one half of the Nation against the other, a solution which saw political antagonism prevail over the humanitarian question."[92] For good measure, he invoked the prevalent Brazilian images of the alleged cost of abolition in "rivers of blood [and] a tremendous civil war the consequences of which cannot be still predicted," which "causes one to retreat with terror before it."[93] At this stage, the US example allowed the Viscount of Rio Branco to justify his opposition to any legislative change regarding slavery.

Just a few years later, however, when the emperor's closest circle decided to put before parliament a bill for the emancipation of children born to slave mothers, the viscount drew upon images of the United States to support an altogether different stance. Rio Branco himself led the state councilors in the battle to persuade planters to join the government in providing a gradual solution for peaceful reform by passing what became known as the "Law of the Free Womb." When discussions began in May 1871, the viscount opened by asking his audience to reflect upon "what the consequences were [in the United States] of not procuring the timely solution which might conciliate the interests of the slave owners with those of the society as a whole."[94] As the opposition of the planters from the Southern coffee-growing areas, who enjoyed a clear majority in the Lower House, became ever more entrenched, Rio Branco openly denounced them for clinging to divisive ideas and turned to the example of their US Southern predecessors to back up his argument. The viscount recalled that in the United States "[t]he ideas of the North entered into conflict with those of the South, and the Southern States, forever unyielding, wanted to subject the legislation of the Northern States to all the requirements of [the slave] institution that [the Northerners] rejected." The result, he pointed out, was secession and civil war. While Brazil, he hoped, had not yet "reached such cruel extremes," the "influences of similar causes and ideas" could clearly be seen.[95] The minister of justice, Francisco de Paula Negreiros Saião Lobato, also invoked the "tremendous lesson" of the US Southerners' rejection of the "fair settlement" offered to them. Citing Lincoln's words: "I neither want nor admit the emancipation of slavery in the Southern States, I only require that adequate measures be taken to modify it," the Brazilian statesman warned that as a result of making "the wrong demand," the slave holders of the American South had "suffered complete ruin."[96] As opinion shifted among Brazil's rulers toward a reluctant acceptance of the need for at least limited change, their choice of images from the US experience changed accordingly.

The second phase of Brazilian abolitionism, which began in the late 1870s with the return of the Liberals to power, was characterized by the elaboration of a full-fledged abolitionist ideology that went beyond the confines of parliament to touch all sectors of society. The overwhelming rejection of a bill for full abolition put before the Chamber of Deputies by Joaquim Nabuco triggered a wave of abolitionist societies, newspapers, and a diverse range of public activities throughout the cities of the Empire. It was at this point that the example of the United States came to the fore for the second time, but in an altogether different way. This time, it was the example of the US abolitionists and their mode of organization that captured attention in Brazil.

During the 1880s, abolition of slavery in the United States came to be seen as a process deriving from a modernizing ethos and ideology that posited free labor as an inescapable condition for modernization, and as such, as a positive example to emulate. Yet there still was no consensus on how slavery should be brought to an end, and the preoccupations of the 1860s re-emerged in new guises. Campaigners were divided between moderates and radicals, both of whom identified with US role models. The most famous Brazilian abolitionist, Joaquim Nabuco, whose accounts of the campaign have been accepted largely uncritically, represented himself as the William Lloyd Garrison of Brazil, signing a whole series of pro-abolition articles with the pseudonym of this "immortal abolitionist,"[97] whom he saw as following in the wise, steady footsteps of Wilberforce and Lamartine, rather than in the impetuous, dangerous leaps and bounds of "Catilina or Spartacus or John Brown."[98] Nabuco reserved the role of Lincoln for his father, Councillor of State José Thomaz Nabuco de Araújo, who drew up the Free Womb Law.[99] In the influential works of Nabuco, who had spent a year in the United States,[100] the labels of "Garrison" and "John Brown" came to demarcate two ways of approaching the struggle for emancipation, the first signifying the assertion of moral pressure in the cause of immediate emancipation, the latter denoting armed servile insurrection. In contrast to the first phase of abolitionism, US images now came to be positive examples emerging as a guide for organizational skills and propaganda tactics to lend substance to these two alternative abolitionist strategies.

If there was one idea that continued to reverberate in the minds of Brazilian abolitionists throughout the process, it was the overwhelming social turmoil involved in the termination of slavery in the United States. This image persisted long enough to make Brazilian abolitionists, even in the second, radicalized phase of the campaign, the champions of reform via legislation rather than direct action. Abolition was routinely associated, by all parties, with social unrest. Once again it was argued by both conservatives and liberals that Brazil was ill prepared to endure a fate similar to that of the United States:

> Wealthy, industrious, with more than thirty millions inhabitants the American Union almost fell in the struggle; poor, without industry and with an insignificant population Brazil will certainly fall.[101]

Stemming from a shared vivid memory of the revolutionary associations of abolition in the United States, "aristocratic" reformers worked hard to minimize the social disruption entailed by the abolitionist campaign, a commitment which actually meant deliberately denying the slaves any place in the movement.

Brazilians did not only draw negative lessons from the US experience about how to reduce the violence involved in such a crucial structural change. The historical example of the United States was also used more positively to work out what the accomplishment of abolition would look like in the Brazilian rural landscape and what complementary measures should be implemented to underpin the work of abolition. The renowned civil engineer, learned analyst of Brazil's socio-economic problems and admirer of the US model, André Rebouças, wrote in 1880 in the *Gazeta da Tarde,* the most uncompromising abolitionist newspaper, that should a land reform be pursued in Brazil to accompany the liberation of slaves: "Brazilian Rural Democracy would be born, predestined to reproduce in the South-American continent the wonders that Yankee Democracy had achieved in North America."[102] The core of Brazil's abolitionist argument had always been grounded primarily on economic arguments about the inefficiency of slavery. Accordingly, Rebouças wrote in 1883 that the day after abolition, "the same thing that happened in the Mississippi Valley after the war of emancipation in the United States will happen on the plateau of São Paulo": the production of coffee will increase. "Ploughed by free men, [these lands] will produce ten times more than those watered by the tears and sweat of miserable slaves."[103]

Rebouças was joined by other liberal ideologues in pointing to postabolition US society as a shining paradigm of liberty and prosperity. Rather than focusing on the loss of wealth by US Southern planters under the Reconstruction era, as pro-slavery sectors preferred to do, abolitionists naturally opted to stress that "the most complete possible proof [of the efficiency of free labor] is the material and economic transformation of agriculture in the [US] Southern states after the war."[104] So much was Nabuco convinced of the increased efficiency resulting from the termination of slavery that he decided to enlighten public opinion at home by calling upon a figure with a controversial background to testify to it. This person was the former US slaveholder and Confederate who served as minister to Brazil between 1877 and 1881, Henry Washington Hilliard. Precisely because Hilliard had been a member of the planter class, Nabuco believed that his opinion was bound to carry weight among those in Brazil who still feared that abolition could cause economic disaster as well as social disorder.[105] At Nabuco's invitation, Hilliard wrote a long letter in which he pointed out that, far from being ruined once free labor had come to the US South, the cotton industry had actually expanded; moreover, race relations had improved.[106] Hilliard's undiplomatic intervention prompted a nationalistic backlash similar to the one that had occurred 30 years earlier when patriotism had been roused against the British after they had brought the Atlantic slave trade to a halt. Yet the incident is telling about the extent to which US abolition was no longer imagined by moderate Brazilian abolitionists as a dangerous political event of far too unpredictable consequences but, rather, as a process deriving from a successful program of economic and social modernization.

Alternative versions of the US experience were circulating among the popular abolitionist organizations that spread rapidly during this period, particularly after 1884. In December 1880 the prominent mulatto abolitionist Luís Gama wrote in the newspaper *Gazeta do Povo:* "I want to be mad like John Brown, like Spartacus, like Lincoln, like Jesus."[107] Gama had been born free to an African woman and a member of the Bahian aristocracy who at the age of ten had sold him illegally into slavery. The inter-provincial slave trade had seen him shipped from Bahia to São Paulo; once there his mulatto appearance spared him from working in the coffee fields and he was bought to serve as a domestic servant in an urban household, as a result of which he learnt to read and write. At the age of seventeen he fled from slavery and became a poet, journalist, editor and self-taught lawyer.[108] Following the publication of his first poems in 1859, Gama gained recognition in elite circles.[109] He came to be seen as the great precursor of the popular Brazilian abolitionist cause and movement. Even though Brazil's most illustrious opponent of slavery, Joaquim Nabuco, was reluctant to recognize Gama's early struggle for unconditional abolition, the ex-slave was the first to initiate successful abolitionist activities when he applied his legal skills to securing the ransoming of the illegally enslaved on the basis of an 1831 law.[110] By the mid-1860s Gama was already helping to establish the two first anti-slavery and anti-monarchy *paulista* illustrated journals,[111] which served as "a Bible of abolition for those who cannot read."[112] He was the one pioneer abolitionist for whom the US experience of building a community of abolitionist practice based on a structured network of societies, publications, and subversive activities served as a blueprint. In 1868, Gama cofounded the abolitionist and republican Masonic lodge of the capital of São Paulo province, "Loja America," the republican and abolitionist ideals of which were influenced by, and paid tribute to, US political doctrine and its post-emancipation social model. Moreover, Gama's motto was "American Brazil and the Cruzeiro lands with neither kings nor slaves" and his dream that Brazil should be called—as indeed it was in the Constitution of 1891—the "United States of Brazil."[113]

After yet another moderate emancipation proposal was defeated in the legislature in 1884, there was a rapid spread of organized popular resistance, adopting ideas and inspiration from what was increasingly merged together in Brazilian abolitionists' minds as the Anglo-American movement, which had successfully taken the abolitionist cause to the people.[114] New abolitionist newspapers were created; the circulation of pamphlets and books gained new momentum; new clubs and societies were established; banquets were held. There was an explosion of conferences, public rallies, benefit dances and bazaar auctions to raise funds for emancipation. Activists traveled around the country to spread the word. By 1886, there was a runaway movement, known as the Caifazes, organized on the basis of the "underground railroad" in the United States. Their newspaper, *A Redenção* (The Redemption), like many other abolitionist publications of the time, serialized *Uncle Tom's Cabin*, which served as a great source of inspiration for Brazilians at a moment when theatrical performances of it had been banned by the authorities. By May 1888 the struggle for abolition was drawing to a close. The death knell for slavery sounded in 1887 when the Armed Forces refused to continue hunting down runaways, an act which was decisive in persuading the majority of the planters to convert to abolition. Yet, interestingly for our purposes, the inexorable defeat of the planter class made the most recalcitrant sectors of it highlight the association of their own fate with that of the Confederates some decades earlier, especially the economic ruin supposedly endured by their US counterparts. On the eve of slavery's demise the contradictions of the process of abolition in the United States were still reverberating in the Brazilian experience. One planter from traditional Bahia argued in the Senate the very day that abolition was passed that although "[he was] convinced that Brazil [would] not die because of the absence of slavery," he did fear for the slaveholders' "fortunes acquired in good faith." Drawing on "the great misfortunes in the South of the United States," the Baron of Cotegipe foresaw a gloomy future for former slaveholders based on the precedent of the US South, where "the misfortunes which [fell on former slaveholders] are so many and great that they might not be repaired in half a century."[115]

Throughout the process of abolition, Brazilian images of the United States were ubiquitous in political debate, and ranged along a spectrum of negative to positive, continually shifting depending on the context. It is conventional in Brazilian historiography to write about the influence of the United States as if it were a unidirectional process. The evidence of the debate about the US model of abolition, however, illustrates one of the larger themes of this book, which is that images of the United States proved so pervasive precisely because they were constituted locally and for highly specific purposes. A highly active role was played by Brazilian observers of the United States who made shameless strategic use of whatever images seemed best to serve their own purposes in promoting their aspirations for their own country.

Conclusion

There was a widespread view during the 1860s—shared by US abolitionists—that US slavery was intrinsically and systematically more brutal than slavery in the Spanish Caribbean or Brazil.[116] This represented a sharp reversal from earlier images, notably among Cuban annexationists or conservative French observers, of slavery in the American South as a relatively harmonious institution because of its reliance on natural reproduction rather than the slave trade.[117] About abolition in the United States, however, there were no such shared imaginings. It is striking that, with the exception of Britain, where US abolitionists were familiar faces on lecture circuits, foreign representations of the US abolitionist movement were highly selective and often badly misinformed. In Cuba, Brazil and, to an extent, elsewhere, the absence of internally generated images of democratic practice shaped images of the role of antislavery politics in the United States. Abolitionist campaigners in general were revered (or feared), but apart from Harriet Beecher Stowe, who was ubiquitously visible, there was appreciable variation in the degree to which other individuals attracted attention: Wendell Phillips was prominent in Cuba, for example; John Brown and William Lloyd Garrison in Brazil.

In all three countries, the pivotal event of emancipation during the US Civil War was interpreted in the light of local circumstances. It was not the only model of emancipation available, but it proved the most influential, even as its meaning was radically contested. Even among abolitionists, a wide variety of images—or lessons to be drawn from the American case—circulated. At the heart of the debate about American emancipation was the feature in which it differed so dramatically from the British and even French colonial precedents, namely its inseparability from a bloody and destructive war. For advocates of gradual rather than immediate abolition, the lesson was that a more cautious approach was preferable. For others, it was proof that violent resistance was not only an effective way to combat entrenched power, but that war could bring moral reformation.

Notes

1. Portell Vilá, *Historia de Cuba en sus relaciones con los Estados Unidos y España*, vol. 2, 170–1.
2. Carwardine and Sexton, eds., *The Global Lincoln*.
3. Bethell, *The Abolition of the Brazilian Slave Trade*; Graham, *Britain and the Onset of Modernization in Brazil*.
4. Serrano García, ed., *España 1868–1874*.
5. Schmidt-Nowara, *Empire and Antislavery*, 162.
6. Gabriel Tassara, Spanish minister in Washington, to the Spanish Dept. of State, July 19, 1865, Archivo Histórico Nacional [AHN], Ultramar, Leg. 3547. Cited in Corwin, *Spain and the Abolition of Slavery*, 162.
7. Rafael M. de Labra, *La abolición de la esclavitud en el órden económico* (Madrid: M. Martinez [Sociedad Abolicionista Española], 1874), viii.
8. Cited in Corwin, *Spain*, 250.
9. Corwin, *Spain*, 224–6.
10. Ferrer, *Insurgent Cuba*.
11. J. A. S. Argudio, "La Nación Española a su parlamento," *La Epoca*, January 2, 1873, and the two subsequent quotations in this paragraph.
12. Gabriel Rodríguez, speech published in *Una sesión de la Tertulia Radical en Madrid. Sesión del 16 de enero del 1873* (Madrid: Imprenta Teodoro Lucuix, 1873), 9.
13. Gabriel Rodríguez, "La abolición de la esclavitud en los Estados Unidos," published in *Conferencias anti-esclavistas del teatro de Lope de Rueda* (Madrid: Publicaciones de la Sociedad Abolicionista Española, 1872), 31–2.
14. Rodríguez, "La abolición," 31–2.
15. Ibid., 17–18.
16. Krausists followed the ideas of the German Karl Christian Friedrich Krause, which were introduced into Spain by Julián Sanz del Río, professor of the history of philosophy at the University of Madrid. For its Spanish followers, who included several of the liberals prominent in this period, Krausism offered a path to national renewal by way of its pantheistic moral imperative to create a hierarchical, yet harmonious society. Society was conceived as an organic whole in which each sector played a distinct part; its ultimate goal of harmony would be achieved when each of these sectors realised, accepted and fulfilled their particular role. The purpose of education and reform, then, was to enlighten sectors of society—whether women, the working class, or the slaves in Spain's colonies in Cuba and Puerto Rico—in order that they could understand and fulfil their potential, but only within the parameters of the subordinate role assigned to them in the natural order.

17. Rafael M. de Labra, *La emancipación de los esclavos en los Estados Unidos* (Madrid: Sociedad Abolicionista Española, 1873), 2.
18. Labra, *La emancipación*, 1–2.
19. Rafael M. de Labra, *La Brutalidad de los Negros (Arguments in disproof of the brutality of negroes)* (Madrid: no publisher given, 1876).
20. The figures used by Labra came from a "semi-official" US report given to him by Ambassador Sickles. Labra, *La abolición de la esclavitud*, 66 and 209–10.
21. Labra, *La emancipación*, 75.
22. On the close links between the abolitionist and free trade movements in Spain, see Schmidt Nowara, *Empire and Antislavery*, chapters 3–5.
23. On the relationship between the "social movements" in mid-to-late-century Spain, see Gil Novales, "Abolicionismo y librecambio."
24. Speech given by Segismundo Moret y Prendegast to the Cortes, June 20th, 1870 in *Diario de Sesiónes de las Cortes Constituyente 1869–1871* (Madrid: J. A. García, 1870) 14: 8998–9. Cited in Schmidt-Nowara, " 'Spanish Cuba,'" 114.
25. Rafael M. de Labra, *La revolución Norte-americana del siglo XVIII* (Madrid: Imprenta De Aurelio J. Alaria, 1881), 373.
26. Labra, *La abolición de la esclavitud*, viii.
27. Rodríguez, "La abolición," 32.
28. The growth in support for abolition in Puerto Rico from the mid-century proved an important impetus for the development of abolitionist sentiment in the metropole, which reinforces the point that the relationship between colony and metropole was one of mutual stimulation and influence. See Schmidt Nowara, *Empire and Antislavery*, 49–50.
29. Joaquín Mará Sanromá, *Mis memorias 1828–1868*, vol. 1 (Madrid: Imprenta de Manuel G Hernández, 1887), 333. Corwin, *Spain*, 158.
30. Gabriel Rodríguez, "La idea e il movimiento antiesclavista en España durante el siglo XIX," in *La España del siglo XIX*, vol. III (Madrid: A. San Martin, 1886–7, cited in Corwin, *Spain*, 162.
31. See, for example, *El Abolicionista*, October 15, 1872; December 30, 1872; and May 26, 1873.
32. "Il manifiesto de la Liga contra las reformas ultramarinos," *El Abolicionista*, January 28, 1873.
33. Schmidt Nowara, *Empire and Antislavery*, 119–22.
34. Portell Vilá, *Historia de Cuba*, vol. II, 135.
35. Emeterio S. Santovenia, "Lincoln, el precursor de la Buena vecindad" [1951], in his *Estudios, biografías y ensayos* (Havana: no publisher stated, 1957), 481–99. For details of 14 individuals who fought for the Union, see http://www.latinamericanstudies.org/Cubans-civil-war.htm (accessed July 23, 2010). On Cubans who fought for the Confederacy, see Tucker, ed., *Cubans in the Confederacy*.
36. F. Fernández Cavada, letter cited in Emeterio Santovenia, "Abraham Lincoln," in his *Estudios, biografías y ensayos*, 435–80, 487.
37. Portell Vilá, *Historia de Cuba*, II, 145.
38. Ibid., 172.

39. Emeterio Santovenia, "Reafirmación del régimen colonial," in *Guerra y Sánchez* et al., ed., *Historia de la nación cubana*, vol. IV, 3–60, 51.
40. *El Siglo* (Havana), August 23, 1863 and January 28, 1864, cited in Foner, *A History of Cuba and its Relations with the United States*, vol. II, 132–3.
41. Cited in Foner, *A History of Cuba*, II, 135.
42. Excerpts from Lincoln's State of the Union Address, December 1, 1862, in *El Siglo*, Año I, nos. 232 and 233, 13 and 15 December 1862, quotation 13 December, 2.
43. *El Siglo*, December 5, 1863.
44. Ibid.
45. Cited in Martínez-Alier, *Marriage, Class and Colour in Nineteenth-Century Cuba*, 31.
46. Santovenia, "Lincoln," 465.
47. Portell Vilá, *Historia de Cuba*, II, 170–1.
48. Antonio María de Zea, to Gabriel García Tassara, minister of Spain in the United States, April 11, 1864, from New York, cited in Emeterio S. Santovenia, "La Popularidad de Mr Lincoln," *Carteles* (Havana), August 31, 1947, www.guije.com/public/carteles/2835/lincoln/index.html (accessed September 5, 2010).
49. Foner, *A History of Cuba*, II, 140–4.
50. Portell Vilá, *Historia de Cuba*, II, 173.
51. Edouard Laboulaye, "Préface," in Porfirio Valiente, *Réformes dan les îles de Cuba et de Porto-Rico* (Paris: Imprimerie Centrale des chemins de fer, 1869), ii.
52. Valiente, *Réformes*, 274–5.
53. The 1862 census listed 368,550 slaves, 221,417 free blacks and 4,521 *emancipados*, out of a total population of 1,359,238. Foner, *A History of Cuba*, II, 128.
54. Foner, *A History of Cuba*, II, 133.
55. Ibid., 164.
56. Carlos Manuel Céspedes, letter to Secretary of State William Seward, October 23–4, 1868, cited in Portell Vilá, *Historia*, II, 217.
57. Miguel Aldama, speaking at a banquet in New York, "Obsequio al Gral. Jordan," in *La Revolución* (New York), no. 142, May 14, 1870, 1.
58. Ponte Domínguez, *Historia de la Guerra de los Diez Años*, 36.
59. Ignacio Mora, *El Mambi* (Guaimaro), May 7, 1869, 1.
60. Portell Vilá, *Historia de Cuba*, II, 240, citing Gonzalo de Quesada, first representative of the insurgents in Washington.
61. *La Sombra* (Havana), Año I, no. 52, September 27, 1874, 413.
62. *El Moro Muza* (Havana), Año 6, no. 49, September 19, 1869, 471.
63. Foner, *A History of Cuba*, II, 199–200.
64. Ibid., 151.
65. Murat Halstead, *The Story of Cuba* (Akron, OH: The Werner Company, 6th edn, 1896), 61.
66. Lisa Brock, "Regreso al futuro. Cuba entre los afronorteamericanos," in Hernández, ed., *Mirar al Niágara*, 87–127, esp. 94–9.

67. Bergad, *The Comparative Histories of Slavery in Brazil, Cuba, and the United States*, 280–1.
68. Pedro de Araújo Lima, Marquês de Olinda, "Ata de 5 de novembro de 1866," in José Honório Rodrigues, ed., *Atas do Conselho de Estado* (Brasília: Senado Federal, 1978).
69. "Fala do Trono de 22 de maio de 1867," in *Falas do Trono desde o Ano de 1823 até o Ano de 1889* (Brasília: Câmara dos Deputados, 1977), 374.
70. Joaquim Nabuco, *O Abolicionismo* (1st edn, Rio de Janeiro: Lamoureux—São Paulo: Publifolha, 2000), ch. XV; translated and edited: Conrad, *Abolitionism*. See also Murilo de Carvalho, *A Construção da Ordem*, 291–328.
71. João Batista Calógeras [member of the Ministry of Foreign Affairs], 30 maio 1865, Arquivo Histórico de Itamaraty (henceforth AHI), Instruções, Minutas, Folder No. 2 (C/I).
72. Joaquim Nabuco, in *O Paiz* (Rio de Janeiro), December 9, 1886. José Murilo de Carvalho, "Liberalismo, radicalismo e republicanismo nos anos sessenta do século dezenove," *Centre for Brazilian Studies* (University of Oxford), 2007. Working paper No. CBS-87–07, 8.
73. *Diário do Rio de Janeiro*, November 7, 1863.
74. Aureliano Cândido Tavares Bastos, "Memória sobre a Imigração," in *Sociedade Internacional de Immigração. Relatório Annual da Directoria. Acompanhado dos Seguintes Annexos: I, Memória sobre a Imigração pelo Director A. C. Tavares Bastos; II, Idem pelo Director Herman Haupt*, No. 1 (Rio de Janeiro: Typographia Imperial e Constitucional de J. Villeneuve, 1867), 7–8, fn 4.
75. José Antônio Saraiva (minister of foreign affairs) to Joaquim Maria Nascentes d" Azambuja (head of the Brazilian Legation to the United States), June 19, 1865. AHI, MDB, Washington, Despachos, Seção Central, s/n. Reservado.
76. "Emigração da América do Norte," on the front page of *Diário do Rio de Janeiro*, October 15, 1865. There were many letters and documents exchanged between the secretary for foreign affairs of the Empire and the Imperial Legation in the United States between 1866 and 1868, now held in the Palácio do Itamaraty, Rio de Janeiro, that attest to the seriousness of the endeavors to attract ex-Confederates to colonize the Empire. See also, "Imigração Norte-Americana para o Brasil," *Revista de Imigração e Colonização* (Rio de Janeiro), 4:2 (Junho, 1943), 264–333 and Antunes de Oliveira, *Movimento de Passageiros Norte-Americanos no Porto do Rio de Janeiro*.
77. Tavares Bastos, "Memória," 7. Estimates of the number of former Confederates to migrate to Brazil vary from contemporary figures of over 1,000 to more recent calculations of closer to 2,000. Tavares Bastos, "Memória," 5–6; Griggs, *The Elusive Eden*, 30; Barros Basto, *Síntese da História da Imigração no Brasil*, 69–70.
78. "Emigração da América do Norte," *Diário do Rio de Janeiro*, October 15, 1865.
79. The Council of State consisted of ten lifetime appointees named by the emperor to assist him to wield the Moderating Power granted by the 1824 Constitution.

80. Marquês de São Vicente, "Ata de 5 de novembro de 1866," in Rodrigues, *Atas.*
81. Nabuco de Araújo, "Ata de 5 de novembro de 1866," in Rodrigues, *Atas.*
82. Visconde de Inhomirim, "Ata de 5 de novembro de 1866," in Rodrigues, *Atas.*
83. "Estados Unidos da América do Norte," *Diário do Rio de Janeiro,* June 4, 1865.
84. Antônio da Silva Netto, *A Corôa e a Emancipação do Elemento Servil* (Rio de Janeiro: Typographia Universal de Laemmert, 1869), 19–23, 21.
85. "Manifesto Republicano," *A Republica* (Rio de Janeiro), December 3, 1870, 1.
86. Joaquim Nabuco promoted this myth at the International Anti-Slavery Conference in Paris in August 1867. Marinho de Azevedo, "Quem Precisa de São Nabuco?," 94.
87. *Jornal do Commércio,* January 3, 1863; *Semana Illustrada* (Rio de Janeiro), 5:232, May 1865; João D. Frick, *Abolição da Escravatura. Breve Noticia sobre a Primeira Sociedade de Emancipação no Brazil (Fundada na Cidade do Rio Grande do Sul em março de 1869)* (Lisboa: Lallemant Frères, 1885), 12.
88. "Ata de 2 de abril de 1867," in Rodrigues, *Atas.*
89. José Maria da Silva Paranhos, Visconde de Rio Branco, "Ata de 2 de abril de 1867," in Rodrigues, *Atas*
90. Visconde de Rio Branco, in Rodrigues, *Atas.*
91. Ibid.
92. Ibid.
93. Visconde de Rio Branco, *Ata de 2 de abril de 1867,* in Rodrigues, *Atas.*
94. Visconde de Rio Branco, *Discussão da Reforma do Estado Servil,* Sessão do 29 maio 1871, 28.
95. Ibid., 176.
96. Francisco de Paula de Negreiros Saião Lobato, *Reforma do Estado Servil,* Sessão do 31 maio 1871, 52–3.
97. Nabuco, "Terceira conferencia no Theatro Santa Isabel a 16 de novembro," in Annibal Falcão, ed., *Campanha Abolicionista no Recife (Eleições de 1884). Discursos de Joaquim Nabuco* (Rio de Janeiro: Typographia de O. Leuzinger e Filhos, 1885), 57–116, 96. Nabuco's articles signed with the nom-de-plume of Garrison appeared in 1884 in the *Jornal de Commércio* and in the *Gazeta da Tarde,* which became the main press organ of the abolitionist movement in 1881.
98. Nabuco, "Terceira conferencia."
99. Joaquim Nabuco, *Minha Formação* (1st ed., Rio de Janeiro: Edições de Ouro/Tecnoprint, 1900), ch. XVIII.
100. Nabuco recollected his thoughts on US society in his *Minha Formação,* 79–105.
101. *O Paiz,* January 28, 1881.
102. André Rebouças, *Gazeta da Tarde* (Rio de Janeiro), December 1, 1880.
103. André Rebouças, "A província de São Paulo depois da abolição," *Gazeta da Tarde,* May 31, 1883.
104. Nabuco, *O Abolicionismo,* ch. XVII.
105. Joaquim Nabuco to Henry W. Hilliard, Rio de Janeiro, October 19, 1880, in *Sociedade Brasileira contra a Escravidão Cartas do Presidente Joaquim Nabuco*

e do Ministro Americano H. W. Hilliard sobre Emancipação nos Estados Unidos (Rio de Janeiro: G. Leuzinger & Filhos, 1880), 3–5. For an English version of these documents, see Henry Washington Hilliard, *Politics and Pen Pictures at Home and Abroad* (New York: G. Putman, 1892).

106. Henry W. Hilliard to Joaquim Nabuco, Rio de Janeiro, October 25, 1880, in *Sociedade Brasileira contra a Escravidão*, ibid., 6–23. This exchange of missives was published in the *Jornal de Commércio* and the *Gazeta de Notícias* on October 31, 1880.
107. Luíz Gama, "A emancipação ao pé da letra," *Gazeta do Povo* (Rio de Janeiro), December 28, 1880.
108. For a comprehensive biography of Luíz Gama, see Mennucci, *O Precursor do Abolicionismo no Brasil*.
109. Getulino [Luíz Gama], *Primeiras Trovas Burlescas* (São Paulo: Typographia Dois de Dezembro, 1859).
110. Nabuco took the view that "the abolitionist movement began in the Chamber in 1879"—see *Minha formação* and Nabuco, *Life of Joaquim Nabuco*, 39–51. Historian Célia Marinho de Azevedo reminds us that contemporary historiography on Brazilian abolitionism uncritically accepts Nabuco's disregard for other contributions to the abolitionist case, which helps to explain why abolitionism before 1880 is rarely studied even today. Marinho de Azevedo, "Quem Precisa de São Nabuco?," 96, fn 6.
111. *O Diabo Coxo* (The Lame Devil, 1864–5) and *O Cabrião* (A troublesome person, 1866–7).
112. Joaquim Nabuco, cited in Alexandre Miranda Delgado, "Aspectos da campanha abolicionista na imprensa," in Wehling, ed., *A Abolição do Cativeiro Os Grupos Dominantes*, 123–7, 126
113. Luíz Gama, Letter to his son Benedito Graco Pinto da Gama, September 23, 1870. Cited in Fonseca Ferreira, "Luíz Gama," 278.
114. Conrad, *The Abolition*, 150–69.
115. João Maurício Wanderlei, Barão de Cotegipe, Senado, May 13, 1888. Cited in Koshiba and Frauze Pereira, *História do Brasil*, 238–9.
116. Both European and Latin American visitors to Cuba spread this idea: see Pérez de la Riva, *La isla de Cuba*, esp. 124 and 178. Julia Ward Howe observed that "The slave laws of Cuba are far more humane than our own," although she was realistic enough to add the caveat that Spanish magistrates were not necessarily "trustworthy in carrying them out," *A Trip to Cuba* (Boston: Ticknor and Fields, 1860), 221–2.
117. Bergad, *Comparative Histories*, 276.

Conclusion

Nicola Miller

The old world, in its experience, and South America, in its youth, both constantly look to Washington's native land. All schools, religions and systems endeavor to enlist the spirit of the United States. All political institutions and constitutional theories tend to be based on the foundations of the American city. Every example of progress, every proof of truth, every imaginable reconciliation of liberty and order, centralization and federation, union and independence, local [...] and national life, all appeal to the spectacle—the magnificent spectacle—of the United States [...]. Chilean intellectual Francisco Bilbao, on US Independence Day, 1858[1]

Many people—both in Europe and in Latin America—were indeed looking to the United States in the second half of the nineteenth century. The results of *the* great experiment in modern nation building were eagerly anticipated by both its champions and its critics. The claims made by many Americans, especially political leaders, that the United States was a universal nation, forging a new society not just for one people but for all humankind, were subjected to widespread, if not always well-informed, scrutiny abroad. It is no coincidence that newspapers throughout Europe and Latin America devoted extensive coverage to the great exhibitions of the period, the Centennial one in Philadelphia and, above all, the World Fair held in Chicago in 1893: such events showcased the United States' official self-definition as the place where all the wonders of the world could be found. Given that the United States often presented itself as a "spectacle," a grand performance of all things modern, it is hardly surprising that anyone who caught even a glimpse of the show felt entitled to pass comment. America was not only a place people felt they knew, at least as part of their imagined life, but it was also a place they felt they had a right to know. This was the state of affairs, above all, perhaps, in Britain, where a self-consciously transatlantic intellectual community developed, at least partly facilitated by the common language, but it was also evident in Cuba, where not only members of the intellectual and political elites but also workers had firsthand experience of the United States, and where dual-language periodicals reinforced a sense of familiarity between the two countries. It was also true elsewhere, if to a lesser extent. In some countries, images of the United States circulated mainly among the elites, or even particular sectors of the elites, for example, Spain and France, but there was surprising social depth to the dissemination of images of the United States, not only in Britain and Cuba. There was popular interest in the United States in Italy (even though—contrary to the common assumption—large-scale migration to the United States did not begin until the start of the twentieth century) and, from the 1880s onward, in Argentina (within the labor movement) and Brazil (because of abolitionist societies). In some places, there were particular periods when images of the United States came to the fore: in Spain, during the six years after the "glorious revolution" of 1868, for example, in Brazil during the 1880s as abolition became a widespread demand, or in France throughout the period of the Second Republic and Second Empire (1848–70). Everywhere, images of the United States were crystallized in the fragments of American English that, from the 1880s onward, were adopted abroad: *self-government, self-made man, go-ahead, comfort, boss, time is money, flirt, miss*. What stands out, however, is the variety of images in play.

The Stuff that Dreams are Made on . . .

In order to understand any particular image of the United States most or all of the following five factors had to be taken into account:

(i) Circulation of images (What were the networks of information, routes of transmission, vehicles of dissemination? What was the extent of social reach, visibility, and receptivity to the images?)
(ii) Carriers of images (Who was producing the images and who were they defined by class, race, and gender? How were they placed in terms of ideology, politics, or economic interest? What were their self-representations?)
(iii) Character of images (Where did they fall on the spectrum from talismanic invocations, for example, of "Lincoln" or "self-government," to multilayered, dense, and sophisticated images? To what extent were things added—or subtracted—locally? How constrained or enhanced were the perspectives on certain phenomena?)
(iv) Context of images (What were the ideological/political debates and events in the receiving country, including US policies and attitudes toward that country?)

(v) Competition of images (Which other countries were present in the social imaginary? What was their relative salience and how did they relate to images of the United States?)

By its nature, this project in comparative cultural history is a survey of a potentially vast field, some areas of which have been well worked while others remain virtually untouched. We found an extraordinary diversity of images that go beyond the well-studied representations of the United States found in literary works, travel writing, and immigrant accounts. There are other themes and many other societies that could be explored, and we hope that other researchers will build upon what we have done here. What our findings have clearly shown is that local conditions shaped horizons of expectation about the United States at least as much as anything the United States itself either was or did. There were some common reference points, but they were relatively few in number, whether we consider events, iconic figures, texts, or sites of imagination. Even those that were widely shared were interpreted in very different ways in different locales. In short, "America" and "American" were highly unstable signifiers.

To take the US Civil War as a revealing example, the following rapid survey, which deliberately focuses only on the most prevalent images, serves to illustrate the range and diversity of the possible meanings generated by even such a widely covered event. In Britain, the outcome was interpreted as confirmation of their protégé's capacity to overcome all obstacles to the consolidation of a strong nation-state. For conservatives, especially, it showed the importance of solid, durable institutions; for radicals, it revived a Paine-ite view of the United States as the crucible of freedom and democracy, an image that testified to the overwhelming importance of Lincoln in the British imagination. The French Left saw the Unionist victory as a vindication of defending the values of a founding revolution, just as they were seeking to do themselves. Popular opinion in France was abolitionist, but often at the same time pro-South, out of a sense of cultural affinity and in the context of relative ignorance about the issues at stake. The contradictions of this position were sustained by romanticized images of slaves in the South being treated better than wage laborers in the North, which were also present in Britain. In Italy, where sympathy for the Unionist cause was widespread, images of the Civil War were almost wholly negative, focused on the extreme violence and high casualties involved, as horror at the very real excesses of the war came to suffuse most Italian representations of it—*feuilletons* circulated (exaggerated) stories about murderous housewives in the Wild West and (entirely fictitious) battalions of ruthless female warriors. The Civil War seemed to confirm the Catholic Church's hostility toward the making of nation-states, while many liberals saw it as a sign that the United States was no longer a valid constitutional model. In Spain, conservatives, who were against both republicanism and colonial reform, also represented the US Civil War as barbaric and as evidence for the inappropriateness of the United States as a role model. Progressives, who advocated US-style abolition and/or a federal republic for Spain, either skirted around the issue of the Civil War or, when they did acknowledge it, painted it as a simple, polarized battle between a "good" abolitionist North and a "bad" slave-owning South. They also seem to have accepted— at least they often repeated—the United States' own official interpretation of the Civil War as the ultimate test of its values and institutions, which had emerged from the war all the stronger.

Argentine liberals also echoed the US view of the Civil War as a hurdle of nation building, although their own problems led them to emphasize the particular importance of civilian authority prevailing over the military, even in wartime, and the overriding importance of unity. In Brazil, both liberals and conservatives saw it as a vision of the horrors that could ensue from too hasty a dismantling of the institution of slavery, although liberals used it to support arguments for reform, albeit gradual, whereas conservatives predictably saw it as proof of the need to preserve the status quo. In Cuba, the US Civil War was interpreted—both approvingly and critically—as emblematic of the connection between all forms of emancipation—from colonial rule, from slavery, from social hierarchy. In both Europe and Latin America, then, the US Civil War was viewed through the lens of local political concerns.

After Lincoln's assassination, which resonated internationally, the next event to feature prominently was the Spanish-Cuban-American War of 1898, which marks the end point of our analysis. In the intervening years, there was great variation in the extent of coverage abroad of other landmark events in US history, such as the disputed election of 1876, the assassination of President Garfield in 1881, the Haymarket Riots of 1886, or the economic panics of 1873 and 1893. For example, the 1876 elections gave further ammunition to Argentines, many of whom were already becoming more critical of the United States, but they were barely discussed in Cuba, where most people still had a benign view of the United States. A few US figures became ubiquitously iconic: Washington (although he was not very visible in Spain); Harriet Beecher Stowe (albeit there was no great interest in Argentina, and she was something of a figure of fun in France, where she was seen as far too earnest); Edgar Allan Poe (but at very different periods in Europe—the 1840s—and Latin America—the 1880s/90s); Mrs Cleveland (but very little in France or Italy); Edison. The idealist writers Longfellow, Emerson, and Whitman attracted attention in Latin America, Spain, and Italy, but there was less interest in them elsewhere. Ulysses Grant was prominent in Britain, Cuba, and Argentina, but not in France, Italy, Spain, or Brazil. Henry George mattered a lot in Britain and Argentina, but was little known in Italy or France. William F. Cody (Buffalo Bill) was a familiar figure in Europe and in Cuba—not least for his speech in support of Cuban independence in 1898—and in Mexico, but less so in other parts of Latin America. The only one who was a ubiquitously towering figure was Lincoln, but, as discussed in chapter 1, what the signifier "Lincoln" meant varied so dramatically as virtually to detach it from any US context.

Apart from some of Lincoln's speeches, mainly the Gettysburg Address, the only two texts about the United States that seemed to resonate virtually everywhere both antedated the Civil War: Tocqueville's *De la démocratie en Amérique* (1835 and 1840) and Harriet Beecher Stowe's *Uncle Tom's Cabin* (1852). The impact of even those works, which of course became international phenomena, varied in timing, social reach, and significance. As for sites of imagination, New York was by far the most prominent throughout the period, supplemented and, to an extent, displaced toward the end of the century by Chicago—the quintessentially modern "American" city. Images of other cities such as Boston, Philadelphia, and San Francisco were also common. California as a whole featured increasingly prominently from the 1850s onward, usually as a microcosm of the extremes of US society, either its potential for boundless largesse or its lust for wealth and consequent disregard for human relations, although there were other interpretations; for example, José Martí saw it as a crucible of benign relations between Hispanics and indigenous people. Beyond that, perhaps the most widely shared images of US locations were of its modes of transportation, especially railroads and steamships, and its hotels, both of which were often represented as microcosms of US society. Rural United States featured relatively little in Spanish or Argentine images (reflecting the strong association of civilization with urbanity among liberals in those societies), although there was interest in US land policy and agricultural techniques in Argentina. Argentina also had its own culture of the frontier in the gaucho, a figure that began to acquire iconic status in Argentine folklore at about the same time as the gauchos themselves were being fought to extinction in order to clear the Argentine pampas for cultivating wheat. In many countries, there was a tendency to focus upon one particular aspect of the US landscape to the exclusion of others: Niagara Falls became a place of ritual pilgrimage for Latin American visitors, particularly Cuban writers, who invested the site with a rich symbolic force, seeing it as a metaphor for the power of nature in the 1820s, the power of industry in the 1860s, and the potential of nature to constrain industry in the 1880s.[2] Both Italian republicans and English land reformers promoted an image of the United States as a country where everybody could own a piece of land, in order to bolster their own campaigns for agrarian reform. Like the Italians, the French were intrigued by the Wild West, as were the British, who were also fascinated by New England villages, with their town meetings, which were represented by some as direct continuities of ancient Anglo-Saxon liberties.

Interpretations of the Spanish-Cuban-American-War varied as widely as had responses to the Civil War, as the following brief sample indicates. In Spain itself, as belligerent rhetoric between the two countries increased from the mid-1890s onward, images of the United States unsurprisingly became more hostile and somewhat one-dimensional. For all but a few progressive liberals, the United States was depicted as a pig or as "a nation of chicken farmers" or, turning New/Old World imagery on its head, as a lecherous old Uncle Sam ogling and manhandling the virginal, innocent female figure of Spain.[3] In France, although the government declared its neutrality, French public opinion was united in favor of Spain, both for economic reasons (France was the most important investor in Spain) and for more cultural and sentimental reasons (a common "Latin" bond). US claims on Cuba and the Philippines were interpreted as final proof of "the American peril."[4] By contrast, British reactions were polarized between the Tories and the jingoistic press, who, in an outpouring of the rhetoric of fraternal Anglo-Saxonism, welcomed the United States as a fellow colonial power that could help to carry the white man's burden, and political radicals, who had until then continued to believe in the United States' own self-image as a force for anticolonialism. They felt appalled and even betrayed by what they represented as the US usurpation of Cuba's struggle for independence. In Argentina there was profound ambivalence: a widespread view that Spain's ejection from the Americas was long overdue vied with an equally pervasive sense that concerns about the power of the United States were amply justified.

Comparing Europe and Latin America

It was not necessarily the case during this period that Latin American countries were more exposed to images of the United States than continental Europeans. Argentina and Brazil had, if anything, less access to images of the United States than France or Spain, at least before the introduction of direct communications in the late 1870s, and indeed they received most of their news about the United States either from European sources or from US sources carried by European ships. There were far more contact zones in Cuba and Mexico, of course, with a wide range of traffic of people and goods each way in both cases, from Cuban mixed-race couples slipping over to Florida, where priests would conduct the marriage ceremony that was banned by the colonial authorities, to US mining engineers in Mexico. The effects of geographical proximity were not always or only what might be anticipated, however. There was certainly a greater visibility of images of the United States in Cuba and Mexico than in the South American countries; whether that necessarily correlated with greater complexity or richness in the images is harder to determine. In Cuba, a survey of the periodicals of the 1880s suggests that the United States was synonymous with two simple messages: self-government and bad manners (the tourists). One way of coping with too much enforced closeness is to enact a simplifying, distancing maneuver; such a strategy can be seen, for example, in the work of José Martí, who, despite the remarkable range and depth of his cumulative writings on the United States, often summed it up in an epigram. It is also worth noting that because of Spanish colonial censorship many of Martí's articles were not published in Cuba but in Buenos Aires or Caracas. Most Cubans, even the educated, did not have full access to the complexity of Martí's analysis of US society until well into the twentieth century.[5] Geographical closeness probably mattered most in that it opened up possibilities for people to take advantage of what the United States had to offer, thereby keeping alive a sense of it as the land of opportunity even as more hostile images developed. Guy Thomson argues that Mexican images of the United States were less negative than the historical record of US seizure of Mexican territory would lead one to expect, partly because of the skill of Mexican political leaders in negotiating the relationship, but partly also because "increasing numbers of Mexicans found material benefit and economic freedom from the opportunities provided, on both sides of the border, by the prodigious expansion of the US economy."[6]

Of course, the United States was directly involved in the politics of Latin America during our period to an extent that it was not in Europe until the twentieth century. Latin American countries embarked upon their independent existence with an acute awareness of the predatory tendencies of the United States: Jefferson had long since identified both Cuba and Mexico as well within US sights, the Monroe Doctrine had been declared (1823), and US entrepreneurs were already casting covetous eyes upon the Amazon basin. By the late nineteenth century, the consequences of the United States' record of interventionism—the annexation of Texas, the Mexican-American War, William Walker's usurpation of Nicaragua, and so on—were manifest in the marked increase in the hostile representations of "Caliban" circulating in Latin America. As noted for the example of Mexico, however, factors beyond US policy have to be adduced to explain the variety of images and to understand why positive—or ambivalent—images persisted. Reactions in Latin America to US expansionism were complicated. During the 1850s, while there certainly were some virulently hostile images of the United States, many Latin American leaders had sufficient confidence in their capacity to defend their own interests, particularly if they could work together, that they continued to produce benign images of the United States as a virtuous republic while at the same time criticizing its adventurism abroad. In any case, these hostile images were largely dispelled by images of Lincoln, which served mainly to reinvigorate the view that the United States still stood for noble ideals. Even in respect of Lincoln, however, there is some evidence that the main reason for Latin American images of the United States becoming more positive after the Civil War was that Lincoln's government had propagated more favorable images of Latin America. The lasting power of the Monroe Doctrine lay in its profound ambiguity: was it a threat of domination or a promise of protection? Latin Americans debated the topic throughout the nineteenth century, many of them continuing to give the United States the benefit of the doubt until Theodore Roosevelt's administrations (1901–09) left no further room for it.

In differentiating Latin American images of the United States from European ones, perhaps the most important factor is that US experiences seemed more meaningful and relevant to Latin Americans than they did to Europeans, a difference that seems to have had less to do with republicanism than has often been assumed. After all, Brazil was a monarchical empire until 1889; France, Italy, and, briefly, Spain all had their own republican experiments. The main two points of Latin American identification with the United States were (i) that they had embarked on comparable experiments in nation building in vast, poorly integrated territories, after colonial rule, with profound social divisions along racial lines and (ii) that they shared a corresponding sense of the utopian promise of the Americas as the place where the ideals generated by Europe, but in degeneration there, would finally be realized. One of the aspects of the United States that particularly commanded attention in Latin America was its policy of assimilating and adapting the best European ideas, practices, and people, just as most of the Latin American countries sought to do. Latin American leaders had their own version of manifest destiny, which was reinforced toward the midcentury by the perception that the United States was no longer worthy of its own founding ideals. With Europe divided, oppressed, and alienated, only Latin America could rise to the challenge of creating a new moral force capable of countering "Yankee individualism."[7] In these broad senses, US experiences invited comparison with Latin American experiences in ways that were not relevant in continental Europe.

Moreover, it is probably fair to claim that Latin American images of the United States were shaped by US images of Latin America to a greater extent than European images of the United States were shaped by US images of Europe. Europeans were far more culturally self-confident than the United States, where intellectuals, above all, often represented their country as culturally inferior to the Europeans. Postcolonial anxieties notwithstanding, it was undeniably harder to counter European contempt for alleged US materialism in the era before the unanswerable successes of twentieth-century US mass culture. Europeans, on the other hand, were largely unconcerned about what anyone from the United States thought of them. In Latin America, many contributors to public debate continued to argue that their nations would in time achieve greater levels of development and civilization than either the Europeans or the Yankees, but as the United States consolidated the Union and shot ahead economically in the three decades after the Civil War, Latin American claims to superiority were increasingly channeled into the cultural sphere. If continental Europeans were sometimes freer in their imaginings of the United States, it was not so much because it was less known there, but more because it did remain irreducibly foreign to them, whereas for Latin Americans the foreignness of the United States was to a considerable extent manufactured as a component of Latin America's own processes of identity creation. Another factor germane to thinking about the mutual constitution of images is the extent to which the United States reciprocated an interest in the other's experiences. It did so above all in Britain and Cuba, to some extent in France, Italy, and Spain, intermittently in Brazil and hardly at all in Argentina. Moreover, US images of others were mixed, too: there was indeed a high level of racist contempt for Latin Americans (to whom the Black Legend of the Spanish as brutal, irrational, and hierarchical was readily transferred), but there was also, as Guy Thomson has pointed out, specifically for the case of Mexico but the point has wider application, a good deal of "adventurous curiosity and romantic attachment."[8] It is no coincidence that many of the midcentury Latin American liberals who disseminated images of the United States as committed to its ideals had met the distinguished minority of US intellectuals who were interested in Latin America and pioneered US scholarship in the field—people like George Ticknor, who wrote the first major English-language study of Spanish literature, and William H. Prescott, famous for his histories of the conquests of Mexico and Peru.

It is tempting to conclude that elective affinities were more important than any material conditions or policy outcomes in differentiating degrees of receptivity to images of the United States. Britain and Cuba are more closely comparable in this respect than, say, Cuba and Argentina or Britain and Spain, because both Britain and Cuba, albeit for very different reasons, experienced a profound sense of identification with the United States. For both countries, America was part of their own histories, a terrain upon which their own experiences were enacted, to an extent that was not so elsewhere. Across the board, the more comparisons between "Europe" and "Latin America" were tested, the less convincing they became.

Transnational Processes of Identity Creation

This book's findings highlight three key points about the role of the foreign in the creation of national identities. First, there are bound to be significant variations in the degree and nature of power wielded by different actors, but it is misleading to assume that images are created or controlled solely by the powerful. Despite the pioneering work of Rob Kroes, mainly on the twentieth century, there is still an assumption prevalent in the historiography that Americanization was what the United States chose to project into the outside world, or that the mere presence of US culture or US goods leads automatically to Americanization. This book has identified many examples of the strategic production of images of the United States, especially—but by no means only—by sectors of the elites, for a variety of ends: to promote their own visions of their country's future; to legitimize policies that they wished to pursue; to discredit those they wished to oppose; to act as a convenient foil to definitions of national identity. In order to make sense of these diverse, contested, and constantly evolving images, comparative history can be, indeed has to be, reconciled with transnational history. While the national context was always significant in accounting for how the United States was imagined by any particular observer, few of these images could have been understood without some knowledge, albeit often regrettably incomplete, of the various—and often indirect—transnational routes by which they traveled.

To a significant extent "the United States" was invented, not in the United States itself, but elsewhere. In the same way, Alastair Bonnett has argued, the idea of "the West," as a shorthand term for the industrialized world, was "not a Western invention. At least, not simply or merely. It was developed and imagined in important, new and influential ways in the non-West."[9] Bonnett's history of the idea of the West set out to challenge the deep-seated assumption that "the West" acts but "the non-West" only reacts. An analogous argument could be made about "the United States" and other countries, including those European countries, such as Italy or Spain—or Hungary or Poland—that are customarily thought of as being mainly reactive in relation to the United States. The point is most obviously applicable to Latin America, however, where it can help to counter the residual tendency to approach the history of any particular country in terms of its relations with foreign powers. The new imperial history has done some very good work in exploring the effects of empire on the histories of the imperial powers themselves, and in drawing attention to the importance of informal modes of power. Yet it is still often assumed that the history of any country that has had any kind of relationship with any imperial power is best understood in the context of that one (implicitly all-determining) relationship—whether it be one of exploitation, collaboration, cooperation, or reciprocity. This leaves the country-that-is-not-the-imperial-power (what word is there to describe it—colonial, postcolonial, neocolonial—that does not relate to the imperial relationship?) as the site—the object—of the struggles of other powers. Tracing the history of how "the United States" was imagined and deployed as a discursive instrument challenges such a conception of both Latin American and European history.

The second point highlighted by a transnational perspective is that, although images of the United States have often been discussed in terms of bilateral relationships with other countries, the evidence in this book shows that there was a complex field of images between Europe, the United States, and Latin America. The relationship between images of Britain and images of the United States in Argentina provides a good illustration. Until the 1870s, when the British consolidated their economic prominence in Argentina, images of both Britain and the United States were predominantly positive. Images of Britain—which were almost exclusively images of upper-class Englishness—were of strong institutions, gentlemanly conduct, and a certain romantic heroism (Byron was an iconic figure among Argentine literati). The United States was associated with education for citizenship and dynamic transformational energy, usually represented as a distillation of the very best of Britishness. During the last quarter of the nineteenth century, however, while Argentine images of Britain remained largely favorable, notwithstanding momentary outbreaks of hostility, such as the Baring Crisis, images of the United States became increasingly hostile. A marked differentiation between Britain and the United States emerged, with the United States becoming the representation of everything that many Argentines disliked about their own experience, namely, the sense that economic growth was not in itself sufficient to create a civilized society. Although there were Argentines who expressed concern about their country's financial dependence on Britain, for the most part Argentine fears about their foreign-dependent approach to modernization were projected onto the United States instead of onto the neo-imperial power itself, Britain.

Thus as Latinity differentiated itself from Anglo-Saxonness, the already established habit of claiming that Argentina and Britain shared certain values (a longing for liberty; a fundamentally civilized way of doing business) meant that the negative elements of Anglo-Saxonness became associated with the United States and the positive aspects with Britain. A series of contrasts was drawn: English adventurers were bold and brave and inspired—even sent a little crazy—by their love of freedom, while American adventurers were selfish and ruthless and motivated by mercenary concerns. English energy was creative, exploratory, and humane; American energy was neurotic, mechanical, and destructive. England was the land of Shakespeare, Ruskin, and other noble souls; the United States lacked poetic genius and took an industrialized approach to culture. Such manipulation of images of the British and the Americans by the supposedly collaborative Argentine elites helped to constrain Britain's room for maneuver in Argentina because it was obliged to preserve a reputation for being gentlemanly. By distancing Argentina from the United States, it also helped to strengthen Argentine claims to lead the hemisphere in resistance against the increasing assertiveness of the United States. At this stage it is not plausible to argue that Argentina was a passive actor in relation to either Britain or the United States, whatever can be said about the interwar years. During the late nineteenth century, the Argentine elite conceptualized itself as part of an international capitalist class, engaged in its own pursuit of advanced modernization, picking and choosing aspects of the various alternative models on offer in the confidence that it would ultimately create the ideal blend to become the greatest modern society of all. Thus, a study of the competition of images can help to prevent an exclusive focus on how external powers acted upon Argentina—whether formally or informally—to create a broader perspective that takes into account the role of internal dynamics in shaping Argentina's responses. Images, particularly when in competition, can serve as sources for the constellation of factors, both internal and external, that created the context in which policy decisions were taken.

The third conclusion in relation to transnational aspects of identity creation is that it is a mistake to assume fixed or frozen perceptions of the foreign, or indeed that the extent of "foreignness" is a given either. For many of the British, images of the United States were not clearly "foreign" at all: their "otherness" was always in question. Even taking into account the particularity of the British situation, the point about the United States being simultaneously exotic yet familiar has resonance elsewhere, at least for certain people and/or at certain times. Images of the United States were found to be competing, changeable, and contradictory to an extent that there was no basis for predicting either uncritical emulation or automatic rejection, which are implicit in the terms Americanism or anti-Americanism. Even when used thoughtfully, with care taken to avoid pathological value judgments that correlate Americanism with health and rationality and anti-Americanism with sickness and irrationality, the very introduction of these terms as tools of analysis tends to be reductive and teleological, mainly because they are applied too sweepingly, for example, summarizing relations between the United States and Latin America as "A Brief History of Hostility, 1783–2005."[10] It is just not the case that all of Latin America was consistently and unremittingly antagonistic to the United States from the late eighteenth century to the twenty-first century, and such claims do not aid understanding of the history of the many instances of opposition to US policies that did take place. Americanism and anti-Americanism both exist, of course, as ideological or political positions worthy of study, but the use of them as analytical terms distracts attention away from the wide range of factors, particularly local factors, that shape perceptions of another society. Looking at images makes it possible to transcend the Americanism/anti-Americanism divide, to appreciate the wider canvas upon which attitudes to the United States were formed, and to gain some insights into how and why perceptions changed. Negative images sometimes mutated into systematic hostility, but at other times they were displaced or eclipsed by positive images, or more often still, simply coexisted alongside them. In most places, at most times, positive and negative interpretations of the United States were juxtaposed, sometimes in the same image. If the range of responses could possibly be captured in a single term, it would be neither admiration nor antagonism but ambivalence.

It is possible, even probable, that such claims could be made about images of any country. It is not at all easy to determine whether or not there was anything distinctive about the reception of the United States. Perhaps a clue can be found in an observation by Chilean playwright Ariel Dorfman, who spent the first 12 years of his life in New York in the 1940s–50s and later recalled "how effortless it was, and still is, to cross over from Yankee-basher to enthralled lover of American culture, [in] a zigzag, back-and-forth path of detestation and adoration."[11] One purpose of this book has been to counter the tendency to read the nineteenth century through the lens of the twentieth century, yet Dorfman's picture of the volatility of twentieth-century attitudes toward the United States serves as a reminder of the instability of the nineteenth-century images analyzed here.

Perhaps, then, the distinctive feature about reception of the United States at any stage of its history is the tendency toward oscillation, often within short periods of time and sometimes within the same people—between one extreme view of what the United States represented and another. Images of the United States acquired the same exaggerated, larger-than-life qualities that were often attributed to "the USA" itself. In casting itself as modernity writ large and bold, the United States to an extent invited foreigners to imagine it as a land in which anything was possible—both supremely good and inordinately bad—a land of excess and horror and wonder, a house of many mansions. It was in the mixture that the potency lay: to echo Martí, the United States was *both* the America of Lincoln *and* the America of Cutting (the New York gangster Bill "the Butcher").

Of course, what happened in the United States and what the United States did or did not do had consequences for how it was perceived abroad, but not necessarily immediately nor in any easily predictable ways, as was illustrated in the chapter on abolition. The US tendency to define itself as a model of modernity meant that it had even less control over how it was interpreted abroad than any other powerful country. Its self-representation as a metaphor of the future meant that everyone felt entitled to build their own utopia or dystopia. Aspects of US society were singled out according to what was deemed relevant in local circumstances, packaged up, and sent on their way, and it was wholly unpredictable where they landed up or what state they would be in when they arrived.

Images of United States in other societies were constructed in a complex field of images that included the self-representations of that society, its images of other societies, US images of that society, and US images of itself. In presenting itself as a universal nation the United States effectively invited everyone to help imagine it, thereby rendering itself an inescapably transnational nation. In some instances at least, images of the United States from abroad in turn reinforced Americans' own image of themselves as exceptional, which was reflected back again in images abroad. If the cultural artifact of "the USA" was often manufactured abroad, correspondingly the image of the United States as a model for other countries was often made in the USA. As noted in the introduction, the idea of the United States as a model for the Italian Risorgimento was at least partly a projection by Americans themselves. We can also see this process at work in Mary Mann's championing of Sarmiento as the man who would turn Argentina into the United States.[12] The cumulative evidence presented in this book therefore supports Ian Tyrrell's arguments that the prism of empire "is only one of the ways in which the United States has connected with [...] world history," and that the nineteenth century is crucial for understanding the transnationality of the American nation-state.[13] Transnational historians tend to focus upon flows of commodities, capital, or people, but this book illustrates that images are also worth studying as a source for understanding the subjective aspects of transnational exchange.

Images always say more about history of subject than of object, as is well known, but there were two common features about images of the United States in Europe and Latin America at the end of the nineteenth century that are worth noting in the light of twentieth-century developments. First, where the United States was still seen as attractive what made it so was its capacity to produce the "wondrous contrivances," in Anthony Trollope's words, that made everyday life enjoyable *for everybody*.[14] The idea that modernity should be democratic in the sense that its benefits should be accessible to all of the people, all of the time, seems to have been more strongly associated with the United States than any particular political rights. Second, the United States was widely seen as culturally lacking, even by those who looked kindly upon it. It was perceived to be good at distribution (literacy, schools, libraries) but not at production, its energy being channeled into material inventions, not artistic creativity. All the glory of Whitman's lofty lyricism could not redeem the United States from the charge of base materialism. It could be argued that elites in other countries, especially in Latin America, had an interest in disseminating such images in order to distract attention from their own failures to achieve the economic success of the United States. Yet such images were also prevalent in labor publications and sources of popular culture.

By the end of the nineteenth century, the cultural artifact of "the United States" had already been invented and reinvented many times over, used as a discursive instrument in specific national debates in ways that often bore scant if any relation to what was happening in the United States itself. Images of the United States were selected, screened, subverted, satirized, and supplemented according to particular social and national contexts. Criticism or praise of the United States did not necessarily entail loathing or love of the United States itself, but was often a convenient quick reference to things people rejected or embraced, such as materialism, mass consumption, or freedom of speech. Yet the association of such qualities with the external referent of the United States could always, not inevitably but potentially, mutate into feelings about the actual United States. US governments of the twentieth century (and indeed the twenty-first century) tended to act as if the rest of the world were a tabula rasa awaiting the benevolent imprint of US values and practices, but our research has shown very clearly that this was not so. A great many doubts had been expressed about the American way of life before the United States became a world power, let alone a superpower. The late nineteenth century, so often glossed over as a prelude to US empire, was a crucial formative period in evaluating the great experiment and in establishing the horizons of expectation for interpreting what was meant by "America."

Notes

1. Francisco Bilbao, "4 de julio—1776. Independencia de los Estados Unidos," 1858, in his *Obras completas,* ed. Manuel Bilbao (Imprenta de Buenos Aires, Buenos Aires, 2 vols., 1866), vol. II, 516–24, 516–17.
2. Luisa Campuzano, "A 'Valiant Symbol of Industrial Progress'?: Cuban Women Travelers and the United States," in *Women at Sea,* ed. Paravisini-Gebert and Romero-Cesano, 161–81.

3. Alvarez Junco, *The Emergence of Mass Politics in Spain*, 86; and Sebastian Balfour, " 'The Lion and the Pig': Nationalism and National Identity in Fin-de-Siècle Spain," in *Nationalism and the Nation in the Iberian Peninsula*, ed. Mar-Molinero and Smith, 107–18, 111.
4. Roger, *The American Enemy*, 143.
5. Guerra, *The Myth of José Martí*.
6. Guy Thomson, "Mexican Liberals and the Uses of the United States, 1829–1910," in *Americanisms*, ed. Steppat, 301–16, 302.
7. Francisco Bilbao, "Iniciativa de la América. Idea de un Congreso Federal de las repúblicas," 1856, in his *Obras completas*, vol. I, 285–304, esp. 292–9.
8. Thomson, "Mexican Liberals," 301.
9. Bonnett, *The Idea of the West*, 163.
10. MacPherson, *Anti-Americanism*.
11. Ariel Dorfman, *What We Think of America* (Special issue of *Granta*, 77, Spring 2002), 32.
12. Cárdenas, *Mary Mann*.
13. Tyrrell, *Transnational Nation*, 7.
14. Anthony Trollope, *North America* [1862] (New York: Alfred A. Knopf, 1951), 120.

Select Bibliography

The bibliography lists major works of secondary literature referred to in individual chapters as well as a small number of primary sources recurring throughout the book. References to works not directly relevant to the book as a whole are given in full in the footnotes.

Adams, Ephraim Douglass, *Great Britain and the American Civil War* (London: Longmans, 1925).
Adams, Willi Paul, "German Translations of the American Declaration of Independence," *The Journal of American History* 85, no. 4 (March 1999), 1325–1349.
Adamson, Walter, *Avant-Garde Florence: From Modernism to Fascism* (Cambridge, MA: Harvard University Press, 1993).
Agulhon, Maurice, *Marianne into Battle: Republican Imagery and Symbolism in France, 1789–1880* (Cambridge: Cambridge University Press, 1981).
Agulhon, Maurice, *The French Republic, 1879–1992* (Oxford: Blackwell, 1993).
Aldrich, Robert, *Greater France: A History of French Overseas Expansion* (Houndmills Basingstoke: Palgrave Macmillan, 1996).
Alvarez Junco, José, *The Emergence of Mass Politics in Spain: Populist Demagoguery and Republican Culture 1890–1910* (Brighton: Sussex Academic Press, 2002).
Antunes de Oliveira, Betty, *Movimento de Passageiros Norte-Americanos no Porto do Rio de Janeiro, 1865–1890: Uma Contribuição para a História da Imigração Norte-Americana no Brasil* (Rio de Janeiro: B.A. de Oliveira, 1981).
Archer, Margaret S., *Culture and Agency: The Place of Culture in Social Theory* (Cambridge: Cambridge University Press, 1988).
Ardao, Arturo, *Génesis de la idea y el nombre de América Latina* (Caracas: Centro de Estudios Latinoamericanos Rómulo Gallegos, 1980).
Arnold, Matthew, "A Word About America," *Nineteenth Century,* May 1882, 681–695.
Arnold, Matthew, "A Word More About America," *Nineteenth Century,* February 1885, 219–236.
Banti, Alberto M., *La nazione del Risorgimento* (Torino: Einaudi, 2001).
Barclay, David E. and Glaser-Schmidt, Elisabeth, eds., *Transatlantic Images and Perceptions: Germany and America since 1776* (Cambridge: Cambridge University Press, 1997).
Barros Basto, Fernando de Lazaro de, *Síntese da Historia da Imigração no Brasil* (Rio de Janeiro: Editôra e Impressora de Jornais e Revistas, 1970).
Bauer, Arnold, *Goods, Power, History: Latin America's Material Culture* (New York: Cambridge University Press, 2001).

Bayly, Christopher A. and Biagini, Eugenio F., eds., *Giuseppe Mazzini and the Globalisation of Democratic Nationalism, 1830–1920* (Oxford: Oxford University Press, 2008).
Belfiglio, Valentino J., "Italians and the American Civil War," *Italian Americana* 4, no. 2 (Spring/Summer 1978), 163–175.
Bell, Duncan, *The Idea of Greater Britain: Empire and the Future of World Order, 1860–1900* (Princeton, NJ: Princeton University Press, 2007).
Belnap, Jeffrey and Fernández, Raúl, eds., *José Martí's "Our America": From National to Hemispheric Cultural Studies* (Durham, NC: Duke University Press, 1998).
Bender, Thomas, ed., *Rethinking American History in a Global Age* (Berkeley and Los Angeles: University of California Press, 2002).
Benjamin, Walter, *The Arcades Project* (Cambridge, MA and London: Harvard University Press, 1999).
Bergad, Laird, *The Comparative Histories of Slavery in Brazil, Cuba, and the United States* (Cambridge and New York: Cambridge University Press, 2007).
Berger, Gottfried, *Amerika im XIX. Jahrhundert. Die Vereinigten Staaten im Spiegel zeitgenössischer deutschsprachiger Reiseliteratur* (Wien: Molden, 1999).
Bethell, Leslie, *The Abolition of the Brazilian Slave Trade: Britain, Brazil and the Slave Trade Question, 1807–1869* (Cambridge: Cambridge University Press, 1970).
Bhahba, Homi K., ed., *Nation and Narration* (London: Routledge, 1990).
Biagini, Eugenio, *Liberty, Retrenchment and Reform: Popular Liberalism in the Age of Gladstone* (Cambridge: Cambridge University Press, 1992).
Billington, Ray Allen, *Land of Savagery, Land of Promise: The European Image of the American Frontier* (New York: Norton, 1981).
Bitterli, Urs, *Die 'Wilden' und die 'Zivilisierten'. Grundzüge einer Geistes- und Kulturgeschichte der europäisch-überseeischen Begegnung* (München: Beck, 1976).
Blackett, R. J. M., *Divided Hearts: Britain and the American Civil War* (Baton Rouge: Louisiana State University Press, 2001).
Bolt, Christine, *The Anti-Slavery Movement and Reconstruction: A Study in Anglo-American Co-Operation, 1833–1877* (Oxford: Oxford University Press, 1969).
Bonnett, Alastair, *The Idea of the West* (Basingstoke and New York: Palgrave Macmillan, 2004).
Boritt, Gabor S., Neely, Mark E. Jr. and Holzer, Harold, "The European Image of Abraham Lincoln," *Winterthur Portfolio* 21, no. 2/3 (Summer-Autumn 1986), 153–183.
Boston, Ray, *British Chartists in America, 1839–1900* (Manchester: Manchester University Press, 1971).
Botta, Carlo, *Storia della Guerra dell'indipendenza degli Stati Uniti d'America* (Paris: Colas, 1809).
Bracewell, Wendy and Drace-Francis, Alex, eds., *Under Eastern Eyes: A Comparative Introduction to East European Travel Writing on Europe* (Budapest and New York: CEU Press, 2009).
Brading, David, *The First America* (Cambridge: Cambridge University Press, 1993).

Brasiliense, Américo, *Os Programas dos Partidos e o Segundo Império* (Brasília: Senado Federal, 1979).
Brent Toplin, Robert, *The Abolition of Slavery in Brazil* (New York: Atheneum, 1972).
Brogan, Hugh, *Alexis de Tocqueville: A Life* (New Haven: Yale University Press, 2006).
Bronstein, Jamie L., "From the Land of Liberty to Land Monopoly: The United States in a Chartist Context," in *The Chartist Legacy*, Owen Ashton, Robert Fryson and Stephen Roberts, eds. (Rendlesham: Merlin, 1999), 147–170.
Bronstein, Jamie L., *Land Reform and Working Class Experience in Britain and the United States, 1800–1862* (Stanford, CA: Stanford University Press, 1999).
Brown, Matthew, ed., *Informal Empire in Latin America* (Oxford: Blackwell, 2008).
Buccini, Stefania, *The Americas in Italian Literature and Culture: 1700–1825* (Philadelphia: Pennsylvania State University Press, 1997).
Buonomo, Leonardo, *Backward Glances. Exploring Italy, Reinterpreting America (1831–1866)* (Teaneck: Fairleigh Dickinson University Press, 1996).
Burk, Kathleen, *Old World, New World. The Story of Britain and America* (London: Little, Brown, 2007).
Burr, Robert N. and Hussey, Roland D., *Documents on Inter-American Cooperation* (Philadelphia: University of Pennsylvania Press, 1955).
Buruma, Ian and Margalit, Avishai, *Occidentalism: A Short History of Anti-Westernism* (London: Atlantic Books, 2004).
Butler, Leslie, *Critical Americans: Victorian Intellectuals and Transatlantic Liberal Reform* (Chapel Hill: University of North Carolina Press, 2007).
Caesar, James W., *Reconstructing America. The Symbol of America in Modern Thought* (New Haven and London: Yale University Press, 1997).
Campbell, Duncan Andrew, *English Public Opinion and the American Civil War* (Woodbridge, Suffolk: Boydell Press, 2003).
Canfora, Luciano, Cardinale, Ugo, eds., *Il Giacobino Pentito. Carlo Botta fra Napoleone e Washington* (Rome/Bari: Laterza, 2010).
Canizares-Esguerra, Jorge, *How to Write the History of the New World* (Stanford, CA: Stanford University Press, 2000).
Cárdenas, María Salomé, *Mary Mann: la amiga incondicional de Sarmiento. Cartas traducidas y comentadas* (Buenos Aires: Círculo Académico de Difusión de Autores Nacionales, 2005).
Carneiro Pessoa, Reynaldo, *A Idéia Republicana no Brasil através dos Documentos* (São Paulo: Editora Alfa-Omega, 1973).
Carr, Raymond, *Spain: A History* (Oxford: Oxford University Press, 2000).
Carwardine, Richard J. and Sexton, Jay, eds., *The Global Lincoln* (New York: Oxford University Press, 2011).
Case, Lynn M., ed., *French Opinion on the United States and Mexico, 1860–1867: Extracts From the Reports of the Procureurs Généraux* (Hamden/Conn: Archon, 1969).
Certeau, Michel de, *L'écriture de l'histoire* (Paris: Gallimard, 1975).
Certeau, Michel de, *L'invention du quotidien* (Paris: Gallimard, 1990).

Cherney, Robert W., *American Politics in the Gilded Age. 1868–1900* (Wheeling, Ill.: Harlan Davidson Inc, 1997).
Chiapelli, Fred, ed., *First Images of America. The Impact of the New World on the Old* (Berkeley, CA: University of California Press, 1976).
Chiaramonte, José Carlos and Buchbinder, Pablo, "Provincias, caudillos, nación y la historiografía constitucionalista argentina, 1853–1930," *Anuario del IEHS* (Tandil) 7, (1992), 93–119.
Claeys, Gregory, "The Example of America a warning to England? The transformation of America in British radicalism and socialism, 1790–1850," in *Living and Learning: Essays in Honour of J. F. C. Harrison*, Malcolm Chase and Ian Dyck, eds. (Aldershot: Scolar, 1996), 66–80.
Clark, Christopher and Wright, Julian, "Regionalism and the State in France and in Prussia," *European Review of History/Revue Européenne d'histoire* 15, no. 3 (2008), 277–293.
Cody Wetmore, Helen and Grey, Zane, *Buffalo Bill. Last of the Great Scouts. Commemorative Edition (1899)* (Lincoln: University of Nebraska Press, 2003).
Cody, William F., *The Life of Buffalo Bill* (Hartford: Bliss, 1879).
Colombo, Arturo, della Peruta, Franco, Lacaita, Carlo G., eds., *Carlo Cattaneo: i temi e le sfide* (Milan: Casagrande, 2004).
Comitato italiano per la storia americana, *Italia e America dall settecento all'età dell'imperialismo* (Venice: 1976).
Conrad, Robert E., *Abolitionism: The Brazilian Antislavery Struggle* (Chicago & London: University of Illinois Press, 1977).
Conrad, Robert E., *The Destruction of Brazilian Slavery, 1850–1888* (Berkeley & Los Angeles: University of California Press, 1972).
Cooper Frederick and Stoler, Ann Laura, eds., *Tensions of Empire: Colonial Cultures in a Bourgeois World* (Berkeley/Los Angeles/London: University of California Press, 1997).
Corwin, Arthur, *Spain and the Abolition of Slavery in Cuba 1817–1886* (Austin and London: University of Texas Press, 1967).
Craiutu, Aurelian and Isaacs, Jeff, eds., *America Through European Eyes* (Pennsylvania: Penn State University Press, 2009).
Craiutu, Aurelian, *Liberalism Under Siege: The Political Thought of the French Doctrinaires* (Lanham, MD: Lexington Books, 2008).
Crawford, Martin, *The Anglo-American Crisis of the Mid-Nineteenth Century: The Times and America, 1850–1862* (Athens: The University of Georgia Press, 1987).
Crespo, Julio, *Las maestras de Sarmiento* (Buenos Aires: Grupo Abierto, 2007).
Croce, Benedetto, *History of Europe in the Nineteenth Century [1932]* (London: Allen and Unwin, 1934).
Crook, David Paul, *American Democracy in English Politics, 1815–1850* (Oxford: Oxford University Press, 1965).
Crouzet, François, "Problèmes de la communication franco-britannique aux XIXe et XXe siècles," *Revue Historique* 99, no. 3 (1975), 105–134.
Crouzet, François, *Britain Ascendant: Comparative Studies in Franco-British Economic History* (Cambridge: Cambridge University Press, 1990).

Cunningham, Michele, *Mexico and the Foreign Policy of Napoleon III* (Houndmills, Basingstoke: Palgrave, 2001).

Czaja, Marek, *Die USA und ihr Aufstieg zur Weltmacht um die Jahrhundertwende: Die Amerikarezeption der Parteien im Kaiserreich* (Berlin: Duncker&Humblot, 2006).

D'Acierno, Pellegrino, ed., *The Italian American Heritage. A Companion to Literature and the Arts* (New York: Garland, 1999) 691–702.

D'Agostino, Peter R., *Rome in America: Transnational Catholic Ideology From the Risorgimento to Fascism* (Chapel Hill: University of North Carolina Press, 2004).

Da Ponte, Lorenzo, *Memoirs* (New York: New York Review of Books, 2000).

Dal Lago, Enrico and Halpern, Rick, eds., *The American South and the Italian Mezzogiorno. Essays in Comparative History* (Basingstoke: Palgrave, 2002).

Dall'Osso, Claudia, *Voglia d'America. Il mito americano in Italia tra Otto e Novecento* (Rome: Donzelli, 2007).

Davidson, Cathy N. and Hatcher, Jessamyn, eds., *No More Separate Spheres!* (Durham and London: Duke University Press, 2002).

Davies, Catherine, "On Englishmen, Women, Indians and Slaves: Modernity in the Nineteenth-century Spanish-American Novel," *Bulletin of Spanish Studies* LXXXII, nos. 3–4 (2005), 313–333.

Davies, Catherine, Brewster, Claire and Owen, Hilary, *South American Independence: Gender, Politics, Text* (Liverpool: Liverpool University Press, 2006).

Davis, David Brion, *The Problem of Slavery in Western Culture* (1966) (New York and Oxford: Oxford University Press, 1988).

De Grazia, Victoria, *Irresistible Empire: America's Advance Through Twentieth-Century Europe* (Cambridge, Mass: Harvard University Press, 2005).

Deconde, Alexander, "Historians, the War of American Independence, and the Persistence of the Exceptionalist Ideal," *The International History Review* 5/3, (August 1983), 399–430.

Degler, Carl, *Neither Black nor White: Slavery and Race Relations in Brazil and the United States* (New York: Palgrave Macmillan, 1971).

Della Peruta, Franco, "Il mito del Risorgimento e l'estrema sinistra," *Risorgimento* XLVII 1–2, (1995), 32–70.

Digeon, Claude, *La crise allemande de la pensée française, 1870–1914* (Paris: Presses universitaires de France, 1959).

Diner, Dan, *Verkehrte Welten. Antiamerikanismus in Deutschland. Ein historischer Essay* (Frankfurt/M: Suhrkamp, 1993).

Diner, Dan, *Feindbild Amerika: Über die Beständigkeit eines Ressentiments* (Berlin: Propyläen, 2002).

Douglass Adams, Ephraim, *Great Britain and the American Civil War* (London: Longmans, 1925).

Doyle, Don H., *Nations Divided. America, Italy, and the Southern Question* (Athens: The University of Georgia Press, 2002).

Dunkerley, James, *Americana: The Americas in the World, around 1850* (London: Verso, 2000).

Edison, Paul N., "Conquest Unrequited: French Expeditionary Science in Mexico, 1864–1867," *French Historical Studies* 26, no. 3 (2003), 459–495.

Ellison, Mary, *Support for Secession: Lancashire and the American Civil War* (Chicago: University of Chicago Press, 1972).

Englekirk, John E., *Bibliografía de obras norteamericanas en traducción española* (Mexico: 1944).

Esdaile, C., *Spain in the Liberal Age. From Constitution to Civil War 1808–1939* (Oxford: Blackwell, 2000).

Evans, John Martin, *America: The View From Europe* (San Francisco: San Francisco Book Company, 1976).

Fauré, Christine and Bishop, Tom., eds., *L'Amérique des Français* (Paris: François Bourin, 1992).

Felski, Rita, *The Gender of Modernity* (Harvard: Harvard University Press, 1995).

Fernández Armesto, Felipe, *The Americas: The History of a Hemisphere* (London: Weidenfeld and Nicolson, 2003).

Ferrer, Ada, *Insurgent Cuba: Race, Nation and Revolution, 1868–1898* (Chapel Hill, NC: University of North Carolina Press, 1999).

Finzsch, Norbert and Lehmkul, Ursula, eds., *Atlantic Communications. The Media in American and German History From the Seventeenth to the Twentieth Century* (Oxford: Berg, 2004).

Fiorentino, Daniele and Sanfilippo, Matteo, eds., *Gli Stati Uniti e l'unità d'Italia* (Rome: Gangemi, 2004).

Foner, Philip S., *A History of Cuba and Its Relations with the United States 2 Vols* (New York: International Publishers, 1962–3).

Fonseca Ferreira, Ligia, "Luíz Gama: Um abolicionista leitor de Renan," *Revista de Estudos Avançados (Universidade de São Paulo)* 21, 60 (2007), 271–288.

Fontaine, Roger W., *Brazil and the United States: Toward a Maturing Relation* (Washington: Smithsonian Institution Press, 1974).

Foucrier, Annick, *Le rêve californien: migrants français sur la côte Pacifique, XVIIIe-XXe siècles* (Paris: Belin, 1999).

Franzina, Emilio, *Dall'Arcadia in America. Attività letteraria ed emigrazione transoceanica in Italia* (Turin: Fondazione Agnelli, 1996).

Franzina, Emilio, *L'immaginario degli emigranti. Miti e raffigurazioni dell'esperienza italiana all'estero fra due secoli* (Paese: PAGUS, 1992).

Frederick, Bonnie, "Harriet Beecher Stowe and the Virtuous Mother: Argentina, 1852–1910," *Journal of Women's History* 18, no.1 (Spring 2006), 101–120.

Freitag, Sabine, *Friedrich Hecker. Biographie eines Republikaners* (Stuttgart: Steiner, 1998).

Friedman, Max Paul, "Beyond 'voting with the feet': Toward a conceptual history of 'America' in European migrant sending communities, 1860s to 1914," *Journal of Social History* 40, no.3 (Spring 2007), 557–575.

Furet, François, *La Révolution Française. II. Terminer la Révolution de Louis XVIII à Jules Ferry, 1814–1880* (Paris: Hachette, 1988).

Garcia Monton, Isabel, *Viaje a la modernidad. La visión de los Estados Unidos en la España finescular* (Madrid: Editorial Verbum, 2002).

Gavronsky, Serge, *The French Liberal Opposition and the American Civil War* (New York: Humanities Press, 1968).
Gemme, Paola, *Domesticating Foreign Struggles. The Italian Risorgimento and Antebellum American Identity* (Athens and London: The University of Georgia Press, 2005).
Gerbi, Antonello, *The Dispute of the New World: The History of a Polemic, 1750–1900* (Pittsburgh: University of Pittsburgh Press, trans, 1973 [1955]).
Gil Novales, Alberto, "Abolicionismo y librecambio," *Revista de Occidente*, no. 50 (1968), 154–181.
Gilbert, James G., *Perfect Cities: Chicago's utopias of 1893* (Chicago: Chicago University Press, 1991).
Gildea, Robert, *The Past in French History* (New Haven: Yale University Press, 1994).
Gilroy, Paul, *The Black Atlantic: Modernity and Double Consciousness* (Cambridge, Mass: Harvard University Press, 1993).
Gladstone, William E., "Kin Beyond Sea," *North American Review* 264 (September-October 1878), 179–212.
Goldstein, Robert Justin, ed., *The Frightful Stage. Political Censorship of the Theatre in Nineteenth-Century Europe* (Oxford: Berghahn, 2009).
González Pagés, Julio César, *En busca de un espacio: Historia de mujeres en Cuba* (Havana: Editorial de Ciencias Sociales, 2003).
González Stephan, Beatriz, "Martí, invenciones tecnológicas y Exposiciones Universales," *Casa de las Américas* (April-June 2006), 25–43.
Graham, Richard, "Causes of the abolition of Negro slavery in Brazil," *The Hispanic American Historical Review* 46, 2 (May, 1966), 123–137.
Graham, Richard, *Britain and the Onset of Modernization in Brazil, 1850–1914* (Cambridge: Cambridge University Press, 1972).
Grandin, Greg, "Your Americanism and Mine: Americanism and Anti-Americanism in the Americas," *The American Historical Review* 111, no.4 (October 2006), 1042–1066.
Gray, Walter D., *Interpreting American Democracy in France: The Career of Édouard Laboulaye, 1811–1883* (Newark: University of Delaware Press, 1994).
Greenblatt, Stephen, *Marvelous Possessions: The Wonder of the New World* (Chicago: Chicago University Press, 1991).
Griggs, William C., *The Elusive Eden: Frank McMullan's Confederate Colony in Brazil* (Austin: University of Texas Press, 1987).
Guerra y Sánchez, Ramiro et al., *Historia de la nación cubana*, 10 vols (Havana: Editorial Historia de la nación cubana, 1952).
Guerra, Lillian, *The Myth of José Martí: Conflicting Nationalisms in Early Twentieth-Century Cuba* (Chapel Hill NC: University of North Carolina Press, 2005).
Gustafson, Susan, "The Religious Significance of Goethe's 'Amerikabild'," *Eighteenth-Century Studies* 24, no.1 (Autumn 1990), 69–91.
Hall, Catherine, McClelland, Keith and Rendell, Jane, *Defining the Victorian Nation: Class, Race, Gender and the Reform Act of 1867* (Cambridge: Cambridge University Press, 2000).

Harris, N. et al., *Grand Illusions: Chicago's World's Fair of 1893* (Chicago: Chicago Historical Society, 1993).

Hazareesing, Sudhir, *From Subject to Citizen: The Second Empire and the Emergence of Modern French Democracy* (Princeton: Princeton University Press, 1998).

Heck, Thomas F., "Toward a bibliography of operas on Columbus," *Notes* 49, no.2 (December 1992), 474–497.

Hegel, Georg Wilhelm Friedrich, *Vorlesungen über die Philosophie der Geschichte* (Frankfurt/M: Suhrkamp, 1986).

Helbich, Wolfgang, Kamphoefner, Walter D., Sommer, Ulrike, eds., *Briefe aus Amerika. Deutsche Auswanderer schreiben aus der neuen Welt, 1830–1930* (München: Beck, 1988).

Hennessy, Alistair and King, John, eds., *The Land That England Lost* (London: British Academic Press, 1992).

Hennessy, Charles A. M., *The Federal Republic in Spain* (Oxford: Clarendon Press, 1962).

Henningsen, Manfred, *Der Fall Amerika. Zur Sozial- und Bewußtseinsgeschichte einer Verdrängung* (München: List, 1974).

Hernández, Rafael, ed., *Mirar al Niágara. Huellas culturales entre Cuba y los Estados Unidos* (Havana: Centro de Investigación y Desarrollo de la Cultura Cubana Juan Marinello, 2000).

Hoggart, Richard, *The Uses of Literacy (1957)* (Middlesex: Penguin, 1965).

Honório Rodrigues, José, "A revolução americana e a revolução brasileira da Independência (1776–1822)," *Revista de Historia de América* (Mexico) no. 83 (Jan.-June 1977), 69–91.

Horsman, Reginald, *Race and Manifest Destiny: The Origins of American Racial Anglo-Saxonism* (Cambridge, Massachusetts: Harvard University Press, 1981).

Houston Luiggi, Alice, *65 Valiants* 'Gainesville, FA: University of Florida Press, 1965).

Humboldt, Alexander von, *The Island of Cuba*, Trans. J. S. Thrasher (New York: Derby and Jackson, 1856).

Hyman, Harold, ed., *Heard Around the World: The Impact Abroad of the American Civil War* (New York: Knopf, 1969).

Isabella, Maurizio, *Risorgimento in Exile. Italian Émigrés and the Liberal International in the Post-Napoleonic Era* (Oxford: Oxford University Press, 2009).

Isnenghi, Mario, ed., *I luoghi della memoria* (Roma and Bari: Laterza, 1997), 1998.

Jackson, Frederick H., "Uncle Tom's Cabin in Italy," *Symposium* 7, (1953), 323–332.

Janz, Oliver, Schiera, Pierangelo, Siegrist, Hannes, eds., *Centralismo e federalismo tra Otto e Novecento. Italia e Germania a confronto* (Bologna: il Mulino, 1997).

Jaume, Lucien, *Tocqueville: les sources aristocratiques de la liberté* (Paris: Fayard, 2008).

Jennings, Jeremy R., "Conceptions of England and Its Constitution in Nineteenth-Century French Political Thought," *The Historical Journal* 29, no. 1 (1986), 65–85.

Jennings, Lawrence, *French Anti-Slavery: The Movement for the Abolition of Slavery in France, 1802–1848* (Cambridge: University of Cambridge, 2000).

Jeune, Simon, *Les Types Américains dans le Roman et le Théâtre français, 1861–1917* (Paris: Didier, 1963).

Jordan, Donaldson and Pratt, Edwin J., *Europe and the American Civil War* (Boston and New York: Houghton Mifflin, 1931).

Klautke, Egbert, *Unbegrenzte Möglichkeiten: "Amerikanisierung" in Deutschland und Frankreich (1900–1933)* (Stuttgart: Franz Steiner Verlag, 2003).

Kohn, Denise, Meer, Sarah, Todd, Emily B., eds., *Transatlantic Stowe. Harriet Beecher Stowe and European Culture* (Iowa City: University of Iowa Press, 2006).

König, Hans-Joachim and Rinke, Stefan, ed., *Transatlantische Perzeptionen: Lateinamerika-USA-Europa* (Stuttgart: Heinz, 1998).

Körner, Axel, "Uncle Tom on the Ballet Stage: Italy's Barbarous America, 1850–1900," *The Journal of Modern History* 83, no. 4 (December 2011), 721–752.

Körner, Axel, ed., *1848: A European Revolution?* (London: Palgrave Macmillan, 2000).

Körner, Axel, *Politics of Culture in Liberal Italy: From Unification to Fascism* (New York: Routledge, 2009).

Koselleck, Reinhart, *Vergangene Zukunft. Zur Semantik geschichtlicher Zeiten [1979]* (Frankfurt: Suhrkamp, 1995).

Koshiba, Luiz and Frauze Pereira, Denise Manzi, *História do Brasil* (São Paulo: Atual, 1996).

Kretschmer, Winfried, *Geschichte der Weltausstellungen* (Frankfurt/M: Campus, 1999).

Kroes, Rob, "America and the European Sense of History," *The Journal of American History* 86, no. 3 (December 1999), 1135–1155.

Kuisel, Richard F., *Seducing the French: The Dilemma of Americanization* (Berkeley: University of California Press, 1993).

La Sorte, Michael, *Images of Italian Greenhorn Experience* (Philadelphia: Temple University Press, 1985).

Laboulaye, Edouard [René Lefebvre], *Paris en Amérique* (Paris: Charpentier, 1863).

Laboulaye, Edouard, *Histoire des Etats-Unis* (Paris: A. Durand, 1855–1866).

Laboulaye, Edouard, *Les États-Unis et la France* (Paris: E. Dentu, 1862).

Lacorne, Denis, Rupnik, Jacques, Toinet, Marie-France, eds., *The Rise and Fall of Anti-Americanism: A Century of French Perception* (Basingstoke: Palgrave Macmillan, 1990).

Lamberti, Jean-Claude, "Laboulaye et le droit commun des peuples libres," *Commentaire* 9, no. 36 (1986/7), 748–758.

Lamberti, Jean-Claude, "Le modèle américain en France de 1789 à nos jours," *Commentaire* 10, no. 39 (1987), 490–498.

Lanero, Juan José and Villoria, Secundino, *Literatura en traducción. Versiones españolas de autores americanos del siglo XIX* (León: Universidad de León, 1996).

Lerg, Charlotte A., *Amerika als Argument. Die deutsche Amerika-Forschung im Vormärz und ihre politische Deutung in der Revolution von 1848/49* (Bielefeld: transcript Verlag, 2011).

Leventhal, Fred M. and Quinault, Roland, eds., *Anglo-American Attitudes: From Revolution to Partnership* (Aldershot: Ashgate, 2000).

Liauzu, Claude, *La société française face au racisme: de la Révolution à nos jours* (Brussels: Complexe, 1999).

Löser, Philipp and Strupp, Christoph, eds., *Universität der Gelehrten – Universität der Experten. Adaptationen deutscher Wissenschaft in den USA des neunzehnten Jahrhunderts* (Stuttgart: Steiner, 2005).

Lowenthal, David, *George Perkins Marsh: Versatile Vermonter* (New York: Columbia University Press, 1958).

Luzzatto, Sergio, *La mummia della repubblica. Storia di Mazzini imbalsamato, 1872–1946* (Milano: Rizzoli, 2001).

Madsen, Deborah, ed., *Visions of America Since 1492* (London: Leicester University Press, 1994).

Margariti, Antonio, *America! America!* (Salerno: Galzerano, 1980).

Margavio, Anthony V., "The Reaction of the Press to the Italian-American in New Orleans, 1880–1920," *Italian Americana* 4, no. 1 (fall/winter 1978), 72–83.

Marinho de Azevedo, Célia Maria, "Quem Precisa de São Nabuco? ," *Estudos Afro-Asiáticos* 23, 1 (Jan.-June 2001), 85–97.

Markovits, Andrei S., *Amerika dich hasst sich's besser: Antiamerikanismus und Antisemitismus in Europa* (Hamburg: Konkret Literatur Verlag, 2004).

Mar-Molinero, Clare and Smith, Angel, *Nationalism and the Nation in the Iberian Peninsula. Competing and Conflicting Identities* (Oxford: Berg, 1996).

Martellone, Anna Maria, "Italian Mass Emigration to the United States, 1876–1930: A Historical Survey," *Perspectives in American History* 1, (1984), 379–423.

Martin, Robert K. and Person, Leland S., eds., *Roman Holidays. American Writers and Artists in Nineteenth-Century Italy* (Iowa: University of Iowa Press, 2002).

Martínez-Alier, Verena, *Marriage, Class and Colour in Nineteenth-Century Cuba. A Study of Racial Attitudes and Sexual Values in a Slave Society* (Cambridge: Cambridge University Press, 1974).

Masiello, Francine, *Between Civilization and Barbarism: Women, Nation and Literary Culture in Modern Argentina* (Lincoln: Univ. of Nebraska Press, 1992).

Masini, Pier Carlo, *Storia degli anarchici italiani nell'epoca degli attentati* (Milan: Rizzoli, 1981).

Matsuda, Matt K., *Empire of Love: Histories of France and the Pacific* (New York: Oxford University Press, 2005).

McPherson, Alan, *Anti-Americanism in Latin America and the Caribbean* (New York: Berghahn, 2006).

McPherson, Alan, *Yankee No! Anti-Americanism in US-Latin American Relations* (Cambridge MA: Harvard University Press, 2003).

Mélonio, Françoise, *Tocqueville et les Français* (Paris: Aubier, 1993), English: *Tocqueville and the French* (Charlottesville: University of Virginia Press, 1998).

Mennucci, Sud, *O Precursor do Abolicionismo no Brasil (Luíz Gama)* (São Paulo: Companhia Editora Nacional, 1938).

Mignolo, Walter, *The Idea of Latin America* (Malden, MA: Blackwell, 2005).

Miller, Nicola, *Reinventing Modernity in Latin America: Intellectuals Imagine the Future, 1900–1930* (New York: Palgrave, 2007).

Moore, Robert Laurence and Vaudagna, Maurizio, eds., *The American Century in Europe* (Ithaca and London: Cornell University Press, 2003).

Murilo de Carvalho, José, 'Liberalismo, radicalismo e republicanismo nos anos sessenta do século dezenove', *Centre for Brazilian Studies* (University of Oxford), Working paper No. CBS-87-07, 8, 2007..

Murilo de Carvalho, José, *A Construção da Ordem. A Elite Política Imperial* (Rio de Janeiro: Civilização Brasileira, 2006).

Murphy, Gretchen, *Hemispheric Imaginings: The Monroe Doctrine and Narratives of US Empire* (Durham and London: Duke University Press, 2005).

Nabuco, Carolina, *The Life of Joaquim Nabuco* (Stanford: Stanford University Press, 1950).

Newton Curtis, Eugene, *The French Assembly of 1848 and the American Constitutional Doctrines*, PhD diss, Columbia University 1917.

Nguyen, Victor, *Aux origines de l'Action Française: Intelligence et politique à l'aube du XXe siècle* (Paris: Fayard, 1991).

Nichols Barker, Nancy, *The French Experience in Mexico, 1821–1861: A History of Constant Misunderstanding* (Chapel Hill: University of North Carolina Press, 1979).

Nicolet, Claude, *L'idée républicaine en France* (Paris: Gallimard, 1994).

Nicolet, Claude, *La Fabrique d'une nation: La France entre Rome et les Germains* (Paris: Perrin, 2006).

Noether, Emiliana, ed., *The American Constitution as a Symbol and Reality for Italy* (Lewiston: Edwin Mellen Press, 1989).

O'Brien, Thomas, *Making the Americas: The United States and Latin America From the Age of Revolutions to the Era of Globalization* (Albuquerque: University of New Mexico Press, 2007).

O'Gorman, Edmundo, *The Invention of America* (Indiana: Indiana University Press, trans, 1961).

Offe, Claus, *Selbstbetrachtungen aus der Ferne: Tocqueville, Weber und Adorno in den Vereinigten Staaten* (Frankfurt am Main: Suhrkamp, 2004).

Oltra, Joaquín, "Jefferson's Declaration of Independence in the Spanish Political Tradition," *Journal of American History* 85, no. 4 (March 1999), 1370–79.

Oltra, Joaquín, *La influencia norteamericana en la Constitución Española de 1869* (Madrid: Instituto de Estudios Administrativos, 1972).

Oltra, Joaquín, "La visita del general Prim a los Estados Unidos," *Atlántida* 9, no. 49 (1971), 61–70.

Pagden, Anthony, *The Fall of Natural Man* (Cambridge: Cambridge University Press, 1982).

Pan, Luis, *Juan B. Justo y su tiempo* (Buenos Aires: Planeta, 1991).

Panick, Käthe, *La Race Latine. Politischer Romanismus im Frankreich des 19. Jahrhunderts* (Bonn: Röhrscheid, 1978).

Papenheim, Martin, "Il pontificato di Pio IX e la mobilitazione dei cattolici in Europa," *Rassegna Storica del Risorgimento* LXXXVIII, (March 2002), 136–146.

Paravisini-Gebert, Lizabeth and Romero-Cesano, Ivelte, eds., *Women at Sea: Travel Writing and the Margins of Caribbean Discourse* (New York: Palgrave, 2001).

Sastre, Pascual and Maria, Isabel, *La Italia del Risorgimento y la España del Sexenio Democrático* (Madrid: Consejo Superior de Investigaciones Cienttíficas, 2001).

Pelling, Henry, *America and the British Left* (New York: New York University Press, 1957).

Pérez de la Riva, Juan, *La Isla de Cuba en el siglo xix vista por los extranjeros* (Havana: Editorial de Ciencias Sociales, 1981).

Pernicone, Nunzio, "Luigi Galleani and Italian Anarchist Terrorism in the United States," *Studi Emigrazione/Etudes Migrations* 30, no. 111 (1993), 469–489.

Pierattini, Maria Giovanna, *'Vien via, si va in America, si parte'. Un secolo di emigrazione pistoiese: storia e storie, itinerari e mestieri* (Pistoia: CRT, 2002).

Pitt, Alan, "A Changing Anglo-Saxon Myth: Its Development and Function in French Political Thought, 1860–1914," *French History* 14, no. 2 (2000), 150–173.

Placido, Beniamino, *Le Due Schiavitù. Per un'analisi dell'immiganizaione americana* (Torino: Einaudi, 1975).

Plessis, Alain, *The Rise and Fall of the Second Empire, 1852–1871* (Cambridge: Cambridge University Press, 1987).

Pollard, John F., *Money and the Rise of the Modern Papacy* (Cambridge: Cambridge University Prerss, 2005).

Polzonetti, Pierpaolo, *Italian Opera in the Age of the American Revolution* (Cambridge: Cambridge University Press, 2011).

Ponte Domínguez, Francisco J., *Historia de la Guerra de los Diez Años* (Havana: Academia de la Historia de Cuba, 1958).

Portell Vilá, Herminio, *Historia de Cuba en sus relaciones con los Estados Unidos y España* (Miami: Mnemosyne Publishing, 1969).

Portell Vilá, Hermino, *Historia de Cuba en sus relaciones con los Estados Unidos y España* (Miami: Mnemosyne Publishing, 4 vols, 1969).

Portes, Jacques, *Fascination and Misgivings: The United States in French Public Opinion, 1870–1914*, Trans. Elborg Forster (Cambridge: Cambridge University Press, 2000).

Rabasa, José, *Inventing America: Spanish Historiography and the Formation of Eurocentrism* (Norman, OK: University of Oklahoma Press, 1993).

Ragionieri, Ernesto, *Politica e amministrazione nella storia dell'Italia unita* (Roma: Editori Riuniti, 1979).

Ramos Mejía, Francisco, *El federalismo argentino* (Buenos Aires: La Cultura Argentina, 1915).

Ramos, Julio, *Divergent Modernities: Culture and Politics in Nineteenth-Century Latin America*, Trans. John D. Blanco (Durham and London: Duke University Press, 2001).

Reid, John T., *Spanish American Images of the United States 1790–1960* (Gainesville FA: University Presses of Florida, 1977).

Rémond, René, *Les Etats-Unis devant l'opinion française, 1815–1852* (Paris: Armand Colin, 1962).

SELECT BIBLIOGRAPHY 253

Riall, Lucy, *Garibaldi. Invention of a Hero* (New Haven and London: Yale University Press, 2007).
Richards, David A. J., *Italian American. The Racializing of an Ethnic Identity* (New York: NYU Press, 1999).
Ridolfi, Maurizio, ed., *La democrazia radicale nell'ottocento europeo. (Annali Fondazione Giangiacomo Feltrinelli, 39)* (Milano: Feltrinelli, 2005).
Robbins, Sarah, *The Cambridge Introduction to Harriet Beecher Stowe* (Cambridge: Cambridge University Press, 2007).
Robertson, Carol E., ed., *Musical Repercussions of 1492* (Washington: Smithsonian Institution Press, 1992).
Roger, Philippe, *L'ennemi américain: généalogie de l'antiaméricanisme français* (Paris: Seuil, 2002). English: Roger, Philippe, *The American Enemy. A Story of French Anti-Americanism* (Chicago: The University of Chicago Press (2002), 2005).
Rolle, Andrew, *The Immigrant Upraised. Italian Adventurers and Colonists in an Expanding America* (Oklahoma: University of Oklahoma Press, 1968).
Rosa, Joseph G. and May, Robin, *Buffalo Bill and His Wild West. a Pictorial Biography* (Lawrence: University Press of Kansas, 1989).
Rosenberg, Emily S., *Spreading the American Dream. American Economic and Cultural Expansion, 1890–1945* (New York: Hill and Wang, 1982).
Rossi, Joseph, "Uncle Tom's Cabin and Protestantism in Italy," *American Quarterly* 11, no. 3 (Autumn 1959), 416–424.
Rossi, Joseph, *The Image of America in Mazzini's Writings* (Madison: The University of Wisconsin Press, 1954).
Rudelle, Odile, "Jules Ferry et le modèle américain," *La Revue Tocqueville/The Tocqueville Review* 17, no. 1 (1996), 193–209.
Rydell, Robert W. and Gwinn, Nancy E., eds., *Fair Representations: World's Fairs and the Modern World* (Amsterdam: VU University, 1994).
Rydell, Robert W. and Kroes, Rob, *Buffalo Bill in Bologna. the Americanization of the World, 1869–1922* (Chicago and London: The University of Chicago Press, 2005).
Rydell, Robert W., *All the World's a Fair: Visions of Empire at American International Expositions, 1876–1916* (Chicago: Chicago University Press, 1984).
Sagala, Sandra K., *Buffalo Bill on Stage* (Albuquerque: University of New Mexico Press, 2008).
Sancton, Thomas A., *America in the Eyes of the French Left, 1848–1871*, (D.Phil-Thesis, University of Oxford 1979).
Sanfilippo, Matteo, *L'affermazione del cattolicesimo nel Nord America. Elite, emigranti e chiesa cattolica negli Stati Uniti e in Canada, 1750–1920* (Viterbo: Sette città, 2003).
Scally Grigas, Carol, "Mission to Spain: Alice Gordon Gulick and a transatlantic project to educate" (PhD thesis, Washington State University, 2004).
Schimdt-Nowara, Christopher and Nieto-Philipps, John M., eds., *Interpreting Spanish Colonialism: Empires, Nations and Legends* (Albuquerque: University of New Mexico Press, 2005).

Schivelbusch, Wolfgang, *Die Kultur der Niederlage: Der Amerikanische Süden 1865, Frankreich 1871 und Deutschland 1918* (Berlin: Alexander Fest, 2001).

Schmidt-Nowara, Christopher, "'Spanish Cuba': Race and class in Spanish and Cuban Antislavery Ideology, 1861–1868," *Cuban Studies* vol. 25, (1995), 101–122.

Schmidt-Nowara, Christopher, *Empire and Antislavery. Spain, Cuba and Puerto Rico, 1833–1874* (Pittsburg: University of Pittsburg Press, 1999).

Schüler, Anja, *Frauenbewegung und soziale Reform. Jane Addams und Alice Salomon im transatlantischen Dialog, 1889–1933* (Stuttgart: Steiner, 2004).

Schwaabe, Christian, *Antiamerikanismus: Wandlungen eines Feindbildes* (München: Fink, 2003).

Scirocco, Alfonso, *Garibaldi. Citizen of the World* (Princeton: Princeton University Press, 2007).

Seliger, Martin, "Race-Thinking during the Restoration," *Journal of the History of Ideas* 19, no. 2 (1958), 273–282.

Serrano García, Rafael, ed., *España 1868–1874. Nuevos enfoques sobre el Sexenio Democrático* (Junta de Castilla y León: Consejería de Educación y Cultura, 2002).

Sewell, Mike, "All the English-Speaking Race is in Mourning: The Assassination of President Garfield and Anglo-American Relations," *Historical Journal* 34, 3 (1991), 665–686.

Sexton, Jay, "The Global View of the United States," *The Historical Journal* 48, no. 1 (2005), 261–276.

Sirinelli, Jean-François, ed., *Histoire des Droites en France. Volume 3: Sensibilités* (Paris: Gallimard, 1992).

Skidmore, Thomas E., *Black Into White: Race and Nationality in Brazilian Thought* (New York: Oxford University Press, 1974).

Smith, Adam I. P., *No Party Now: Politics in the Civil War North* (New York: Oxford University Press, 2006).

Smith, Adam I. P., *The American Civil War* (New York: Palgrave, 2007).

Snyder Yost, Nellie, *Buffalo Bill. His Family, Friends, Fame, Failures, and Fortunes* (Chicago: Sage, 1979).

Solé, Jacques, *Les Révolutions de la fin du XVIIIe siècle aux Amériques et en Europe* (Paris: Seuil, 2005).

Stephan, Alexander ed, *The Americanization of Europe: Culture, Diplomacy, and Anti-Americanism After 1945* (New York: Berghahn, 2006).

Steppat, Michael, ed., *Americanisms. Discourses of Exception, Exclusion, Exchange* (Heidelberg: Universitätsverlag Winter GmbH, 2009).

Stewart-Steinberg, Suzanne, *The Pinocchio Effect. On Making Italians (1860–1920)* (Chicago and London: Chicago University Press, 2007).

Storm, Eric, *La perspectiva del progreso. Pensamiento político en la Espana del cambio del siglo (1890–1914)* (Madrid: Biblioteca Nueva, 2001).

Stowe, Harriet Beecher, *Uncle Tom's Cabin* (New York: Barnes&Noble, 2003 [1852]).

Strauss, David, *Menace in the West. the Rise of French Anti-Americanism in Modern Times* (Westport, CT: Greenwood Press, 1978).

Summers, Mark Wahlgren, *The Era of Good Stealings* (Oxford: Oxford University Press, 1993).
Surwillo, Lisa, "Representing the slave trader: Haley and the Slave Ship or, Spain's Uncle Tom's Cabin," *PMLA* 120, no. 3 (May 2005), 768–782.
Swart, Koenraad W., *The Sense of Decadence in Nineteenth-Century France* (The Hague: Martinus Nijhoff, 1964).
Tavares Bastos, Aureliano Cândido, *Os Males do Presente e as Esperanças do Futuro* (São Paulo: Companhia Editora Nacional, 1976).
Témime, Emile, "Un journaliste d'affaires: Gabriel Hugelmann, propagandiste au service de Napoléon III et homme de confiance de Thiers," *Revue d'Histoire Moderne et Contemporaine* 18, no. 4 (1971), 610–629.
Thadden, Rudolf von and Escudier, Alexandre eds., *Amerika und Europa – Mars und Venus? Das Bild Amerikas in Europa* (Göttingen: Wallstein, 2004).
Thaller, Manfred, *Studien zum europäischen Amerikabild. Darstellung und Beurteilung der Politik und inneren Entwicklung der Vereinigten Staaten von Amerika in Grossbritannien, Deutschland und Österreich im Vergleich zwischen 1840 und 1941*. Inaugural Dissertation zur Erlangung des Doktorgrades an der Philosophischen Fakultät der Karl-Franzens-Universität in Graz, 1975.
Thelen, David, "The Nation and Beyond: Transnational Perspectives on United States History," *Journal of American History* 86, no. 3 (December 1999), 965–975.
Thier, Maike, "The View from Paris: 'Latinity', 'Anglo-Saxonism', and the Americas, as discussed in the *Revue des Races Latines*, 1857–64," *The International History Review* 33, 4 (Decembr 2011), 627–644.
Thiesse, Anne-Marie, *Ecrire la France: le mouvement littéraire régionaliste de la langue française entre la Belle Epoque et la Libération* (Paris: Presses universitaires de France, 1991).
Thompson, Edward P., *The Making of the English Working Class* (London: Gollancz, 1963).
Thomson, Guy, "Garibaldi and the legacy of the revolutions of 1848 in Southern Spain," *European History Quarterly* 31, (2001), 352–395.
Tocqueville, Alexis de, *De la démocratie en Amérique [1835]* (Paris: Flammarion, 1981; 1993); English: *Democracy in America and Two Essays on America, Trans. Gerald Bevan* (London: Penguin, 2003).
Todd, Nigel, *The Militant Democracy: Joseph Cowen and Victorian Radicalism* (Whitley Bay: Bewick Press, 1991).
Todorov, Tzvetan, "'Race', Writing and Culture," *Critical Inquiry* 13, no. 1 (1986), 171–181.
Todorov, Tzvetan, *La Conquête de l'Amérique. La question de l'autre* (Paris: Seuil, 1982).
Todorov, Tzvetan, *Nous et les Autres: la réflexion française sur la diversité humaine* (Paris: Le Seuil, 1989).
Toinet, Marie-France, ed., *Et la Constitution créa l'Amérique* (Nancy: Presses universitaires de Nancy, 1988).
Tombs, Robert, *France 1814–1914* (London: Longman, 1996).

Tombs, Robert and Tombs, Isabelle, *That Sweet Enemy: The French and the British from the Sun King to the Present* (London: William Heinemann, 2006).

Trauth, Mary Philip, *Italo-American Diplomatic Relations, 1861–1882. the Mission of George Perkins Marsh, First American Minister to the Kingdom of Italy* (Washington: The Catholic University of America, 1958).

Trocmé, Hélène, "Les Etats-Unis et l'Exposition Universelle de 1889," *Revue d'Histoire Moderne et Contemporaine* 37, no. 2 Special Issue "L'Histoire de l'Amérique du Nord vue de France (1990), 283–296.

Tucker, Phillip Thomas, ed., *Cubans in the Confederacy* (Jefferson, NC: McFarland & Co., 2002).

Tulloch, H. A., "Changing British Attitudes towards the United States in the 1880s," *Historical Journal* 29, 4 (1977), 825–840.

Turgeon, Laurier, Delâge, Denys, Ouellet, Réal, eds., *Transferts culturels et métissages Amérique/Europe XVIe-XXe siècle* (Paris: L'Harmattan, 1996).

Tyrrell, Ian, "Reflections on the transnational turn in United States history: Theory and practice," *Journal of Global History* 4, (2009), 453–474.

Tyrrell, Ian, *Transnational Nation: United States History in Global Perspective Since 1789* (Basingstoke and New York: Palgrave Macmillan, 2007).

Vance, William L., *America's Rome* (New Haven: Yale University Press, 1989).

Vann Woodward, Comer, *The Old World's New World* (New York: Oxford University Press, 1991).

Villerbu, Tangi, *La conquête de l'Ouest: le récit français de la nation américaine au XIXe siècle* (Rennes: Presses universitaires de Rennes, 2007).

Viñat de la Mata, Raquel, *Luces en el silencio. Educación femenina en Cuba (1648–1898)* (Havana: Editora Política, 2005).

Wagnleitner, Reinhold and Tyler May, Elaine, eds., *"Here, There and Everywhere." the Foreign Politics of American Popular Culture* (Hanover and London: University Press of New England, 2000).

Walch, Jean, *Michel Chevalier: Économiste Saint-Simonien* (Paris: Librairie Philosophique J. Vrin, 1975).

Warren, Louis S., *Buffalo Bill's America. William Cody and the Wild West Show* (New York: Alfred Knopf, 2005).

Wehler, Hans-Ulrich, *Der Aufstieg des amerikanischen Imperialismus. Studien zur Entwicklung des Imperium Americanum 1865–1900* (Göttingen: Vandenhoeck & Ruprecht, 1974).

Wehling, Arno, *A Abolição do Cativeiro Os Grupos Dominantes* (Rio de Janeiro: Instituto Histórico e Geográfico Brasileiro, 1988).

Weinstein, Cindy, ed., *The Cambridge Companion to Harriet Beecher Stowe* (Cambridge: Cambridge University Press, 2004).

Williams, Linda, *Playing the Race Card. Melodramas of Black and White From Uncle Tom to O.J. Simpson* (Princeton: Princeton University Press, 2001).

Wilson, Alexandra, *The Puccini Problem. Opera, Nationalism and Modernity* (Cambridge: Cambridge University Press, 2007).

Wolfe, Patrick, "Land, labor and difference: Elementary structures of race," *The American Historical Review* 106, 3 (June, 2001), 866–905.

Wright, Julian, *The Regionalist Movement in France: Jean-Charles Brun and French Political Thought* (Oxford: Clarendon, 2003).
Wright, Nathalia, *American Novelists in Italy. The Discoverers: Allston to James* (Philadelphia: University of Pennsylvania Press, 1965).
Wyck Brooks, Van, *The Dream of Arcadia. American Writers and Artists in Italy, 1760–1915* (New York: Dutton, 1958).
Zeldin, Theodore, *A History of French Passions* (Oxford: Oxford University Press, 1993).
Zululeta, Carmen, *Misioneras, Feministas, Educadoras. Historia Del Instituto Internacional* (Madrid: no publisher given, 1984).

Index

Note: Page numbers with 'n' refer to notes, numbers in *italics* refer to figures, and numbers in **bold** refer to definitions or detailed discussions.

Acton, Lord, 24–5
Adams, Henry, 105
Adams, John Quincy, 10
Adams, W. E. (William Edwin), 39
Adee, Alvey A., 73
Africa, 7, 8, 162, 181, 205
Agriculture, 2, 10, 98, 209, 214, 229
Alberdi, Juan Bautista, 62, 63, **103–4**, 166
Alem, Leandro, 63–4
Altamirano, Ignacio, 100
Amadeus I, King of Spain, 199
Amazon Basin, US interest in, 231
American and Foreign Bible Society, 23
American Philo-Italian Society, 23
American way of life, 4, 14, 91, 92, 100, 126, 129, 161, 162, 171, 239
  see also United States of America
Americanism, 6, 161, 162, 183, **236–7**
Americanismo, 167
Americanization, 3, 9, **14**, 88, 125–6, 234
Anarchism, 27, 33, 144, 147–8, 158 n. 136, 176, 208
Anglo-Saxonism, **13**, 21, 141, **162–74**, 175, 177, 180, 182, **183**, 230
  compare Latinity
Anti-Americanism, 3, **4**, 161, 162, **178**, 183, **236–7**
Arenal, Concepción, 85, **86**, 164
Argentina, **10–11**, 20, **27–8**, 29, 33, 35–6, 43, 53, **55–6**, 60, **61–4**, 67, 72, 73–5, 82, 87, **88–9**, 92, 93, 98, 102, 103–4, 105–6, 126, 130, 143, 147–8, 149, 166, 167, 208, 226, 228, 229, 230, 233, **235–6**
Argentine National Exhibition (1870), 98, 104
Arnold, Matthew, 73, 127
Asia, 7, 8, 162, 181
Austria, 57, 128, 141
Avellaneda, Nicolás, 28, 104
Azcárate, Gumersindo de, 57, 58, 64, **65–6**, 71, 164

Balkans, 8, 151
Ballet, 38, **127–8**, 152 n. 9, 154 n. 41
Baltimore, 97
Barbarity, 11, **12–13**, **125–52**
Barcelona, 97, 141
Barcia, Roque, 60
Baudelaire, Charles, **144–5**
Bauman, George, 89
Beecher, Catherine, 88
Beecher, Henry Ward, 136
Beecher Stowe, Harriet, 2, 13, 83, **84**, 106, 108, *121*, **127–33**, 136, 152 n. 15, 217, 229
Beesly, E. S., 24, 64
Belasco, David, 142
Belgium, 8, 57
Bellini, Vincenzo, 139
Benjamin, Walter, 6
Bentzon, Thérèse, 91

Beresford-Hope, Alexander, 137
Biagini, Eugenio, 39
Bilbao, Francisco, 21, 23, 149, 225
Bigelow, John, 180
Blackwell, Elizabeth and Emily, 89
Blaine, James, 105
Bolívar, Simón, 74
Bonnett, Alastair, 234
Boston, 90, 97, 229
Botta, Carlo, 134
Boulanger, Georges Ernest Jean-Marie, 141
Boutmy, Émile, 71, 74
Brazil, 1, **11**, 13, 20, 23, 53, 60, 67, 68, 100, 108, *123*, 131, 134, 137, 170, 172, 179, 188 n.101, 191–2, 193, **207–18**, 221 n. 77, 223 n. 110, 226, 228, 229, 230, 233
Brewster, Harriet, 198
Bright, John, 24
Britain, 2, 8, **9**, 10, 20, 22, **24**, 26, **30–2**, **39–41**, 51, 52, 53, 58, 59, 60, 65–6, 73, 74, 84, 85, 86, 91, 92, 93, 95, 129, 132, 138, 140, 141, 164, 170, 172–3, 176, 199, 217, 225, 226, 227, 228, 229, 233, 235–6
Brown, Ella, 89
Brown, John, 213, 215, 217
Bryce, James, 25, **59**, 65
Buffalo Bill, 14, 31, 127, 128, **140–3**, 144, 157 n. 111, 173, 229

Cabrera, Raimundo, 97, 106–7
Caccia, Antonio, 134
California, 4, 22, 28, 84, **95–6**, 167, 169, 229
  Gold Rush, 28, 167
Caminhal, Adolfo, 100
Canada, 31, 178
Cané, Miguel, 106
Canel, Eva, 96, 110
Cánovas del Castillo, Antonio, 57, 74
Capellini, Giovanni, 135
Capitalism, 3, 26, 28, 33, 39, 41, 73, 151
Carlyle, Thomas, 127

Carnegie, Andrew, **41**, 97, 106
Carnot, Nicolas Léonard Sadi, 141, 176
Carrasco Albano, Juan Manuel, 169
Carroll, Anna, 85
Casanova, Giacomo, 138–9
Castelar, Emilio, 176
Castillo de Gómez, Aurelia, 98
Castro, Carlos María de, 97
Catholic Church, 23, 58, 133–4, 136–7, 157 n. 100, 227
  see also Papal States
Cavalotti, Felice, 176
Cavour, Camillo Benso, Count of, 23, 136
Central Europe, 9–10, 142
Certeau, Michel de, 1, 6
Chamberlain, Joseph, 71, 145
Chambrun, Adolphe de, 64, 71
Channing, William Ellery, 204
Charleston, 97
Chartists, 20, 23–4, 39, 40, 44 n. 17, 72
Chasles, Philarète, **168**
Chateaubriand, François René de (Viscount), 101
Chevalier, Michel, 161, **165–6**, **168**, **175**
Chicago, 27, 33, 100, 229
  World Fair of 1893, 15, 98, 110, 144, 225
  see also Haymarket Affair
Chile, 21, 23, 90, 103, 104, 105, 113–14 n. 63, 149, 166, 169, 201, 225, 237
Church and State, relationship between, 8, 20, **23**, 44 n. 13, 64, 75
Civil society, 12, 59, 65, **67–9**, 75, 171
Clemenceau, Georges, 130
Cleveland, Grover, 31, 107
Cleveland, Mrs Frances (née Folsom), **107–8**, 228
Cody, William F. (Buffalo Bill), 31, **140–3**, 156 n. 98, 229
Columbus, Christopher, operas about, 132
Comparisons, 7
  Europe and Latin America, **230–33**
  Europe and the United States, 167–8

INDEX 261

Latin America, Africa and Asia, 7, 8
Latin America and the United States, 21, 170, 232
United States and Argentina, 10, **28**, 55, **62–4**
United States and Brazil, 208, 211
United States and Britain in Argentina, 235–6
United States and Britain in Brazil, 108
United States and Cuba, 206–7
United States and Italy, 132
United States, France and Britain in Spain, 65
Confederacy, the, 24, 136, 137, 193, 201, 202, 216
see also South, the American
Confederate migrants to Brazil, 209, 221 n. 76 and n. 77
Constitution, English, 53, 59, 65–6, 74
Constitution, US, 2, 9, 10, 12, 20, 25, 31, 51, 52, **53**, **54–66**, 67–8, 74, 75, 77 n. 24, 86, 126, 134–5, 138, 171, 191, 197, 203, 205, 225, 227
Constitutions
  in Argentina, 10, **55–6**, **62–4**, 67–8, 77–8 n. 37, 130
  in Brazil, 191, 216, 221 n. 79
  in Cuba, 205
  in France, 25, **56**
  in Italy, 61
  in Spain, **54–8**, 60–1
Consumption, of US goods, 99, 100, 109, 111, 150, 239
Cook, Thomas (travel agent), 140
Cooper, James Fenimore, 2, 14, 128, 135, 155 n. 60
Corruption, 13, 26, 27, 30, 31, **32**, 53, 69, **70–4**, 75, 79 n. 76, 94, 142, **145–8**, 157 n. 108
Cotegipe, Baron of (João Maurício Wanderley), 216
Cousin, Victor, 86
Cowen, Joseph, 24
Croce, Benedetto, 133

Cuba, 2, 4, 9, **10**, 11, 12, 13, **29–30**, 33, 34, **36–7**, 38, 53, 82, **83**, 84, **85–6**, 87, **89–90**, 92, **96–8**, **100–1**, 105, **106–7**, 108, **109**, 128, 130, 143, 144, 149, 150, 169, 174, 179, 183, 191, **192–207**, 208, 211, **217–18**, 223 n. 116, **225–6**, 228, 229, **230–1**, 233
Cucheval Clarigny, Phillippe Athanase, 71
Cutting, Bill, 237

Da Ponte, Lorenzo, 138–9
Darío, Rubén, 105, 106, 107, 109, 149, 158–9 n. 43
Davis, Jefferson, 136, 137
De Amicis, Edmondo, 150
Death penalty, 146
Decadence, 13, 97, 106, **167–8**, 183
Delany, Martin Robinson, 206
Democratic practice, 51, 56, 60, 63, **66–9**, 70, 73, 171, 217
Dickens, Charles, 2, 14, 90, 126–7
Dilke, Sir Charles, 170
Divorce, 95
Dobson, John and James, 27
Dolz y Arango, María Luisa, 86
Domesticity, 11, **12**, **82–3**, 90, **96–102**, 111
Dominican Republic, 201, 205
Donizetti, Gaetano, 132
Dorfman, Ariel, 237
Douglass, Frederick, 206–7
Drouyn de Lhuys, Édouard, 180–1
Duden, Gottfried, 22
Dupuy de Lôme, Adela de, 96

Edison, Thomas, 109–11, 182, 228
Education, 10, 12, **22–3**, 24, 29, 35, 55, 67, 82, 85, **86–90**, 96, 131, 139–40, 171, 196, 197, 204, 205, 218 n. 16, 235
Eiffel, Gustave, 182
Emerson, Ralph Waldo, 105, 106, 228
Engels, Friedrich, 28
Engineering, US, 38, 89–90, 98, 183

Enlightenment, the European, 1, 4, 7, 10, 102, 132–3, 171
Epstein, James, 170
Equality, 20, 21, 23, 26–7, 28, 31, 34, 41, 68, 99, 106, 193
  see also Inequality; Social mobility
Estrada, José Manuel, 63

Federalism, 9, 13, 53, 59, **60–4**, 75, 77 n. 32, 135
Fernández y Cavada, Adolfo and Federico, 201
Fidel y López, Vicente, 62, 63–4
Figuera, Fermín, 203
Figueras, Estanislao, 60
Filibustering, 149, 167, 199
Finch, John, 22
Fish, Hamilton, 205
Flaubert, Gustave, 175
Flirtation, 93–4
Florida, 10, 29, 97, 199, 230
France, 1, 4, 5, **8**, 10, 16 n. 7, 22, 25, 30, 52, 53, **56**, 64–5, 66, 67, **71**, 74, 84, 86, 93, **94**, 95, 98, 99, 115 n. 90, 116 n.120, 126, 129, 151, 157 n. 108, 161, **162–5**, **167–8**, 170, 171, **173–4**, 175, **176–7**, 178, 180, 182, 185 n. 34, 189 n. 114, 199, 202, 226, 227, 228, 229, 230, 232, 233
Franchetti, Alberto, 132
Franklin, Benjamin, 37, 102, 103, *118*
Freedom, 19, 24, 30, 34, 35, 37, 40, 54, 63, 68, 74, 79, 110, 137, 144, 151, 177, 192, 193, 204, 205, 206, 210, 227, 231, 235, 239
  religious, 22, 23, 133, 134
  women's, **90–5**, 108
  see also Liberty
Freiligrath, Ferdinand, 142
Frontier, Argentine, 143–4, **229**
  US, 8, 39, 43, 140, 142, **143–4**, **229–30**
Future, concepts of, 1, 2, 20, 26, 30, 37–8, 42–3, 56, 68, 82, 90, 232, 238

Gama, Luís, **215–16**
Garfield, James A., 32, 147, 172, 228
Garibaldi, Giuseppe, 44 n. 13, 52, 61, 134, 136, 137, 176
Garrison, William Lloyd, 213
Gauguin, Paul, 141
Gender, 3, 11, **12**, **81–117**, 130, 226
Geography, 1, 7–8, 156 n. 80, 180, **230–1**
George, Henry, **41**, 42, 43, 229
Germanic race, 169
Germany, German States, 4, 5, 8, **9**, 10, 17 n. 28 and n. 35, **21–2**, 26, 29, 30, 57, 88, 98, 115 n. 90, 128, 129, 134, 141, **142–3**, 151, 169, 170, 171, 175
Gladstone, William, 5, 24, 31, 38–9, 57, 58, 65, 71, 140, 173
Gómez, Máximo, 109
González, Florentino, 62
Gorman, Mary, 88
Gorriti, Juana Manuela, 93, 167
Gramsci, Antonio, 6
Grant, Ulysses S., 32, 145, 172, 199, **205–6**, 207, 228–9
Grazia, Victoria de, 110
Grimke, Frederick, 63
Guizot, François, 181
Gulick, Alice Gordon, 86–7
Gutiérrez, Juan María, 74

Habsburg monarchy, 4, 10, 128, 150, 177
Haiti, 1, 130, 194, 201
Hamilton, Alexander, 64
Harney, George Julian, 24
Hayes, Rutherford B., 32, 64, 70–1
Haymarket Affair, 27, **33**, 151, 228
Hecker, Friedrich, 134
Helm, Charles, 201
Hilliard, Henry Washington, 215
Hoggart, Richard, 6
Homestead Act, US (1862), 40
Hotels, **99**
Household appliances, 97
Howe, Julia Ward, 84, 223 n. 116

INDEX 263

Hugelmann, Gustave, 178, **179–80**
Huizinga, Johan, 8
Humboldt, Alexander von, 96–7
Hungary, 234
Hyndman, Henry Mayers, 27

Idealism, US, 12, 13, 34, 40, 82, 83, 105, 106
Imperialism, 4, 110, 147, 149–50, 178, 181
Industrialization, 2, 19, 22, 38, 39, 41, 43, 74, 168, 169, 198, 214, 215, 229
Inequality, 21, 25, 39
  see also Equality; Social mobility
Intellectuals, 10, 23, 31, 35, 39, 54, 75, 102, 103, 106, 130, 166, 167, 232–3
Inventions, mechanical, 109–10, *119*, 126, 169, 239
Irving, Washington, 52
Isabella II, Queen of Spain, 141
Italy, 4, 8, **9**, 15, **25–6**, 30, 32, 38, **43–4**, 53, 60, 115 n. 90, 125, 126, 128, 129, 130, **132–8**, 141, 151, 152 n. 12, 156 n. 80, 163, 167, 176, 178, 181, 226, 227, 228–9, 232, 233, 234

James, Henry, 128
Jannet, Claudio, 58, 73, 74
Jefferson, Thomas, 10, 42, 197, 231
Jennings Bryan, William, 42
Jews, 8, 133, 163
Johnson, Andrew, 32, 57–8, 66
Jordana y Morera, José, 69
Juárez, Benito, 202
Justo, Juan Bautista, **27–8**, 30, 144

Kaplan, Amy, 82–3
Koselleck, Reinhart, 5
Kossuth, Lajos, 10
Krausism, 197, 218 n. 16
Kroes, Rob, 14, 234
Ku Klux Klan, 146
Kürnberg, Ferdinand, 26

Labor movement
  in Argentina, 144, 147–8, 226, 227
  in the United States, 30, **32–3**, 41, 148, 168, 173
  see also Haymarket Affair
Laboulaye, Edouard, 4, 8, 12, **56–7**, 66, 67, **68**, 74, 95, 165, 170, **171**, 172, **173–4**, 177, 178, 186 n. 56, 204
Labra, Rafael María de, 51, 61, 65, 86, 172, 195, **196–8**
Lamartine, Alphonse de, 164, 181, 213
Land, 12, 19, **37–42**, 229–30
Latinity, 13, 21, 110, 150, **161–2**, 163, **164–70**, **174–83**, 184, 187 n. 67, 235
  see also Anglo-Saxonism
Le Bon, Gustave, 163
Leisure, 4, **99–100**
Lemoine, Jean, 131
Leo XIII, Pope, 141
Lesseps, Ferdinand de, 182
Levi, Carlo, 43
Liberalism and Liberals, 3, 4, 9, 10, 20–1, 23, 25–6, 28, 29, 31, 38–9, 44 n. 13, 51, **52–6**, 58, 59, 61, 62, 63, 67–70, 71, **74**, 75, 85, 86, 94, 100, 104, 110, **130–1**, 133, **136–8**, 145, 149, 150, 165, 171, 173, 174, 192, 194, 195, 196, 197, 198, 199, 202, 203, 205, 209, 213–14, 218 n. 16, 227, 228, 229, 230, 233
Liberty, 25, 26, 56, 60, 61, **64–6**, 68, 75, 82, 95, 96, 100, 107, 108, 144, 164, 165, 167, 171, 173, 174, 177, 187, 197, 198, 204, 214, 225, 235
  see also Freedom
Liebknecht, Wilhelm, 29
Lincoln, Abraham, 21, **34–7**, 48 n. 91, 102–3, 106, 108, 191, 226, 227, 228, 229, 232, 237
  Gettysburg Address, 31, 36, 193, 203, 229
  "House divided" speech, 195

Lincoln, Abraham—*continued*
  images of: in Argentina, 2, **35–6**, 47 n. 79, 130; in Brazil, 191, 210, **212**, 213, 215; in Britain, 2, 31, 34, **35**, 47 n. 78, 172, 173, 227; in Cuba, 2, **36–7**, 191, 202, **203–4**, 207; in Italy, 9, 34, **35**, **135–6**, **137**, 147, 155 n. 65 and 67; in Mexico, 202; in Spain, 85, 191, 193, 194, 195
Lombroso, Cesare, 102, 147, 158 n. 136, 163
London, design of, 97
London, Jack, 14
Longfellow, Henry Wadsworth, 106, 228
Loria, Achille, 39
Louis Armand, Baron de Lahontan, 1
Louis Philippe, King of the French, 134
Luz y Caballero, José de la, 36, 87
Lynch, John, 146
Lynching, 13, **146**

Macaulay, Thomas, 59
McKinley, William, 42, 96
Mac-Mahon, Patrice de, 66, 78 n. 48
Madrid, design of, 97
Maine, Sir Henry, 25
Malatesta, Errico, 147
Malvinas, Las (Falkland Islands), 166
Manifest destiny, in Latin America, 232
"Manifest domesticity", 82–3
Mann, Mary Peabody, 84, 88
Manners, 74, 81–2, 88, 100, 126, 135, 161, 231
Mansilla, Eduarda de García, 35–6, 92, 93–4, 98, 99–100, 105–6, 109, 116 n. 123
Manso, Juana, 88, 90, 93
Manzotti, Luigi, 38
Marriage, 94–6
Martí, José, **29–30**, 34, **36–7**, 83, 95, 98, 100, 105, 107, 108, 109, 149, 229, 231, 237
Marx, Karl, 2, 28, 29, 34, 151

Marx-Aveling, Eleanor, 29
Mass culture, **14–15**, 233, 239
Materialism, of US way of life, 13, 73, 82, 83, 98, 105, 109, 126, 134, 233, 239
Maximilian I, Emperor of Mexico, 177, 181, 205
May, Karl, 14, *121*, 128, **142–3**, 157 n. 107 and n. 108
Mazzini, Giuseppe, 34, 35, 61, 127, **134–5**, 136
Mexico, 100, 104–5, 174, 177, 180, 192, 229, 230–1, 233
  French intervention in, 162, 167, 175, 177, 179, 180–1, 201, 202
  see also War, Mexican-American
Michelet, Jules, 164
Migration, to the United States, 7, 11, 16 n. 22, 17 n. 35, **22**, 28, 43, 134, 141, 147–8, 158 n. 136, **150–2**, 170, 177, 179–80, 188 n. 100
  Confederates to Brazil, **209**
Minghetti, Marco, 70
Mistral, Frédéric, 176
Mitre, Bartolomé, 62
Modernization, 3, 72, 82, 93, 104, 105, 143–4, 213, 215, 235, 236
Monroe Doctrine (1823), **166–7**, 181, 194, 202, 231, 232
Montégut, Émile, 165, 170
Mora, Ignacio, 205
Morales Lemus, José, 205, 206
More, Thomas, 1
Moret, Segismundo, **194**
Morley, John, 58–9
Mozart, Wolfang Amadeus, 138
Munch, Edvard, 141
Music, 6, 36, 107, 138
  see also Ballet; Opera

Nabuco, Joaquim, 207, **213–15**, 222 n. 86, 223 n. 110
Nabuco de Araújo, José Thomaz, 213
Napoléon III, 162, 171, 179, 181, 201
Nast, Thomas, **73**

Nation building, 20, 55, 203, 224, 228, 232
Nationalism, 111, 176, 177
Native Americans, 84, 105–6, 116 n. 123, *123*, **142–4**, 157 n. 108, 174, 229
Nature, US and, 3, 38, 110, 229
Negreiros Sayão Lobato, Francisco de Paula, 212
Netherlands, the, 8, 57
New England, 68, 84, 100, 104, 170, 230
New Mexico, 4
New Orleans, 10, 97, 100, 139, 209
New York, 10, 30, 32, 67, 70, 71, 73, 83, 84, 89, 90, 91, 93, 94, 97, 99, **100**, 106, 134, 136, 138, 139, 144, 151, 182, 199, 204, 207, 209, **229**, 237
Coney Island, **100**
Nguyen, Victor, 168
Niagara Falls, 229
Nicaragua, 149, 167, 231
Noailles, Paul de, 6th Duke, 56, 57, 71, 74
Norway, 57

Offe, Claus, 162
Opera, 107, 132, **139**, 142
Orense, José María, 55, 75
Ory, Pascal, 178
Ottoman Empire, 8

Palanca, Manuel, 54, 57
Palma di Cesnola, Luigi, 136
Panama Canal, 182
Papacy, 141
Papal States, 132, 133, 153 n. 37, 155 n. 67
Paraguay, 115 n. 90, 208, 210
Paraguayan War, *see* War, of the Triple Alliance
Pardo Bazán, Emilia, 85
Paris, 83, 90, 99, 166, 179
 design of, 97
 World Exhibitions, 107, 140, 141, 166, 168, 182
Parker, Theodore, 36

Pedro II, Emperor of Brazil, 207, 209
Pelling, Henry, 26, 27
Penn, William, 106, 144
Philadelphia, 10, 20, 61, 87, 90, 97, 144, 225, 229
Phillips, Wendell, 217
Phylloxera, **2–3**
Pi y Margall, Francisco, 60, 61
Pierce, Franklin, 167
Pitt, Alan, 177
Plácido (Gabriel de la Concepción Valdés), 206
Poe, Edgar Allan, 14, 106, 116 n. 129, **144–5**, 228
Poland, 234
Polk, James Knox, 4
Portugal, 53, 57, 176, 180
Prefabricated housing, 97
Prescott, William H., 103, 106, 233
Prim y Prats, General Juan, 54, 192
Progress, 1, 11, 13, 15, 38, 79, 89, 106, 110, 126, 129, 133, 138, 146, **167–8**, 169, 172, 173, 179, 182, 183, 191, 197–8, 225
Protestantism, 161, 175
 see also Religion
Publishing and book trade, 30, 54, 74, 129, 216
Puccini, Giacomo, 142
Puerto Rico, 4, 130, 192, 193, 194, 195, 198, 199, 200, 204, 219 n.28

Race, 3, 11, 34, 84, 105–6, 111, 131, 146–7, **160–4**, **194**, 203, 215, 226, 230
 see also Anglo-Saxonism; Germanic race; Latinity
Railroads (railways), 68, 99, 103, 107, 143, 229
Ramos Mejía, Francisco, 63
Rawlins, John, 205
Rebouças, André, 214

Reception, theories of, 6, **14–15**, 184, 237
Reid, Thomas Mayne, 14, 140
Religion, 3, 21, **23**, 55, 58, 64, **133–4**, 163, 165, 177, 225
Renan, Ernest, 163
Republicanism and Republicans, 8, 9, 12, 24, 25, 26, 29, 30, 31–2, 35, 41, 42, 48 n. 101, **51–2**, 53–4, 58, 60, 61, 82, 88, 92, 106, 134, 136, 138, 148, 150, 151, 166, 171, 176, 177, 204, 205, 211, 212, 216, 228, 229, 232
Revolution, American, 8, 58, 59, 65, **68**, 126, 141
Revolution, French, 8, 25, **68**
Revolutions of 1848, **3–4**, 9, 25, 56, 60, 142
Ricàsoli, Bettino (Baron), 136
Rieneck, Louise, 143
Rio Branco, Viscount of, 211–12
Risorgimento, Italian, 150, 238
Rodó, José Enrique, 110, 150
Rodríguez, Gabriel, 195
Roebling, Emily Warren, 89
Roebling, Washington, 90
Roger, Philippe, 164
Romanticism, German, 126
Roosevelt, Theodore, 232
Rosas, Juan Manuel de, 130
Rota, Giuseppe, 127, 128, 132
Ruskin, John, 127, 236
Russia, 8, 57, 154 n. 42, 166
Rydell, Robert W., 14

Sáenz Peña, Roque, 149
Said, Edward, 6
San Francisco, 167, 229
Sanromá, Joaquín María, 198–9
Sardou, Victorien, 94
Sarmiento, Domingo Faustino, 10–11, 23, **35**, 37, **55–6**, **61–2**, 63, 67, **68–9, 72**, 74–5, 82, 87, **88**, 92, 94–5, 98–9, 103, 115 n. 97, 130, 131, 149, 203, 238
Scandinavia, 8
Schiller, Friedrich von, 139
Scott, Walter, 135
Seward, William, 104–5, 108, 201–2
Sexuality, 12, **93**, 100, 109, 111
Shakespeare, William, 236
Sickles, Daniel, 200
Slave trade, 127, 130, 131, 193, 202, 208, 209, 215, 217
Slavery
  in Argentina, 130
  in Brazil, 131
  in the United States, 13, 23–4, 40, 51, 84, **127–33**, 137, 151, **191–223**, 227, 228
  see also Beecher Stowe, Harriet; Slavery, abolition of
Slavery, abolition of
  in Brazil, 100, 131, **191–2, 207–17**
  in Cuba, 36, **192–3, 201–7**
  in Puerto Rico, 192
  in Spain, 85, 192, **193–9**
  in the United States, 13, 56, 130, 136, 149, 173, **191–223**
Smith, Goldwin, 72
Social Darwinism, 25
Social mobility, 12, 21, 29, 35, 39, 43
South, the American, 12, 100, **136–7**, 177, 195, **196–8**, 201, 209, 211–12, 214–16, 217, 227, 228
South, the French (*le Midi*), 176
South, the Italian (*Il Mezzogiorno*), 135, 136, 147, 151
Spain, 4, 8, **9**, 12, 13, 25, **32–3, 52**, 53, **54–8**, 60, 61, **69**, 70–1, 73, 75, **84–5, 86–7**, 90, 97, 98, 99, 130, 137, 141, 145, 146, 149, 167, 169, 171–2, 176, 179, 182–3, 192, **193–201**, 202, 205, 207, 218 n. 16, 219 n. 22, 226, 227–9, **230**, 232, 233, 234
Spanish American unity, 167
Spontini, Gaspare, 139

Steamships, 99, 151, 229
Staël, Madame Germaine de, 175
Statue of Liberty, 181–2
Stendhal (Marie-Henri Beyle), 138
Stoker, Bram, 29
Story, Joseph, 62–3
Street, Revd. J. C., 172
Suffrage, 20, 24, 29, 35, 54, 58, 68, 145, 147, 148, 192
  women's, **85–6**
Swett Marden, Orison, 81
Switzerland, 8, 57, 61

Taine, Hippolyte, 163
Tammany Hall, 70, **73**
  see also Tweed, William
Tassara, Gabriel, 193
Tavares Bastos, Aureliano Cândido, **23**, 68, 209
Technology, 4, 14, 19, **37–8**, 42–3, 93, 95, 98, 106
Ten Years' War (Cuba), 85, 87, 192, 195, 196, 200, 207
Texas, US annexation of, 24, 89, 149, 169, 181, 231
Theatre, 94, 127, 130, **138–40**, 141
Thierry, Augustin, 163
Ticknor Curtis, George, 62–3, 103, 233
Tilden, Samuel J., 70
Tocqueville, Alexis de, 2, 7, 8, 25, 27, 54, 59, 67, 68, 70, 81, 93, 104, 113 n. 63, 128, **165**, 184 n. 10, 229
Toscanini, Arturo, 132
Tourists, US in Cuba, 34, 105, 231
Transnational history, 7, 11, 13–14, **234–7**
Travel in the United States, 98–9
Travel writing, 7, 16 n. 22, 126, 141, 227
Trollope, Anthony, 14, 238
Trollope, Mrs Frances (Fanny), 14, 113 n. 63, **126**
Trumbull, General Matthew M., 59
Turgot, Anne-Robert-Jacques, 1
Turner, Frederick Jackson, 39, 43
Twain, Mark, 14, 70

Tweed, William, 32, **73**, 145
  see also Tammany Hall
Tyrrell, Ian, 238

Umberto I, King of Italy, 147
United States of America
  as Caliban, 105, 109, 149–50, 158–9 n. 143, 174, 231
  as plutocracy, 42
  as Uncle Sam, 109, 161, 174, 206, 230
  as universal nation, 3, 54, 57, 125–6, 225, 238
  Bill of Rights, 75
  Declaration of Independence (1776), 1, 39, 75, 140
  economic success of, 4, 14, 165, 239
  election of 1876, 32
  exceptionalism of, 11, 15, **37–42**, 43, 238
  expansionism of, 4, 9, 82, **149**, **167**, **231–2**
  "Gilded Age", 12, 26, 53, 70, 72, 75
  mediocrity of, 13, 74
  natural abundance of, 12, 21, 22, **38–9**
  prosperity of, 1, 9, 11–12, 21, 22, 23, 24, 30, 43, 88, 109, 126, 138, 150, 169, 172, 173. 214
  public libraries in, 30
  Reconstruction, 24, 71, 75, 126, 214
  robber barons in, 30
  vulgarity of, 13, 73, 92, **126–7**
  War of Independence, 8, 126, 133, 134
Uruguai, Viscount of (Paulino José Soares de Sousa), 67, 68
Uruguay, 91, 150, 166, 208

Valiente, Porfirio, 204
Varela, José Pedro, 91
Victoria, Queen of the United Kingdom of Great Britain and Northern Ireland, 66
Vicuña Mackenna, Benjamín, 90, 103, 105, 115 n. 97

Vittorio Emanuele II, King of Italy, 135
Vizcarrondo, Julio, 198–9

Walker, William, 103, 167, 231
War, Franco-Prussian (1870–1), 94, 126, 175, 181
War, Mexican-American (1846–8), 3–4, 103, 174, 231
War, of the Desert (Argentina, 1879–80), 105
War, of the Triple Alliance (Argentina, Brazil and Uruguay against Paraguay, 1865–70), 208
War, Spanish-Cuban-American (1898), 108, 182, 228, **230**
Warner, Charles Dudley, 70
Washington DC, 73, 105
Washington, George, 41, 64, 102, 103, 106, 134, 137, 203, 225, 228
Weininger, Otto, 147
Wheelwright, William, 103–4
White Mario, Jessie, 136
Whitman, Walt, 106, 228, 239
Wild West, 31, 140, 141, 144, 227, 230
Wilson, John, 34
Wood, Fanny, 89

CPSIA information can be obtained
at www.ICGtesting.com
Printed in the USA
BVOW08s0957111117
500072BV00024B/1697/P